BOWLING
BEYOND
THE BASICS

BOWLING
BEYOND
THE BASICS

WHAT'S *REALLY* HAPPENING ON THE LANES, AND WHAT YOU CAN DO ABOUT IT

JAMES FREEMAN AND RON HATFIELD

BowlSmart

Every inquisitive, truth-seeking human being is solicited by innumerable beliefs, old and new. The past generations, out of which we spring, have been believing many undemonstrated and undemonstrable things; and we inherit their beliefs. Every year new beliefs appeal to us for acceptance, some of them clashing with the old.

– Charles W. Eliot, The Happy Life, 1895

TABLE OF CONTENTS

PREFACE

THIS BOOK OWES its genesis to my coauthor, United States Bowling Congress Gold Coach Ron Hatfield. I started bowling rather late in life. In an effort to understand the game better and thereby improve my own average, I read everything I could find on the topic and queried everyone I met who seemed knowledgeable. Like most bowlers, I accepted the explanations given if the source seemed credible, but I soon found that much of what I read or was told just didn't seem to work as advertised. I decided to cut out the middlemen standing between me and real bowling knowledge and go straight to the authorities, so I signed up for a USBC Bronze level coaching class, which happened to be taught by Ron.

During class, a discussion ensued regarding ball weight and speed. Ron stated his belief that ball speed is more important than ball weight in terms of knocking down the pins, but he couldn't explain why this should be so. During our break I sheepishly approached him, wrote out the formula for kinetic energy, and performed some simple math to demonstrate not only that he was correct, but also why. Rather than recoiling at the impertinence of a mere student daring to think he knew more about something than a career Gold Coach, Ron instead was genuinely thankful for the new information. I went home and wrote out a many pages long essay explaining the basics of both rotational and translational kinetic energy, and how bowling ball weight, speed, and rev rate affect total kinetic energy.

From there, I began trying to apply the same simplified scientific approach to other bowling problems. As I dug into the problems, I quickly discovered that the widely repeated bowling knowledge that is shared so freely doesn't work on the lanes because these ideas, though they sound so plausible, just don't comport with simple math and physics. Worse yet, they are countered by observational evidence that is right in front of us, but that sometimes occurs too quickly for us to see. There is an apocryphal quotation I enjoy, attributed to 16th century French philosopher and essayist Michel de Montaigne—"I write to keep from going mad from the contradictions I find among mankind—and to work some of these contradictions out for myself." I began working out these bowling contradictions, and writing up the results as essays intended mostly for my own benefit. As the essays piled up, I decided to compile them into a small book, with no real target audience in mind.

Most of the essays were of the "myth busters" variety. I would examine common bowling wisdom, ideas such as leaving a 10-pin because one's angle to the pocket is wrong, or leaving a 9-pin because one's ball was still hooking. I'd disprove the diagnosis, and demonstrate that even were the diagnosis correct, the common prescriptions could not cure the problem. In discussing my project with Ron, we came to the realization that we could combine this unique and unbiased analysis technique with our real-world coaching experience, which in Ron's case is truly elite level.

After many years of research, two solid years of writing, and more time, discussion, and even argument devoted to revising, rewriting, and editing than either of us care to recall, the result of our effort is this book, which is unlike anything written on the subject of tenpin bowling to date.

ACKNOWLEDGMENTS

WE WOULD LIKE to acknowledge and thank several people and companies that helped us bring this book to fruition by generously providing answers, advice, and resources. We'd first like to thank our illustrator, M.D. Eqramor Rabbi. He went above and beyond the call of duty, absorbing lots of bowling esoterica in order to clearly illustrate what were sometimes extremely technical concepts. We'd also like to thank Revan Riendanitra, who also provided illustrations, and Siddarth K., who did our photo editing and worked his magic to make frame captures from low resolution video at least somewhat suitable for print.

Thank you to the Bowling Palace at Columbus Square for generously allowing us access to their lanes, facilities, and personnel for our experiments and photo shoots. Thanks also to all of the bowlers who generously volunteered their time participating in the experiments and providing data; Chad Roberts, Duane Joseph, Evan Hammond, Blair Blumenscheid, John Davidson, Pennie Davidson, and Jay Hendershot.

A special thank you to Brian Crater, not only for dressing up in his fancy PBA duds and modeling for our photos, but also for serving as a human guinea pig for many of our experiments. His adaptability and high level of bowling skill allowed him to repeatedly alter his game to test out our sometimes heretical ideas.

We owe a debt of gratitude to the late Todd Kurowski, who answered innumerable questions on bowling ball construction, layout, and drilling, and who gave me my introduction to bowling ball dynamics. Your knowledge, kindness, and generosity are sorely missed.

We would like to thank Dr. Michael Lisch, who not only proofread this book, but also served as devil's advocate, questioning and challenging us on some of our more controversial findings. His tenacity and insight made this a better book.

Finally, we want to thank a number of companies and individuals who generously answered questions, provided information, or allowed us to reproduce and adapt their copyrighted images; Kegel LLC, Ebonite International, Brunswick Bowling, Bowling Digital, the United States Bowling Congress, World Bowling, the Polyurethane Manufacturers Association, Marko Luksa, Victor Marion, and Parker Bohn III.

— James Freeman and Ron Hatfield

I wish to thank my coauthor, Ron Hatfield. Without his encouragement, I would not have continued in this sport or pushed forward with my research. Without his contributions, this book could not have happened.

Most importantly I want to thank my beloved wife, Julia, for her patience and understanding. She never once grumbled about the years I spent wading through scientific journals, crunching numbers, and sitting in front of a monitor typing away until all hours. I promise, now that this project has concluded, I will finally finish building the house!

– James Freeman

My sincere gratitude goes to my coauthor, James Freeman, for doing this project with me. Because of him, I have learned more about bowling by writing this book than I ever did by reading one. He has made me a better coach.

I would never have been able to write this book, or do pretty much anything in coaching, were it not for my two mentors, Fred Borden and Jeri Edwards. Many thanks to them for giving me the opportunities and advice early in my career that helped shape me as a coach, and for providing me with the knowledge base I needed to be able to write this book.

Though it may sound a little cliché, without my Mom and Dad (late), I would never have started bowling or made a career in the sport I love. The time, money, and energy they invested in me will never be forgotten. Thank you.

Without any doubt, my main influence, and the reason I could even contribute a single word to this book, is the love of my life, Michele. She was always there to offer encouragement, understand the sacrifice, and offer unconditional support while I worked on this project. As with everything else, I couldn't have done it without her. I love you, Michele.

– Ron Hatfield

INTRODUCTION

CLAUDIUS GALENUS, BETTER known as Galen of Pergamon, was the greatest physician and medical researcher in the Roman Empire. Building upon the ideas of the Greek physician Hippocrates, Galen determined that the human body ran of four fluids, called humors, and that disease and illness were the result of an imbalance between these humors. He created an intricate and very precise system of adjustments to the levels of the humors, which involved removing a certain portion of the patient's blood based upon his or her age, physical constitution, the weather, the time of year, and even upon geographic location. The blood had to be drained from a certain vein or artery depending on the specific illness to be treated, and the amount of blood to be drained depended on the severity of the illness.

Galen's system was both elegant and specific, and was taught to nearly all physicians for the next 1300 years, persisting well into the early 1900s. It offered precise prescriptions for any possible problem. Well, any problem except one—the human body contains no humors. Since Galen had the cause of the problem wrong, his prescriptions could not possibly offer an effective cure.

We have the same problem in bowling. Ask any accomplished bowler why something happens on the lanes and what to do about it, and you will get an answer. But they won't ever say "I *think* it happens because of X," or "I have heard that Y will cure it," or that "I read somewhere that Z will change it." Much like Galen, we share our bowling knowledge as though it were fact, as though we had a firm basis for making our claims. If we are to be brutally honest with ourselves, we will have to admit that we don't really have any firm basis for most of our claims. In some cases we just built a plausible-sounding explanation in our head based on limited data and limited understanding. In others, we simply heard the ideas from someone else and we assumed that our source had done the research, but in a great many cases they were just repeating something they had heard or read.

In Hindu, Chinese, and some Native American mythology there is the idea that the Earth is held up by a giant turtle. What holds up that turtle? Another turtle. And what does that turtle stand on? Why, another turtle still. As we delved into some of the common bowling prescriptions and pronouncements looking for a credible primary source based in physical fact, we never were able to locate one. No experiments, no equations, no photographic evidence, not even a step-by-step logical explanation about why it should be so. Nothing. Just one person repeating another person repeating another person. It was "turtles all the way down."

Neither Ron nor I are engineers or physicists by training, but I had a pretty fair layman's understanding of classical physics. Quite a bit of the common and widely shared bowling knowledge just didn't seem to comport with logic or physical law. So we started digging. We dragged out textbooks and calculators. We read through dusty tracts, and crawled through obscure and forgotten corridors in research libraries. We conducted experiments. We analyzed video with a forensic detective's eye. We slogged through dense and esoteric research papers long hidden behind formidable paywalls. We chipped away, melded, and refined, until finally some form began to emerge, some light through the mist.

The result of our labors is this book. Did we get everything right? We think so. Everything we say is backed up by something solid—no turtles at all. For the first time, bowlers and coaches can base their decisions on facts and evidence rather than hearsay and conjecture. We share all of our reasoning, computations, and proof sources for anyone who wishes to "check our work." We want to end the practice of blind acceptance of ideas based only on the reputation of the source, even if that source is us. We are sure we have gored a sacred ox or two somewhere along the way, so we ask that you keep an open mind. As the famed composer Gustav Mahler said, "Tradition is tending the flame, not worshiping the ashes." We have only followed the evidence where it lead us. We offer this book not as the be-all and end-all, but rather as a starting point, and it is our sincere hope that others will take our first humble steps even further.

This is not a "how to bowl" book. There are plenty of those already on the market. Our book is instead an exploration into what actually causes less than desirable results from seemingly good pocket hits. It looks into what is really happening on the lane and how things actually work, and separates out conjecture from fact. Just as Galen couldn't cure disease because he had the cause completely wrong, we cannot cure our bowling issues unless we understand what really caused them. Once we have correctly diagnosed the problem, we can prescribe an effective cure. We demonstrate what the various "cures" available to the bowler really do, how to properly perform each one, and how to decide which to apply in any given situation.

This book is organized into three sections. In Part I we dismantle many of the common bowling myths and misconceptions. We go on to demonstrate that most of the reasons cited by even high-level bowlers, coaches, and commentators for why one left this or that on what they thought was a pretty good strike shot, are incorrect. If the cause of the problem is incorrectly identified, any advice bowlers receive on how to fix the problem, however well-intentioned, simply cannot work. If you've misdiagnosed the disease, you've probably prescribed the wrong medicine to cure it.

While Part I examines what *doesn't* work, Part II addresses what *does* work. We take the reader through all of the possible changes a bowler can make to their shot, including equipment changes and alterations, zone and line changes on the lane, and ways to change the shape of one's shot by altering various release characteristics. We explain what each change does, and when and how to apply it. We then discuss how to read the result of your shot to determine what really went wrong and what needs to change. Finally, we help you organize all of your new skills and adjustments into a Bowler's Tool Kit. When you know what really caused your carry issue, what the ball really needs to do differently to start striking again, and what all of your possible changes really do to the path of the ball, you will be able to quickly select the right tool for the right situation.

In Part III, we help you organize everything you have learned, and show you how to put it all together and take your game to a much higher level. We discuss lane play issues and considerations which will let you determine where and how to best attack a given bowling condition, and how to stay one step ahead of the inevitable changes in those conditions as the game progresses. We teach you advanced strategies and tools to deal with especially tough, problematic, or rapidly changing conditions. Finally, we present a new and unique way to look at spare targeting and shooting that will quickly optimize your spare game.

Bowling books are typically targeted toward a very specific audience, which in most cases is beginning and intermediate bowlers. Our book is different. There is something here for all bowlers regardless of skill level, from beginners through elite touring professionals. There is information that will prevent beginning and intermediate bowlers from falling into common traps or applying ineffective remedies to bowling problems, and new ways of looking at and addressing common carry issues that even the most high-level pros likely haven't considered.

This book will also prove beneficial to bowling coaches at all levels. Whether you are a high school or college bowling coach, a pro shop owner, a USBC Certified Bronze, Silver, or Gold coach, or even just a high average bowler who dispenses advice or gives lessons, there is new information here that will give you a fresh perspective on the game. Nobel Prize-winning physicist Richard Feynman said that, "A scientist looking at nonscientific problems is just as dumb as the next guy." While we may all be wonderful and knowledgeable bowlers and coaches, we need to turn that quotation on its head, and recognize that statements about why things happen on the lanes and what will happen when we make certain changes are really not coaching issues at all—they are problems in geometry, physics, and engineering. This book will help you examine and reevaluate the cause/effect beliefs you have been operating under, and perhaps give you a better understanding of the tools and solutions available to you. With better knowledge of the true causes of carry issues, and of the proper application of the various tools available to a bowler, coaches who read this book will be in a much better position to help their students.

While we examine the game from a fairly advanced perspective, we have tried to present the information in an accessible and easily understood manner. Several of the chapters contain some math. In a couple of the chapters the math gets so hairy that we chose to relegate it to appendices at the end of the book. We know that many people dislike math, but please don't let it turn you off. It is there mostly to show you where our ideas come from and what backs them up, and to prove that our proclamations are not mere opinion. If you are able to follow and understand the math, you will have a deeper understanding of the issues being addressed. Even if you can't or don't wish to truly grasp the math, please at least read through it in order to follow the logic. But if you really just can't stand math, feel free to skip over it and jump right to the conclusions. Many people don't care about the details behind the proof of an idea so long as they know that actual proof does exist, and that's perfectly fine with us.

We organized this book in such a way that each chapter builds on the ones that came before, so ideally you will read it straight through. We know, however, that many readers will skip around, jumping directly into the topics that interest or concern them most, going back through the rest when time allows. With that in mind, you will find a bit of repetition from chapter to chapter. We wanted to give those who skip around enough background on the concepts to proceed unimpeded. We tried to keep the repetition to a minimum, and have provided chapter references for those who want more detail. We hope that those who read the book straight through will forgive the occasional repetition, or perhaps view it as a refresher.

So with the preliminaries out of the way, let's get to the good stuff! Find a comfortable chair, sit back, and we'll begin. We promise you a long and interesting journey.

PART I

DISMANTLING COMMON BOWLING MYTHS AND MISCONCEPTIONS

WHAT DOESN'T WORK.

CHAPTER 1

LUCK *IS* A FACTOR IN BOWLING

PHILOSOPHERS, THEOLOGIANS, AND bowlers have argued about luck for centuries. Superstitious people insist that luck is an actual, tangible force, much like gravity or electricity. They attempt to influence it by playing lucky numbers, wearing their lucky shirt, or making sure to always use their lucky bowling towel. Others deny that luck even exists. Everything has a cause, they say, even if we cannot yet figure out what that cause might be.

Our view is somewhere in the middle. "Luck" is just a name we give to anything that happens that could not have reasonably been expected to happen.[1] If you are walking down the road, minding your own business, and a meteor falls from the sky and knocks you on the head, that's definitely bad luck. There is nothing you did to cause it. It just randomly happened. If you stand on one foot atop a ladder while stretching to change a light bulb, and then fall, that's not bad luck at all. Anyone could have seen that coming, and you got just what you deserved.

Since random, unforeseeable things happen in any sport, it would be tough to claim that luck doesn't exist, and bowling is no exception. Most bowlers we talk to believe they have more bad luck than good when they bowl. You threw a beautiful shot but left a 10-pin? Bad luck. You hit your mark, but left a 7-10 split? Bad luck. Blasted the pocket but left an 8-pin? Bad luck. Bad luck just seems to follow us around the lanes.

Why do we believe we have more bad luck than good? Mostly because we humans are genetically programmed to remember our bad breaks and forget our good breaks. We dwell on our bad luck five times longer than we think about our lucky breaks.[2] All of our grumbling over our bad breaks makes us remember our bad experiences while quickly forgetting the good ones.[3] Worse yet, the happiness we feel after a lucky break quickly fades away, but the negative emotions from a bad break lingers and festers.[4] Since we quickly forget our good breaks but remember our bad breaks pretty much forever, is it any wonder we think we have more bad luck than good?

"I SEES 'EM LIKE I CALLS 'EM."

The idea that we have more bad luck than good is made even worse because bowlers often don't even recognize when they've gotten a lucky break. Most of us think that if our ball hit the headpin and all ten pins fell, it was a good shot. The truth is, a great many of our good, solid strikes weren't really good at all, and carried due only to luck.

Even when there is all kinds of evidence telling us that we got a very lucky break, we tend not to see it. We all recognize good luck when it is painfully obvious, such as when we yank the ball all the way over to the Brooklyn side but it carries anyway, but we tend not to notice more subtle cases of good luck, such as when a messenger takes out the 10-pin or when the 4-pin falls late. We are programmed by experience to believe that if the ball hits near the 1- and 3-pins and strikes, we threw a good shot, and a reasoning error known as *confirmation bias* prevents us from ever looking any deeper.

All humans are subject to confirmation bias. Confirmation bias is a tendency to seek out evidence that supports our pre-existing conclusions, and to ignore contrary evidence.[5] Confirmation bias causes us to see "bad luck" when a shot we thought was right in the pocket fails to carry, and it prevents us from looking for evidence that might point out that it wasn't such a good shot after all. The flip side of confirmation bias is that it also prevents us from seeing good luck in action when we carry a strike we probably should not have. Since our preconceived opinion was that the shot was in the pocket, confirmation bias makes us simply see a strike, not a *lucky* strike.

WHY RECOGNIZING LUCK IS IMPORTANT

Our biases make us see bad luck everywhere, and blind us to good luck. There are certainly some flat out bad breaks in bowling, as in any other sport. The truth, though, is that we have far more good luck than bad. It is very important that we learn to recognize good luck in action, and that we realize that most of our bad luck wasn't really bad luck at all. Unless we accept responsibility for the outcome of every shot, we will never be able to understand what is really happening on the lane. We will go on making excuses and placing blame where it doesn't belong.

We must accept that bad luck rarely affects our pin fall, and that if we left pins standing, we more than likely got exactly what we deserved. Until we accept that our failure to carry is because of a bad shot rather than bad luck, we will not take ownership of our game. We will curse, and smack the ball return instead of making the quick, well-informed, confident, and effective adjustments we need to get back to striking.

THE DIFFERENCE BETWEEN GOOD LUCK AND GOOD SHOTS

A hard truth to accept is that we carry an awful lot of bad shots. Many of the shots that you think are pocket hits are not in the pocket at all. When we start to recognize our lucky breaks for what that they are, they begin to give us valuable information that can help avoid leaving pins standing on the next shot when our luck runs out.

How many corner pins did you leave last week in league on what you thought were good pocket shots? How many strikes did you get where pins fell late, or fell forward, or were tripped out by others? All of these pins are are trying to talk to you. When we bowl, we are presented with real-time information showing how we need to attack or adjust to the lanes, but we are either blind to it or we don't understand what we are seeing. If we fail to see the clues that are before us, or fail to even recognize that they *are* clues, we will forever be one step behind the lane transition. We will make "total guess" adjustments instead of decisions based on real data.

In Chapter 10 we will explain what the pocket really is and what it isn't. In Chapter 12 we will show you why you leave the pins you leave on certain hits—hits that you currently think are good but will soon understand could be better. Bad carry doesn't mean your shot wasn't physically well executed. It often has little to do with that. Carrying your strike or leaving pins standing is simply a function of where your ball is positioned on the lane when it impacts the headpin.

Once we start basing our adjustments on the ball's position on the lane when it impacts the headpin, this game becomes a lot simpler. When you watch where the ball hits the headpin and then see which pins are left, you begin to clearly see what adjustment you need to make. And you will make your adjustments far more quickly, because you no longer blame the outcome on bad luck.

HOW DO I APPLY GOOD LUCK TO MY GAME?

There is a difference between a shot that is great because you physically executed it well, and a shot that is great because it was both physically well-executed *and* hit the headpin where it is supposed to. We have all thrown physically great shots that completely whiffed the headpin. We have thrown less than great shots that somehow still found the pocket and managed to strike. Some of us have even thrown shots that were nowhere near the pocket, but somehow resulted in a strike anyway.

If a great shot strikes or a bad shot doesn't, we're sure we can all agree that no luck was involved, good or bad. If a poorly executed shot or a shot that misses the true pocket manages to strike, we have to chalk it up to good luck. That's one to nothing in favor of good luck!

Is there any bad luck in bowling? Sure, but not very much. There is a very small statistical chance of leaving a single back row pin standing on a good, solid pocket hit, but the odds are quite low. The vast majority of the time we leave a back row pin, the ball simply did not hit the true pocket. That single pin isn't bad luck at all. Like the guy standing on one foot atop the ladder, we got exactly what we deserved. The problem is, most of us don't know what a true pocket hit looks like. We think our shot was in the pocket when it wasn't, and we erroneously attribute these completely deserved single pins to bad luck.

We've all thrown great shots, but there is a big difference between throwing a bowling ball well and actually being a *great bowler*. There are many other pieces to the puzzle, including the mental game, equipment knowledge, lane play strategies, physical fitness, and more. Beyond these facets, a very important component of being a great bowler is knowing the difference between good luck and bad luck. A great bowler is going to see those single pin leaves as information, as the pins telling you to make an adjustment now, not later. A great bowler is going to realize that even if the shot resulted in a strike, luck was a factor. If a pin fell late or the ball didn't hit the headpin exactly where intended, an adjustment is needed, regardless of the outcome. A great bowler does not wait until a horrible leave before making an adjustment. A great bowler sees that late pin or that sloppy strike as a clear warning that a horrible leave is on the way. A great bowler is going to recognize just how many lucky strikes he or she carried, because that is really the only luck that matters. Almost everything else that occurs happens exactly as it should.

BOWL WITHOUT FEAR

If you want to become a great bowler you needed to have an open mind, an open eye, and a lack of fear. An open mind means being willing to withhold judgment, and allowing your preconceived ideas to be challenged. It means accepting new evidence and changing your ideas accordingly, just as we did many times while researching this book. It means accepting that there is very little bad luck and a great deal of good luck in our sport.

An open eye means watching more closely as your ball makes its way through the pins, carefully noting not only where it hits the headpin, but also where it exits the pin deck. We will explain in later chapters exactly what to look for and what it all means, but you're still not finished.

An open mind and an open eye will set you up for success and start you on your journey toward becoming a great bowler, but success ultimately depends on what you do with the new information you are gathering. If you strike on an off hit, will you be proactive and make an adjustment, or will you roll the dice and leave well enough alone? If your "great" shot leaves a ringing 10-pin, will you grumble about bad luck, or will you accept what the pins are telling you and make an adjustment? Once you understand what is and isn't "luck", are you still going to be afraid to take action, or will you bowl without fear?

Bowling without fear means being aggressive in your decision making and your adjustments. There are not many examples in any sport where being passive or cautious paved the way to greatness. An ancient Roman proverb says that fortune favors the bold. Bowling without fear, being bold and staying aggressive in your physical game and your mental attitude, puts you in line with the champions we try to emulate.

Bowling without fear becomes easier once you see pin carry for what it really is— simply the inevitable result of where your ball impacts the headpin. The beauty of no longer blaming bad luck for what happens on the lanes is that it enables you to be confident and aggressive with your adjustments. You see a clear cause and effect relationship when the pins are not falling. You are no longer taking shots in the dark and hoping something works, but are instead making sound, educated adjustment decisions based on solid visual evidence.

Believing in bad luck makes us lazy and complacent. If bad carry is just due to bad luck, we don't need to do anything about it. This laziness and complacency leads to always being one step behind the lane transition, and never consistently getting those true pocket hits. A strategy of complacency is not going to lead to winning or to solid bowling performance.

There is no guarantee of success in bowling or in any other endeavor. The best you can hope for is the *chance* to succeed. In the balance of this book we will present real, solid information based on science, mathematics, careful observation, and logic in place of supposition, opinion, and conjecture. Replacing opinion with fact will arm you with the tools you need for a real chance at success.

Making quicker decisions and adjustments doesn't mean you will be right every time. If that were true, the same people would win every tournament. Some days your quick, well-informed decisions will work and some days they will seem futile, but by sticking with it you guarantee yourself at least a chance at success.

Without a solid foundation of knowledge and a well-understood set of tools, your game will fall into the insanity trap—doing the same things over and over but expecting a different result. How many times has that worked out for you? Start working to become a great bowler, and not just someone who knows how to throw a bowling ball well. Start watching your ball going through the pins. Start watching the pins that fall late on a strike. Start staring fear and bad luck right in the face. Conquer your fear as you make immediate adjustments based on solid visual evidence, and start striking more!

CHAPTER 2

DOES A HEAVIER BALL REALLY HIT HARDER AND CARRY BETTER?

THE ESSENCE OF tenpin bowling is attempting to knock down 35 pounds of pins with a ball weighing less than half of that amount. Pound for pound, it seems like a fight the ball can't win. Common knowledge therefore suggests that a bowler should use the heaviest ball he or she can handle. Obviously a heavier ball hits the pins harder than does a lighter ball, right? Even if we throw a 16 pound ball, the heaviest allowed by the United States Bowling Congress, the pins still have in excess of a two-to-one weight advantage over the ball. Beyond weight, the rolling ball possesses two other factors to help tilt the odds in its favor; ball speed, and spin, most often referred to as *revs*.

So does a heavier ball really hit the pins harder than does a lighter ball? How do ball speed and rev rate affect the ball's hitting power? Which of these three factors have the most effect on hitting power, and to what extent? In this chapter we shall explore what is happening when we roll the ball down the lane, and how ball weight, speed, and spin contribute to hitting power. In order to make our exploration a bit less daunting we will simplify the ball's motion, and ignore complicating factors such as the ball's loss of energy to friction. We will also take some liberties with our units of measure. While a physicist or engineer might cringe a bit, for our purposes these simplifications will suffice, allowing us to gain an understanding of what is actually going on out on the lanes.

DRIVE THROUGH THE PINS

If we look at the case of a simple massive sphere rolling down the lane and impacting the pins, two main facets of "hitting power" come into play. The first facet we will discuss is momentum. Momentum can be defined as the ball's resistance to change in its path or speed. It is what bowlers think of as the ball's ability to drive through the pins.

Momentum is calculated by multiplying the object's mass by its velocity, or in simple terms, ball weight times ball speed. As such, it is easy to compute that an 8 pound ball traveling down the lane at 10 miles per hour will possess momentum of 8 x 10, or 80 units. If we were to double our ball speed to 20 miles per hour, our momentum would likewise double to 8 x 20, or 160 units. If instead we were to leave ball speed unchanged at 10 mph but double our ball's weight to 16 pounds, our momentum will again simply double to 16 x 10, or 160 units.[6] We see, then, that changes in weight or speed have precisely the same proportional effect on momentum. That is, a certain percentage change in either one will have an identical effect on total momentum.

Momentum, or more loosely, drive through the pins, is important in bowling, but not in precisely the way we may imagine. Since momentum describes the ball's resistance to change in direction or velocity, it is often assumed that it controls how much the ball deflects from its trajectory as it impacts various pins. In reality, momentum has a rather more complex relationship to deflection, as we will discover in Chapter 4. Even aside from that, the fact is we do need a certain amount of deflection in order to strike.

In a classic or "textbook" strike, our ball impacts the headpin, deflects to the right in order to hit the 3-pin (in the case of a right-handed bowler), deflects to the left off of the 3-pin in order to hit the 5-pin, then again deflects to the right off of the 5-pin, colliding with the 9-pin (Figure 2.1). Without all of this deflection, such a strike would not be possible. Given the complex and indirect relationship between momentum and deflection and the fact that some degree of deflection is necessary, momentum cannot be the prime factor affecting our ball's fight with the pins. If momentum is not the dominant factor, what is?

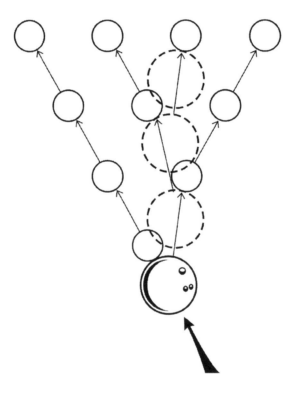

Figure 2.1: Textbook Strike

HITTING POWER

The main force we are concerned with in bowling is *kinetic energy.* Kinetic energy is the energy that an object possess due to its motion, in our case the motion of the ball down the lane. It can be thought of as the ability of the moving ball to carry the energy you imparted to it through your swing and delivery, and to transfer that energy to the pins in order to knock them over. As with momentum, kinetic energy, or "hitting power," is dependent on ball weight and ball speed, but not in the same simple, linear way. Momentum treats ball speed and ball weight the same. In terms of kinetic energy, though, ball speed is of profoundly more importance than is ball weight, as the following discussion will demonstrate.

The kinetic energy of a simple moving object is defined as $1/2$ x (Mass x Velocity^2). Unlike our calculation of momentum where we simply multiplied mass times velocity, in the case of kinetic energy we first square the velocity, or multiply it by itself, before multiplying the result by our mass. Because we first square the velocity, even a small increase in ball speed makes this part of the equation get very big very fast, and thus adds far more to the kinetic energy than does the ball's weight. As was the case with momentum, any increase in ball weight results in a small arithmetic increase in kinetic energy, but unlike with momentum, a similar increase in ball speed results in a proportionally much larger increase in kinetic energy. Perhaps a few simple examples will clarify this and demonstrate the magnitude of the difference. This is all easy math, so stay with us!

Let's again take the case of an 8 pound bowling ball rolling at 10 miles per hour. In this example the kinetic energy of our ball is:

$1/2$ x (Mass x Velocity^2), or
$1/2$ x (8 pounds x 10mph^2), or
$1/2$ x (8 x 10 x 10), or
$1/2$ x (8 x 100), or
$1/2$ x 800, or
400 units of Kinetic Energy

We already saw that doubling our ball weight to 16 pounds while keeping our speed constant resulted in a doubling of momentum, but what is the effect of this same doubling of ball weight on kinetic energy? Let's find out:

$1/2$ x (Mass x Velocity^2), or
$1/2$ x (16 pounds x 10mph^2), or
$1/2$ x (16 x 10 x 10), or
$1/2$ x (16 x 100), or
$1/2$ x 1600, or
800 units of Kinetic Energy

Just as with momentum, doubling our ball weight while keeping the speed the same results in an equal doubling of our kinetic energy. Watch what happens, however, when we instead double our ball speed to 20 miles per hour while keeping the weight constant at our initial 8 pounds:

1/2 x (Mass x Velocity^2), or
1/2 x (8 pounds x 20mph^2), or
1/2 x (8 x 20 x 20), or
1/2 x (8 x 400), or
1/2 x 3200, or
1600 units of Kinetic Energy

Doubling our ball weight resulted in an equal doubling of our kinetic energy from 400 to 800 units, but doubling the ball's speed instead of its weight increased our kinetic energy from 400 to 1600 units, a quadrupling of the ball's kinetic energy.[7]

This exercise shows us that any decrease in ball weight, so long as it is made up for with a sufficient increase in ball speed, will have no negative effect on kinetic energy, and may actually result in an increase. The question, then, is will we automatically throw a lighter ball faster than we would a heavier ball? We all know that we can throw a baseball much faster than we can throw, say, a medicine ball, but does this also hold true for bowling balls of different weights? Given our own level of strength and delivery force, will we throw a 15 pound bowling ball faster than we throw a 16 pound ball? Let's find out.

We send the bowling ball down the lane by applying force to it. That force derives from a combination of factors including the speed of our footwork, the height of our backswing, and the muscular effort we apply during the forward portion of our arm swing. The actual amount of force applied by any given bowler's delivery is fairly easy to calculate. Warning: There is a bit more math here. You don't need to digest the actual computations though. Just follow along so you can see where our results and conclusions come from.

CALCULATING FORCE

Force is defined as mass multiplied by acceleration. Mass is easy; in our case it is simply the weight of our bowling ball. Figuring out our acceleration, though, requires a bit of work. Acceleration is defined as the change in an object's velocity divided by the amount of time it took to make the change. The change in velocity is simply the object's final velocity minus its starting velocity. In the case of bowling, since our ball is essentially at rest at the top of our backswing our starting velocity is zero, and thus our change in velocity is our ball speed minus zero, or merely our ball speed.[8] The "time" aspect of the acceleration calculation is the amount of time elapsed between the top of our backswing and the point at which the ball leaves our hand. This is the interval during which we are applying force to the ball via gravity, legwork, and our muscles. For our calculations we will use as an example a young bowler we have worked with rather extensively. We will call him Brian.

Brian typically throws his ball at a speed of about 16 miles per hour.[9] He rolls a 15 pound ball, and we timed his swing from the top of his backswing to the point of release at 0.533 seconds.[10] While Brian is an extremely versatile bowler possessing the ability to alter most aspects of his physical game, let's assume for the purposes of this discussion that the above numbers represent his maximum release power, employing all of his tricks and giving it everything he's got. We now have enough information to calculate acceleration.

Brian's 16 mile per hour ball speed converts to 7.153 meters per second, and his 15 pound ball weight converts to 6.8 kilograms.[11] Since acceleration is change in velocity divided by change in time, Brian's acceleration is 7.153 meters per second divided by 0.533 seconds, or 13.42 meters/sec^2.

With this calculation of rate of acceleration, we are now able to determine force. Since Force = Mass x Acceleration, the force Brian imparted to his 15 pound ball via the combination of all of the components of his approach and release is the 6.8 kilogram weight of his ball multiplied by his 13.42 meters/sec^2 acceleration, which is 91.26 kilogram-meters/ sec^2, or more properly, 91.26 Newtons.

CALCULATING BALL SPEED

Since we now know precisely how much force Brian is able to apply via his approach, swing, and release, we can work backward and calculate what ball speed would result from that same level of force applied to a lighter bowling ball. We will start with our Force = Mass x Acceleration formula, but will turn it on its head. Since we already know the force, we can solve the equation for acceleration by dividing both sides by mass. Thus, Acceleration = Force ÷ Mass. We already know that if Brian applies his maximum release force of 91.26 Newtons to his 15 pound ball, it will travel down lane at 16 miles per hour. Let's see what happens if we move him up to a 16 pound, or 7.26 kilogram ball:

Acceleration = Force ÷ Mass
Acceleration = 91.26 kg-m/sec^2 ÷ 7.26 kg
Acceleration = 12.57 m/sec^2

We have stated previously that acceleration equals change in velocity divided by change in time. Since we know acceleration, and since we already measured the time of his release at 0.533 seconds, we can solve for velocity by multiplying both sides of the equation by time.

Velocity = Acceleration x Time
Velocity = 12.57 m/sec^2 x .533 seconds
Velocity = 6.7 meters/second

Converting meters per second to miles per hour, we get:

Velocity = 6.7 meters per second x 3600 seconds per hour x .00062
            miles per meter
Velocity = 14.95 miles per hour

Thus, when ball weight increases from 15 to 16 pounds, Brian's ball speed drops more than a full mile per hour, from 16 MPH down to less than 15 MPH.[12] Let's now figure out which ball hits the pins harder.

CALCULATING KINETIC ENERGY

Since kinetic energy equals 1/2 of (Mass x Velocity²) Brian's kinetic energy with his 15 pound ball is:

Kinetic Energy = 1/2 x (Mass x Velocity²)
Kinetic Energy = 1/2 x (15 pounds x 16 mph²)
Kinetic Energy = 1/2 x (15 x 256)
Kinetic Energy = 1/2 x 3840
Kinetic Energy = 1920 units

...while his kinetic energy when throwing a 16 pound ball with equal force is:

Kinetic Energy = 1/2 x (Mass x Velocity²)
Kinetic Energy = 1/2 x (16 x 14.95²)
Kinetic Energy = 1/2 x (16 x 223.5)
Kinetic Energy = 1/2 x 3576
Kinetic Energy = 1788 units

Thus, the 16 pound ball actually hits the pins with significantly less kinetic energy than does the 15 pound ball. In fact, using the 16 pound ball would result in a nearly 7% reduction in kinetic energy or "hitting power." Like many other things that "everybody knows" and takes for granted, it turns out that the idea that a heavier ball hits the pins with more force is actually a myth and has no basis in fact. Indeed, the opposite is true.

BUT WHAT IF I JUST THROW IT HARDER?

It is easy to fall into a mental trap here. We might think, "I'll just throw the heavier ball harder, applying more force to it to make it go just as fast." Unfortunately, force doesn't work that way. As we said earlier, force is the inevitable result of the factors that make up your swing and release. These factors include the speed of your footwork, the height of your backswing, and the amount of muscle you apply during your swing and release. You can certainly back off on these factors to decrease your force, but if you already have them at your maximum—or as we described it before, "using all of your tricks"—then there is simply no way to increase the force any further. Think of it like the volume knob on your radio; once you have it turned all the way up, there is nowhere left to go and the radio simply cannot get any louder. If you give a shot with a 15 pound ball everything you've got and it goes 16 miles per hour, then a 16 pound ball thrown with that same combination of factors can never go as fast.

Another way to look at this is to imagine that you own a 200 horsepower engine. If you put that engine in a 6000 pound truck, it will accelerate at a certain rate and travel at a certain speed. If you now transfer that same 200 horsepower engine to a 2400 pound sports car, the lightweight car will naturally accelerate much more quickly and go much faster than did the heavy truck. If you buy a more powerful engine, say 300 horsepower, the truck will now go faster than it did with the smaller engine, but the sports car with the same 300 horsepower engine will go faster yet. No matter how much force you are able to generate with your delivery—no matter how powerful of an engine you buy—the lighter ball will automatically travel faster and hit harder than will the heavier ball. As Scotty said to Captain Kirk, "You cannot change the laws of physics!"

Given what we've now learned—that for any given bowler, kinetic energy increases as ball weight decreases—then wouldn't it make sense to use the lightest ball possible? This idea will be explored in Chapters 3 and 4.

CHAPTER 3

DOES A LIGHTER BALL REALLY DEFLECT MORE?

CHAPTER 2 DEMONSTRATED that, contrary to popular opinion, a heavier ball does not hit the pins harder than does a lighter ball. In fact the opposite was proven to be true; other things being equal, a lighter ball actually hits the pins with more kinetic energy than does a heavier ball. Even with this objection to lighter equipment gone, surely there must still be a drawback to throwing a lighter ball. What about deflection? We all know that lighter balls deflect more, leaving lots of 5-pins, strange splits, and weird random messes. But is this really true? Do lighter balls actually deflect more than do heavier balls? Let's find out.

In Chapter 2 we used the example of Brian, a young bowler who throws his 15 pound ball at 16 miles per hour. From his ball speed and the duration of his swing we calculated that his release generates 91.26 Newtons of force. From this data we were able to demonstrate that if Brian were to apply his full 91.26 Newtons of force to a heavier 16 pound ball, his ball speed would drop from 16 miles per hour to less than 15, and the resulting kinetic energy at the pins would drop by almost 7 percent. The 15 pound ball travels faster and hits harder than does the 16 pound ball for any given release, but does this relationship hold as ball weight decreases further? Do we reach a point where the decrease in ball weight overshadows the increase in speed and energy?

Chapter 2 and its endnotes covered all of the math involved in calculating ball speed and kinetic energy. We won't bore you by repeating the calculations here, and will instead simply provide you with the numbers. Table 3.1 below lists Brian's resulting ball speed and kinetic energy as he applies his consistent 91.26 Newton release to progressively lighter bowling balls.

Ball Weight (pounds)	Ball Speed (miles per hour)	Kinetic Energy (Joules)
16	14.95	163
15	16.00	174
14	17.10	186
13	18.40	201
12	19.96	218

Table 3.1: Ball speed and kinetic energy as ball weight varies

Table 3.1 shows that with each decrease in ball weight, the resulting increase in ball speed was more than enough to offset the lighter weight. In fact, kinetic energy increased at a faster rate than ball weight declined. There seems to be no point at which a lighter ball loses its kinetic energy advantage over a heavier ball for any given delivery force. Think of yourself as a bowling pin standing in the road. A huge Greyhound bus hitting you at 30 miles per hour will certainly ruin your whole day, but a Ferrari hitting you at 200 miles per hour will spread your splinters across the entire intersection! Mathematics dictates that in terms of kinetic energy, light and fast beats slow and heavy every time.

As enlightening as this information is, Table 3.1 also reveals another very interesting fact. In Chapter 2 we touched on the subject of momentum. We defined momentum as an object's resistance to change in its path or speed, and described it loosely as the ability of our ball to drive through the pins. You will recall that momentum is calculated by multiplying the object's mass by its velocity. To help clarify the concept of momentum, let's borrow an example from another game. If we look at football, momentum tells us why a 280 pound lineman will blast through a line of defenders more readily than would a 200 pound player running at the same speed. Momentum also explains why a 280 pound lineman running 9 miles per hour will break through the line more easily than will the same sized player running only 4 miles per hour. Since the relationship between weight and speed is linear, a 280 pound player running 6 miles per hour has precisely the same momentum as does a smaller 200 pound player running 8.4 miles per hour (280 x 6 = 1680; 200 x 8.4 = 1680). In short, as long as any decrease in the object's weight is made up for by a sufficient increase in speed, that object's momentum is maintained.

In addition to what Table 3.1 told us about Brian's automatic increase in ball speed and the resulting increase in kinetic energy as he threw lighter and lighter equipment, it also provides us with enough information to calculate the momentum that each shot will possess. Since momentum is mass multiplied by velocity, or more simply ball weight times ball speed, we can perform the calculation for each combination of weight and speed. Table 3.2, below, adds a fourth "Momentum" column to the data from Table 3.1. Ball speed was first converted to meters per second and ball weight to kilograms, and then momentum was calculated in the proper units (kilogram-meters per second).

Ball Weight (pounds)	Ball Speed (miles per hour)	Kinetic Energy (Joules)	Momentum (kilogram-meters per second)
16	14.95	163	48.5
15	16.00	174	48.5
14	17.10	186	48.5
13	18.40	201	48.5
12	19.96	218	48.5

Table 3.2: Ball speed, kinetic energy, and momentum as ball weight varies

Notice anything strange or unexpected? No matter which ball Brian threw, the ball's momentum was the same. As counterintuitive as it may seem, it is nonetheless true that for any given delivery force we might apply to the ball, the ball's momentum will be almost exactly the same regardless of the weight of the ball that is thrown.

Since any ball that Brian throws possesses approximately the same amount of momentum, does this mean that deflection of the ball after it hits the headpin will also be the same? The short answer is yes, almost. Recall that we defined momentum as an object's resistance to change in its path or speed. In actuality, the lighter, faster ball will transfer a bit more of its momentum to the headpin during the collision than will the heavier ball, so it will experience a very tiny and almost completely meaningless increase in deflection. We will explore this deflection in greater depth in Chapter 4. For now, though, we can safely say that within reason the lighter ball will not experience any meaningful increase in deflection.

SHOULD WE ALL THROW LIGHTWEIGHT BALLS?

We've now dispelled two prevalent myths surrounding the weight of a bowling ball. We have demonstrated mathematically that for any given delivery force, a lighter ball hits the pins with more energy than does a heavier ball, and it will possess the same amount of momentum as does the heavier ball. Since a lighter ball will always have an energy advantage over a heavier ball without a detrimental increase in deflection, logic would seem to dictate that a bowler should use the lightest possible ball in order to generate the most energy at the pins. So should we all drop down to 12 pound balls? 8 pound? Little pink 6 pound balls like the kids use? It seems there must be some flaw in this logic, and indeed there are several. None, however, are related to hitting power or deflection.

So what is the ideal ball weight? As much as we may desire an easy answer, there is unfortunately no "one size fits all" solution to the question. The proper ball weight is different for different bowlers, and it depends on a number of factors beyond merely maximizing kinetic energy. Let's first look at the problems with using a ball that is too heavy.

"THIS PORRIDGE IS TOO HOT."

We all see bowlers, both men and women, struggling with a ball that is clearly too heavy for them based on the now thoroughly debunked notion that it will hit the pins harder and carry better. Some of us, even after we know better, still stick with a too-heavy ball out of little more than a sense of machismo. "Real men throw 16 pound balls!"

Beyond the loss of hitting power, a ball that is too heavy brings with it a host of other problems. A too-heavy ball will typically result in a lower backswing, and a weaker wrist position and weaker release. It will result in lower ball speed, causing not just decreased kinetic energy, but also a more jumpy and less controllable ball reaction for any given rev rate. A heavy ball will also result in decreased revs, creating a smaller and weaker hook.

Perhaps most detrimental of all, a too-heavy ball also causes serious balance and accuracy issues. We all hold and swing the ball more or less off to one side of our body, away from our body's center of gravity. This imbalance, present to some degree in every bowler's swing, is greatly exaggerated when ball weight is increased beyond what our own body weight and strength level can compensate for, allowing any minor flaw in our swing to more easily pull our arm off line and away from our intended target.

"AND THIS PORRIDGE IS TOO COLD."

So once again it seems that a lighter ball is the answer, but of course we can't get "something for nothing." Just as with a ball that is too heavy, there are a number of problems with using a ball that is too light for you, and these problems tend to fall into one of two categories which we will call *physical* and *technical*.

The physical problems introduced by a too-light ball are different from those produced by a too-heavy ball, but they are at least as damaging to our game. In order to understand these physical problems, we must first gain an understanding of the concept of *inertia*. We hear the groans already! "Not another physics lesson!" Rest easy, friends, there is no math involved with this one.

Most of us are familiar with Isaac Newton's First Law of Motion: "An object in motion tends to remain in motion unless acted upon by an outside force. An object at rest tends to remain at rest unless acted upon by an outside force." This law is commonly referred to as the law of inertia. Inertia is the resistance any object has to a change in its state of motion. Whatever the object is doing at the moment, Newton insists that it will keep doing precisely that unless some outside force acts to change it. If our bowling ball is sitting still on the approach, it will tend to stay right there unless something gives it a push. If the ball is rolling down the lane, it will tend to keep rolling at the same speed and in the same direction unless something acts to stop it, slow it, or pull it onto another course.

The amount of inertia an object possesses is a direct function of its *inertial mass*, which for our purposes is simply the weight of the ball.[13] The more weight an object has, the more inertia it possesses. Think of how easy it would be to push a small child on a swing, but how much more difficult it would be to push the swing if it held a 200 pound adult. This is because the 200 pound person possesses more inertia than does the small child. The heavier the object, the harder it is to change its state of motion, including its speed and its direction of travel. Likewise, if a small child were running in a straight line, it would be fairly easy to push him or her off course. If an NFL linebacker were running in a straight line, we're not sure we could push him off of his path no matter what we did. The small child possesses very little inertia, so it takes very little outside force to alter his or her direction. The linebacker possesses a tremendous amount of inertia, so tends to remain on his path even in the presence of an outside force.

Though most coaches tell us to maintain a free arm swing, no bowler truly possesses one. Every swing of the ball entails a very complex coordinated set of muscle movements, any one of which could go slightly awry. We also swing the ball on a far from optimal pivot. In fact, our shoulder joint is not a pivot at all; we just try to use it as one when we bowl. Unlike the pivot on a bowling robot such as that used by the USBC, which is highly constrained and can only move in one predetermined direction, our shoulder joint is a ball-and-socket arrangement. It is almost completely unconstrained, and is capable of movement across a fantastic range. For the most part, the only things serving to keep our swing on our desired straight path are a highly choreographed and constantly changing interplay between the myriad muscles pulling on our shoulder joint, and the inertia of the bowling ball, which, by trying to maintain its own direction of motion, also serves to drag our arm and shoulder joint in a straight line right along with it.

The delicate dance our shoulder muscles perform in order to keep our arm swing in line happens completely subconsciously. If any little calculation performed by our subconscious mind is incorrect, an inconsistency in the direction of our swing will occur. If we try to consciously control our swing plane or even consciously think about it during our approach, an inconsistency is pretty much guaranteed to occur. Since a pendulum has a stable pivot point, all we have to do is line it up, pull it back, and the weight has no choice but to hit the target. Our shoulder joint, however, makes a rather poor pendulum because the pivot is far from fixed. Though we line up correctly and pull our ball straight back, if any errant force acts on the joint it will pull the swing to one side or the other and our shot will miss the target.

If so many things can go wrong with our swing plane, why don't we miss our target more often? The answer is in the ball's inertia. As our bowling ball begins to fall from the top of our backswing due to the force of gravity, it will travel in a direction determined by how our shoulder is lined up. Provided that the ball is not too heavy for the bowler, the heavier the ball is—the more inertia it possesses—the more it will fight any little errant pulls or pushes away from this line that the shoulder muscles may introduce, and thus the more accurate the shot will be. The first physical problem, then, with employing a ball that is too light is that its inertia will be lower, so it will be easier for any little mistake in our swing to pull the shot off line and cause a miss.

Another physical problem stemming from a too-light ball has to do with the direction of our backswing. Though we have said that no bowler's swing is truly free, our backswing and the first part of our downward swing should be relatively so if we wish to maintain any degree of accuracy. If our form is good, we line up our shoulders and push our ball away toward our target. We then let the ball fall toward the floor and swing backward, pivoting on our shoulder joint, with our arm serving only to passively connect the ball to the pivot. If the ball is relatively heavy it will stay pretty much on this line, so at the top of the backswing it will be in the right place, still lined up toward our target. People tend not to be comfortable with free movement though, and in most physical endeavors control is mandatory, so our natural tendency is to try to control the ball's motion. If the ball is heavy enough it will not be easy to overpower, so our backswing will remain in line. If the ball is too light, it is easier to overpower it and pull it into our backswing rather than letting it passively arrive there. Once we do this, the ball can very easily end up in the wrong place at the top of the backswing, setting up our forward swing on the wrong line.

A too-light ball also causes a couple of physical problems in our release. As we will learn in Chapter 5, a high rev release requires a certain amount of wrist motion. If the ball is too light, the tendency will be to keep the wrist in its initial strong position throughout the release, thus costing us revolutions. Also, due again to the light ball's decreased inertia, there is the real possibility that the mere act of flipping the ball from our fingers during release can drive it off line and away from our intended target. There is also an increased likelihood that we will *throw* the light ball rather than *roll* it, thus ensuring a poor delivery.

Even if our swing and delivery is so smooth and consistent that we are not adversely affected by the light ball's lack of inertia, we are still left with a sometimes serious technical problem which stems from how bowling balls are designed and manufactured. A modern bowling ball is constructed of three parts, a dense coverstock, a lightweight filler material, and at its center a very heavy weight block or "core." It is this method of construction, and specifically the characteristics of the weight block, that cause the technical problem with using a too-light ball.

As we will discuss in detail in Chapter 8, the weight block contributes to the "shape" of your ball's path down the lane, and it is what your ball driller manipulates as he or she lays out your new ball. The weight block is made of a hard and dense plastic which is given even more mass by the addition of very heavy filler materials such as powdered rock or occasionally powdered metal. Ball manufacturers reduce the amount of heavy additive or substitute a less dense additive in order to make successively lighter weight blocks, and this is the way they make lighter balls. There is a problem with this, though. As the weight block gets lighter, its physics characteristics, and therefore its affect on the ball's path, change. It in effect becomes a slightly different ball. Further, a given weight block can only be reduced in weight to a certain point before it reaches its physical lower limit. For most weight blocks, the weight can only be reduced enough to make a 14 pound ball. Below 14 pounds the ball will still look the same on the outside, but it will have a completely different "generic" weight block of a different shape and size within, with very different characteristics. Worse yet, some of these lightweight generic weight blocks themselves can only be reduced in weight enough to make a 12 pound ball, so some 10 and 11 pound balls don't have any real weight block at all, and instead have only a rudimentary "pancake block" placed just below the ball's surface to make up for weight lost when drilling the gripping holes.

An advertisement for a new high-end bowling ball from a major manufacturer aptly demonstrates this technical problem. The 15 pound version of the ball—likely the benchmark weight the engineers used when designing the weight block—has a Radius of Gyration, or RG, of 2.48 inches. Moving up to the 16 pound version, the heavier weight block caused the ball's RG to decrease by a small amount, to 2.47. Moving down to the 14 pound version, the lighter weight block causes the ball's RG to jump to 2.53, still close, but definitely not the same ball. The 13 pound version of this ball no longer contains the fancy weight block. It is instead built around a very simple and very different generic weight block. The RG of this ball jumps up to 2.59 inches. At 12 pounds, the generic weight block is so light that the RG of the ball leaps all the way up to 2.65 inches. We will discuss the concept of RG in detail in Chapter 6. For now, just know that as RG changes, so does the shape of the ball's path down the lane.

As big as these RG changes are, the differences between the heavy and the light balls are even more profound if we look at another technical aspect of ball design called *RG differential*. Our bowling ball possesses more than one RG axis. The one we have been discussing so far is properly called the *low RG axis*. The low RG axis is typically located near the ball's pin, an imaginary line that runs through the center of the ball, one end of which is marked on the ball's surface by a small plastic dot ordinarily located in the vicinity of the finger holes. The ball's *high RG axis* is located somewhere near the thumb hole, and runs through the side of the ball at roughly 90 degrees to the low RG axis. The various RG axes will be addressed more fully in later chapters. It is enough now just to know that the two axes exist, and that they are different.

The difference between these two measures of RG is called the *RG differential*. Without getting into it too deeply, RG differential influences a phenomenon called *track flare*—made visible by the pattern of oil rings on your ball after you throw it. Track flare is touted as being an important factor contributing to hook. We will address this idea more fully in Chapter 9 and determine what, if anything, track flare actually does. It is enough at this point just to know that RG differential influences the amount of track flare. Returning to the ball advertisement, it lists the RG differential for the 15 and 16 pound balls at .048, which is very high, indicating a strongly flaring ball. When you get down to the 12 pound version the differential drops all the way to .035, which, while certainly not down in spare ball territory, is nonetheless firmly in the low-flare range.

While every one of these balls, from 16 down to 12 pounds, looks the same and carries the same name, they are clearly not the same ball. The usual rationale used to justify this state of affairs is that the people throwing lighter balls are probably also throwing them slower, so the higher RG and lower differential are actually a good thing, making the light ball thrown by a less powerful player act in a similar manner to the heavier ball thrown by a stronger bowler. In our case though, that rationale, even if true, does not hold. We are exploring the consequences of a given bowler employing a lighter ball in order to generate more kinetic energy. In this situation, Chapter 2 shows us that lighter weight will cause ball speed to significantly increase, while Chapter 6 will show us that higher RG will cause the bowler's rev rate to decrease. This increase in speed and decrease in revs will cause the light ball to react differently than would the heavier ball.

"BUT THIS PORRIDGE IS JUST RIGHT!"

Let's sum everything up. While a too-heavy ball can easily overpower the bowler and pull his or her shot off of the intended line, it is equally true that a bowler can him or herself easily pull a too-light ball off of the intended line. While a too-heavy ball can lead to a stunted, strained, and weak delivery, a too-light ball can lead to a mechanical and inconsistent "herky-jerky" delivery. Though a lighter ball undeniably hits the pins with more kinetic energy than does a heavier ball, the physical and technical drawbacks to using a too-light ball may well outweigh the kinetic energy gains. So where does that leave us? The usual advice is to use the heaviest ball you can comfortably throw. However, the material in this and the previous chapter demonstrates that better advice might be to use the lightest ball you can accurately and effectively throw, staying at 14 pounds or greater if you can in order to utilize the weight block the designer intended, but dropping lower without hesitation if you must, trusting a skilled and qualified ball driller to compensate for the technical differences inherent in a lighter ball. The idea that "heavier is better" is nothing but a myth. Don't let a bunch of macho nonsense keep you using a ball that is too heavy for you.

CHAPTER 4

FOLLOW THE BOUNCING BALL
DEFLECTION, AND WHAT INFLUENCES IT

IN CHAPTER 2 we talked briefly about the so-called *textbook strike*. In a textbook strike, knocking down all of the pins is dependent on our ball deflecting properly after it hits the 1-, 3-, and 5-pins. Bad carry from seemingly good pocket hits is often attributed to too much or too little deflection—"The ball deflected too much and missed the 8-pin," or "The ball hooked right past the 9-pin." Too much or too little deflection is blamed for a great many bad outcomes in bowling, but is it really an issue?

We've already dispensed with the idea that a heavier ball hits the pins harder, but what of those bowlers who struggle with a ball that is obviously too heavy for them in the belief that a lighter ball would deflect too much? Does a heavier ball really punch through the pins better and deflect less than does a lighter ball, or is this too just another fairy tale? Can we just throw the lighter ball faster to decrease deflection?

The easy thing here would be to just rely on video evidence to show deflection as we changed different parameters. Such an approach would always be open to argument, though. No two shots would ever be released identically, and doubters would launch a never-ending stream of "what if" or "what about" challenges to the results. You simply can't film every possibility, so the door is always open to challenge. And this is as it should be. Throughout this book we emphasize that bowlers need to stop accepting ideas and explanations so uncritically. Our basic premise is that any explanation or prescription, any "this causes that," or "such and such will cure so-and-so," should be ignored or at least seriously discounted unless it is backed by hard evidence and physical law.

So if we can't make categorical statements about deflection from video, and if we discount anecdote, is there a way to determine with certainty what effect ball weight and ball speed have on deflection? Unlike video and anecdote, math cannot lie, and there is indeed a way to mathematically determine the ball's deflection angle after it hits the headpin. The problem, though, is that the math required to complete these calculations is extremely complex. By extremely complex, we mean exceedingly, maddeningly complicated and headache-inducing, probably just shy of causing an aneurysm! My own head nearly exploded while working through this problem. It literally took me an entire day and several beers to figure out how to set up the equations and to work through the math, and I'm pretty sure smoke was coming from my calculator by the time I finished.

If we were to present the math here, most of you would simply close the book and put it down. The calculations require a tremendous amount of rather difficult algebra and trigonometry, and a lot of explanation. Most of us had little interest in higher math when we were forced to learn it in school, and we're certainly not going to suffer through it now just to be able to make better bowling decisions. What to do? The math is how we reached our conclusions, and it absolutely supports our contentions, but therein lies the problem: If we present the math, we lose most of you, but if we don't present it you would have to just take our word for it, which is something we have already asked you not to do.

Our solution is to present this chapter somewhat inside-out. We've already described our problem. We need to determine if a lighter ball deflects more and a heavier ball less, and if increasing speed will decrease deflection. Instead of working through the proof with you, we'll just jump right to our conclusions. From there we can discuss the implications of deflection on our game. All of the supporting math, which backs up everything we say, can be found in Appendix A, at the back of the book. If you are able to follow the math, you will have a far greater understanding of what is happening on the lane. You can even work through your own variations of the problem to explore deflection in as great a depth as you desire. Even if you only skim through the math, you will at least be able to see where our ideas came from, and satisfy yourself that our conclusions are based in fact and that we didn't just make this stuff up!

CALCULATING DEFLECTION

We know that when our ball hits the headpin, the pin will fly off in one direction at some speed and the ball will deflect in the other direction at some speed. Great, but how can we determine these angles and velocities?

Once again, Isaac Newton provides us with the tools we need—his laws of Conservation of Momentum and Conservation of Energy. Newton tells us that the amount of energy and momentum coming out of a collision is equal to the amount that went into it. Before the collision the headpin had no momentum or energy because it was standing still, so all of the momentum and kinetic energy had to come from the ball. After the collision, the ball will keep some of its momentum and energy, but it will transfer some of it to the pin in order to send it flying off.

The angle at which the pin deflects is determined only by where on its surface it was hit by the ball. The deflection angle of the ball is determined not only by the point of impact, but also by how much of its energy and momentum it gave to the pin, and by the direction it was traveling at the instant it hit the pin. From these facts, plus some trigonometry and an insane amount of complicated algebra, we can calculate the deflection angle and velocity of both the ball and the headpin after a collision.

Let's again use Brian as our test subject, the young man we introduced you to in Chapter 2. Recall that Brian is a right hander who delivers his 15 pound ball at 16 miles per hour, exerting 91.26 newtons of force to do so. To keep the math as simple as possible, we will have him roll a shot straight up board 17-1/2, where it strikes the headpin.

Working through all of the math—which we suggest you review at this time in Appendix A—we calculate that after the ball hits the headpin, the pin deflects off to the left at an angle of 23.55 degrees and at a velocity of 23.88 miles per hour. Brian's ball deflects to the right at an angle of 11.54 degrees, and at a velocity of 11.1 miles per hour.

LIGHTER AND HEAVIER BALL

Now that we know how to calculate the deflection angle of the ball, let's see what happens when Brian throws a heavier 16 pound ball and a lighter 14 pound ball with his same 91.26 newton delivery force, and again straight up board 17-1/2.

Recall from Chapter 2 that when a bowler applies his given delivery force to a lighter ball, that ball will travel faster than will a heavier ball. In Chapter 3 we computed Brian's ball speed as he applies his 91.26 newton delivery force to balls of various weights. For convenience, that data is reproduced here as Table 4.1.

Ball Weight (pounds)	Ball Speed (miles per hour)	Kinetic Energy (Joules)
16	14.95	163
15	16.00	174
14	17.10	186
13	18.40	201
12	19.96	218

Table 4.1: Ball speed derived from 91.26 newton delivery force, as ball weight varies

We can calculate the deflection angle for any weight of ball by performing the same Appendix A calculations all over again, but substituting in the new ball weight and the appropriate computed ball speed. The headpin will deflect at the same angle regardless of ball weight, but its velocity after the collision will change. Table 4.2 presents the resulting final pin velocity, final ball velocity, and the ball deflection angle as Brian throws a 14 pound, 15 pound, and 16 pound ball.

Ball Weight (pounds)	Initial Ball Speed (MPH)	Final Pin Speed (MPH)	Final Ball Speed (MPH)	Ball Deflection Angle (Θb)
16	14.95	22.49	10.62	10.69°
15	16.00	23.88	11.10	11.54°
14	17.10	25.09	11.62	12.47°

Table 4.2: Deflection angles and speeds as ball weight varies

Table 4.2 reveals that the ball's deflection angle did, in fact, increase as ball weight decreased. The increases, however, are quite small, less than a degree for each one pound decrease in ball weight. We said in Chapter 3 that a lighter ball would not experience any meaningful increase in deflection over a heavier ball. Isn't nearly a full degree meaningful?

A change in course of one degree would indeed cause a meaningful change in ball position over a relatively great distance. For example, a one degree change in course over the entire 60 foot length of a bowling lane would cause the ball to end up over a foot away from our intended target. Keep in mind, however, that after our ball deflects away from the headpin it will only travel a very short distance, a matter of inches, before encountering the 3-pin. Over this very small distance between the headpin and the 3-pin, the amount of lateral movement caused by our extra less-than-one-degree deflection will be insignificant. Let's do the math. We know we promised no math, but this is actually simple!

The USBC specifies that the 3-pin must be 10.39 inches behind the headpin. According to Table 4.2, our 15 pound ball deflects off of the headpin at an angle of 11.54 degrees. We can set up a triangle between the headpin and the 3-pin. Our ball deflection angle, which we have labeled Θb (pronounced theta sub B), forms the angle at the bottom of the triangle, while the USBC's 10.39 inch down lane distance between the headpin and the 3-pin forms the triangle's adjacent side.[14] The base of the triangle represents the distance the ball deflects to the right off of the headpin (Figure 4.1).

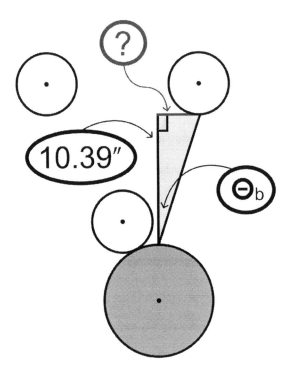

Figure 4.1: Calculating deflection to 3-pin

Trigonometry tells us that the length of our triangle's base—the lateral distance the ball will deflect on its way to the 3-pin—will be equal to the tangent of the ball's deflection angle multiplied by the length of our adjacent side, which is just the distance back from the headpin to the 3-pin. We don't even need to understand what the tangent of an angle is. We can just look up the number in a tangent table, or easier yet, just ask Google. The tangent of our 11.54 degree ball deflection angle is 0.204. Plugging our known data into our formula, we get:

Deflection Distance = Tangent of Deflection Angle x Adjacent Side
Deflection Distance = 0.204 x 10.39 inches
Deflection Distance = 2.12 inches

Thus, if our 15 pound ball deflects off of the headpin at an angle of 11.54 degrees, it will move to the right approximately 2.12 inches before striking the 3-pin. We can carry out similar calculations for our 14 and 16 pound balls. The relevant figures are listed in Table 4.3, below.

Ball Weight (pounds)	Ball Deflection Angle (Θb)	Deflection Distance (inches)
16	10.69°	1.96
15	11.54°	2.12
14	12.47°	2.30

Table 4.3: Lateral ball movement at various deflection angles

As Table 4.3 shows, the small increase in the ball's deflection angle caused by a full pound decrease in ball weight results in increased deflection of only slightly more than 1/8 inch before the ball hits the 3-pin. Even if we were accurate enough to hit precisely the same point on the headpin every single shot, this tiny 1/8 inch additional movement would not impact our pinfall in any meaningful way. When we factor in slight variations from shot to shot and variations in pin placement by the pin-setting machine, this 1/8 inch difference becomes meaningless. Even if we were to drop all the way to a 12 pound ball, the increased deflection would only be about half a board.[15]

A PICTURE IS WORTH A THOUSAND WORDS

We can sense your disbelief from here! Though the numbers clearly demonstrate that a lighter ball does not deflect materially more than does a heavier ball when thrown by the same bowler, real life has to be different, right? Everyone knows that lighter balls deflect more. We can't all be wrong, can we?

Some years ago, Ebonite International, the world's largest manufacturer of bowling balls, produced a series of videos comparing 14, 15, and 16 pound balls as they hit the pins. Other than weight, the balls were identical. One video in particular employed a ramp to deliver the ball in order to remove all possible variation between the shots. The following images are frames captured from this video.

Figure 4.2, below, shows the three balls as they make nearly identical impact with the headpin. In Figure 4.3, the balls have all deflected to the right from the headpin, and are just making contact with the 3-pin. We can clearly see that all three balls contact the 3-pin in almost precisely the same spot, thus demonstrating that deflection was nearly identical despite the weight differences. The final photo, Figure 4.4, shows the three balls as they exit the back of the pin deck following numerous collisions. Again, their positions, and thus their subsequent deflection off of the 5-pin, are almost precisely the same.

Figure 4.2: 14, 15, and 16 pound ball, impact with headpin

Copyright Ebonite International. Adapted with permission.

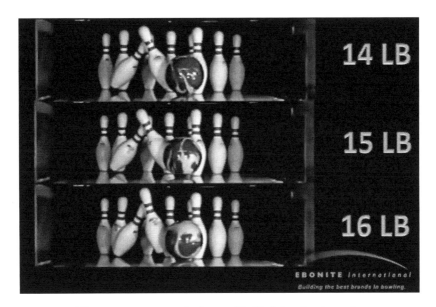

Figure 4.3: 14, 15, and 16 pound ball, deflection to 3-pin

Copyright Ebonite International. Adapted with permission.

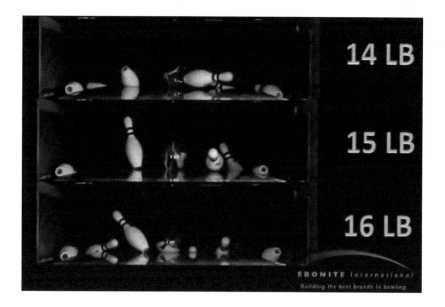

Figure 4.4: 14, 15, and 16 pound ball, leaving pin deck

Copyright Ebonite International. Adapted with permission.

ADVANTAGE: LIGHTER BALL?

The data in Table 4.2 also point to another advantage a lighter ball has over a heavier ball. Table 4.4, below, contains the final ball speed and pin speed data from Table 4.2 after the ball hits the headpin. From this data, we can compute the amount of kinetic energy that both the pin and the ball will possess following the collision, which we recall is equal to 1/2 x Weight x Speed^2. We will not bother with converting to proper units, so while the numbers thus calculated will not be meaningful in and of themselves we can nonetheless compare them to each another.

Ball Weight (pounds)	Final Pin Velocity (MPH)	Pin Kinetic Energy	Final Ball Velocity (MPH)	Ball Kinetic Energy
16	22.49	885	10.62	902
15	23.88	998	11.10	924
14	25.09	1102	11.62	945

Table 4.4: Final ball and pin velocities and kinetic energy following collision with headpin

We have already learned in Chapter 2 that a lighter ball possesses more kinetic energy than does a heavier ball when thrown by any given bowler. The data in Table 4.4 demonstrates that this advantage holds true even after the ball hits the headpin, though not to as great a degree. While the lighter ball does possess a higher kinetic energy than does the heavier ball following the collision with the headpin, it amounts to only slightly more than a two percent increase. Since the lighter ball had a large kinetic energy advantage going into the collision but has only a minor advantage coming back out, where did the extra kinetic energy go?

Mr. Newton tells us that kinetic energy is conserved in a collision, so if the ball lost a significant amount of energy, we know that it still has to be in our collision system somewhere. Table 4.4 shows us where the ball's lost kinetic energy went.

Notice the values in the Pin Kinetic Energy column. The lighter ball transfers far more kinetic energy to the pin than does the heavier ball, and all while maintaining a slight kinetic energy advantage for itself. In fact, for each pound decrease in ball weight, the headpin gains over 10 percent more kinetic energy. Since the pin driven by the lighter ball travels at a much higher velocity and with far greater kinetic energy, it will in turn cause much more violent collisions with subsequent pins. These violent collisions are what we colloquially refer to as *pin action*, and more pin action leads to greater carry as pins splash around the deck taking out any stragglers remaining from less than perfect pocket hits.

The conclusions are clear. A lighter ball not only hits the pins harder, it also creates more pin action than does a heavier ball, and all without any meaningful increase in deflection. Once more, it seems that we should throw the lightest ball we can get away with rather than the heaviest ball we can handle. We are beginning to rethink our own 15 pound arsenals!

A STORY

We admonish you throughout this book that stories and hearsay don't count as evidence and don't prove anything. Since the numbers have already proven our contention that a lighter ball will not deflect too much, we offer the following only as an interesting aside. A recently departed friend was a bowler possessed of an extremely high degree of skill, and he also, through his position with a ball company, had access to equipment and drilling at no cost. At one point in his career he drilled up a series of balls for himself with weights of 6-, 8-, 10-, and 12-pounds, just to see what would happen when he threw them. He said that while it took all of his skill and restraint to keep from overpowering the lighter equipment, he nonetheless was able to roll a 279 game with the 8-pound ball, and averaged over 200 with the 6-pound ball. He said that the strikes "sounded funny," but they definitely still carried.

DEFLECTION AND BALL SPEED

We've just dispensed with the notion that a lighter ball will deflect materially more than will a heavier ball. Another common notion is that ball speed also affects the amount of deflection. We have heard bowlers say that if their ball is deflecting too much, they just increase their ball speed to help it "drive through the pins" rather than deflecting to the side.

We can use the same series of calculations to test this idea. All we have to do is arbitrarily change ball speed to some higher value, and then follow the mathematical procedure laid out in Appendix A but with this new speed value in place of the old.

Recall that our calculations above were based on a 15 pound ball traveling with an initial velocity of 16 miles per hour, which resulted in the ball deflecting off of the headpin at an 11.54 degree angle to the right. What happens if we run through the same calculation, keeping everything the same but decreasing the ball speed to 15 miles per hour? We come up with a new ball deflection angle of—Are you ready for it?—11.54 degrees! What if we increase ball speed to 17 miles per hour? Again, crunching all the numbers yields a ball deflection angle of 11.54 degrees. Feel free to double-check our math. Slow the ball down to one mile per hour, or speed it up to 50. No matter how you vary the numbers, you will find that the ball's deflection angle, in addition to being only minimally affected by ball weight, is also completely independent of ball speed.

DEFLECTION AND THE "SIZE OF THE POCKET"

Our calculations thus far have been limited to the case of a straight ball traveling directly in line with the lane boards, which is a zero degree angle of entry to the pocket. While this zero degree ball path simplified our computations, few bowlers beyond rank beginners would ever employ such a path. Even those who throw a straight ball recognize that they carry more of their hits when throwing the ball on an angle toward the pins rather than straight up the boards. Indeed, the USBC conducted a study some years ago in which they tallied the strike percentage of several hundred shots based on both the ball's position when it hit the pins and on the entry angle—or amount of hook—on each shot. The result of their Pin Carry Study is the now famous chart in Figure 4.5, below.

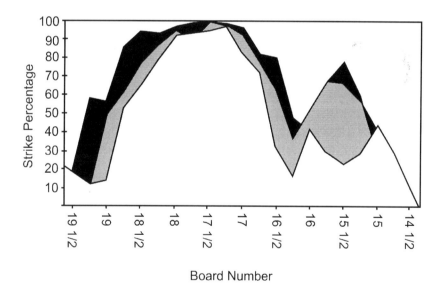

Figure 4.5: Strike percentage as a function of impact position at 2, 4, and 6 degrees of entry angle
Copyright United States Bowling Congress. Adapted with permission.

Figure 4.5 shows the likelihood of achieving a strike based on where the ball impacts the headpin. It is further broken down by entry angle to the pocket, which is another way of saying "more hook." The front graph in white represents an entry angle of 2 degrees, the middle grey graph, 4 degrees, and the black graph at the back, 6 degrees. We will discuss this graph and the study from which it derives in much greater depth in later chapters, but for now let's just look at the peak area of the chart which represents the area on the lane with the greatest strike percentage.

We see from the white 2 degree graph that we can expect a 90 percent or greater chance of striking if our ball impacts the headpin anywhere from board 17-1/4 to board 18-1/4, or an area roughly one board in width. If we switch to the grey 4 degree chart we see a much wider area that still maintains this 90 percent plus chance of striking, extending from about board 17 almost to board 18-1/2. This gives us nearly half a board more room to the right and almost a quarter of a board more to the left than what the 2 degree bowlers enjoy. An extra half board of area doesn't sound like much, but it represents a nearly 50 percent increase in the size of the high-percentage strike zone.

Things get even more extreme when we look at the black 6 degree chart. At the 90 percent level, this chart covers an area from about board 16-3/4 all the way to board 18-3/4. Those bowlers with a 6 degree entry angle to the pocket have almost two full boards of area at the pins with a 90 percent probability of a strike, which is twice the area available to our 2 degree bowlers.

Why should this be so? Why does a big hook give you so much more miss room? While there are likely a number of physical differences between bowlers who throw big hooks and those who throw smaller hooks which could certainly impact strike percentage, an important difference between the results achieved by various ball paths comes down to deflection.

It is certainly possible to calculate the deflection angle of the ball as it impacts the headpin on an angled path rather than straight up the boards, but the math involved is even more daunting and complex. Those well-versed in mathematics will readily see how to do so by shifting our frame of reference when performing the calculations, and those who hate math will not care how to do it, so we will completely skip over the methodology and just provide you with the answers. Table 4.5 presents the ball's deflection angle to the right resulting from our same 15 pound, 16 mile per hour ball impacting the headpin on board 17-1/2, but at an entry angle of 0, 2, 4, and 6 degrees.

Entry Angle	Ball Deflection Angle
0°	11.54°
2°	8.92°
4°	6.24°
6°	3.47°

Table 4.5: Ball deflection angle as entry angle increases

The table shows that as entry angle increases, ball deflection decreases. What does this decrease in deflection mean? Let's look at shots that miss to the right, resulting in the ball hitting too light on the headpin. If our ball hits the headpin head on, it will continue rolling straight back without deflection. As the ball hits the pin farther and farther to the right it will deflect more and more. Let's first look at a straight ball with a zero degree entry angle. The increased deflection from the light hit causes the ball to hit too high on the 3-pin, meaning that the 3-pin does not get driven far enough to the right to properly take out the 6- and the 10-pin. It also results in the ball not deflecting leftward enough off of the 3-pin to send the 5-pin into the 8-pin.

Suppose now that we increase our entry angle from zero to 2 degrees. We see from Table 4.5 that the 2 degree ball deflected 2-1/2 degrees less than did the zero degree ball. On a slightly light hit, this 2-1/2 degree decrease might just be enough to prevent our ball from hitting too high on the 3-pin. Likewise, a 4 degree entry angle results in over a 5 degree decrease in deflection, which means that the 4 degree ball could hit the headpin even lighter still without over-deflecting. The more entry angle a bowler has, the further to the right he or she can miss the pocket and still have a good chance of carrying the strike.

What about shots that miss to the left and hit too high on the headpin? A straight up the boards shot that hits high on the headpin is a nearly head on collision, so the ball will tend to follow the headpin straight back leaving a wide open split. As entry angle increases, the ball has a greater chance of deflecting a bit to the left. With luck, the ball will deflect enough to sweep out the left-hand side of the split, and if we are very lucky some of those left side pins will bounce toward the right where they might trip the other half of the split. Such pinfall won't be pretty and the results will be far from textbook, but the increased entry angle reduces the likelihood of a split on a high hit, and increases the chance of a sloppy strike.

So do the big hook bowlers really have a bigger pocket than do straighter players? It's not really fair to say that. Figure 4.5 shows us that the center of the target is the same for all bowlers, and that center point *is* the pocket. It's just that as entry angle increases, the size of the bulls-eye painted on the target gets bigger. Everyone strikes when they hit the pocket, but geometry conspires to let those with bigger hooks carry more of their bad shots. Far more.

CHAPTER 5

YOU SAY YOU WANT A REVOLUTION
THE MYTH OF THE UNLOADED WRIST, THE FRISBEE, AND THE YO-YO.

I AM REMINDED of an old joke I heard from a college professor: Two engineering professors, on their way out of the building after work, are arguing over what they consider to be the most amazing invention in the history of the world. The first professor insists that the wheel is the most amazing invention, arguing that it revolutionized not only transportation, but in fact lead to the invention of most all of our mechanical contrivances. The second professor argues that the most amazing invention in the world is the transistor, in that it not only revolutionized the field of electronics and data processing, but also enabled the automated control and regulation of the very mechanical devices engendered by the wheel. An old janitor who had been mopping the hallway overheard their conversation, and was smiling smugly and shaking his head. One of the professors turns to the old man and says, "I suppose you have something to add to this discussion?" "Yeah," replies the old man. "You're both wrong. The most amazing invention in the world has to be the Thermos. It has no batteries, no moving parts, no nothing, but if I put hot food in it, it keeps it hot, and if I put cold food in it, it keeps it cold." "What, pray tell, is so amazing about that," enquires one of the professors? The old man replies, "How does it know which to do?"

When I first began bowling I was having trouble picking up my 10 pins. I did not yet own a plastic spare ball, and just used my regular ball for everything. Though I had very little hook at the time, it always seemed to be just enough to make me miss the 10-pin to the left or to drop the ball into the gutter in trying to get it out far enough to hook back into the pin. The proprietor of the bowling center gave me a bit of advice; allow my wrist to bend back as I release the ball, which would take revolutions off the ball and would make it go straight. This trick—which is common bowling knowledge—is widely shared, and in fact works. If you allow your wrist to bend backward as you release your ball, it will have far lower revolutions and will tend to go very straight rather than hook.

Some time later, I wanted to develop a good hook. My ball displayed a rather slow and moderate fade to the left, as opposed to the hard left turn I saw in both the pros and the high average bowlers on my league. Understanding that it was relatively high revolutions which caused the desired dramatic hook, I set out to figure out how to achieve such revs. In watching the league bowlers who enjoyed big hooks, I observed people putting spin on the ball through various ungraceful and forced quirks, people employing a wicked snap of their wrist at the point of release, and one young man who had the most graceful and seemingly effortless release, yet his ball positively sizzled as it touched down on the lane surface. Whatever these bowlers were doing to obtain their revs, it happened far too quickly for me to see with the naked eye. Nor did video help, as the release occurs far too quickly to be captured by the slow cameras in most electronic devices. At 30 frames per second, in one frame the bowler's thumb is still in the ball while in the next frame the ball is already gone from their hand.

Unable to observe how to achieve respectable revs on my own, I sought professional help. A very well credentialed coach told me that elite bowlers achieved their high revolution rates by rapidly "unloading" their wrist during their release. That is to say, by rapidly and forcefully snapping their wrist backward, moving from a strong, flexed, cupped position—ostensibly "loaded"— to a fully extended, bent back, "unloaded" position once the thumb exits the ball. I heard this claim again in a bowling tips video released by a major ball manufacturer, and yet again from a league bowler who was explaining to me how he was working to increase his rev rate. "Just like throwing a Frisbee," he stated. I heard it again just days ago while watching a video of an old televised tournament featuring the young bowling phenom, E.J. Tackett. The color commentator stated of Tackett, "You wonder how you can generate that much power from such a small stature. Easy. Get your feet going fast, cup that wrist, and bend that elbow right before you let go of the bowling ball, *and snap that wrist open.* You'll throw it fast, you'll generate a lot of revs." The idea that revs are created by bending the wrist back during the release is seemingly everywhere.

This, of course, leads us to a contradiction. In the first instance, uncupping the wrist on release *decreases* revs and makes the ball go straight, while in the second instance uncupping the wrist on release *increases* revs and makes the ball hook more. Huh? Like the old janitor's Thermos bottle, "How does it know which to do?"

In answer to the question of "How does it know which to do?", we have heard speculative hypotheses ranging from "The difference is in when your thumb comes out of the ball relative to when you uncup your wrist," to "The difference is in forcefully uncupping versus passively uncupping your wrist," and several even more tenuous guesses along the lines of "uncupping the wrist lets the ball roll off your fingers," whatever that might mean. The most honest, but unfortunately least convincing explanation we heard was, "It just does"! None of these ideas hold much water. We have already seen, and can readily demonstrate to ourselves, that passively uncupping our wrist during the release decreases revs and makes our ball go straight, not hook. How, then, could the same motion increase revs and increase the amount of hook, even if we did it more quickly? It's sort of like saying that tipping a bucket of water slowly will empty it, but tipping it quickly will somehow fill it.

We find the "unloading the wrist to create revs" idea repeated in books, videos, and magazine articles, many by famous and respected personalities. It is easy to see where this idea comes from. If you watch video of the more powerful professional bowlers as they release their ball, it sometimes does look as if that is exactly what they are doing, at least from a casual viewing—and unfortunately human nature and basic psychology conspire to prevent us from ever looking any deeper.

A psychological concept called *priming* has a powerful effect on what we see and what we retain when viewing complex data. Stated simply, priming says that once an idea is in our head, it tends to stay there and to influence how we perceive the world. When the widely respected coach or the well-known commentator on a PBA telecast tells us that power players create revs by snapping their wrist open, they have primed our brain to see exactly that. But the perception problems don't stop there. Once we have convinced ourselves that we have personally witnessed it, another psychological demon, our old friend *confirmation bias*, kicks in to reinforce the idea.

Confirmation bias causes us to unconsciously seek out confirming data, and to stop looking as soon as we have found anything that seems to back up our preconceived ideas. Worse yet, it also causes us to ignore or rationalize away any conflicting evidence that comes our way, and to accept confirming evidence unquestioningly. Thus, when a respected authority tells us that bending the wrist back during the release creates revs, priming causes us to see it even if it's not really there, and confirmation bias causes us to stop looking once we think we've seen it, and to ignore anything that doesn't fit our newly adopted worldview.

All of us are subject to the effects of priming and confirmation bias, and most of the time we are completely unaware that they are skewing our perception. It takes a great deal of intellectual effort to get past them in order to see things as they really are, and it is imperative that we put forth that effort if we wish to truly understand our sport. If we are willing to look more closely and analytically at bowling releases on a frame-by-frame basis, we will see that high rev bowlers are not "snapping their wrist open" during their release at all, and that quite the opposite is actually happening. Despite what it may look like at first glance, and despite the great many voices to the contrary, the facts and the evidence simply do not support the unloaded wrist idea, as we will soon discover.

WHAT ARE REVS, AND WHERE DO THEY COME FROM?

In bowling, our desire is to create topspin, meaning that the top of the ball is spinning away from us and toward the pins as the ball travels down the lane (Figure 5.1). Our topspin is measured in Revolutions Per Minute (RPM), which bowlers refer to as *rev rate* or simply as *revs*. The higher the rev rate, the faster the ball is spinning. Revs is just another name for topspin.

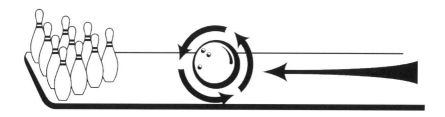

Figure 5.1: Down lane travel coupled with topspin

Note that our topspin need not be in precisely the same down lane direction as our ball trajectory. In fact, in order for the ball to hook, the topspin must be at some angle to the direction of ball travel. This angle away from the direction of travel is referred to in bowling as *axis rotation*, and it plays a significant role in the eventual path of our ball. Axis rotation and other factors affecting the degree of hook will be covered in detail in later chapters. For this discussion of revolutions, we will ignore axis rotation. As we are concerned at this point only with the *amount* of topspin created by our release, we don't really care right now in what direction the ball is pointing as we create that topspin.

In order to impart topspin, we must accelerate the ball in such a way that the top of the ball travels down the lane and away from our body at a faster rate than we are accelerating the ball itself. This effect is achieved through the action of our fingertips carrying the finger holes up or forward faster than the arm is carrying the ball up or forward. If our fingers do not propel the finger holes up or forward faster than our arm is pushing the ball down the lane, the ball will simply slide rather than spin, and no meaningful hook will be possible. Perhaps an illustration will help clarify.

In Figure 5.2 below, a rocket is attached directly to the back of a bowling ball. When the rocket fires, it will project the ball forward without spin. In Figure 5.3, the rocket is attached to the ball via a pivot, and a smaller rocket is attached directly to the back of the ball. In this case, while the main rocket still serves to propel the ball forward, the smaller rocket provides extra forward push to the top of the ball, causing the ball to spin as it travels. In both cases the large rocket provides only down lane velocity, with no spin. It is only when we add a second component of force perpendicular to the ball, via the smaller rocket, that we can get the ball to spin forward as it travels down the lane.

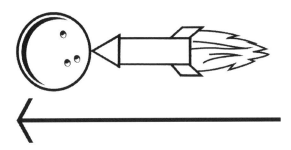

Figure 5.2: Down lane force

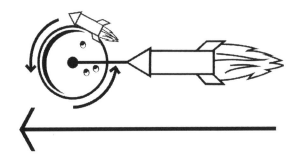

Figure 5.3: Down lane force with spin

We create the energy which we impart to the bowling ball through our delivery. Our delivery is a combination of our footwork, our arm swing, and our release. This energy needs to do two things to the ball. The simplest function of our delivery is to project the ball down the lane with a certain velocity just as the large rocket did in the illustration above, and bowlers of every skill level do this. For those bowlers who wish to hook the ball, a required secondary function of the delivery is to impart topspin to the ball, just as the small rocket did above.

SPIN

The portion of the energy generated by our delivery and release that projects the ball down lane is called *force*, and the portion that spins the ball is called *torque*.[16] In everyday language, torque can be thought of as a twisting force. In engineering terms, torque is a force applied to an object *at some distance from the object's axis of rotation*, and *at an angle away from that axis of rotation*. This definition sounds complex, but it really isn't, and it will become more clear over the course of our discussion.

A bowling ball's axis of rotation passes through its geometric center. In our illustration of the ball and the rocket, though the large rocket fulfills the first torque requirement by imparting its force at a distance from the ball's axis of rotation, it does so directly in line with the axis. Since it fails the second requirement to apply the force at an angle to the axis of rotation, it cannot cause the ball to spin. The second smaller rocket is also attached at a distance from the ball's axis of rotation, but in this case it provides its thrust at an angle away from the axis rather than directly in line with it. Since the small rocket fulfills both requirements, it imparts torque to the ball and causes it to spin. In bowling, our legs and arm can be thought of as the large rocket providing down lane force to the ball, while our wrist and fingertips play the part of the small rocket, imparting spin. Let's make this clearer by looking at the example of trying to turn a stuck bolt.

To remove a stuck bolt, we need to apply torque, or twisting force, to it. It is very difficult to remove a bolt by just twisting it with our fingers. To make the task easier we put a wrench on the bolt, and then push on the side of the wrench handle. We said that torque is a force applied to an object at some distance from the object's axis of rotation and at an angle away from that axis of rotation. The wrench lets us apply more torque to the bolt than we possibly could with our bare fingers because rather than twisting the bolt directly we instead apply our force *at some distance from the object's axis*—this distance being the length of the wrench handle—and *at an angle away from that axis of rotation* by pushing on the side of the wrench handle rather than on the end. From an engineering standpoint, the wrench handle would technically be called our torque system's *lever arm* or *moment arm*. The longer the lever arm—that is, the longer the wrench handle—the more twisting force we can apply to the bolt for any given level of force applied to the wrench (Figure 5.4).

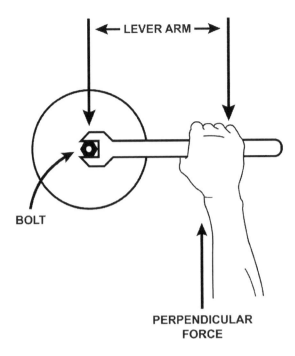

Figure 5.4: Torque system, bolt

We employ precisely the same mechanism to spin our bowling ball. When holding the ball prior to release, our fingertips do not reach all the way to the center of the ball. Instead, they reach only part way into the ball, and the distance from the ball's center to our fingertips is analogous to the length of our wrench handle. During our release, we must apply energy to the finger holes in a direction perpendicular to the ball's lever arm, that is, perpendicular to the line drawn from the ball's center out to the finger holes. The inertia of the ball acts as a pivot point, much as our bolt did, which allows the force we apply to the finger holes to convert to torque and spin the ball rather than merely adding to the down lane force supplied by our arm swing (Figure 5.5).

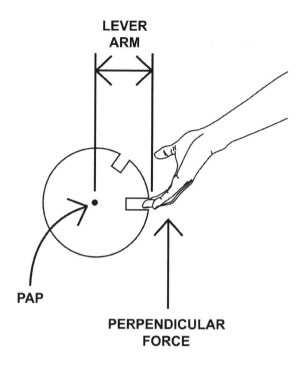

Figure 5.5: Torque system, ball

CONVENTIONAL GRIP VERSUS FINGERTIP GRIP

As a side note, the above discussion of our bowling ball's torque system explains very neatly why a bowler generates more revolutions with a "fingertip grip" than with a "conventional grip" drilling. We said that the amount of twisting force we can apply to a bolt is a function of the length of the wrench or *lever arm* we employ—the longer the wrench, the greater the torque. In bowling, we can change the length of the lever arm, our "wrench," through alteration of the length of the grip drilled into our ball.

In a conventional grip, the finger holes and thumb hole are very close together, and our fingers are buried in the holes up to the second knuckle. This puts our fingertips about two inches below the surface of the ball. Since a bowling ball has a radius of just over four inches, we have cut the length of our lever arm, the point at which our fingertips push on the handle of the wrench, almost in half. If we change our ball drilling to a longer "fingertip" grip, our fingers will only go into the ball up to the first knuckle, or about 1/2 inch or so. This puts our fingertips about 3-1/2 inches from the center of the ball, so we have increased the length of our lever arm—our wrench—by well over 50 percent (Figure 5.6). Just as with a longer wrench, the increased lever arm length provided by a fingertip grip as opposed to a conventional grip allows more of our muscle strength to convert to torque in order to spin the ball faster with any given release.

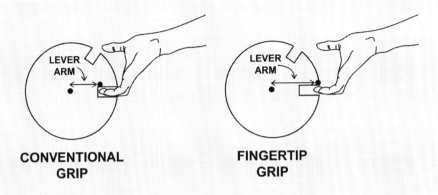

Figure 5.6: Lever arm length, conventional grip vs. fingertip grip

This line of reasoning was carried to its extreme in the old-school "stretched" grip, which was a layout so long that the very tips of the fingers were just barely able to grasp the edge of the finger holes. A stretched drilling did increase the lever arm length to the maximum possible given the fixed size of a bowling ball, thus increasing possible torque to the maximum. Unfortunately it also put the hand and thumb in a highly stressed position which led to injuries, particularly at the base of the thumb. It also required the bowler to tightly grab the ball, which adversely affected his or her release. These problems caused the stretched grip to fall from favor. Despite this, you will still see some bowlers, mostly old-timers, employing a stretched grip. You can often recognize stretched drillings by rubber finger hole inserts with a flat side, so-called "lifts," facing the thumb hole, rather than the simple oval inserts used by most fingertip grip bowlers. Since the fingertips are barely in the ball with a stretched grip, these undercut flats help the bowler hang onto the ball during the swing.

There also exists a fourth though rarely used drilling known as the *Sarge Easter* grip, named for professional bowler and career military man Ebber "Sarge" Easter. In the Sarge Easter grip, the middle finger hole is laid out for a fingertip grip while the ring finger span is shortened to a conventional grip. By this method the ball driller tries to achieve an intermediate lever arm length which is an approximate average of the two individual holes. All four grips are illustrated in Figure 5.7, below.

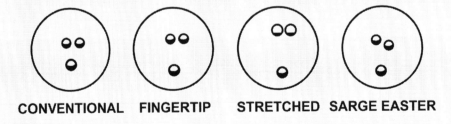

Figure 5.7: Conventional grip, fingertip grip, stretched grip, and Sarge Easter grip

HOW DOES A BOWLER CREATE TOPSPIN?

We said that topspin is a condition wherein the top of the ball is spinning in a forward, down lane direction faster than the ball is traveling down the lane (Figure 5.8).

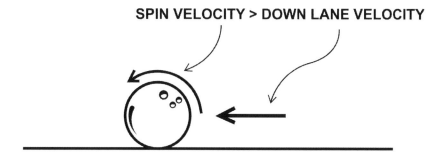

Figure 5.8: Ball with forward motion and topspin

In order to make the ball spin forward, our engineering definition requires that we impart a force to it in a direction *perpendicular to the its axis*, and *at some distance from the its axis*. In bowling, we impart this force via the finger holes after our thumb has released its grip on the ball. As Figure 5.9 illustrates, the only way to propel the finger holes in the proper down lane direction is to pull up on the finger holes if they are on the back of the ball, to push forward if they are on top of the ball, to pull downward if they are on the front of the ball, or to pull backward if they are under the ball—or an averaging of two of those movements if the finger holes are at some intermediate position. Any other motion of the fingertips, say pushing downward on the finger holes when they are on the back of the ball, would clearly spin the ball in the wrong direction.

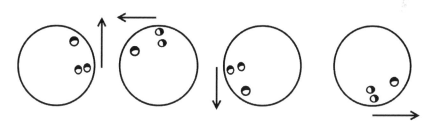

Figure 5.9: Imparting spin via the finger holes

You are probably beginning to see just why the common notion that we can impart spin by "snapping that wrist open" cannot be true. To hammer the point home, let's perform a little experiment. Place a bowling ball on the floor with the finger holes somewhere between the back and top of the ball. While kneeling behind the ball, insert the tips of your fingers into the finger holes while your wrist remains straight, as in Figure 5.10. Now, let's "snap that wrist open" by bending it back. What happens? When we bend our wrist back, our fingernails push backward against the lower side of the finger holes, and the ball rolls *toward* us rather than away from us as would be required to create topspin.

In kinesiology, snapping that wrist open is properly called *extension* of the wrist joint. If we extend the wrist joint while our fingers are in the ball anywhere along the back or top of the ball, *our fingertips will impart force in precisely the wrong direction* for the creation of topspin, and we will instead create backspin.

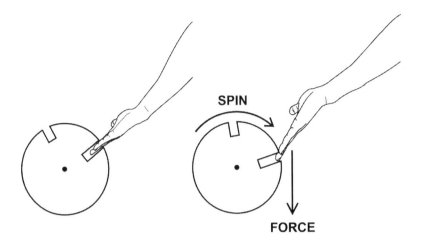

Figure 5.10: Wrist extension causes spin in wrong direction

How, then, can we create topspin? Place your fingertips back in the ball, but this time snap your wrist upward, into a cupped position. What happens to the ball? By snapping the wrist "closed" rather than open—bending it forward rather than back—our fingertips now produce force against the front of the finger holes, driving them away from us and causing the ball to roll away from us in the proper down lane direction (Figure 5.11).

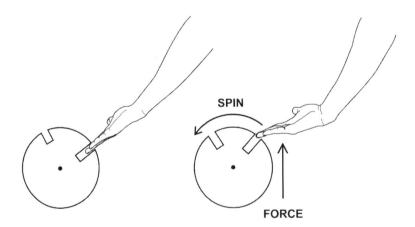

Figure 5.11: Wrist flexion causes spin in proper direction

Here's an even more convincing demonstration. Place a bowling ball on the floor. Put your hand on the back of the ball with your fingers in the holes, and the holes at or a bit above the ball's equator, as in Figure 5.12a. Leave your thumb out of the ball. Now, holding your arm and fingers stationary, "snap that wrist open" by bending back your wrist joint (Figure 5.12b). What happened? If you indeed held your arm and fingers stationary, all that happened was that your fingers pulled out of the ball as your hand bent back, and the ball just sat there. No revs, no roll, no topspin, no nothing. Now place your hand back on the ball, but this time "close" your wrist instead of "opening" it, bending it toward your forearm while again holding your arm and fingers stationary (Figure 5.12c). This time, the ball rolls forward. By bending the wrist forward, even without any movement of the arm or fingers, we created topspin.

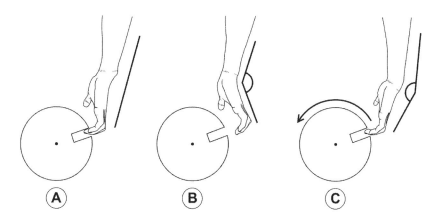

Figure 5.12: Result on topspin of wrist extension and flexion

If you were a believer in the idea that "snapping that wrist open" creates revs before you read this chapter, you are at this point likely thinking, "Yes, but if I bend my wrist back while both my fingers and my thumb are in the ball, the ball will rotate in the proper direction. Doesn't this count as creating revs?" This line of reasoning isn't uncommon. We were recently sent a YouTube video in which a coach was reviewing release footage with a bowler. As the coach slowly advanced the video, he pointed out that when the bowler bent his wrist back prior to release, the hand moved toward the top of the ball and the ball rotated less than one eighth of a turn. The coach then said, "You wouldn't think such a small turn of the ball could create so many revs, but it does." The coach should have stopped after the first part of his sentence—"You wouldn't think such a small turn of the ball could create so many revs"—because it can't. Most of us have been taught the old adage "If something seems too good to be true, it *is* too good to be true," and that advice is certainly sound in regard to rev creation.

    The easiest way to dispel the idea that the small rotation of the ball resulting from bending back the wrist can create revs, is to try it, or more safely, to picture it in your head. If we were to bend our wrist back with our fingers and thumb both in the ball, and were to then let go of the ball, no spin would occur at all. The ball would simply crash to the floor. Even though bending your wrist back did slightly rotate the ball, as soon as you stopped extending your wrist, the rotation stopped too. You cannot get your fingers and thumb out of the holes quickly enough to let the ball continue rotating, and they act instead as a brake. Even if you could somehow instantaneously get your fingers and thumb out of the ball after extending your wrist, the amount of rotation your wrist extension imparts will be negligible. The only thing that bending back the wrist does is reposition the ball relative to your hand, not spin it. Topspin requires us to apply meaningful force to the finger holes, and we see no way that bending the wrist back can do this.

While bending the wrist back is properly called *extension* of the joint, bending it forward into a cupped position is called *flexion*. If we bend our wrist back, we *extend* it. If we bend it forward, toward our forearm, we *flex* it. It is only by applying force to the finger holes with our fingertips, and in the proper down lane direction, that we can impart topspin to the ball. In terms of wrist joint motion, meaningful topspin can only be created by flexing the wrist forward into a cupped or at least a less extended position. Extending the wrist into an open, bent back position simply cannot drive the finger holes forward as is required.

"Snapping that wrist open"—or "unloading the wrist," as it is more often called—with the fingers behind or atop the ball, cannot create topspin since it would spin the ball in the wrong direction or not at all. Even if it somehow *could* produce topspin, we do not believe it would be physically possible to forcibly "snap that wrist open" even if we wanted to, because the muscles controlling wrist extension are far weaker than those controlling flexion. Wrist flexion and extension are brought about through the action of six relatively slender muscles in the forearm. The muscles which bring about flexion, the cupping of the wrist, are over 20 percent stronger than those which extend or "open" the wrist.[17] More importantly, the amount of flexion force these muscles generate, the amount of force they can exert against a resistance such as a heavy bowling ball, increases dramatically as the wrist is flexed. That is to say, the more our wrist is moved from extension to flexion—from bent back to cupped—the more force we are able to generate to maintain or even increase that flexion.[18] In fact, with the wrist bent back to full extension, the average male is able to generate 45 newtons of flexing force. As the wrist moves forward into flexion the amount of force we are able to generate increases steadily, averaging 90 newtons once the wrist is fully flexed forward. When strongly flexed (cupped), our wrist is able to generate *twice* as much force as when it is extended (open), which also nicely bolsters our use of the bowling term "strong" in describing a flexed (cupped) wrist position, and "weak" in describing an extended (open) wrist.[19]

It is also pretty much meaningless to refer to "loading" or "unloading" the wrist regardless of which direction we move it. Unlike a hydraulic cylinder, muscles can only exert force in one direction, and can only do so by contracting. In order to move a joint in the opposite direction, opposing muscles must contract, which also serves to stretch out the muscles that originally contracted to "close" the joint. If we extend, or bend the wrist back, we contract the muscles on the back of the forearm but simultaneously stretch the opposing muscles on the front of the forearm. Likewise if we flex the wrist forward into a cupped position we contract the muscles on the front of the forearm while simultaneously stretching the opposing muscles on the back of the forearm. Do we "load" a muscle by contracting it, or by stretching it out, ready to be contracted again? Since movement of a joint requires one muscle to contract as another stretches, how can we load or unload a joint? Regardless of how we choose to define the terms, any movement would require one muscle to load as the opposing muscle unloads. The terms "load" and "unload" are simply not descriptive in this regard, and should be dispensed with. We should instead stick with the proper terms from kinesiology, "flex" and "extend."

OTHER SOURCES OF TOPSPIN

While topspin can be created by flexing the wrist, the fingers, or both, bowlers can also impart topspin to the ball without any active movement of the wrist at all, through the simple action of our arm swing moving forward against the inertia of the ball. Think back to our example of a wrench turning a bolt as was depicted in Figure 5.4. When we push on the side of the wrench handle, that is, perpendicular to the wrench, all of our effort converts to torque to turn the bolt. If instead we were to push on the end of the wrench handle, directly toward the bolt, then the bolt would not turn and our effort would instead merely push the object containing the bolt away from us. If we push on the wrench handle at any angle in between those two extremes, some of our effort will convert to torque to twist the bolt and some will convert to force to push the object away.

The same thing happens to your bowling ball during your delivery. When your hand is behind the ball during your swing all of your effort converts to force to push the ball down the lane and none of it produces torque to spin the ball. As soon as you release your thumb from the ball, the ball will begin to fall from your hand toward the floor. As the ball falls toward the floor, it has the effect of moving your fingers more toward the top of the ball. Because your fingers are no longer directly behind the ball, the effort of your arm swing is no longer entirely toward the center of the ball. Your swing instead now causes your fingertips to apply force at some angle to the ball, so while some of your effort converts to down lane force, the rest of it pushes against the inertia of the ball and converts to torque, creating topspin (Figure 5.13). If your wrist remains firm during this part of the swing, quite a bit of your effort can convert to torque and topspin. If your wrist bends back during this motion, then some of your potential topspin will be lost to damping effects, which we will discuss later in this chapter. Regardless of wrist position though, at least some of your swing will convert to torque, so even those bowlers with relatively weak releases will enjoy at least a bit of topspin so long as their thumb comes out of the ball before their fingers do.

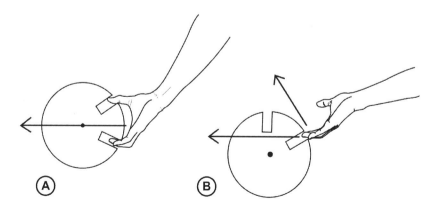

Figure 5.13: (a) Swing producing force, (b) Swing producing force plus torque

Beyond the passive topspin created by the arm swing operating through the fingertips against the inertia of the falling bowling ball, and any active topspin created by the forceful flexing of the wrist into a less extended or more closed, cupped position, bowlers also add topspin to the ball through the action of the fingers themselves. Think back to Figure 5.9, which showed us that the only way to create topspin is to drive the finger holes rapidly upward or forward with the fingertips. Let's temporarily eliminate the topspin created by our arm swing and our wrist by holding both straight. How can we produce the required topspin using only our fingers? The only way to do so is to forcibly curl our fingers up toward the palm of the hand, as we might do in order to grip an object. That is to say, we must *flex* our fingers.

Our fingers are incredibly strong, but curiously they contain no muscles.[20] Instead, our fingers are attached via long tendons to 17 muscles in the palm of the hand and 18 muscles in the forearm. The flexion of the fingers is controlled by two subgroups of these muscles, and together they are able to apply a significant amount of force to our bowling ball through our fingertips. When closed into a full grip, our fingers can flex with about five times more force than can our wrist. Even without flexing that far, our fingers can still impart significant force to the finger holes of the ball, making the curling of the fingers a potentially powerful contributor to topspin.

So we have four sources of force available to us in bowling; our footwork, arm swing, wrist flexion, and finger flexion, all propelling the ball forward, with some of their effort converting to down lane velocity and some to topspin. All bowlers must employ at least one of these four sources of force or the ball will not move down the lane. Most every bowler uses footwork plus an arm swing, though there are even exceptions at this basic level. We sometimes see children and the elderly who just stand at the foul line, swing their arm back and forth a few times, and let the ball roll. It is our assumption, though, that most every bowler reading this book employs both an approach and an arm swing.

Better bowlers will add to the approach and arm swing at least some forward motion of their wrist, their fingers, or both. The more pieces of the delivery we have working in a forward direction, the more force we impart to the ball in the form of velocity and topspin (rev rate). In his book *Sport Science*, professor of physics Peter J. Brancazio similarly describes the swing of a baseball bat: "Swinging the bat requires rapid angular acceleration. The torque needed to accelerate the bat is supplied by the batter's hips, shoulders, arms, and wrists, each of these rotating in a proper sequence that builds one rotation on another." To understand why we get more velocity and revs by employing more sources of force—by *building one upon another* and all in the same direction—we need to examine the curious case of the 40 mile per hour cockroach.

THE 40 MILE PER HOUR BUG

The average human walks at a rate of about three miles per hour, and can run at about 15 miles per hour. Our approach on the bowling lane is ordinarily something faster than a walk but well short of a run, so let's assume that our approach speed is about five miles per hour. If we make our approach but don't do anything else to the ball, merely dropping it to the floor as we near the foul line, the ball will certainly roll down the lane, though not very powerfully. Since at least some of our five mile per hour foot speed will convert to torque as the ball falls away from our fingers, the remaining effort will propel the ball at something less than our original five miles per hour. We are unlikely to win many tournaments with such a low ball speed and rev rate, so we need a way to add some power to our delivery. The only way to propel the ball with more force is to somehow get our hand and fingers moving forward at a much faster rate than our body is moving during our approach.

How can our fingertips possibly move forward at a faster rate than does the arm and body they are attached to? Part of our problem in visualizing this comes from our common idea that our bowling delivery is essentially a pendulum—our ball, attached to our shoulder pivot by our arm, swinging freely in more or less of an arc. In reality this is a rather poor analogy. Our arm swing is far from free, and our delivery more closely approximates the compound motion of the cracking of a bullwhip than it does the swinging of a simple pendulum. To better understand this idea, let's look at an analogy.

Suppose a dog is standing on the back of a railroad flatcar attached to a train. The train is traveling at a rate of 20 miles per hour, so our dog is also traveling at 20 miles per hour relative to the ground. Now, as the train is traveling forward the dog starts to run forward on the flatcar at his maximum speed of 17 miles per hour. He is traveling at 17 miles per hour relative to the flatcar, but since that flatcar is also moving forward at 20 MPH our dog's speed relative to the ground is the sum of the two velocities, or 37 MPH. By adding his own speed to that of the train, the dog is able to move faster relative to the ground than either he or the train are able to travel on their own. Now let's add a third factor. A cockroach is standing on the dog's back near his tail. The roach is capable of running at a rate of three miles per hour. If the roach runs forward on the dog's back at his maximum speed of three MPH, as the dog runs forward at 17 MPH, atop a flatcar traveling at 20 MPH, then that little bug is traveling at the blistering rate of 40 MPH relative to the ground even though none of the individual parts of our system are moving anywhere near that fast.

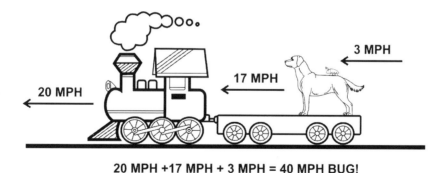

20 MPH +17 MPH + 3 MPH = 40 MPH BUG!

Figure 5.14: The 40 MPH bug

The phenomenon of the 40 mile per hour bug is called the *Principle of Additive Velocities*, and derives from the work of the great 17th century mathematician and physicist, Galileo.

In essence, the bug walks forward at three MPH regardless of how fast the dog is going, and the dog travels forward at 17 MPH regardless of how fast the train is going. In bowling, think of your footwork as the train, your arm swing from the shoulder as the running dog, and your wrist and finger flexion as the bug on the dog's back. As long as the train, the dog, and the bug are all traveling in the same direction, their individual velocities will add together. Additive Velocity can be thought of like compound interest for your ball speed. Because of the Principle of Additive Velocities, as we add more and more sources of force in the proper down lane direction we are able to propel the ball down the lane far faster than either our arm, legs, or fingers alone would be capable of. More importantly the Principle of Additive Velocity allows us to spin the ball by driving the top of the ball forward at a faster rate than we are propelling it down the lane, and this spin is of course our revs.

OF DOGS, BUGS, AND TRAINS

Now that we understand how all of the parts of our delivery add together to create our ball speed and revs through the Principle of Additive Velocities, let's look at a few different delivery styles in terms of dogs, bugs, and trains.

We have observed a large number of bowlers, from casual recreational bowlers, through league, high school, collegiate, and national team players, all the way to elite PBA professionals. While there are all sorts of releases, some clean and textbook, others bordering on the bizarre, for the most part they fall into one of three general camps which we have termed *passive, static,* and *active,* and these camps, with few exceptions, vary significantly from one another in terms of the rev rates they are able to generate.

PASSIVE RELEASE

In a passive release the wrist is not held rigid during the swing, whether due to forearm weakness or wrist injury, or simply to inexperience or inefficient technique. Because little or no flexion effort is applied to the wrist, the heavy ball causes the wrist to bend back into a very extended, weak position, often happening right from the push away (Figure 5.15). We call this release *passive* because the bowler does pretty much nothing to control the wrist position during the swing or the release, instead passively letting the weight and inertia of the ball assume control.

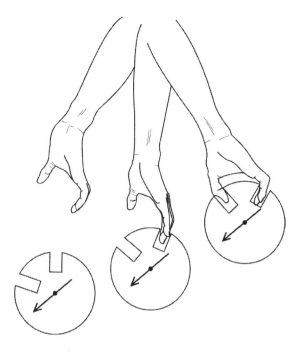

Figure 5.15: Passive release.

Because the wrist is bent backward quite a bit, the hand will tend to be more toward the top of the ball rather than behind it during the release. Since the hand is atop the ball, the ball will fall away very quickly once the thumb exits, giving the bowler very little time or opportunity to apply torque with his or her fingers. Worse yet, since little effort is put into keeping the wrist joint straight, the effort put into trying to drive the finger holes forward to generate topspin often instead results only in the wrist bending back even more. In effect, the passive wrist dampens and cancels out most of our attempt to generate torque. Passive bowlers obtain forward force with their legs and arm swing, but the wrist and fingers add pretty much nothing to the equation. That is, the train is moving forward, the dog is running forward, but the bug is dead! The dead bug may just lay there on the dog's back as he runs, adding nothing, or worse yet may actually be blown backward, subtracting velocity. Since all of the forward force ordinarily provided by wrist and finger flexion is missing from their delivery, bowlers employing a passive release tend to exhibit a relatively low rev rate, with little or no hook unless their ball speed is also extremely low.

STATIC RELEASE

In a static release, the bowler's wrist and fingers neither flex nor extend to any meaningful degree as he or she releases the ball. The wrist is relatively immobile, whether due to a wrist device or merely from very strong forearms, and the wrist and fingers remain in essentially the same position relative to the forearm throughout the swing and release. Think of the static release as a "stiff wrist" release, as it never varies much from its starting flexure, whether straight, cupped, or slightly bent back. Instead, the bowler's hand forms sort of a claw, allowing for some of the delivery forces of the legs and arm to convert to revs as the bowler pulls up or forward on the finger holes once their thumb exits the ball. In this stiff-wrist, *static*, claw-like release, the bowler's legs and arm swing both add force to the ball, but while the static wrist and fingers keep the bowler from losing effort as happens with a passive release, they do nothing active to add to the forward motion. In this case the train is moving forward, the dog is running forward, and while the bug is at least not dead, he's certainly not running forward as quickly as he might.

While much of the energy imparted to the ball in a static release is converted to force which propels the ball down the lane, some portion is still converted to torque, providing the topspin which our ball needs in order to hook. We call this a static release because the topspin on the ball is created without any meaningful wrist or finger movement. It is instead mostly the result of the rigidly held fingertips resisting the falling ball, and typically also providing "lift," or extra spin as the arm and hand move upward and claw through the ball. Perhaps an illustration will help to clarify what is happening during a static release.

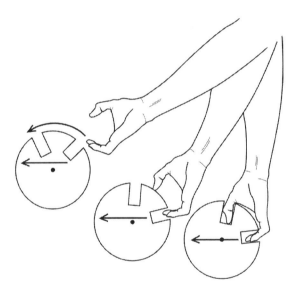

Figure 5.16: Static release.

Examine figure 5.16, above. While the thumb is in the ball, all of the energy imparted to the ball is converted to force, propelling the ball down lane. As the thumb begins to release, the fingers are still for the most part pushing the ball forward. As the ball falls away from the hand the tips of the rigid fingers resist that drop, creating torque which causes the ball to spin forward.

The static release, though quite respectable and far stronger than the passive release, typically does not create the large amount of torque or spin often associated with the so-called power players, though there are exceptions. In fact, if the bowler's arm swing is rather forceful, a significant amount of topspin can be created via a static release, and there are a number of PBA bowlers who do so. The "suitcase" release, popular many decades ago, was in fact a static release, but with the hand turned sideways rather than being more behind the ball as in the modern game.

Since much of the energy imparted via a static release is in the down lane direction, with only some of it converting to torque, the more "physical" bowlers employing a static release will often be *speed dominant*. Speed dominant bowlers are those who do not have enough revs for their ball speed, so ball speed dominates the revs, resulting in a relatively straight ball path and a late hook. Some bowlers who are less physical in their game but who employ a static release, often via a wrist device, will have lower ball speed, so these bowlers can obtain a respectable amount of hook. However, since this hook comes at the expense of ball speed, such bowlers can suffer from poor carry. Because of the low speed, the ball does not convey enough kinetic energy to spray pins around the deck to knock down the stragglers on less than perfect shots.

ACTIVE RELEASE

In an active release, not only are the feet and the arm propelling the ball forward, but the bowler's wrist, fingers, or both also add forward impetus to the delivery. As we have discussed, the wrist and fingers can only impart force to the ball in the proper down lane direction by flexing, that is, by the wrist bending forward toward the inside of the forearm and by the fingers curling in toward the palm of the hand (Figure 5.17).

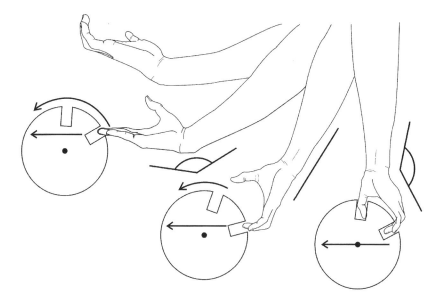

Figure 5.17: Active release

If you watch very carefully as PBA bowlers release their ball, perhaps by viewing a video frame-by-frame, you will see that the vast majority of them do indeed flex their wrist, their fingers, or both, after their thumb has exited the ball. Figure 5.18 depicts PBA great Parker Bohn III at various stages during his release. The photos clearly reveal that far from "snapping that wrist open" or "unloading" his wrist, Mr. Bohn instead employs an active release, moving his wrist from a slightly extended, to a straight, and finally to a flexed position while simultaneously flexing his fingers in a forceful manner.

Figure 5.18: Parker Bohn III active release
Copyright Bowlingdigital.com/Flavio Cuva. Adapted with permission.

With an active release, the bowler's legs, arm, and wrist/fingers are all moving in the required down lane direction. Since the train, the dog, and the bug are all running forward, the Principle of Additive Velocity works to enable the bowler to impart the maximum force and torque to the ball that his or her strength and form will allow, thus creating the highest combination of revs and ball speed.

ELBOW BEND

As you may have noticed, most of the power players flex their elbow to one degree or another during the forward portion of their arm swing. Pundits tend to attribute great powers to this motion. Some claim that it adds overall power to the delivery, some believe that it adds ball speed, and others cite it as another source of increased revs. This slight bending of the elbow is sometimes referred to as "creating a flat spot" in the arm swing, because when viewed from the side the flexing of the elbow raises the ball slightly during the lowest portion of the swing, thus flattening out the bottom of the arc. Great powers are also sometimes credited directly to this flat spot, and we have even heard bowlers being advised to intentionally develop such a flat spot in order to gain revs and power.

It is easy to imagine that flexing the elbow during the arm swing could add to ball speed and revs. After all, in the context of the 40 MPH bug, doesn't the flexing elbow add a fourth component of down lane force to add to the other three? Sadly, an analytical look at the situation will reveal that the elbow bend adds pretty much nothing to the delivery, and human biomechanics would suggest that it isn't even an intentional motion.

First, let's define the term "power player." We view a power player as one who employs a great deal of muscle in their forward swing and release (Compare Ryan Ciminelli's massive left arm with his much smaller right before you say "free arm swing"!). Whether this power converts to significant revs, like Robert "Maximum Bob" Smith, or mostly to speed, like Eugene McCune, depends upon the nature of the bowler's release. In both cases, though, a great deal of muscular effort is put into the forward swing, and usually also into the release.

We reviewed video of a great many elite bowlers' arm swing. All of the power players we looked at bent their elbow during the downward or forward portion of their swing, and all of them straightened it out again somewhere near or slightly after the low point in the swing where the ball passed their legs. Indeed, many elite bowlers who are not ordinarily thought of as power players also exhibit this trait, though typically to a lesser degree.

If every power player seems to bend their elbow during their swing, there must be a reason, right? If the power players do it but the more "free" players do not, then can't we assume that the elbow bend is adding power? As reasonable as this assumption may sound, it is a leap that is completely unsupported. Reaching such a conclusion is a classic case of a very basic but common flaw in reasoning known as *post hoc, ergo propter hoc*—"after this, therefore because of this." Post hoc reasoning says that if some event follows some other event, then it must have been caused by that other event. A classic example of post hoc reasoning is, "the rooster crows just before the sun comes up, therefore the crowing *causes* the sun to come up." Just because the elbow bend occurred before revs were created, we cannot assume that the elbow bend caused the revs to be created any more than we can assume that the rooster's crowing caused the sun to rise.

The idea that elbow bend adds to power seems to have arisen some time in the 1980s, and has been taught ever since. We do not know how the idea started, but our guess is that someone noticed that the power players bent their elbow, and asked them why they did it. Instead of saying "I have no idea, I'm not doing it on purpose, and truthfully I didn't even know I was doing it before you told me," they, or some pundit, decided that it was a source of power, and everyone then started repeating it. As any propagandist would tell you, repeat something often enough and it becomes accepted as fact, even if it never had any solid basis to begin with.

Since the bent elbow straightens out again well before the power player releases his or her ball, it cannot add force to the delivery. While flexing the elbow during the swing adds some small amount to down lane force due to the Principle of Additive Velocity—the train, dog, and bug principle—the subsequent straightening out of the elbow would subtract this gain right back out of the equation. As long as the elbow straightens back out prior to release, the net result of the elbow action is precisely zero. If bending the elbow cannot add to delivery force, why do power players do it? Why do bowlers with more free arm swings tend not to do it? The answer seems to simply come down to the way the human body is put together and the way our muscles function. In short, power players bend their elbow because they can't help but do so.

The act of swinging the arm forward is called shoulder flexion. Shoulder flexion is caused for the most part by contraction of a group of muscles on the front (anterior) part of the shoulder girdle, including the anterior deltoid and a few smaller muscles. These aren't the only muscles involved in the motion, though. Indeed, the entire concept of muscle isolation is overly simplistic, and many other muscles not ordinarily thought of as being associated with any given movement play a significant supporting role.

The biceps brachii, most often referred to simply as the biceps, are the big, showy muscles on the front of the upper arm. The biceps is often described as controlling elbow flexion, as in curling a barbell. That is certainly its major function, but it is also a significant contributor to twisting of the forearm, and more importantly to this discussion, to arm flexion at the shoulder. How can a muscle that primarily flexes the elbow also contribute to shoulder flexion?

Muscles cause joint flexion because their ends attach to two different bones, and muscle contraction serves to pull those two bones closer together causing bending of the joint between them. Most muscles span only one joint, so only act on that single joint. The biceps brachii, however, is what is known as a *bi-articular* muscle, meaning that it spans two joints rather than just one, and therefore acts on both of them at once. While the biceps' insertion is in the forearm, the other end of the muscle has both points of origin not on the upper arm, but rather on the shoulder blade (scapula). Thus, when the biceps contracts it does not pull the lower arm toward the upper arm per se, but rather pulls the lower arm toward the shoulder, with the bone in the upper arm—the humerus—acting to separate the two.

Medical studies have demonstrated that the biceps is activated along with the deltoids during shoulder flexion.[21] Given this, when the biceps contracts to aid the deltoid in flexing the shoulder in the highly muscled "power" delivery, it cannot help but to also pull against the lower arm, causing some degree of elbow flexion. Another muscle called the brachialis is even more strongly involved in elbow flexion than is the biceps. Curiously, the brachialis is also activated during shoulder flexion though it is not even connected to the shoulder, adding even further to involuntary elbow flexion when the shoulder is flexed.[22] Physical therapists and physical conditioning trainers refer to this situation as a "kinetic chain," or more specifically in this bowling example as an "open kinetic chain." One cannot isolate a single muscle, and all of the muscles in the chain fire to one extent or another. In an open kinetic chain, muscle recruitment begins at the point closest to the body, in our case at the shoulder. Activation then travels step by step along the chain through the biceps and the brachialis.

This explains the elbow flexion; it is an involuntary byproduct of a muscled flexion of the shoulder. So why might a power player's elbow straighten back out at the bottom of the arm swing? We could not locate any studies that might explain this and we certainly lack the facilities and medical knowledge to conduct the research ourselves, but we can think of a few reasons that probably account for it. One hypothesis is that the centrifugal force of the heavy bowling ball as it is rapidly accelerated at the end of our swing might simply become too much for the muscle to overcome, thus pulling the elbow joint straight. Another possibility is that the bowler's subconscious focus shifts from swinging the ball to revving the ball, so the neural call for muscle contraction likewise relaxes to some extent. Perhaps the most likely cause might be the bowler subconsciously switching from "swing" mode to "drive and follow through" mode, so he or she simply starts to reach out. Whatever the underlying cause, the evidence supports the idea that both the elbow flexion and subsequent relaxing are subconscious and unintended.

People saw the power, saw the elbow flexion, and decided in a case of the "correlation is causation fallacy" that the flexion must be an important part of obtaining that power. Instead, the common cause principle would suggest that whatever is causing the power is also what is causing the elbow flexion, and that common cause is simply a muscled arm swing.

DOGS, BUGS, AND TRAINS, AND "SNAPPING THAT WRIST OPEN"

The Principle of Additive Velocities also points out another fatal flaw in the idea that we can impart revs to our bowling ball by "unloading" the wrist, or "snapping that wrist open." Suppose for a moment that despite all of our previous discussion we somehow found a way to actually rapidly and forcefully bend our wrist back during our release. In such a case our legs are moving in a down lane direction, our arm swing is in a down lane direction, but our hand will now be moving away from the pins rather than toward them. In effect, the train is moving in the right direction, the dog is running in the right direction, but the darned bug is running the wrong way! Instead of the bug adding to our velocity and revs as in an active release or just sitting there quietly neither adding nor subtracting as in a static release, he is actually subtracting. Extending or "unloading" the wrist during our release, whether passively or rapidly, would decrease both revs and ball speed, not increase them.

We can gain a better understanding of how rapidly bending the wrist back would cut down on revs and ball speed by performing a little thought experiment. Imagine that you are standing on solid ground with your feet firmly planted as you square off with a rival bowler. If you now give him a shove, he will fall away from you with some amount of force.

Now, lets perform the same task, but this time you are standing on a sheet of ice. What happens when you push on your opponent? Some of your effort will still push him away, but certainly not with as much force as before. Isaac Newton tells us that every action has an equal but opposite reaction. Since you are standing on ice your feet can no longer resist that reaction to the same extent, so some of your pushing effort against your opponent will instead be lost in pushing you backward.

The first iteration of our thought experiment is analogous to the static release. Your firm and solid stance is like the bowler's firm wrist, so all of the effort of your footwork and arm swing goes into the ball. The second iteration, the one on ice, is very much like letting the wrist bend backward, either forcefully or passively. When your stance wasn't firm, some of your push effort against your opponent served instead to push you backward, leaving less force to push him away. Likewise, during a passive or a hypothetical "snap that wrist open" release some of the force of your footwork and arm swing, rather than being applied to the ball, will instead be lost by moving your wrist backward.

Let's perform a third iteration of our thought experiment. This time, rather than standing still as you push your opponent, you instead run toward him as you push. In this case the force of your run will add to the force of your push, and your hapless opponent will go flying. This case is analogous to the active release, where your wrist and fingers moving forward *add* to the forward force of your footwork and arm swing to propel the ball away with the maximum combination of speed and revs.

SO, WHY EXTEND THE WRIST?

"But," you are likely thinking, "I can clearly see the pros' wrists bend back during their swing." This is true, at least some of the time. Some professional bowlers such as Chris Barnes extend their wrist back a fair bit. Some, such as Wes Malott and Mike Fagan, do so to only a very minor degree. Still others, such as Ryan Ciminelli, do not allow their wrist to extend at all, keeping it in a very strong and flexed "cupped" position throughout the entire swing and release. All of these bowlers display very high rev rates, yet there seems to be little correlation with the amount they allow their wrists to extend. This is not surprising, since we have already demonstrated that bending back the wrist cannot create topspin. What is consistent among them is in *when* they extend their wrist during the sequence of events that constitute their delivery. None of them do so during the release portion of their delivery, as the unloaded wrist idea would imply.

It would be useful at this point to define what we mean by the word "release," as there seems to be no standard definition. We view the release as beginning when the thumb lets go of the ball and is no longer preventing the fingers from creating topspin, which in a conventional delivery is the point at which the thumb starts to lose contact with the thumb hole. The release ends when the fingers lose contact with the ball. During a conventional delivery the fingers cannot spin the ball so long as the thumb remains in opposition, and likewise can no longer spin the ball after they lose contact with it. The portion of the delivery during which the fingers can impart spin to the ball constitutes the release phase.

The release phase is a bit trickier to define when bowlers do not use their thumb, which includes the two handers, the no-thumb one handers, and the half-thumb one handers. In these cases we define the release as beginning when the ball begins to drop away from the hand, and it ends, just as with the conventional delivery, at the point where the fingers lose contact with the ball. With this definition in mind, let's see what some top-level pros do with their wrist as they release the ball.

Figure 5.19 is a series of captured video frames. It depicts Chris Barnes, Wes Malott, and Ryan Ciminelli at various points prior to and during their release. These three bowlers are typical of the variations on the active release often employed at an advanced level of play. Though these bowlers vary in the degree to which they allow their wrist to extend, if at all, in all cases we can clearly see their wrist, their fingers, or both, flexing *forward* in the required down lane direction during their release. Those who do allow their wrist to extend do so *well before* their release, while their thumb is still in the ball. In none of the cases do we see any evidence of "snapping that wrist open" or rapidly uncupping the wrist during the actual release.

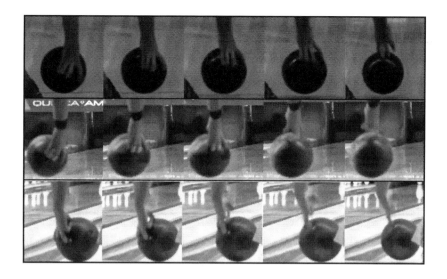

Figure 5.19: Barnes (top), Malott (center), and Ciminelli's (bottom) release

Barnes: Copyright Marko Luksa. Adapted with permission
Malott, Ciminelli: Copyright United States Bowling Congress. Adapted with permission

If extending, or bending back the wrist cannot create revs, why do some of the pros do it? We believe that in most cases the wrist extension is entirely unconscious, and they may not even be aware of it. When we asked Parker Bohn whether the slight extension of his wrist prior to release was intentional, he replied that it was just "something that fell into place."

We can think of a couple of reasons why a bowler's wrist may unintentionally extend just prior to release. The simplest explanation is that the bowler simply unconsciously relaxes their wrist muscles a bit as the brain switches focus away from maintaining a strong wrist position and becomes more occupied with the upcoming active portion of the release. Another likely cause is one of simple body mechanics. Think of what happens to a fishing rod when an angler makes a cast. As the arm moves the rod forward, the rod bends backward. It does so because the slender fishing rod is not strong enough to resist the backward pull of inertia and wind resistance against the line and lure. Make the same overhead casting motion with a broomstick and no bending occurs, because the rigid broomstick is strong enough to resist the forces attempting to hold it back (Figure 5.20).

Figure 5.20: Fishing rod and broomstick vs. inertia

Likewise a very strong bowler may, if he or she so chooses, be able to maintain a straight or cupped wrist during a powerful forward arm swing against the strong backward pull of the inertia of the heavy bowling ball. If the bowler is not physically strong enough or does not actively resist the backward pull of the ball's inertia, something has to give way and bend backward just as the fishing rod did. Of all the muscle and joint systems involved in swinging the ball forward—the shoulder, elbow, wrist, and fingers—the wrist joint is by far the weak link in the system. If something has to give, it is going to be the wrist.

A TWO-EDGED SWORD

We have demonstrated that extension or bending back of the wrist during the release cannot create topspin, and indeed will actually reduce topspin and revs because it is moving in the wrong direction. In terms of wrist motion, only forward, down lane motion—wrist flexure rather than extension—can create revs and topspin. There is a bit of a paradox at work here, though. While only forward motion can create revs, more revs will be created when that forward motion begins from an extended position than from a straight or flexed position, but this is only true if the bowler's arm, wrist, and fingers are very powerful.

In bowling, extending the wrist prior to release does not create revs, and in fact retards them. But once the wrist is put into this extended condition, a strong bowler will be able to create even greater topspin through the subsequent *forward* flexion of his or her wrist and fingers. That is to say, if your wrist is very strong and fast, you can drive the top of the ball forward with your wrist and fingers to a greater degree starting from an extended position than you can starting from a straight position. Wrist extension merely puts you in a favorable extended position, and it is still the subsequent forward flexion that creates your revs.

How does extending the wrist backward prior to release set the bowler up to create higher revs? We see two ways that a small extension of the wrist prior to release could set a bowler up to generate a higher rev rate through their subsequent forward flexion.

BOWLING BEYOND THE BASICS

We have already demonstrated that bending the wrist back during the delivery reduces the amount of force the delivery creates. While this is true, this initial decrease in energy can be more than made up for if the bowler has a very strong or a very fast wrist. To understand how this can be, let's look at the analogy of a bow and arrow.

To shoot an arrow we must pull back on the bow string. If we pull back to only a small degree the arrow will not obtain much velocity. If we pull the string back quite far, the arrow will be propelled with significantly greater energy. This is because when the bow is bent back and the string stretched to a greater degree, it will not only transfer a greater amount of force to the arrow as it springs back forward, but will apply this force over a greater distance. We can liken this to the active bowling release. Beginning your release with your wrist bent back is similar to pulling back the bow string. By bending the wrist back we stretch the flexor muscles on the front of the forearm. Stretching out the wrist flexors allows these muscles to flex the wrist back forward with even greater force than had the wrist remained straight, because in addition to the ordinary contractile force of the muscles we also get some elastic force as the stretched muscle fibers spring back to their normal length.

Bending your wrist back prior to release is a dangerous game, though. The benefit of extending the wrist prior to release is only available to those bowlers with sufficient wrist strength to quickly power their wrist forward again during their release, and the level of strength required to do so is rather substantial. Even with sufficient strength, the bowler also needs to be blessed with muscles capable of contracting at a very rapid rate.

The speed at which our muscles contract is an accident of birth, and an athlete either has fast muscles or doesn't. Muscle fibers fall into two general categories, Type I, or "slow twitch," and Type II, or "fast twitch." Type II fibers are further broken down into Type II-a and Type II-b. While Type I muscle fibers contract relatively slowly, they display great endurance, and can maintain their strength for long periods of time. Type II fibers contract far more quickly, but they lack the endurance of Type I fibers. While Type II-a fibers contract far more quickly than do Type I, Type II-b fibers contract even more rapidly than do Type II-a. Type I muscle fibers are red in color, and tend not to grow in size in response to exercise. They can certainly get stronger, but they do not get bigger. Type II-a fibers are pink, and Type II-b white, and both grow in size, or *hypertrophy*, in response to effort.

Humans display great variation from one individual to another in the relative proportion of the three types of muscle fiber making up their bodies. Some people's bodies are composed of mostly slow twitch fibers while others are composed of mostly Type II-a or II-b fast twitch fibers. These proportions do not change in response to training or exercise. They are pretty much fixed over time, and are the result of genetics and biological sex. Essentially, we are either born with the propensity for muscle speed, or we aren't. Some sports such as distance running favor slow twitch muscles, while others such as boxing and weightlifting favor fast muscles. At least in terms of rev rate, bowling definitely favors fast twitch muscles.

All of this makes extending your wrist back prior to release a dangerous proposition. If you lack the speed and strength necessary to drive the top of the ball forward from an extended wrist position, then you are left with the loss of revs caused by the wrist extension, with nothing to make up for it. Lacking sufficient wrist strength or fast enough muscles, you are better served by maintaining a straight or slightly cupped wrist.

The second potential benefit of extending the wrist back prior to release has to do with how force translates to torque, and with what the extended wrist does to the position of the bowler's fingertips relative to the ball's axis of rotation. Earlier in this chapter we learned that torque is created by applying a force at some distance from the object's axis of rotation and at an angle away from that axis. We also learned that the amount of our force that gets converted to torque to spin the object is a function of the length and position of the lever arm—the wrench handle—in the torque system.

Look at the three photos in Figure 5.21, below, which depict a bowler's wrist in three different positions. If the wrist remains flexed or "cupped" prior to release as in the first photo, the fingers are initially below the equator of the ball (marked with a white line). Since we begin to release our bowling ball somewhere near the bottom of our arm swing, most of the force generated by our footwork and arm swing is in the down lane direction. With the fingers below the ball's equator the force of our delivery is transmitted by the palm of the hand rather than the fingers and does not initially act at an angle to the ball's axis of rotation, so at least during the early part of the release no meaningful torque is generated. Note that significant torque will eventually be generated by such a release, just not during the initial phase, as we will explain later.

With the wrist straight, as in the second photo, the fingers are at or slightly above the ball's equator, so some torque will be generated in the early part of the release. However, since the lever arm is almost directly in line with the force of our delivery, the amount of initial torque will not be terribly great. As with the flexed wrist, most of the force of the delivery, at least initially, acts in line with the ball's axis of rotation and so converts to ball speed rather than revs. Again, meaningful torque will still be generated later in the release, just not during the initial part.

Figure 5.21: Finger position prior to release with wrist flexed, straight, and extended.

Contrast the location of the fingers relative to the ball's equator in the third photo, which depicts an extended wrist prior to release, with the first two photos. The third photo reveals that an important side effect of extending the wrist is that it moves the fingers up toward the top of the ball, placing them some meaningful distance above the ball's equator just prior to release. The first two photos show that with the fingers at or near the ball's equator, the effective lever arm in our torque system is more or less horizontal. It is as though our fingertips were pushing on the end of the wrench handle rather than the side, so very little torque is produced. Once we move our fingers up above the equator, the angle of our lever arm increases dramatically. Since our fingertips are now applying force at least partially to the side of the wrench handle rather than to the end, it is easy to see how any motion of the arm, wrist, or fingers in the forward, down lane direction will translate into revs rather than just into ball speed.

SHOULD I EXTEND MY WRIST, OR NOT?

If extending the wrist just prior to release puts you in a position to be able to generate increased revs, shouldn't everyone do it? Once again the devil is in the details. As we have already stressed, this tactic will only work for those bowlers who have a very fast wrist, fingers, or both, or for those who have a very powerful and rapid arm swing. Why should this be so?

We know that in order to generate revolutions on the ball, the arm, wrist, or fingers, or some combination of the three must powerfully flex forward in order to drive the top of the ball forward in a forceful manner. The problem, as we can see from the third photo in Figure 5.21, is that with the fingers so far above the equator, as soon as the bowler's thumb exits the ball, the ball quickly begins to drop toward the floor. The higher up the hand is, the faster the ball will fall away.

With the wrist extended, the ball will fall away so quickly that there is very little time for the hand to drive the finger holes forward. The wrist, arm, or fingers must therefore be able to snap forward even more quickly than the ball is falling away. Again, if you are blessed with a fast wrist and fingers or a very powerful arm swing you may be able to do this. If so, you will indeed have the possibility of achieving a higher rev rate by extending the wrist prior to release and then rapidly powering everything forward into a flexed position during the actual release.

If you do not have very fast wrists and fingers or a very powerful arm swing—and most of us don't—extending the wrist to any large degree prior to release will not help your cause. The ball will drop from your fingers far too quickly for your hand to do much in the way of imparting torque, and the ball will rotate rather lazily as it makes its way down the lane. We have all seen bowlers of lesser skill do precisely this, allowing their wrist to bend back during their release only to see the ball drop to the lane with a thud, and with no real force or torque. In fact, this is precisely the less than desirable situation we described in our discussion of the passive release. If you allow your wrist to extend without possessing a fast release, you will not be able to apply significant forward force to the finger holes before the ball drops away from your grasp. What, then, should we mere mortals do? How can we achieve meaningful torque without first extending the wrist and moving the fingers up above the ball's equator?

While the ball dropping away from the hand hurts those who bend their wrists back unless they have very fast muscles, the falling ball actually helps in the creation of revs for those bowlers whose wrist remains in a stronger position. The simple fact of the ball falling after the thumb has released but while the fingers are still in place will serve to effectively move the fingers up above the ball's equator without any wrist extension at all. This automatic repositioning of the fingers creates our required lever arm, allowing some of the force of delivery to convert to torque and spin the ball (Figure 5.22). As long as the bowler's thumb exits the ball before his or her fingers do, a reasonable rev rate will be achieved just by maintaining a firm wrist.

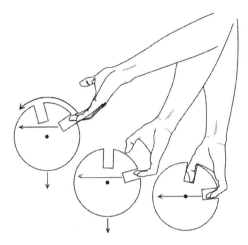

Figure 5.22: Automatic creation of torque as the ball falls away from the hand

WHY DO TWO HANDERS HAVE MORE REVS?

Our discussion thus far helps to explain why two handers, and one handers who don't use their thumb, have higher rev rates than do conventional bowlers. It is fairly easy to see that meaningful revs cannot be created while the thumb remains in the ball, because while our fingers might be trying to drive the top of the ball forward, our thumb stands in opposition and holds it back. Once our thumb exits the ball, our fingers are free to create topspin (revs) until such time as the ball falls away and the fingers lose contact. The longer our fingers remain in the ball following the thumb's exit, the more torque we can apply to the ball to create revs.

In physics, the concept of a force or torque applied over a length of time is called *impulse*. Think of a rocket ship. If the engine burns for say 10 seconds, the rocket will reach a certain velocity. If that same engine instead burns for 10 minutes, the rocket will obviously attain a much higher velocity. The same thing happens to our bowling ball. The longer we apply our given torque, the more impulse we apply to the ball and the more revs we create.

So how does impulse help no-thumb bowlers achieve such high rev rates? Figure 5.23 depicts the releases of PBA bowlers Dick Allen and Osku Palermaa. Mr. Allen employs a conventional release, while Mr. Palermaa is a two-hander who does not use his thumb. The photos on the left are the moment each bowler begins to apply torque to the ball, and those on the right are the point where their fingers lose contact with the ball. The white line indicates the position of the fingertips, making it easier for us to see the degree of rotation.

Figure 5.23: Range of torque application, Allen (top) and Palermaa (bottom)
Copyright United States Bowling Congress. Adapted with permission

We see in the top photos that Mr. Allen's thumb exits his ball when his fingers are at roughly the one o'clock position, and that they lose contact with the ball at about 12:30. He thus applies torque to the ball through only 15 degrees or so of rotation, lasting only 0.13 seconds. Mr. Palermaa, in contrast, never employs his thumb, and so applies torque to the ball as soon as it begins to fall from his hand, from roughly the six o'clock position all the way to about 1:30. His release covers over 67 degrees of rotation and continues for 0.36 seconds. Thus, even if both bowlers applied precisely the same amount of force with their arm swing, wrist, and fingers, our no-thumb bowler applies this effort for almost three times as long, so his revs are driven by significantly more impulse than the conventional bowler is capable of generating.

EXTEND, OR NOT? WHAT DO THE PROS DO?

What do the pros do as they release the ball? They do all sorts of things! One can find among the PBA and PWBA players examples of most every variation on the static and the active release. There are elite bowlers who extend their wrist to varying degrees, and those who keep their wrist completely rigid, either straight or cupped. There are those who power the ball forward by flexing only their wrist or only their fingers, and those who actively flex both. There are power players who extend their wrist dramatically prior to release and then simply rip forward on the top of the ball with the force of their arm swing, seemingly never flexing their fingers or wrist at all. There are players who employ a completely static release, both with a wrist device and without. We can even find one or two who against all odds employ what appears to be a completely passive release.

PWBA star Diana Zavjalova gets all of her revs via her wrist, flexing it from a bent back position into a cupped position, with almost no help from her fingers. Norm Duke and Francois Lavoie use the opposite approach, keeping their wrists straight throughout their release and only flexing their fingers powerfully forward. Dick Allen and Dom Barrett also derive most of their revs via their fingers all while holding their wrists static in a slightly extended position. E.J. Tackett creates his torque by slightly extending his wrist to move his fingers toward the top of the ball well prior to release, then ripping forward on the finger holes via a fast and powerful arm swing coupled with finger flexion once his thumb has exited the ball. All of these bowlers either flex their wrist forward or hold it static in a straight or extended position during their release.

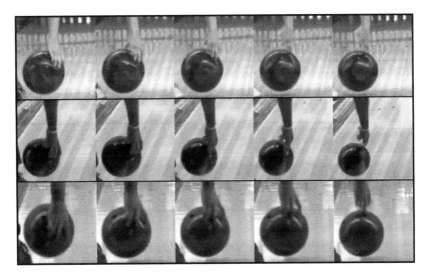

Figure 5.24: Releases: Zavjalova (top), Duke (center), and Tackett (bottom).
Copyright United States Bowling Congress. Adapted with permission

Pete Weber and Amleto Monacelli derive their revs from both their wrist and fingers, but they both flex their wrist forward from a straight to a cupped position, never letting it extend at all. Ryan Ciminelli also obtains his revs via both his wrist and his fingers. His wrist never relaxes from a flexed state, instead moving from slightly cupped to strongly cupped as he simultaneously rips forward with his fingers. Tommy Jones and Robert Smith likewise employ both their wrist and fingers, but while Ciminelli moves from a slightly cupped to a very cupped position, Jones and Smith flex their wrist forward from an extended, bent back position to a straight position. Marshall Kent flexes his wrist forward through the full range of motion, beginning in an extended, bent back position and powering forward into a fully cupped position. All of these bowlers flex their wrist forward during their release, though they do so from different starting positions and with different finishing positions.

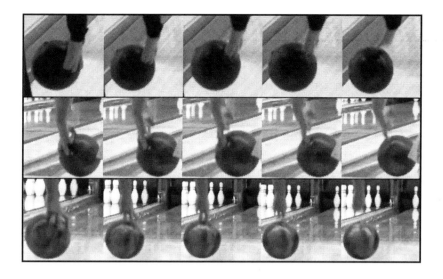

Figure 5.25: Releases: Weber (top), Ciminelli (center), and Kent (bottom).

WHOSE EXAMPLE SHOULD I FOLLOW?

So what should you do to maximize your rev rate, assuming that is your goal? That, of course, depends upon you. While our discussion in this chapter points to some very useful guidelines, there is unfortunately no *one size fits all* solution.

If you have very fast wrists, fingers, or both, or a very rapid and powerful forward arm swing, the rules governing how torque is generated would dictate that you allow your wrist to slightly extend prior to release in order to move your fingers to a higher position on the ball, and then to powerfully and rapidly snap your wrist and fingers forward.

If you have muscles which operate more slowly, as most of us do, the best thing you can do to maximize revs is to maintain a firmer wrist, never letting it bend back beyond a straight or slightly extended position, as in the photos of Parker Bohn's release in Figure 5.18. This will keep your fingers lower on the ball than what the power players do, but this is necessary because your slower wrists and fingers need more time to apply torque to the ball before it falls away from your grasp. You still need to flex your wrist and fingers forward just as those with fast wrists do, though your slower movements will be more of a push than a snap.

If you have weaker or very slow wrists, it is best to strive for the strongest, most flexed wrist position you can. Even with weaker wrists, by telling yourself to keep your wrist cupped you may at least be able to trick yourself into not letting it bend back too far. This will keep your fingers as low on the ball as possible, giving you the most possible time to apply torque to the ball. With your wrist as firm as your musculature will allow, try to flip the ball forward with your fingertips or just via the force of your arm swing.

For those with extremely weak wrists, whether due to injury, age, arthritis, carpal tunnel syndrome, or any other physical or medical issues, a chat with your doctor or physical therapist is certainly in order. Bowling balls are heavy, and the forces generated during your delivery and release are substantial even in the softest and most gentle of deliveries. Subject of course to your doctor's advice, the best way to generate revs for those with weakened or damaged wrists or fingers is to use a high quality and very supportive wrist device to take the strain off of your wrist, and to then lift up and through the ball with a static release. As long as you do not allow your wrist to bend back too far and you get your thumb out of the ball before your fingers exit, you will still be able to generate a reasonable and effective rev rate.

The one common theme in all of these approaches is that you need to get as many parts of your delivery and release as you are able to—arm, elbow, wrist, and fingers—operating in the same down lane direction. That is, everything needs to flex forward. Snap that wrist and those fingers closed, not open, if you wish to maximize your rev rate.

WHAT ABOUT FRISBEES AND YO-YOS?

We often hear pundits compare rolling a bowling ball to throwing a Frisbee or spinning a yo-yo. When we throw a Frisbee or a yo-yo, we do indeed "snap that wrist open," or rapidly bend the wrist back from a flexed to an extended position in order to impart spin or revs to the object. If snapping that wrist open works for Frisbees and yo-yos, why doesn't it work for a bowling ball? If we examine the entire physical act of throwing a Frisbee, the answer to this question will become clear.

Figure 5.26, below, depicts a top down view of a person throwing a Frisbee. The first drawing illustrates the thrower in the starting position. Notice that in his starting position his shoulder, elbow, wrist, and even fingers are tightly flexed, and all in a direction opposite to the intended path of the Frisbee. This is similar to how you cock a pistol by pulling the hammer back prior to firing. Recall the physics professor's description of how a batter's swing generates force in baseball: "The torque needed to accelerate the bat is supplied by the batter's hips, shoulders, arms, and wrists, each of these rotating in a proper sequence that builds one rotation on another." Our Frisbee thrower must do the same thing. Since he starts with his joints tightly flexed, he must now rapidly *extend* his shoulder,[23] elbow, wrist, then fingers in the same down range direction, "building one rotation on another." In terms of motion, throwing a yo-yo is identical to throwing a Frisbee, but in the body's sagittal (up and down) rather than transverse (side to side) plane. To throw the yo-yo, you again begin with your shoulder, elbow, wrist, and fingers tightly flexed, and then must rapidly *extend* your shoulder, elbow, wrist, and fingers, all in the same downward direction.

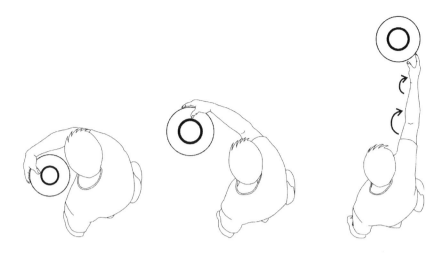

Figure 5.26: Extension of shoulder, elbow, wrist, and fingers when throwing a Frisbee.

Contrast throwing a Frisbee or a yo-yo with rolling a bowling ball. In the case of the Frisbee and yo-yo, all of the joints involved start out *flexed* to one degree or another in the direction opposite to the object's intended path, and all are then *extended* in the desired direction of travel. Conversely, when rolling a bowling ball all of the joints begin in an *extended* position in the direction opposite to the ball's intended path, and all are then *flexed* in the desired direction of travel. Both actions propel the object away from the body with both rotation and velocity, but do so using completely opposite motions. The Frisbee started out with the arm, wrist, and fingers *flexed* and curled around the body, and so needed to *extend* them to push the object forward. The bowling ball starts out with the arm, wrist, and fingers *extended* behind the body, so they must *flex* to push the ball forward. There is simply no comparison between the two deliveries. They are complete opposites of one another. With the false analogies to throwing a Frisbee or a yo-yo dispensed with, we turn our attention to a third and equally false comparison that crops up from time to time.

UNDERHAND FOOTBALL SPIRAL

We have heard some well-meaning bowlers advise others that putting revs on a bowling ball is "just like throwing an underhand spiral with a football." To throw an underhand spiral with a football, the hand must be underneath the ball with the palm facing upward, and the forearm must then *pronate*, or rotate inward as the ball is released. You probably already see the problem with trying to apply this movement to a bowling ball.

The problem with the football analogy is that while the hand is underneath the lightweight football during this toss, a bowler's hand is pretty much never underneath the ball once past the initial push away. While some no-thumb bowlers do position their hand more or less underneath the ball during the forward swing, conventional one-hand bowlers do not. As we saw in the photos of the various PBA bowlers' releases, a conventional bowler's hand will ordinarily be somewhere in the top rear quadrant of the ball prior to release. With the hand in this position, pronating the wrist would result only in spinning the ball like a top. In fact, this is precisely what the "Asian helicopter spinner" bowlers do during their release, since their goal is vertical spin rather than down lane revolutions.

It is technically possible for a conventional bowler to throw a bowling ball in an underhand football spiral, though it would require a tremendous amount of wrist strength. In fact, I did throw a ball in this manner for demonstration purposes. It resulted in the ball's oil track being completely horizontal and above the finger holes, and my PAP, or Positive Axis Point was below the thumb hole, both of which are far from normal or desirable. We have also seen several self-taught no-thumb and two-handed bowlers release their ball this way due to a misunderstanding of what the mechanics of the no-thumb release are supposed to be. Since a ball thrown like an underhand football spiral is so undesirable, it is fortunate that very few bowlers even possess the strength to attempt it.

Despite the fact that we do not want our bowlers to actually throw the ball anything even remotely like an underhand football spiral, this analogy is still sometimes useful in a limited way as a coaching tool. We employ it on occasion when trying to get a bowler who throws a backup ball to start turning their hand inward. Those who throw a backup ball *supinate* their wrist, or turn it outward rather than *pronating* it inward during their release, resulting in a ball that hooks to the right for a right-handed bowler and to the left for a lefty. While we are well aware that our bowlers will not in fact throw their bowling ball anything like an underhand football spiral, a few spirals with a Nerf football can help to trick them into getting their wrist moving in the required direction during their release. The football spiral analogy is also useful with beginner bowlers who want to learn to hook the ball, as it can help them to understand that their wrist needs to be an active part of the release and that it should be turning inward rather than outward.

CHAPTER 6

MY REV RATE IS...

A GENTLEMAN I occasionally bowl with asked me to teach him the basics of laying out a bowling ball for drilling. The next time I saw him, he showed me his new ball with his proposed layout marked in grease pencil and asked me what I thought. I told him that the ball would likely go very long, and not hook very much. "No," he replied, "I saw this layout on YouTube and it hooked a ton." I asked him what the YouTube bowler's specs were. "About the same as me; 15 miles per hour, 375 RPM." When I informed him that based on observation his own rev rate was just a little over 200 RPM, he was in complete disbelief.

This gentleman is not alone in overestimating his rev rate. We often hear bowlers discussing their own rev rates, throwing around rather unlikely numbers in the 450 to 550 RPM range. A series of ball reaction videos on the Internet lists one of their ball testers, an old-school, fairly low-rev stroker, as a medium-rev "tweener." A ball review website posts videos of their three ball testers, listing a gentleman who seems to have a 200 RPM rev rate as a 275 RPM bowler, and rating their high-rev guy, who appears to have a very respectable release in the 425 RPM range, at a staggering 600 RPM. Strokers often see themselves as tweeners, tweeners see themselves as crankers, and very many of us believe we have more revs and a bigger hook than we really do.

None of these people are liars. We are sure they sincerely think their rev rates are what they say they are. A lot of the error comes from making our own estimates by comparing our revs against a flawed comparison base. You may see a bowler on TV whose rev rate looks very similar to your own. Suppose the color commentator says this bowler's rev rate is 400 RPM even though it's really closer to 300. Can you be blamed for then thinking that your own rev rate was 400 RPM too?

Another source of error is comparing your own rev rate against calculations performed using a flawed methodology. For example, there are a series of videos on the Internet purporting to measure rev rate by counting the number of revolutions the ball makes over the entire lane before hitting the pins, and measuring the time it takes the ball to do so. This sounds like it should be right, but as we will learn in Chapter 7, the very high rev rate during the last portion of the ball's journey has little to do with the revs the bowler actually put on the ball with his or her own hand. Including these unearned high revs in the calculation leads to a drastic overstatement of rev rate. After recalculating from one of those videos while ignoring the revolutions occurring after the ball "revved up" on the back portion of the lane, the bowler's actual rev rate was 50 RPM lower than what the video stated.

To get an idea of real world rev rates, we assembled a group of bowlers ranging from recreational level, through fairly typical league bowlers, and on to very competitive "scratch league" and tournament-caliber players. Our group represented the range of bowlers one might find at a local bowling center. After warming up, we had each bowler roll three shots. We measured their rev rate on each shot, and then averaged the results. We do not claim that our survey was in any way scientific or statistically authoritative, but we offer the results for purposes of illustration.

Our recreational bowler displayed a rev rate well below 200 RPM. Our average league-type bowlers had rev rates in the 200 to 300 RPM range. Our high-caliber, competitive bowlers with conventional one-handed releases achieved rev rates in the 350 to 400 RPM range, and our lone competitive-level two hander produced an extremely high 550 RPM rev rate. Bowlers' actual rev rates, even at the PBA level, are not nearly as high as we are lead to believe.

DETERMINING REV RATE

Guessing at our rev rate is unnecessary in this modern age where most everyone has access to a cellular telephone or a tablet computer with a built-in video camera. The procedure for determining rev rate from cellphone video is quite simple and is reasonably accurate. In fact, with a better quality video camera with a higher frame rate, the video method of determining rev rate is extremely accurate.

The first step in measuring your rev rate is to determine the location of your ball's PAP (positive axis point), or what a physicist would call its *initial spin axis*. The PAP is one end of an imaginary axis that runs through your ball. Your ball spins around this axis as you release it onto the lane. Think of this axis of rotation as being like the axle of a bicycle wheel. Your ball spins on its axis just as the bicycle wheel spins on its axle.

The location of your PAP depends upon how you release your ball, so can be different from one bowler to another. Your PAP can even change over time as your physical game evolves. The key to locating your own PAP is the first oil ring that forms on your ball as it skids down the lane, the one closest to the finger and thumb holes. Your PAP is one of the points on the surface of the ball at the very center of this oil ring.

There are two main ways to locate your PAP from the first oil ring. The most accurate method is to trace over the oil ring with a grease pencil, then ask your pro shop operator to mark your PAP based on this traced line using a tool called an *armadillo* (Figure 6.1). If you don't have access to an armadillo, a "quick and dirty" method is to place your ball on a ball cup or a towel with the traced oil ring below the equator of the ball and as level all the way around as you can get it. Your approximate PAP will now be at the very top of your ball (Figure 6.2). Once you've marked your PAP (we use a bit of white bowling or electrical tape), throw a shot or two to verify you have the location right. If you've located your PAP correctly, the taped spot should be quite visible and very stable during the initial portion of the ball's travel down the lane.

Figure 6.1: Marking PAP with an armadillo.

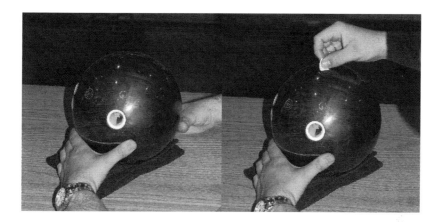

Figure 6.2: Marking PAP, quick method.

Regardless of the method you use to locate your PAP, place a strip of electrical tape of a contrasting color onto the surface of your ball, beginning at your PAP and ending at a point just above your finger holes (Figure 6.3). Now have someone video your ball from behind you and close to the lane surface as you throw a shot (Figure 6.4).

Figure 6.3: Ball taped for rev rate measurement.

Figure 6.4: Videotaping marked ball.

You need to know the frame rate of the camera you are using. Most cell phones and tablets shoot at a rate of 30 frames per second. Many video cameras shoot 60 frames per second. Higher quality cameras are often able to shoot at much higher frame rates. Transfer the video to your computer, and open it with any viewing or editing software that will allow you to advance the video one frame at a time. Most computers come with some sort of free "movie maker" software that will work, and there is also a way to view a video frame by frame with the media player that comes pre-installed with Windows.

As you advance your video, you will be able to observe your tape strip rotating around your PAP much like the hands on a clock. From the point at which the ball first contacts the lane, count the number of frames it takes for the tape strip to make two complete revolutions. As an example, let's say that the ball made two revolutions as you clicked through 15 frames, and that your cell phone camera shot at a rate of 30 frames per second.

The first step in calculating your rev rate is to divide the number of revolutions the ball made—in our case, two— by the number of frames it took to make them. This will give us the fractional number of revolutions per frame:

2 Revolutions ÷ 15 Frames = 0.133 Revolutions per Frame

Revolution per frame isn't a terribly meaningful number, so we need to do a bit of simple math to convert it into revolutions per minute. Since our camera shoots 30 frames per second, we can multiply our revolutions per frame by 30 frames per second to obtain our revolutions per second:

0.133 Revolutions per Frame x 30 Frames per Second = 4 Revolutions per Second

Since there are 60 seconds in a minute, we can multiply our revolutions per second figure by 60 to obtain our rev rate in RPM:

4 Revolutions per Second x 60 Seconds per Minute = 240 Revolutions per Minute

Putting this all together, our rev rate formula becomes:

(Number of Revolutions ÷ Number of Frames) x Frame Rate of our camera x 60

Thus, if it took only 10 frames for the ball to make two complete revolutions, our rev rate is:

2 ÷ 10 x 30 x 60, or 360 RPM

Likewise, if it took 18 frames for the ball to complete two revolutions, our rev rate is:

2 ÷ 18 x 30 x 60, or 200 RPM

To increase the accuracy of our measurement of rev rate, it is best to record and analyze three or more shots and then to average the results together. Note also that the higher the frame rate of the camera used, the more accurate will be the results obtained. There are other variations on this method, such as reading the time component directly from the playback counter of your video editing software rather than computing it from frame rate, but all such methods will get you to the same place. And do not think of this video method of calculating rev rate as being somehow inferior or second rate. It is the most accurate method available to us, and is in fact a form of optical tachometry, a method of revolution measurement widely used in science and industry.

A QUICK AND DIRTY METHOD FOR ESTIMATING REV RATE

While the video procedure is very accurate, it does take a bit of work and time. If you just want an approximation of your rev rate, there is a simple way to make a rough estimate while you are out on the lanes. This method requires no video equipment or preparation at all; only your eyeballs and a calculator. The formula to make the calculation is very simple, but the math we had to go through to create it was a little more complex. We'll work through the math for you just to show you where our formula comes from and why it is valid, but you won't have to work through it all yourself when you calculate rev rates. All you'll need to do is write down the final formula, and plug in the numbers. First, a bit of explanation.

Most of us have noticed that when our ball comes back after a strike shot, there is a pattern of oil rings spaced fairly evenly across the portion of the ball adjacent to the gripping holes (Figure 6.5). Each one of these rings represents one complete revolution of the ball as it traveled in the oiled portion of the lane, and the rings stop forming when the ball hits the dry area at the end of the lane. By counting these oil rings, we know how many times the ball revolved in the oil. This gives us a rough measure of revolutions, but determining revolutions per minute requires some sort of time measurement too.

Figure 6.5: Oil rings.

It would be impossible to measure the time element directly with a timer or stopwatch, since we cannot determine exactly where or when the ball leaves the oil pattern just by watching it. Even if we could see the end of the pattern, no one's reflexes are fast enough to start and stop the stopwatch at even close to the right moments. We therefore need a method to figure out the time factor without directly measuring it. Fortunately, most bowling centers provide enough information to make a good estimate.

On most score-keeping systems, ball speed is displayed after each shot. Since speed is distance divided by time, we can determine the time if we know the distance the ball traveled. We are looking for the distance the ball travels in the oil, so all we need to do to obtain an estimate of this distance is to ask the bowling center's lane technician for the length of the oil pattern. Since we know how many miles per hour the ball is traveling, and that there are 5280 feet in a mile, we can easily estimate the amount of time our ball spent in the oiled part of the lane as it formed its oil rings.

Let's look at an example to make it all clear. Fair warning: This is where the math is! It would be great if you followed along, but we've put it all in a grey box to make it easy to skip if you just want to trust us.

Suppose we count seven distinct rings of oil on our ball. The monitor said that our ball traveled at a speed of 16 miles per hour, and the lane technician told us that the oil pattern on the lane is 38 feet in length. Our first step is to calculate how long it takes a 16 mile per hour ball to travel 38 feet, so we need to convert our ball speed from miles per hour to feet per minute. Since there are 5280 feet in a mile, we can multiply 16 miles per hour by 5280 feet per mile to yield:

16 miles per hour x 5280 feet per mile = 84,480 feet per hour

There are 60 minutes in each hour, so we can divide our 84,480 feet per hour by 60 to give us feet per minute:

84,480 feet per hour ÷ 60 minutes per hour = 1408 feet per minute

Of course, our ball was not in the oil for a full minute, and it traveled only 38 feet, not 1408 feet. We determine the amount of time the ball spent in the oil by dividing the 38 foot pattern length by the 1408 feet the ball would have traveled in a full minute:

1408 feet per minute = 38 feet ÷ X minutes
X minutes x 1408 feet per minute = 38 feet
X minutes = 38 feet ÷ 1408 feet per minute
X = 0.027 minutes

So now we know that our ball revolved seven times (seven oil rings) in 0.027 minutes. Knowing that the ball revolved 7 times in 0.027 minutes is still not very meaningful. We instead need to know how many times the ball would have revolved in a full minute, which is of course our RPM measurement. Again, the math is simple:

X revolutions per minute = 7 revolutions ÷ .027 minutes
X = 259 RPM

Thus, if your ball forms seven oil rings over the course of a 38 foot shot at 16 miles per hour, your ball revolved at a rate of approximately 259 RPM.

Using some math tricks that we won't bore you with, we can compress all of the previous computations down into the following simple formula, which you can write down and keep in your bowling bag:

Rev rate in RPM = (Number of oil rings x Ball speed in MPH x 88) ÷ Pattern length (feet)

Let's rework the original calculation with this new formula just to demonstrate that it yields the same results without all the runaround. Again, we had seven oil rings, and our ball traveled 16 MPH over the 38 foot oil pattern:

Rev rate = (7 oil rings x 16 MPH x 88) ÷ 38 feet
Rev rate = 9,856 ÷ 38
Rev rate = 259 RPM!

If your ball had instead formed nine oil rings at the same speed, your approximate rev rate is

9 x 16 x 88 ÷ 38, or 333 RPM

Six oil rings with the same speed and pattern length translates to

6 x 16 x 88 ÷ 38, or 222 RPM

Outside of the USA, ball speed is often displayed in kilometers per hour rather than miles per hour, though pattern length is still measured in feet. For readers bowling in countries employing the metric system, the formula becomes:

Rev rate in RPM = (Number of oil rings x Ball speed in KPH x 55) ÷ Pattern length (feet)

While this quick and dirty system is certainly simple to use, there are a couple of caveats that prevent it from ever being more than a rough estimate. First, the speed registered by the bowling center's scoring system is only an approximation, and worse yet it is an approximation taken at a point roughly 45 feet down lane. Since a bowling ball slows down somewhere in the neighborhood of two miles per hour as it rolls down the lane, we need to add perhaps one mile per hour to the speed registered by the score keeper to get closer to the ball's true average speed. If you don't make this adjustment, the formula will give you a result that is low by about five percent or so. The second caveat is that it is sometimes difficult to count the oil rings. The oil is typically lighter in volume toward the end of the pattern so the last ring can sometimes be very faint. Regardless of its shortcomings though, it's still better than just guessing based on comparisons with other bowlers in YouTube videos!

C.A.T.S. VIDEO-BASED BALL MOTION MEASURING SYSTEM

During Professional Bowlers Association tournament telecasts, the commentators often cite the competitors' rev rates. Most seem to be quoted in the 400-500 RPM range, with the power players and those who do not put their thumb in the ball often approaching an incredible 600 RPM or more. We would watch these players' releases, and wonder how they were able to generate such phenomenal rev rates when even the strongest bowlers we had personally measured, whose releases appeared to be just as powerful and whose ball hooked just as much or more, seemed to max out at far lower levels. Are the PBA pros really such a quantum leap ahead of we mere mortals in terms of rev rate? As it turns out, the lofty rev rate numbers we hear on the telecasts are pretty much fantasy.

When we calculated rev rate using the video method described in the beginning of this chapter, we obtained hard, verifiable numbers, the result of the actual rotation of the ball over some segment of time. In fact, most measurements of RPM in machinery are performed in a similar manner, either by optically counting as index marks pass by a lens or sensor, by counting electrical pulses, or by some other method of counting actual rotation over time. These numbers are as "real" and tangible as we can get them. In contrast, the rev rate numbers reported on TV seem to come from data provided by a motion sensing system called the *Computer Aided Tracking System*, or *CATS*. So wouldn't the rev rate measurements performed by a computerized tracking system be even more accurate and reliable than the rates we compute using electrical tape and a video camera? The answer is that yes, they probably would be, *if* the CATS system[24] actually measured rev rate, but the truth is that it does not. So what is the CATS system, and what does it measure?

The CATS system was invented by employees of the American Bowling Congress— the predecessor to today's USBC, the governing body of our sport—some time in the 1980s. According to our research, it was patented in 1996. In 2003 the USBC transferred the rights to the system to Kegel, LLC, and they have been maintaining and marketing CATS ever since.

CATS is a system of sensors installed at various points along the lane. The sensors read the precise down lane and cross lane position of the ball at each point, and record the elapsed time between each sensor reading. Applying a bit of math to the position and time data allows the system to report on ball velocity at any point on the lane, and basic trigonometry combined with the position data allows the system to accurately report on the angle of the ball's path, be it during the launch of the ball, during the hook phase, or as the ball enters the pin deck. In short, anything having to do with the speed or position of the ball during its trip down the lane will be accurately measured by CATS. It is a brilliant system.

As amazing and useful as the CATS system is, one thing that it specifically does *not* measure is the ball's rev rate. In the system's patent application, the inventors proposed a camera placed behind the foul line which would capture video footage of the ball, marked with a strip of tape as a visual reference, as it traveled down the lane.[25] Does this sound familiar? It is exactly the same method of calculating rev rate that we described in the first part of this chapter, the very procedure you can perform with your cell phone. Some time between the filing of the patent application and the actual implementation of the commercial system, the camera and the ball markings were eliminated, and the CATS system now has no method at all to measure the ball's rev rate. If no measurements are taken but the system still reports rev rate, where do these numbers come from?

Since the CATS system knows the exact position of the ball at various points along the lane, it knows how many boards it covered as it hooked. According to a representative at Kegel, the system's algorithm then simply makes an educated guess as to what rev rate might have caused that particular amount of hook at that ball speed. It bases this estimate on a set of assumptions and on a database of measured shots by different bowlers using different equipment, on different lanes, with different amounts of oil, at different times. Most seriously, CATS does not factor in the coefficient of friction of the actual ball being thrown, which of course is the single most important factor influencing hook. Nor does it look at the bowler's axis tilt or axis rotation, two factors that greatly influence hook quite independently of rev rate. As it turns out, the system's imputed estimate of rev rate suffers from these and other shortcomings, and is not very accurate. Just how inaccurate is it?

In 2008 a group of mechanical engineering researchers and professors at the University of Michigan developed a wireless electronic angular velocity and force sensor, and worked with Ebonite Corporation to embed it into an actual bowling ball.[26] They were thus able, for the first time, to take direct measurements of not only the forces imparted to the ball as it is released onto the lane, but also of the actual rate at which the ball was spinning. This measured rate as the ball leaves the bowler's hand is, of course, the bowler's actual rev rate. Ebonite now markets the device, or at least a version of it, as the Ebonite Powerhouse Bowler ID. They had well-known professional bowlers throw the instrumented ball, and measured their actual rev rates. They reported the following results in their marketing presentation on the device, stated to be within 1% accuracy:[27]

Bowler	Rev Rate	Bowler	Rev Rate
Mike Scroggins	229 RPM	Mika Koivuniemi	397 RPM
Liz Johnson	262 RPM	Jason Couch	403 RPM
Walter Ray Williams	277 RPM	Chris Barnes	429 RPM
Kelly Kulick	290 RPM	Bill O'Neill	437 RPM
Mike Fagan	388 RPM	Tommy Jones	453 RPM

Table 6.1: Actual measured rev rate of select PBA pros

These numbers are probably *far* lower than you would have expected, and certainly much lower than what is regularly reported during PBA telecasts and in other sources. They do, however, comport with video rev rate measurements we have taken of other bowlers who exhibit similar hook and ball speed. In fact, Ebonite compared these measured rev rates with those reported by the CATS system, and determined that the CATS rev rate numbers were high by 50%. Thus, if CATS reports a rev rate of, say, 450 RPM, the bowler's actual rev rate is closer to 300 RPM. That's quite a difference! Instead of feeling discouraged when you hear the phenomenal rev rates quoted on PBA telecasts, just knock about a third off of the number and realize that these folks, as good as they are, are not superhuman after all.

None of this discussion is intended as a knock against the PBA, their players, or against the CATS system. Not at all. CATS is a terrific tool that provides bowlers and coaches with invaluable speed, position, accuracy, and repeatability information not obtainable in any other way, and the Kegel corporation is performing a valuable service to the bowling community by maintaining the system. CATS does not, however, measure a bowler's rev rate.

NOW THAT WE KNOW WHAT OUR ACTUAL REV RATE IS...

By employing the video analysis method discussed in the first part of this chapter, we know what our true rev rate is and have no more need to guess. Or do we? As it turns out, while the general rev rate range we achieve is a function of the speed and power of our wrist and fingers and the efficiency of our release, the actual rev rate of any given shot is highly dependent on the specific ball we throw.

In Chapter 2 we introduced the concept of Radius of Gyration, or RG. Recall from that chapter that RG determines how difficult it is to rev up a ball of any given weight, and also how stubbornly that ball, once revved up, will resist any change in those revolutions. We most often think of the ball's RG as a factor controlling length. The RG of the ball very definitely affects both the length of the ball's skid phase and the length of the hook phase, but RG also affects hook in an even more profound way.

We said that a higher RG ball is more difficult to rev up. If we accept that the amount of force our hand can impart to the ball during any given release is relatively fixed by our strength, musculature, and technique, then it would follow that as RG increases, our rev rate must necessarily decrease. Returning to our radio analogy from Chapter 2, once the volume is turned all the way up the radio simply cannot get any louder. Likewise, once we apply all of our force to a low RG ball, there is no way to increase this force beyond our maximum when throwing a higher RG ball. The question then is, how and to what extent does increasing RG cause a decrease in rev rate? The "how" question is easy to answer: It's Isaac Newton's fault! Determining just how much an increase in the ball's RG will decrease the bowler's rev rate, however, will unfortunately involve some more math. Again, we've highlighted the math in grey if you aren't terribly interested in it. Reading through it will let you see that we're not making this stuff up, but the choice is yours.

CALCULATING THE EFFECT OF RG ON REV RATE

In Chapter 3 we briefly touched on Newton's First Law of Motion: "An object in motion tends to remain in motion unless acted upon by an outside force. An object at rest tends to remain at rest unless acted upon by an outside force." We said that the tendency of an object to retain its state of rest or motion is called *inertia*. Since RG is the dominant factor affecting the ball's moment of inertia, the higher the ball's RG, the slower it will spin for any given application of force. Mr. Newton will also help us determine the extent of the resulting decrease in rev rate.

Newton's Second Law tells us that the force acting upon an object is equal to that object's mass multiplied by its acceleration;

Force = Mass x Acceleration

The above formula works for linear ball speed, but we are instead concerned here with revolutions imparted to the ball. When dealing with "spinning force," the same formula, with slight modification, applies. The spinning force we apply to the ball in order to generate revolutions is called *torque*.[28] Just as force = mass x linear acceleration, when addressing spin rather than linear travel the formula becomes:

Torque, or spinning force = Moment of Inertia x Angular Acceleration

Angular acceleration, which replaced linear acceleration in our formula, is simply the rate at which our ball is revved up by our fingers and wrist. Moment of inertia, which replaced mass in our formula, is the ball's mass multiplied by the square of the RG. Our formula can therefore be rewritten as

Torque = (Mass x RG^2) x Angular Acceleration

Wonderful physics lesson, but what does any of this mean? The torque, or spinning force, we apply to the ball during our release creates angular acceleration, and this angular acceleration, applied over a segment of time, causes the ball to spin. Our ball's rev rate, more properly called its *angular velocity*, is equal to the amount of angular acceleration we apply to the ball multiplied by the amount of time during which we apply it, which is simply the amount of time our fingers remain in the ball as we snap our wrist or flick our fingers forward after our thumb has exited. If we attach a rocket engine to a sled, the longer that engine burns, the faster our sled will go. Likewise, the longer our fingers remain in the ball during release, the longer we can apply torque to the ball and the faster our ball will spin. Let's examine a hypothetical bowling scenario in order to make this concept clear.

Our subject bowler throws a 15 pound ball with a medium RG of 2.54, and we measure his rev rate using our video method at 275 RPM, or 275 revolutions per minute. We time his wrist snap, and determine that it occurs over one quarter of a second, or 0.25 seconds.[29] From this data, we can calculate the amount of Torque his release imparted to the ball. Torque is ordinarily measured in Newton-meters (Nm), or sometimes a bit more loosely in pound-feet, kilogram-meters, or similar units. Performing our computations in Newton-meters would require us to convert most of our input measurements, such as converting our RPMs to radians per second and our RG into meters rather than inches. Instead, we are going to ignore our units, which will greatly simplify our calculations. Since we are not looking at absolute values, but only at relative values as we change the RG of our ball, the units become irrelevant, so this simplification is valid.

In order to calculate Torque—the force our bowler applies toward spinning the ball—we need to convert our 275 RPM angular velocity into angular acceleration. We said that angular velocity is equal to angular acceleration multiplied by the amount of time over which this acceleration is applied. This can be written as

Angular Velocity = Angular Acceleration x Time

Since angular acceleration is our unknown, we isolate it by dividing both sides of the equation by time. Thus,

Angular Acceleration = Angular Velocity ÷ Time, or
Angular Acceleration = 275 RPM ÷ 0.25 seconds, or
Angular Acceleration = 1100 spin units per time unit squared, or for our purposes, simply 1100.

Now, back to Mr. Newton's Second Law of Motion. We have already learned that torque is equal to the ball's moment of inertia multiplied by its angular acceleration. Since we also know that moment of inertia is equal to our ball's mass multiplied by the square of its RG, we can substitute those terms, and our formula becomes:

Torque = Mass x RG² x Angular Acceleration

Plugging in our numbers, we get,

Torque = 15 lb x (2.54")² x 1100 spin/time², or
Torque = 15 x 6.4516 x 1100, or
Torque = 106,451.4 units (whatever those Frankenstein units may be!)

Thus, if our bowler's release imparts 106,451.4 units of torque to his 15 pound, 2.54 inch medium RG ball, it will spin at a 275 RPM rev rate. Let's see what happens to our bowler's rev rate if the same 106,451.4 units of torque are applied to a low RG ball, say 2.47 inches.

APPLYING OUR RELEASE TO A LOWER RG BALL

To compute this rev rate, we must first calculate the angular acceleration resulting from our applied torque. We have already learned from Newton's Second Law that,

Torque = Moment of Inertia x Angular Acceleration

Solving for angular acceleration by dividing both sides of the equation by moment of inertia, we get:

Angular Acceleration = Torque ÷ Moment of Inertia

Again, since Moment of Inertia = Mass x RG², we get:

Angular Acceleration = Torque ÷ (Mass x RG²)

Plugging in our numbers, including our new lower RG, we get:

Angular Acceleration = 106,451.4 ÷ (15 x 2.47^2), or
Angular Acceleration = 106,451.4 ÷ (15 x 6.1009), or
Angular Acceleration = 106,451.4 ÷ 91.514, or
Angular Acceleration = 1163.23

Since we said that angular velocity, our rev rate, is equal to angular acceleration multiplied by the amount of time this acceleration is applied, and since we said our time, or wrist snap occurred over 0.25 seconds, our formula becomes:

Angular Velocity = 1163.23 x 0.25, or
Angular Velocity = 290.8 RPM

This is a rather significant increase! By throwing a low RG ball, our bowler's rev rate increased from 275 to approximately 291, a gain of almost 6 percent. Note that this gain was automatic. It was not the result of anything the bowler did differently. The increase in rev rate was the result of simply applying his same release to a lower RG ball.

APPLYING OUR RELEASE TO A HIGHER RG BALL

What would happen, then, if our bowler instead threw a high RG ball, say 2.60"?

Angular Acceleration = Torque ÷ (Mass x RG^2)
Angular Acceleration = 106,451.4 ÷ (15 x 2.60^2)
Angular Acceleration = 106,451.4 ÷ (15 x 6.76)
Angular Acceleration = 106,451.4 ÷ 101.4
Angular Acceleration = 1049.817
Angular Velocity = Angular Acceleration x Time
Angular Velocity = 1049.817 x 0.25
Angular Velocity = 262.454

Again, this is a significant change. By moving to a high RG ball, our bowler's rev rate dropped from 275 to approximately 262, a decrease of almost 5 percent. The USBC currently allows balls to have an RG ranging from a low of 2.46 inches to a high of 2.8 inches. Though we might be hard-pressed to find actual bowling balls possessing these extremes, in theory our bowler could obtain a rev rate ranging from 226 RPM to 293 RPM just by changing bowling balls, with every other part of his release remaining constant.

In our example above using the extremes of RG allowed by the USBC, our bowler, employing precisely the same release, saw his rev rate range from 226 to 293. So is he a 226 RPM low rev bowler, or a 293 RPM medium rev bowler, or is he something in between? We can see now that when we said in our setup to the problem that our bowler's rev rate was 275, this number was in fact largely arbitrary, depending as it does upon the RG of the ball chosen when the measurement of rev rate was taken. Thus, any discussion of rev rate any more specific than low-rev, medium-rev, or high-rev, isn't terribly descriptive. In fact, in the Ebonite Bowler ID presentation cited earlier, they define "low-rev" as 0-270 RPM, "medium-rev" as 271-350, and "high-rev" as 351 and higher. While these ranges are arbitrary, they nonetheless serve to demonstrate that it is more meaningful to speak of rev ranges than of specific rev rates.

Since RG has such a powerful influence on rev rate, and since rev rate translates almost directly into hook, the above study allows us to see quite clearly why lower RG balls are easier to hook than those possessing a higher RG. Compound this with the fact that manufacturers often provide their lower RG balls with high-end and more "grippy" coverstocks while the high RG equipment gets the lower friction, harder, or "old school" coverstocks, and this divergence in hooking power becomes even more pronounced.

The significant effect that RG exerts on our realized rev rate also points up a problem with bowling ball recommendations. Higher RG, weaker coverstock balls are typically marketed as "entry-level" balls, but since entry level bowlers tend to have fairly weak releases and limited hook, sticking such a bowler with a high RG ball would only serve to compound his or her problems and quite possibly cause discouragement. Such "entry level" equipment is almost singularly unsuited to an entry level bowler, who in most cases would do much better with a "mid-grade" or "intermediate" piece of equipment with a more moderate RG and a somewhat more aggressive coverstock. So-called entry level equipment is actually far better suited to more skilled players for difficult situations where excessive lane friction or other such conditions require them to tame their release or get the ball farther down the lane. Higher RG and lower friction "entry level" balls are also suitable for players who throw a reasonable hook, but whose ball speed is very low causing stronger equipment to overreact.

CHAPTER 7

DOES A HIGH REV BALL REALLY HIT THE PINS HARDER?

IN CHAPTER 2 we discussed kinetic energy, and determined that a lighter bowling ball actually hits the pins harder than does a heavier ball when thrown by any given bowler. As compelling as that determination was, it really only tells part of the story. The kinetic energy we described in Chapter 2 is that of a moving, non-rotating object, and is referred to as *translational kinetic energy*. Translational kinetic energy would provide a complete description only if our ball merely skidded down the lane, but very few bowlers release their shot without also imparting some measure of spin. A rotating object possesses a second form of kinetic energy, and this *rotational kinetic energy* exists apart from and in addition to the translational kinetic energy of our moving bowling ball. The total kinetic energy which our ball can impart to the pins is the sum of the translational and the rotational kinetic energy. We have learned that translational kinetic energy is influenced primarily by ball speed and in a lesser way by ball weight, but what factors influence rotational kinetic energy?

WHAT IS ROTATIONAL KINETIC ENERGY?

Rotational kinetic energy is the energy conveyed by an object because of its spin rather than because of its travel. The rotational kinetic energy of our bowling ball is computed in a manner similar to that of translational (down lane) kinetic energy. While our now familiar formula for translational kinetic energy is:

Translational Kinetic Energy = 1/2 x (Mass x Velocity^2),

...the formula for rotational kinetic energy is:

Rotational Kinetic Energy = 1/2 x (Moment of Inertia x Angular Velocity^2)

We can see that the formulas are almost identical, but with moment of inertia substituted for mass, and angular velocity substituted for velocity. Angular velocity is simply a fancy way of describing how fast our ball is spinning. In bowling, spin is measured in RPM (revolutions per minute), more commonly referred to as *revs*.

Moment of inertia is a measurement of the resistance of an object to any change in angular velocity. In simple terms, it is a measure of how hard it is to rev up a stationary object, or conversely of how stubbornly our now spinning object wants to keep those revs it already has. An object's moment of inertia is dependent on its weight and upon how that weight is distributed within the object.

In bowling, a given ball's moment of inertia is a function of its radius of gyration, or "RG." Inside of a bowling ball, the weight is not distributed evenly. A typical bowling ball is composed of a very heavy and dense but oddly shaped weight block near the center of the ball, a relatively lightweight filler material, and a dense and heavy outer covering. If we could somehow average out the weights and locations of these three different materials and condense them into a uniform hollow sphere, this smaller but averaged imaginary sphere would have precisely the same moment of inertia—or resistance to changes in spin—as would our much larger but more randomly constructed bowling ball (Figure 7.1). The radius of gyration is simply a measurement, in inches, of the radius of that averaged, idealized hollow sphere.[30]

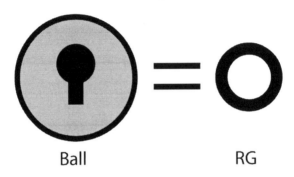

Figure 7.1 Visualizing radius of gyration

What does it mean when the specification sheet that came with our new ball lists an RG of, say, 2.50? An RG of 2.50 means that if we averaged the weights and their locations within our ball and made it all into a uniform hollow sphere, that sphere would have a radius of only 2.50 inches, as opposed to the roughly 4-1/4 inch radius of the typical bowling ball.

The moment of inertia of our bowling ball is calculated as the ball's weight multiplied by the square of its RG, or Mass x RG^2. Therefore, the higher the RG of a ball of any given weight, the greater its moment of inertia, and thus the harder it is to either rev up or slow down. So what does all of this mean to us?

CALCULATING ROTATIONAL KINETIC ENERGY

Let's look again at the formula for rotational kinetic energy:

Rotational Kinetic Energy = 1/2 x (Moment of Inertia x Angular Velocity^2).

If we use common bowling units of measure in place of proper scientific units and substitute our bowling terms for the physics terms, we can turn that formula into something much easier to understand:

Simplified Rotational Kinetic Energy = 1/2 x (Ball Weight x RG^2) x Revs^2

Due to our ignoring of proper units, the results from this simplified formula for rotational kinetic energy will not be terribly useful on their own but will still be suitable for our present demonstration. We learned two important things in our discussion of translational kinetic energy in Chapter 2. First, that the weight of the ball has a limited influence on the kinetic energy of our shot, and second, that ball speed, since it is squared in the formula, has a profound effect. Likewise with rotational kinetic energy, the moment of inertia of the ball will have limited influence, but the revs, being squared like ball speed was, will have a profound effect. Let's look at some examples. Again, don't let the math get in your way. It's really very simple, and it is enough just to read through it.

In order to keep the math simple, let's use a not terribly realistic example of an 8 pound ball with an RG of 2.50. We'll have an average bowler throw it at 200 RPM. The (simplified) rotational kinetic energy of that ball would be:

1/2 x (Ball Weight x RG^2) x Revs^2, or
1/2 x (8 x 2.50^2) x 200^2, or
1/2 x (8 x 2.50 x 2.50) x (200 x 200), or
1/2 x (8 x 6.25) x 40,000, or
1/2 x 50 x 40,000, or
1 million units of rotational kinetic energy.

If that same ball is now thrown by a power player at 400 RPM, the resultant rotational kinetic energy is:

1/2 x (Ball Weight x RG^2) x Revs^2, or
1/2 x (8 x 2.50^2) x 400^2, or
1/2 x (8 x 2.50 x 2.50) x (400 x 400), or
1/2 x (8 x 6.25) x 160,000, or
1/2 x 50 x 160,000, or
4 million units of rotational kinetic energy.

Just as doubling our ball speed in Chapter 2 resulted in a quadrupling of translational kinetic energy, a doubling of our rev rate results in the same quadrupling of the rotational kinetic energy of our bowling ball. If our power player and our average bowler throw the same ball at the same speed, they will both have precisely the same down lane translational kinetic energy. Our power player, however, will hit the pins with four times as much rotational kinetic energy as will the average bowler. Since kinetic energy is what knocks down the pins, other things being equal, it would seem that the power player, with four times as much rotational kinetic energy, will always win. Why, then, is this not the case in real life?

CALCULATING TOTAL KINETIC ENERGY

The actual numbers we calculated above and in Chapter 2 are not meaningful in and of themselves due mostly to our foregoing of proper units within each computation. But since each calculation was carried out the same way, we can still compare the numbers on a relative basis, that is translational to translational, or rotational to rotational. We cannot, however, simply combine those rotational and translational kinetic energies to obtain total kinetic energy without first converting to proper units.

In physics, kinetic energy is measured in units called Joules. One Joule is defined as the amount of energy required to apply one Newton of force over a distance of one meter, which admittedly doesn't mean much to a typical bowler. For our purposes it is enough just to know that a Joule is a unit of kinetic energy. If we wish to calculate the actual kinetic energy of our rolling and spinning bowling ball in Joules, we first need to convert all of our bowling units into proper scientific units. We then need to plug the appropriate numbers into our formulas for translational and rotational kinetic energy, and then add the two forms of energy together. Performing all of these conversions and calculations is not terribly difficult, but we won't bore you with the math here. We will instead just present you with the results. The complete calculations are shown in the endnotes to this chapter if you wish to walk through the problem with us.[31] In either case, let's look at a couple of kinetic energy examples using the actual rather than the simplified formulas.

Bowler A is an average bowler with revs of 200 RPM. Bowler B is a power player with a 400 RPM release. Both utilize the same 15 pound ball with an RG of 2.60, and in this example both will throw the ball at 16 miles per hour. Bowler A's ball will hit the pins with 180.6 Joules of kinetic energy. Bowler B's ball hits the pins with 200.3 Joules. What?!? If we just demonstrated that doubling the ball's rev rate from 200 to 400 RPM results in a quadrupling of the rotational kinetic energy, why does the power player's ball hit the pins with only about 10 percent more kinetic energy than does that of the average bowler? The sad fact is that with the small size and weight of a bowling ball, and at our relatively low RPM range of perhaps 100 to 500, the amount of rotational kinetic energy a bowler can generate is fairly insignificant when compared to the translational kinetic energy from the ball simply traveling down the lane. In our example above, both bowlers generated 174 Joules of translational kinetic energy. Bowler A's 200 RPM rev rate added just over 6.5 Joules of rotational kinetic energy, and our 400 RPM power player's revs added only 26 Joules. Though Bowler B's rotational kinetic energy was indeed four times that of Bowler A, the difference in total kinetic energy amounted to less than 20 Joules.

SO WHERE DOES THE REAL ADVANTAGE COME FROM?

If a power player's additional revs do not add very much to his ball's total kinetic energy, where does his or her real advantage come from? We know there must be an advantage or no one would expend the extra energy or incur the extra wear and tear on their body from a powerful release, and we wouldn't see most of our league awards and tournament victories going to the high rev bowlers.

In fact, high rev bowlers have many advantages over average rev players. As we learned in Chapter 4, high rev bowlers enjoy a significantly larger "lucky strike" zone on either side of the pocket due to their increased entry angle to the pins. They also have the ability to play a far greater portion of the lane and far more lines of attack, the ability to effectively utilize higher RG equipment thus experiencing less roll out, and a number of other advantages more or less unavailable to the low rev player. In addition, and despite our previous discussion, high rev bowlers typically do hit the pins with far more kinetic energy than do low rev players. If increased revs do not directly add significant energy to the shot, what, then, is the actual source of their kinetic energy advantage?

To be an effective bowler your rev rate and ball speed need to be in balance. Too many revs for a given ball speed can result in the ball reading the lane too soon, losing energy too soon, overreacting to friction, reacting erratically, or any number of other potentially undesirable outcomes. Too much speed for a given rev rate results in a relatively straight ball path with its resultant decrease in the entry angle to the pins, which causes an increase in deflection and a reduction in the size of the "lucky strike" zone. It also results in an inability to play deeper or more aggressive lines of attack, and tends to preclude the use of higher RG equipment.

Striking the proper balance between rev rate and ball speed will result in a smoother, more predictable ball reaction. Unfortunately though, there are no hard and fast rules governing the proper ball speed for any given rev rate. There is probably a way to calculate the ideal ball speed, but it would be highly dependent on many factors besides rev rate. Even if we could incorporate these additional factors, the math would almost certainly be daunting. In the absence of solid data, the following table contains what we use as target speed ranges when working with bowlers. These speeds are those read by the down lane sensors and displayed on the score keeping monitor at most bowling centers. By the time the ball has reached these sensors it has slowed down to some degree, so speed "off the hand" will probably be a couple of miles per hour faster. The numbers in the table represent our opinion based on observation of a great many bowlers. Given that these are only opinion, and that many other factors come into play when trying to balance ball speed with rev rate, these numbers should be used only as a rough guide.

Rev Rate (RPM)	Ball Speed (MPH)	Ball Speed (KPH)
200-250	14-15	21-23
250-300	15-16	23-25
300-350	16-17	25-27
350-400	17-18	27-29
400+	18+	29+

Table 7.1: Balanced rev rate and ball speed (down lane)

Maintaining balance between revs and ball speed points out the true source of the high rev bowler's kinetic energy advantage. The high rev bowler's kinetic energy advantage comes down to his or her greater rev rate allowing for significantly greater ball speed while still maintaining the required balance, and we have already determined that ball speed is by far the predominant factor affecting the ball's kinetic energy.

Let's look again at our two bowlers. To remain in balance, our 200 RPM bowler should have a ball speed in the neighborhood of perhaps 15 miles per hour, while our 400 RPM bowler has enough revs for a ball speed of roughly 19 miles per hour. If we have both bowlers roll an identical 2.50 RG ball with their given revs and at their balanced ball speeds, let's see what happens to their kinetic energy:

Bowler A:

> 15 pound ball @ 15 MPH has a translational kinetic energy of 153 Joules.
> 200 RPM and 2.50 RG has a rotational kinetic energy of 6 Joules.
> Total kinetic energy equals 159 Joules.

Bowler B:

> 15 pound ball @ 19 MPH has a translational kinetic energy of 245 Joules.
> 400 RPM and 2.50 RG has a rotational kinetic energy of 24 Joules.
> Total kinetic energy equals 269 Joules.

Bowler B, our high rev bowler, hits the pins with 110 more Joules, or 70% more kinetic energy than does our low rev bowler, but note that only 18 Joules of this increase resulted directly from his extra revs. Almost all of his increase in kinetic energy, nearly 85 percent, resulted from the increased ball speed which his higher revs allowed.

This entire exercise is just theoretical, though. As we will soon discover, even the small 18 Joule kinetic energy increase attributed to the increased revs is largely a phantom, and for the most part vanishes when we look more deeply at what happens to our ball as it travels down the lane.

WHAT REALLY HAPPENS TO REVS AND SPEED AS THE BALL TRAVELS DOWN THE LANE

The above discussion contained a simplification. It assumed that our ball retains the revs and speed that we impart to it via our release. That is, a 200 RPM release at 15 miles per hour hits the pins at 200 RPM and 15 miles per hour, and a 400 RPM release at 19 miles per hour hits the pins at 400 RPM and 19 miles per hour. This, however, is not the case. In reality, the revolutions a bowling ball possesses when it hits the pins are entirely dependent on ball speed, and the original rev rate at release has no direct effect on the final rev rate. How can this be?

We've all observed that as a bowling ball travels down the lane it seems to "rev up," spinning faster and faster the closer it gets to the pins. This revving up is not an illusion. Our bowling balls do, in fact, spin far faster as they approach the pins than they did when we released them onto the lane. But why, and how, does our ball rev up?

WHY DOES MY BALL REV UP?

As our ball begins its path down the lane, it spins at a rate dictated by our release. As it approaches the pins it begins to spin faster and faster. The most common explanation we have heard is that the bowling ball's powerful core design somehow has the ability to rev up the ball, but absent a power source, this idea can pretty much be discarded. If not the ball's core design, what, then, is the cause of this "revving up" phenomenon?

Our initial thought was that the revving up must be related to the ball's various RG measurements. Most of us have observed that when a figure skater spins on the ice with her arms extended, she spins rather slowly. When she pulls her arms in, she spins much faster without any additional application of force. This is because with her arms extended she has a high RG. In this position, her mass is more spread out away from her center. This gives her a higher moment of inertia, or resistance to changes in spin. With her arms pulled in—with her mass concentrated more toward her center—she has a much lower RG, and therefore a much lower moment of inertia and less resistance to changes in spin. In effect, our figure skater "revs up" by decreasing her RG.

If our bowling ball had a perfect sphere for a core, the ball would not have a low and a high RG axis. It would have precisely the same RG regardless of how the ball was spinning since the weight in such a ball would be uniformly distributed. However, since a real bowling ball has an oddly shaped core, which is also usually at least a bit off center within the ball, it will exhibit very different RG characteristics depending upon which axis it is spinning. We are for the most part concerned with only three of these possible axes; the axis that runs through the ball's *pin*, the ball's so-called *preferred spin axis*, and the axis that runs through our PAP as we release the ball.

Our bowling ball has its low RG axis along its pin, that is, along a line drawn from the pin locator dot on the surface of the ball, through the long dimension of the ball's core, and out the other side of the ball. When rotating on this axis our ball has it's lowest moment of inertia—its lowest resistance to spin—and thus will spin at its fastest rate for any given input of torque. The ball's high RG axis typically runs roughly perpendicular to the low RG axis, more or less through the side of the core. This high RG axis—the end of which will ordinarily be located somewhere in the vicinity of the thumb hole in a drilled ball—is called the *Preferred Spin Axis* or *PSA*, though bowlers often refer to it as the *Mass Bias*. When spinning along this high RG axis our ball has its greatest moment of inertia, and will thus spin at its slowest rate for any given application of torque.

Our ball's initial spin axis, or what bowlers refer to as the *Positive Axis Point* or *PAP*, is the point around which we spin the ball as we release it. The PAP is ordinarily located four to five inches to the right of the gripping holes (for a right-handed bowler), and roughly in line with the center of the grip. The ball's RG value when spinning about the PAP is typically somewhere in between the ball's high RG preferred spin axis and low RG pin, so we can think of the PAP as a medium RG axis. When we release our bowling ball with some given torque, it will spin about the PAP at a certain rate. If the ball's rotation point migrated from our medium RG PAP to the ball's much lower RG pin, the ball would rev up to a faster rate in precisely the same manner as does the figure skater when she pulls her arms in. Sounds logical, right?

The problem is, while the ball's rotational axis does indeed migrate away from our PAP as the ball travels down the lane, it does not migrate toward the pin. Instead, the ball's rotational axis migrates along what is called an RG plane. The RG plane is that set of points along the ball's surface that happen to possess roughly the same RG as did our initial spin axis, or PAP. In the case of our bowling ball, those points typically form a curving line that starts on our PAP and then travels in between our thumb hole and finger holes (Figure 7.2). This line sometimes curves slightly upward toward the low RG pin and sometimes slightly downward toward the high RG PSA, but never reaches either. Further, since every point along this RG plane possesses almost precisely the same RG as did our PAP, then a change in RG could not possibly account for our ball revving up. In the case of a rolling bowling ball, our figure skater never pulls her arms in.

Figure 7.2: Axis migration along RG plane

If there is no magical revving power provided by the ball's core, and if the ball is not migrating to a lower RG axis, how then does it rev up? The answer is both simple and somewhat disappointing. The revving is not some positive feature stirred into the mix when the ball was manufactured, nor is it due to anything your pro shop operator did. The revving up is instead a mere byproduct of the ball rolling following the hook phase rather than skidding as it was doing before it hooked.

SKID VS. ROLL

Most coaches teach that at the point of release, our ball possesses its highest ball speed and its lowest rev rate. This probably isn't precisely true, but it's close enough. Our ball definitely loses ball speed to friction as it travels down the lane, as would any other object. Let's see, though, what this lane friction does to the ball's rev rate.

When our bowling ball travels down the lane it first skids in the oil, then hooks as the oil tapers off, and then rolls in a straight line once friction between the ball and the lane takes over. We all know intuitively what "skid" and "roll" are, but in order to gain an understanding of ball dynamics we need to know the true definitions. Both skid and roll reference the relationship between a rotating object and the surface the object is traversing.

Rolling, or more properly *pure rolling*, is a state where there is a one-to-one relationship between the circumference of the rotating object—the distance around the object's perimeter—and the amount of distance the object travels as it rotates. This is not as confusing as it sounds. Let's use the example of a car tire to illustrate. The average car tire is a bit over two feet in diameter. If we were to wrap a tape measure all the way around the tire's tread, we would find that it had a circumference of about seven feet. This means that every revolution of the tire presents seven feet of rubber to the road. If our car were traveling on a dry road, then each revolution of the tire would propel the car forward by this same seven feet. This situation describes a state of pure roll, a one-to-one relationship between the surface of the tire and the surface of the road.

Skid is the opposite of roll. Skid is the state where there is a difference between the amount of surface presented by the rotating object and the amount of distance the object travels. Suppose we are driving our car on a snow covered road at a safe and prudent speed when a hapless squirrel ignores the traffic light and runs out in front of us. We slam on the brakes, but since the road is slippery our car slides for 30 feet, right through the intersection, and unfortunately also right through the squirrel. Since our brakes were firmly engaged our tire did not rotate at all. The stationary tire presented only a few inches of rubber to the road, but it still traveled 30 feet. This disconnect between the amount of surface presented by the object and the distance the object travels is the very definition of skid.

Just as when our car tires were sliding on the icy road, during the initial skid phase of the ball's journey there is no correlation between the amount of surface the ball presents to the lane and the amount of distance covered. We can demonstrate this very easily by counting the oil rings on our ball after a trip down the lane. Suppose our 200 RPM bowler threw his or her ball in an "end-over-end" manner at 15 miles per hour on a 40 foot long oil pattern. The ball will pick up six oil rings over this 40 feet, meaning that it rotated six times as it traveled 40 feet. A bowling ball has a circumference of roughly 27 inches. If it rotated six times, it presented 6 x 27 inches, or 162 inches of coverstock to the lane. 162 inches is equal to only 13-1/2 feet of ball surface contacting the lane while the ball traveled 40 feet, which is very far from a one-to-one relationship. Our 400 RPM bowler's shot would present twice as much ball surface to the lane, but even his 27 feet of surface falls far short of the 40 feet the ball traveled. During the initial skid phase, the ball is traveling much faster than it is spinning.

While the ball is skidding during the first part of its journey down the lane, it possesses more or less whatever rev rate our release created. As the ball enters the hook phase it skids less and rolls more, and when it exits the hook phase it is simply rolling along the lane with very little or no skid at all. When the ball is rolling rather than skidding, there will be a one-to-one relationship between the amount of distance the ball covers on the lane and the amount of ball surface that contacts the lane. That is, if the ball rolls one foot, it will have presented one foot of its circumference to the lane. This is the same situation as our example of the car traveling on a dry road. Since the tires are not spinning, every seven feet of travel results in the tire making one full revolution. Since a bowling ball has a circumference of roughly 27 inches, once the ball enters the roll phase, every 27 inches of travel will result in one full revolution of the ball.

Let's assume that when our 200 RPM ball exits the hook phase and begins simply rolling, it is traveling at a rate of 14 miles per hour. Since there are 60 minutes in an hour and 63,360 inches in a mile, this means that our ball is now rolling down the lane at a rate of 14,784 inches per minute. Since our ball's circumference is 27 inches, every 27 of the inches covered while rolling down the lane results in the ball spinning one complete revolution. 14,784 inches per minute divided by 27 inches per revolution means that merely by rolling down the lane, our 14 mile per hour ball will spin at a stunning 548 RPM![32] This 548 RPM rev rate far exceeds the 200 RPM we put on the ball when we released it. What we are actually observing as our ball revs up is simply the transition from our relatively low 200 RPM release rev rate to the staggering 548 RPM rate that the ball's roll provides.

Suppose instead that we are a high rev *power player*, and that we rip the cover off the ball with our 500 RPM release and launch the ball at 19 miles per hour. 19 miles per hour is equal to 20,064 inches per minute. Dividing this by 27 inches per revolution yields a simple rolling rev rate of 743 RPM, again easily dwarfing our powerful 500 RPM release. The following Table lists the rate at which your ball will spin due only to simple rolling at various ball speeds. In all cases we can see that the rolling rev rate is far higher than whatever our release may be able to impart to the ball.

Ball Speed	Rev rate due to rolling, in RPM
12 MPH	469
13 MPH	508
14 MPH	548
15 MPH	587
16 MPH	626
17 MPH	665
18 MPH	704
19 MPH	743
20 MPH	782

Table 7.2: Ball rev rate due to simple rolling

As unsatisfying as it may feel, your ball revving up had little to do with the spin you put on the ball when you released it, nor with any magic power of the ball's core, nor with anything your ball driller did. The revving up phenomenon, and the ball's final rev rate as it hits the pins, are instead merely side effects, the inevitable byproduct of the ball rolling rather than skidding.

SO WHAT DOES THIS MEAN IN TERMS OF KNOCKING DOWN PINS?

In our previous examples we assumed that the ball maintained a rev rate equal to that which we imparted to it during our release. We demonstrated that even when the rev rate doubled, the kinetic energy at the pins was not much greater, since ball speed has a far bigger impact on kinetic energy than does rev rate. We now learn that even this small rotational kinetic energy advantage disappears in real life, because *two bowling balls rolling at the same final speed will possess precisely the same rev rate regardless of what their initial rev rate was when they were released*. The final rev rate of a rolling bowling ball is determined solely by its rolling speed.

If a ball thrown at 500 RPM and one thrown at 200 RPM both hit the pins at, say, 18 miles per hour, and assuming that the ball is rolling when it hits the pins, then both balls will hit with precisely the same rev rate and precisely the same kinetic energy. This would imply that higher revs confer no kinetic energy advantage, but as with pretty much every other aspect of bowling, the truth is not quite so simple.

Let's look at the case of a 500 RPM power player and a 200 RPM stroker who both throw the ball at an *initial* velocity of 18 miles per hour. We said that both balls will rev up as they transition from skid to roll. Since no energy is added to our system by a magic weight block, a top secret ball drilling, or by any other means, then the law of conservation of energy tells us that the energy required to rev up the ball has to come from somewhere. Since the only two meaningful components of our ball's motion are spin and down lane speed, the energy required to rev up the ball has to come from our ball speed. That is, our ball must burn off speed and slow down in order to fuel the increase in rev rate.

Imagine your car accelerating from 20 miles per hour up to a speed of 70 miles per hour as you enter a freeway, a 50 mile per hour increase. This acceleration will burn a certain quantity of gasoline. If instead your car was already going 50 miles per hour, it is obvious that it would burn far less gasoline to accelerate to the same 70 mile per hour final speed, since in this second case the engine only had to add 20 miles per hour of speed instead of 50. Just as your car burned off more gas accelerating from 20 miles per hour up to 70 than it did accelerating from 50 miles per hour up to 70, your bowling ball will burn off far more speed in accelerating its rev rate from 200 RPM up to 600 or 700 RPM than it would in revving up from 500 RPM to the same 600 or 700 RPM.

In short, though both balls were delivered with the same 18 mile per hour initial velocity, the 200 RPM ball will burn off more speed as it revs up than will the 500 RPM ball, and so will hit the pins with far less velocity and with a lower final rev rate. Since we know that velocity is the major contributor to kinetic energy, it is clear that the 200 RPM ball will hit the pins with significantly less energy than will the 500 RPM ball even though they were delivered with the same initial velocity. Again, the higher initial rev rate did not create the final kinetic energy advantage, it just gave the shot a head start. The higher initial rev rate simply allows for a higher final velocity and final rev rate as the ball hits the pins, and this higher final velocity and resulting higher rev rate creates the high rev player's kinetic energy advantage.

A high rev bowler clearly has a huge kinetic energy advantage over a lower rev bowler, both because he or she can throw the ball with a higher initial velocity while still retaining a reasonable hook potential, and because regardless of initial velocity the high rev bowler's ball will lose far less of that velocity on its way to the pins. Higher speed equals higher kinetic energy. Higher kinetic energy leads to more pin action, more powerful messenger pins, and more randomly spinning and flying pins to help take out any strays left behind by less than perfect shots.

So can we mere mortals compete against the high-rev power players? Of course, but we must recognize that we operate at a fairly significant disadvantage, and must take steps to try to compensate to the extent possible. While the balanced high rev bowler undeniably generates significantly more kinetic energy than does the balanced low rev bowler, the fact is that the amount of kinetic energy required to knock down all ten pins on a proper pocket hit is not terribly high, and most every bowler generates enough kinetic energy to strike so long as he or she is able to deliver the ball to the pocket on given lane conditions. Lower rev bowlers need to hit the pocket to strike, while high rev bowlers only need to get close. Bowling is a game of kinetic energy and targeting. To overcome the high-rev bowler's kinetic energy advantage, those of us with less than stellar rev rates just need to be more accurate than the high rev players!

CHAPTER 8

WHY DOES MY BALL HOOK?

WHY DOES A bowling ball hook? There are dozens of books, magazine articles, and websites, and thousands of coaches, pro shop operators, and high average bowlers offering answers. We hear lots of different ideas, and some of these ideas even conflict with others.

Hook is often credited to modern bowling ball coverstocks and cores, and ball manufacturers oblige these ideas with a constant parade of new coverstock formulations, different surface finishes, and new and ever more complex core shapes. In fact, we often hear bowlers blessed with high rev rates and big hooks disparage modern bowling balls as "hook in a box," as though the ball manufacturers are somehow allowing those with lesser hand to "cheat," and obtain hook they are not entitled to. A recent coaching article in a bowling magazine even claimed that "modern bowling balls hook all by themselves," a sentiment that we have heard expressed many times.

Pro shop operators often credit hook to variables within their own control. They attempt to influence the magnitude of the hook by changing the amount of track flare. They try to alter the shape of the ball's path by manipulating the location and value of the various RG axes or the ball's surface roughness, or until the practice was recently outlawed, by drilling an extra hole in a strategic location. Bowlers and coaches, while acknowledging the above, tend to focus on what they are able to control, including variables such as rev rate, ball speed, axis tilt, and axis rotation. Do any of these things actually cause the ball to hook? If they don't actually cause or create hook, do they at least influence the shape or magnitude of the hook?

The Internet supplies a wealth of information on many aspects of the game of bowling. Most of it is stated quite authoritatively, but proof sources are rarely provided. Even when they are provided, they tend to point only to other unsubstantiated writings, or to misinterpreted equations and skewed observations. All of the information we found on websites, blogs, videos, and discussion forums seemed quite well-intentioned, and we are certain that the authors believe they are stating truth. Most, however, also seem to be merely restating common bowling folklore and offering no proof at all to back up their statements.

An extreme example of this parroting of ideas can be seen in discussions of a dubious concept called "core torque." One finds several mentions of bowling ball core torque on the Internet, but curiously all share almost verbatim wording, indicating that they were all merely copied from the same source. These writings reference a core's "internal lever arms" as providing this torque. The problem with this concept is that a bowling ball core has no torque and cannot create torque, and has no lever arms, internal or otherwise.

It seems that one pundit invented the concept, it sounded "science-y" enough to be convincing, and so it was repeated by others as though it were fact.

Since our common bowling folklore is stated so emphatically, and since we hear the same reasons repeated over and over to explain this or that issue, the rest of us simply assume that it is correct and we then repeat it ourselves. A great many of us have done it, and we were both as guilty of this as anyone else when we started out in this sport. If the guy on TV said it, or the guy with the stellar reputation on the bowling chat site said it, or the guy on our league with the monster rev rate said it, it must be true!

Since these ideas are so widely held and since we have repeated them ourselves, we tend to become invested in them. We respond negatively when these ideas are challenged. We react as though it were an attack against ourselves, and we never admit to ourselves that we do not, in fact, *know* these things to be true at all. We accept these passed-down bits of bowling wisdom based on purely anecdotal evidence at best, which is just stories and is not really evidence at all. Worse yet we even accept them based solely on the reputation of the person making the claim. We repeat this folklore as truth though we have never questioned these ideas, never pulled out a physics text to see if they comport with known laws of motion, never thought them through logically, and never rigorously tested them on the lane. It is as though "bowling knowledge" simply means how much of the common folklore we've memorized and can repeat.

As such, we need to be very careful when seeking bowling information, especially on the Internet. Unless it is backed up with hard evidence, we must recognize all such information for what it is—opinion. It may be opinion from a highly credible source, perhaps a PBA professional, a well-known coach, or a highly experienced ball driller, but it is still only opinion and must always be open to questioning.

It is fine to state "I *believe* that hook is controlled by X," or "*I have read* that track flare does thus-and-so to the path of the ball," but unless we or the author have done the research and checked the premises against physical law, we should refrain from stating that "hook *is* controlled by X" or "track flare *does* thus-and-so." In short, we must be ever vigilant to separate real knowledge from belief. In the absence of real knowledge, belief and opinion are all we've got to go on. Certainly belief and opinion from a credible source is better than just making a wild guess, but where there is actual science, that science has to trump opinion.

Charles Eliot, a past president of Harvard College, said in an 1895 speech, "The first steps toward making a calm choice are to observe strictly the line of demarcation between facts on the one hand and beliefs on the other, and to hold facts as facts and beliefs as nothing more than beliefs." Let's therefore look past the folklore, which may or may not be correct, and look at the actual science that has been published on the topic of bowling. Sadly though, there is not much of it.

SPHERICAL CHICKENS

We scoured the scientific literature looking for answers. It seems that bowling is not a terribly interesting subject to scientists, and very little real research on the game has been conducted. Those few papers we did uncover offer some help, but often miss the mark for a couple of reasons. Several of the scientific papers did not actually attempt to model the motion of a real bowling ball at all, and instead used bowling merely as a convenient backdrop to build high school or college physics lessons. These and other papers also tend to break down when applied to real-life situations due to their reliance on spherical chickens. Allow us to explain via a bad physics joke.

A farmer's chickens had all stopped laying eggs, and the poor man had no idea as to why. He tried all of the old-time remedies, but nothing worked. He consulted the folks at the feed mill, he consulted the town veterinarian, but no one could figure out how to get his chickens to again lay eggs. As he sat sulking at the counter of the local diner, another man at the counter introduced himself as a physicist and offered to take a look at the problem.

The farmer figured he had nothing to lose, so he drove the physicist out to the farm. The physicist examined the chickens, the roosts, and the nesting boxes. He took samples of the feed, and of the air and water. He weighed and measured some eggs from other sources, then asked if there was somewhere quiet where he could work. The physicist pulled out his calculator and proceeded to fill page after page in his notebook with complex diagrams and calculations. Working diligently, he kept churning through his formulas until finally, with a satisfied smile on his face, he boldly underlined the final set of numbers. The physicist turned to the farmer and said, "I've figured out a method to get the chickens to lay eggs again. The only problem is that it will only work with spherical chickens in a vacuum."

While those familiar with physics are rolling on the floor and laughing hysterically right now, the rest of you are scratching your heads and wondering how that story even qualifies as a joke. The reason this story is so uproariously funny, at least to scientists, is that physicists quite often make simplifying assumptions in order to make the math less daunting, to make the problem comprehensible to students, or to make seemingly intractable problems at least somewhat approachable. The problem with this approach, of course, is that each simplification takes us farther and farther away from a real world situation, and if we take the simplifications too far we will end up with an answer that is mathematically correct but is completely inapplicable. Though the physicist in our joke came up with a mathematically correct solution to the farmer's problem, it only worked when he simplified chickens to perfect spheres and removed the influence of the atmosphere. Since there are no spherical chickens, and since chickens, spherical or otherwise, require air, the physicist's elegant and correct solution to the problem yielded nothing useful.

Of the dozen or so papers on the physics of bowling that we were able to uncover, all seemed to suffer from the spherical chicken problem to one extent or another. One of the common spherical chicken assumptions employed, and which takes the results far from real world applicability, is to assume a bowling ball of uniform density. We know that a bowling ball is far from uniform in construction, being composed as it is of a very heavy and oddly shaped core, a dense coverstock, and a relatively light filler material between the two. Another common spherical chicken is the assumption of uniform lane surface friction. In real life, of course, the lane is very oily and slippery in the front portion, very dry and high friction in the portion just before the pins, and varying from low to high friction throughout the middle. Even worse, the oil is placed differently in terms of volume and location from house to house and is constantly being moved and absorbed over various portions of the lane as play progresses, making the true coefficient of friction next to impossible to model.

In fairness, several of the published papers we reviewed were never even intended as accurate models of bowling ball motion. Such papers purposely oversimplified the situation on the lane, merely using a very stripped down look at bowling as a foil to illustrate and teach physics concepts related to torque, friction, and rotation. These papers certainly fulfill their educational purpose, but because of the simplifications, they don't offer much we can apply to real-world bowling. Other papers were likely intended as very basic models of actual ball motion, but the simplifying assumptions were too severe to let them reveal anything other than very rough information. The bottom line seems to be that far too many variables affect the path of a bowling ball to ever fully model it, and to accurately account for them all would be close to impossible. We can, nevertheless, use the research that does exist to support or disprove some of the folklore surrounding ball motion and thereby get us closer to a real understanding of the major factors involved. By eliminating the sometimes widely shared dead-end paths, we can focus in on the variables that can truly make a difference. Let's examine some of the variables and see if we can begin to sort them out.

HOOK

We agree with the USBC's definition of hook. Through their Ball Motion Study, the USBC demonstrated experimentally that the laws of motion apply to bowling the same way they apply to the rest of the physical world; that a bowling ball first skids in a straight line along the trajectory upon which we release it, then curves away from this skid path over a short distance, and then once more merely rolls on a new straight path which is at an angle to the original skid path.[33] The short, curved portion of the ball's path is the hook. As we discussed in previous chapters, hook begins gradually with a gentle curve while the ball is still in the oil. The curve tightens into a smaller radius when the ball encounters greater friction, and then quickly becomes more gradual again as high friction causes the ball's path to once more straighten out. The point in the curved portion of the path where the radius is the tightest is defined as the breakpoint. It is important to recognize that hook is not the entire path from the breakpoint to the pocket, but is only the curved portion of the path.

In previous chapters we have studied many of the factors that go into making a bowling ball hook. Summing it all up, we can say that a useful hook requires three conditions; a ball that is designed to allow for hook, a lane surface oiled so as to have a low coefficient of friction (COF) over the front part of the lane and a high COF over the back portion, and finally a release that imparts topspin to the ball on an angle away from the ball's initial launch trajectory. If any one of these factors is missing, the ball will not hook, or at least not by a great amount or in a helpful way. Contrary to claims that modern bowling balls hook all by themselves, even the most aggressive and high-performance ball will travel straight if released with all forward roll or if thrown on a lane that is heavily oiled over its entire length.

These three factors required for hook can be looked at as those the ball provides, those the lane provides, and those the bowler provides. There is nothing we can do about the lane-specific hook factors. The bowling center chooses their lane surface, and each surface has its own set of frictional characteristics. The mechanic or the tournament director specifies the oil pattern and the resultant variability in surface coefficient of friction. Since we have no control over the lane-specific aspects of hook, we shall not discuss them further here. We will, however, discuss how to deal with different and changing lane conditions in later chapters.

We have also adequately covered the bowler-specific factors in previous chapters. We know that the bowler must impart topspin to the ball, and that this topspin must be in a direction away from the ball's initial trajectory. In later chapters we will discuss how the amount and direction of this topspin affects the ball's path, and how, when, and why to vary these factors. For now we will simply assume that the bowler is at least meeting the minimum required conditions. The balance of this chapter will focus on the ball-specific factors required for hook and how these factors influence hook. In later chapters we will discuss how to select a ball for given conditions and how to alter the ball's frictional characteristics.

There are really only two aspects of ball construction that have a material affect on hook; coefficient of friction (COF), and radius of gyration (RG). Giving the bowler choices between various combinations of COF and RG is why bowling ball manufacturers have so many different balls in their product lines, and why they are constantly trying to improve coverstock chemistry and weight block design. In fact, almost all of your pro shop's alterations to the ball, including drilling layout and surface changes, are attempts to customize either RG or coefficient of friction.

WHAT THE BALL CONTRIBUTES TO HOOK

Put quite simply, hook is a function of friction, and friction is a function of the ball's coverstock. Specifically, we are referring to friction between the ball and the lane surface. In fact, according to the results of the USBC Ball Motion Study, the top five factors affecting ball path are all related to the ball's coverstock. Many of the hook-influencing factors the USBC examined were specific to the lane, or the weather, or other non-ball variables. If we look only at those factors related to the construction of the ball itself, about 75 percent of the resultant ball motion comes down to coverstock.[34] Given the overwhelming importance of coverstock factors, some analysis is in order.

Modern bowling ball coverstocks fall into three broad categories; plastic, urethane, and reactive resin. Plastic balls are typically employed as spare balls because they hook very little if at all. Urethane balls are generally described as exhibiting moderate hooking capability, and to be rather gentle and gradual in terms of ball motion. Reactive resin balls are thought of as "strike balls," with the ability to hook significantly and sometimes even aggressively. It is at this broad categorization level that the confusion surrounding bowling ball coverstocks begins, because none of these terms—plastic, urethane, and reactive resin—are accurate from a scientific standpoint, and all three are technically forms of plastic. Let's look at each category and see if we can make some sense of it.

PLASTIC BALLS

Plastic bowling balls are made of a polymer called polyester. Yes, this is the same polyester found in our plaid double-knit bell-bottom pants and our disco-era leisure suits. Polyester tends to be rather hard and dense, with a very smooth surface. When polyester balls were first introduced in 1958 they were considered big-hooking strike balls. Indeed, on the very soft lacquer finish used on bowling lanes at the time, polyester balls could grab the lane and out-hook the old rubber bowling balls. Polyester continued as a high-performance coverstock until the early 1970s, when polyurethane varnish began replacing lacquer as a lane finish. Polyurethane varnish exhibited far less friction than did shellac or lacquer. As such, polyester balls—which exhibit very little friction themselves—could not obtain enough friction with the lane surface even on the dry portion of the lane. Hook began to disappear, shots tended to skid forever, and scores started to drop. In 1973 a resourceful professional bowler named Don McCune figured out that if he soaked his bowling ball in a dangerous industrial solvent called butanone or methyl ethyl ketone, the polyester coverstock would become very soft and sticky, allowing it to grab the polyurethane lane surface with more friction than ever before. With the aid of his "soaker" ball, McCune rocketed from the middle of the pack to PBA Player of the Year. Soaker balls and factory-made, soft, "bleeder" balls dominated the lanes until 1976, when a new rule by the American Bowling Congress banned soft bowling balls, and polyester returned to its previous status as a low-friction coverstock.

Since polyester exhibits such low friction, polyester balls cannot hook much on modern lanes even if the other two conditions necessary for hook are present. The relatively straight ball path exhibited by polyester balls therefore makes them an ideal choice for spare shooting, and despite originally being marketed as a strike ball, spare shooting is the primary purpose for which they are sold today. While the industry would prefer that we all refer to these balls as "polyester," the less accurate terms "plastic ball" and "spare ball" are not likely to go away. They are simply too ingrained into bowling terminology to ever change, so we will succumb to inaccuracy and continue to refer to them as plastic balls right along with you.

URETHANE BALLS

The first thing you need to know about urethane balls is that they are not made of urethane. Urethane, technically called ethyl carbamate, is not a plastic. It is a carcinogenic chemical that no longer has any industrial applications, but curiously can be found naturally in fermented foods and beverages including beer, wine, and bread. Urethane bowling balls are instead made of *polyurethane*, which is a far different chemical. Confusingly, though poly-urethane literally means "many urethanes," polyurethane does not contain any urethane either. Without getting technical, polyurethane is a long, chain-like molecule wherein the bits of stuff that make up the molecule are held together by a type of chemical bond called a *urethane bond*. Thus, polyurethane means "many urethane bonds." Despite the inaccuracy, the word "urethane" has become a polymer industry shorthand for polyurethane. When you hear the word "urethane" used today in reference to any plastic-like substance, know that they are really talking about polyurethane.

Polyurethane is a polymer that can take on many forms, from hard and dense like our bowling balls, to stretchy and rubber-like, to rigid or flexible foam. Basic polyurethane is made up of two chemicals, an isocyanate and a polyol. There are many different isocyanates and polyols, and the physical traits of the final polyurethane depend on which particular versions are selected as raw ingredients. Various additives to the basic isocyanate/polyol mix can further alter the physical properties of the finished polymer. These additives modify the basic polyurethane, and it is the particular set of additives used in the formulation that makes one polyurethane bowling ball coverstock differ from another, whether from product line to product line or from manufacturer to manufacturer. In fact, the specific additive mixtures used are among the ball manufacturer's most closely guarded trade secrets, and we had a difficult time gathering the information necessary to gain even a basic understanding of coverstock chemistry.

The polyurethane used to make urethane bowling balls is not modified much from its basic form. It probably contains a plasticizing agent to make it a bit more resilient and impact resistant, but that's about it. Urethane balls therefore have a rather smooth and dense surface, but not nearly as smooth and dense as polyester. Urethane is also much softer than polyester, so exhibits far greater lane friction and hook.

Urethane bowling balls were first patented in 1966, but it wasn't until the advent of urethane skateboard wheels in the 1970s that ball manufacturers really started to take a hard look at the possibilities. The first commercial urethane bowling ball was introduced in 1981, and urethane quickly supplanted polyester. In very short order polyester balls were relegated to spare ball status. While urethane balls significantly out-hook polyester, they do not exhibit the strong and angular-appearing hook that we identify with today's game. Urethane balls tend to take a longer, more gentle and continuous path than reactive resin balls. Though they represent "old technology," urethane balls still find use today. We often see them employed by PBA and collegiate bowlers on very short or low-volume oil patterns. They also see frequent use on many different patterns by the hyper-rev bowlers who don't use their thumbs, in order to cut down and even out their ball reaction.

REACTIVE RESIN

Like the word *urethane*, "reactive resin" is a misnomer. Reactive resin balls, like urethane balls, are made of polyurethane. The "resin" half of the term "reactive resin" is largely meaningless. "Resin" is simply a chemical definition of one of the two building block groups in polyurethane, and the polyester in spare balls is also made from a resin. The "reactive" half is just a marketing term, and doesn't seem to have any chemical meaning at all. Since such balls respond particularly well to friction, they are said to "react" with the dry part of the lane, hence "reactive resin."

While urethane balls tend to exhibit a more or less gently curving path, reactive resin balls can display a variety of reactions, from a very early start to the hook and a gradual arc-shaped path, to a straight path far down the lane and a seemingly violent turn back toward the pins. If both urethane balls and reactive resin balls are made from polyurethane, what makes them behave so differently? The answer is in the chemistry.

Polyurethane has a structure made of a great number of long strands, or "polymer chains." These strands bind chemically to one another, forming a big, tangled mass. In fact, the cover of your bowling ball is really one single very large molecule. Picture a plate of cooked spaghetti noodles. Wherever they touch their neighbor, they stick together. They also intertwine and wrap around each other, and stick to greater and lesser degrees depending on how much contact they make. All of this sticking and intertwining means that if you try to pull out one noodle, you tend to move all of the noodles on the plate. Polyurethane has a similar structure, and all of this interlocking and bonding is what makes it so tough and dense.

In order to obtain more lane friction than urethane provided, chemists needed to open up this dense structure. By adding another chemical called a *blowing agent* to the mix, they were able to introduce a matrix of microscopic bubbles into the polyurethane. Under an electron microscope the surface of a urethane ball looks sort of like a rippled sand dune, while the porous surface of the reactive resin ball looks more like a sponge, all covered in tiny pits and craters. Technically speaking, the coverstock of a reactive resin ball is a microcellular foam—a foam with extremely tiny bubbles—though of a particularly stiff and dense variety. These microscopic bubbles give the reactive resin ball a much higher coefficient of friction than that of the unmodified urethane balls. As a side effect, the sponge-like nature of reactive resin causes it to absorb lane oil, which according to bowling ball marketing has the potential to further increase lane friction by reducing the amount of oil between the ball and the lane.

Though the idea of increased hook through oil absorption is a widely held belief, we have our doubts for two reasons. First, the fact that there is still oil on your ball when it comes back to the ball return implies that the oil absorption is occurring far too slowly to make any material difference during an actual shot. As a test, we placed a single drop of oil on a relatively new, very dull and porous high-end ball, and started a stopwatch. After ten minutes, the drop of oil was still sitting on the surface of the ball. It had spread out a bit, but was otherwise unchanged. Even after wiping the oil drop away with a clean cloth, it took almost ten seconds for even the remaining thin residue of oil to be absorbed by the ball. Considering that a ball takes less than three seconds to traverse the entire lane, this very slow oil absorption seems not to be a factor. Second, once a portion of your ball contacts the lane and picks up oil, that portion never again contacts the lane surface during that shot, as evidenced by the flared pattern of oil rings on your ball (more on this in Chapter 9). Thus even if your ball could instantaneously absorb the oil, it simply wouldn't be a factor.

We believe that it is the physical porosity of reactive resin that increases the friction with the lane, and that the oil absorption is merely a byproduct of this porosity. While oil absorption could arguably serve to increase friction for subsequent shots, especially if the bowler fails to wipe off the ball between shots, we see no mechanism by which it could increase friction while the ball is actually traveling down the lane. Indeed, we see oil absorption as a detriment, with the ball absorbing enough oil over time to dramatically decrease hook. We believe that oil absorption is what causes a ball to eventually "die," and that attempts to extract the oil will also extract the plasticizers—which are not chemically bound to the polyurethane—also leading to ball death.

At the time of this writing, the USBC announced a new rule regulating the rate of oil absorption. The new rule takes effect August, 2020, and specifies that the oil absorption rate must be slower than two minutes, fifteen seconds. While it is always dangerous to predict the future, we will go out on a limb and say that this new specification will not affect the game in any material way. If any balls are actually affected by the new rule, it will likely be only the very high-end, dull, solid "hook monsters." Since these balls are not terribly well suited to league and house shot play, bowlers who don't play on heavy oil sport shots should not be affected.

FRICTION

While the porosity of reactive resin seems to add greatly to friction, the friction-enhancing modifications to the polyurethane don't stop there. Reactive resin balls also have a friction advantage over their simpler urethane cousins through another trick the chemists perform.

We all understand what friction is on an intuitive basis, and we easily recognize its effects, from stopping our car, to starting a fire by rubbing two sticks together, to getting a rug burn if we trip while running. Friction can be thought of as two objects gripping one another, and it works by slowing down the relative motion of one object over the other and converting that lost motion to heat. While we understand what friction is and what it does, and can even make accurate calculations predicting its effect on a moving body, the truth is that science really doesn't have a terrific understanding of how friction actually works.

We tend to think of friction as a mechanical sort or gripping, like the knobby treads of an off-road motorcycle tire digging into the soft dirt, or the very fine treads on the bottom of a basketball shoe grabbing the smooth gym floor. This is indeed one aspect of friction, but it mostly affects things on a macro (large scale) level. We will refer to this sort of real world friction as *physical friction*. At the microscopic level, friction seems to work through chemical rather than physical forces, with molecules in one surface actually grabbing onto molecules in the other through various types of atomic bonding. Think of how an insect or a tree frog can walk straight up your glass window though neither their feet nor the glass has any appreciable texture or tread with which to grab. We refer to this type of friction as *chemical friction*.

Chemical friction seems to play a big part in determining ball motion, and ball manufacturers devote a significant amount of time and research dollars to devising ways to enhance it and to set their coverstocks apart from those of their competitors. It is not terribly hard to figure out how to formulate a basic polyurethane suitable for a bowling ball coverstock, or even how to get it to foam enough to create the needed microscopic porosity. That's not the part you are really paying for when you buy a bowling ball. The real magic comes into play when the chemist develops a cocktail of additives which increase chemical friction, making the coverstock more "sticky" while still maintaining the required hardness and durability.

This advanced coverstock chemistry is what is really increasing the on-lane performance of your ball, and the research, formulation, and testing doesn't come cheaply. Have you ever wondered why a high-end bowling ball costs so much more than an entry level version, when both are just 15 pounds of plastic? It is because the lower end ball has far less work and expense put into its coverstock formulation, or is using older, tried-and-true research that has long since been paid for through ball sales. Ball manufacturers even tout this recycling of research as a benefit to the consumer, with sales pitches such as, "We brought back our proven Super-Turbo 3 coverstock and coupled it with our tried-and-true Master Blaster weight block." If you want the benefits of the tremendous amount of time and money that goes into research and development of the most advanced coverstock formulations, you've got to be willing to pay for it. As with most everything else in life, you get what you pay for.

PHYSICAL FRICTION VS. CHEMICAL FRICTION

Coverstock friction is influenced by both physical and chemical means. Think of chemical friction as the basic level of stickiness that the manufacturer built into the ball. Think of physical friction as what your pro shop contributes via sandpaper, rubbing compound, and polish. While both means of achieving friction definitely affect ball motion, ball selection becomes much easier if we consider chemical friction to be intrinsic to the ball itself, and physical friction to be only a modification to that intrinsic chemical friction. Perhaps an example will help to clarify.

Imagine two sets of car tires. Both sets have identical tread patterns carved into them, but one set is made out of rubber while the other is made of a hard plastic. If we put these tires on two identical cars on identical roads and have the drivers stomp the gas pedal, what will happen? Obviously, the car with the rubber tires will accelerate at a far greater rate than will the car with the plastic tires. The rubber tires will grip the road fairly well while the hard plastic tires will spin and smoke, and this is despite their having identical tread patterns. We can equate the tread pattern carved into the tires to our bowling ball's surface finish. The composition of our test tires can be likened to the ball's coverstock chemistry, which can be chemically sticky, smooth and dense, or somewhere in between. Just as the rubber tire exhibited far more friction than did the plastic tire despite having the same tread pattern, a chemically sticky reactive resin ball will exhibit more friction than will a urethane or a plastic ball, even if they all have an identical surface finish.

So how can you determine how chemically sticky and porous a reactive resin ball is? Sadly, you can't. We reviewed the published specifications for every major ball manufacturer, and none of them report coefficient of friction or any measure of the level of porosity. Though these chemical properties of the ball's coverstock were by far the most important determinants of ball path in the USBC ball motion study, consumers are left completely in the dark.

With no way to compare the actual frictional characteristics of one ball versus another, we need a method to at least sort them out in some rough and general way. Fortunately, if we trust our manufacturers to price their equipment fairly, reflecting the cost of the chemical research and compounding that went into the ball's production, we can use relative price as a surrogate for chemical friction. Since there is very little difference from one weight block to another, at least in terms of research and manufacture, we can assume that the price difference between balls comes down to either coverstock chemistry or marketing. There are definitely a few balls on the market that are priced at a much higher level than their technology would seem to dictate, but these seem to be the exception, not the rule. Since we have no way of knowing how much of the difference in price is due to marketing rather than technology, this method is very far from perfect. Unfortunately though, it's the best we've got.

The various manufacturers market their balls within broad categories with names such as *Premier, High-Performance, Pro Performance*, or other such terms at the top, *Entry Level, Lower Mid Performance*, or *Hot* at the lower end, and *Performance, Master*, or *Upper Mid Performance* in the middle tier. We need to be very careful not to accept these category names literally, and especially not to think that "performance" relates directly to amount of hook. As we will learn later, all balls are high performance on certain conditions and all are low performance on others, and it is entirely possible, sometimes even probable, that a bowler will obtain more overall ball motion from a lower grade ball than from a higher one.

In a pub, the high quality, premium liquor is up on the "top-shelf," the low grade booze is in the "well," down by the bartender's knees. The middle-grade product sits on the "mid-tier" or "call brand" shelves, and all three tiers are priced accordingly. We can sort out the various grades of bowling balls the same way, and indeed many pro shops even display their inventory in precisely this manner, with high-end balls on the upper shelves and more moderately priced balls on the lower shelves. At the time of this writing, top-shelf bowling balls have a manufacturer's suggested retail price (MSRP) in the $220 to $280 range, mid-tier runs from about $150 to $200, and the bottom shelf balls list for around $120 to $150. Most pro shops discount bowling balls by various amounts and some build the cost of drilling into their selling prices, so the actual price in your local shop will likely differ from list price, but you can still use relative price as a surrogate for coverstock chemistry. Balls in your shop's highest price range will likely be more chemically sticky than those in the middle tier, and middle tier balls will likely be stickier than those on the "bottom shelf." Again, definitely not perfect, but it's unfortunately the best we've got.

SURFACE FINISH

The chemical friction of the ball is controlled by the chemist and there is no legal way for a bowler to modify it, but physical friction is another matter. Physical friction can be thought of as the surface texture of the ball, which is comprised of the porosity of the polyurethane mixture used and the pattern of scratches we put on top of that porosity. The pattern of scratches, or lack thereof, is called surface finish, and is applied via sandpaper, rubbing compound, and polishing compound. While the greater part of friction is set by the ball's chemistry and is beyond our control, as is the porosity, we are still able to alter surface finish in an attempt to modify the friction level.

The coverstock porosity and the pattern of scratches act in a similar manner to the treads on a tire. When a knobby tire is used on an extremely soft surface, like a dune buggy riding on soft sand, the tread works by increasing the amount of contact surface between the tire and the sand. Since a bowling ball and lane are very similar in hardness, this effect of surface texture is not likely to be a major factor in increasing friction. While we could find no relevant research, we instead believe that the porosity and scratch pattern act in a manner similar to the treads on a road tire, increasing the amount of coverstock in contact with the lane surface by channeling away some of the lane oil just as the tread on a car tire channels away water and road grime.

Any surface finish can be applied to any ball. Balls come from the manufacturers with one of three finishes, sanded dull, polished to a high gloss, or a satin rubbing compound finish somewhere in between. It is helpful to equate these three general surface finishes to automotive tires. Think of dull, sanded surfaces as off-road mud tires, satin rubbing compound finishes as street tires, and polished balls as being like smooth racing tires.

There are many ways to measure surface roughness, with each focusing on a different aspect of surface texture. The most commonly employed is a measure called Ra (pronounced "R sub a"). Ra measures the average height or depth of the pits or bumps—called asperities—on the object's surface. A higher Ra number indicates greater surface roughness. Ra does not factor in the shape of the bumps or pits, and does not even differentiate between a bump and a pit. As such, a smooth ball covered in evenly spaced one millimeter deep pits would register precisely the same Ra as another ball covered in one millimeter tall similarly spaced spikes, even though the two balls would obviously display very different frictional characteristics. This rather serious shortcoming means that roughness measurements using the Ra method are not terribly predictive of friction, and there are even scientific studies demonstrating that Ra has no statistical correlation with coefficient of friction.

If Ra is not a good predictor of coefficient of friction, why do we use it when measuring the roughness of common objects such as bowling balls? The unsatisfying answer is that it is the easiest and cheapest way of measuring surface roughness. We trade accuracy and predictive value for ease and economy. The assumption underlying the use of Ra is that a ball that is rougher in Ra will also be rougher in other aspects of surface texture, and though Ra is not correlated with coefficient of friction, some of these other aspects of roughness will be. And indeed this assumption seems to hold in many cases, and is at least close enough for the not terribly precise world of bowling balls. We don't need to delve any deeper into the fascinating science of surface roughness measurement. For our purposes we just need to know that a higher-end coverstock will in general have a higher Ra value than will a lower-end ball, that a dull ball will have a higher Ra than will a satin ball, and that a satin ball will have a higher Ra than will a shiny ball, other things being equal.

EFFECTS OF SURFACE FINISH ON FRICTION

Most studies of friction are conducted on uniform surfaces. A bowling lane, however, possesses variable frictional characteristics. As we have discussed in previous chapters, the front part of the lane is covered in a relatively thick film of oil, the back part of the lane is completely dry, and the middle portion of the lane has a light coating as the residual oil on the lane machine's brush is buffed out thinner and thinner. Unfortunately for the bowler, each of these conditions has its own unique relationship between surface roughness and coefficient of friction. Simply put, things that increase friction on one part of the lane may well cause decreased friction on another. Let's look first at the oiled portions of the lane.

Friction under lubricated conditions is very different from ordinary friction, so different in fact that there is a unique field of study dedicated to it called *tribology*. Tribology differentiates between two lubricated states. Under *hydrodynamic lubrication*, a layer of oil exists thick enough to separate the two sliding objects, which in our case are the ball and the lane. Under *boundary lubrication*, the oil has thinned sufficiently to allow the two oily surfaces to start to touch. Bowlers refer to these two states as heavy oil and light oil. We tend to experience heavy oil in the front part of the lane, light oil mid-lane, and dry conditions on the back portion of the lane. As the oil begins to taper from heavy in the front part of the lane to light oil mid-lane, tribology describes the resulting condition as *mixed lubrication*.

In the heavily oiled, hydrodynamically lubricated portion of the lane, surface roughness surprisingly has little if any effect on coefficient of friction.[35] Recall that surface roughness essentially measures how "spiky" the ball is, but since there is a layer of oil on the lane thicker than the spikes are tall, there is nothing for them to grab onto. In heavy oil, any friction generated will for the most part be between the ball and the oil (and also between the oil and the lane). While little friction and little hook will occur in the heavy oil, any traction the ball does manage to get will likely be the result of a chemically sticky, higher-end coverstock formulation rather than of surface texture.

As the ball leaves the heavy oil and enters the mixed-lubricated middle portion of the lane the spikes and ridges on the ball—the asperities—begin to reach through the oil and physically contact the lane surface. It is here that surface roughness has its greatest impact on friction. Think of this like the deep tread on a mud tire reaching down through the slippery muck to try to grab onto something more solid below. In this second section of the lane, higher surface roughness equates directly to greater friction and greater ball movement.[36]

In the mid-lane, the buffed out boundary-lubricated area toward the end of the oil pattern, the relationship between surface roughness and friction becomes muddied and not well understood. While theory holds that increased surface roughness *should* lead to increased friction under boundary lubrication on the buffed area, experimental results show that at least sometimes, it does not.[37] As in the heavy oil, on the buffed part of the lane it seems to be the chemical stickiness of the coverstock that controls the coefficient of friction.

On the dry back end portion of the lane, after the end of the oil pattern and covering the remaining distance to the pins, tribology no longer applies and ordinary dry friction controls the ball path. Under dry friction, the effects of surface roughness are completely reversed. While surface texture helped to increase friction on the lubricated portions of the lane by channeling away the oil and allowing at least some physical contact to occur, surface texture instead leads to a *decrease* in friction on dry surfaces.[38] On dry surfaces, friction is determined by how much physical contact there is between the two objects, in our case between the ball and the lane. Let's go back to our tire example to help clarify.

We know that in muck a deeply treaded mud tire will give us a friction advantage, where a smoother road tire would just spin. If we run those mud tires on a dry road, however, the opposite will happen and we will get low friction. We would not be able to accelerate rapidly without spinning the tires, and we would not be able to corner sharply without sliding and losing control. This is because on a dry road only the ends of the blocks of rubber forming the tread pattern actually contact the pavement. While the big gaps between these rubber blocks aided friction in the mud, they provide absolutely no friction against the dry road. Contrast this with race cars that run on dry pavement. Such cars use smooth tires with no tread at all. The smooth tire contacts the road everywhere it touches rather than just at the ends of some rubber blocks. This relative lack of surface texture leads to the maximum possible contact area between the tire and the road, which translates into maximum friction. This same effect occurs when our bowling ball is on the dry part of the lane. A ball with a lot of surface texture will only make contact with the lane at the points of its asperities, while a smooth shiny ball will contact the lane over a much greater portion of its surface.

PEARL VS. SOLID

Thus far we have looked at the effects on friction of chemically sticky and porous "top-shelf" balls versus less sticky mid-tier and bottom shelf balls, and of dull, medium, and shiny surface finishes. The last variable in bowling ball coverstock formulation is the difference between so-called solid, hybrid, and pearl variants.

Solid coverstocks are made from the polyurethane resin just as the chemist formulated it. Solid coverstocks display the highest degree of porosity, the largest pore structure, and the highest degree of chemical stickiness which that particular formulation is capable of achieving.

A *pearl* coverstock is made from the same chemicals as is the solid polyurethane, but with powdered mica added to the resin as a filler material. Mica is an extremely soft, flaky mineral. When ground to a powder, mica is the silvery sparkle you see in things like eye makeup and automotive paint. While mica does add sparkle to pearl bowling balls, that is not its primary function. When mica powder is added to the polyurethane resin it acts as a filler, partially clogging and rounding over the coverstock's pores. This serves to decrease the coverstock's surface roughness, which decreases the ball's coefficient of friction. Additionally, since mica is soft and slippery, everywhere it is exposed on the ball's surface it also decreases the chemical friction between the coverstock and the lane. Think of a pearl coverstock as a solid that has had slippery powder stirred into the mix.

Hybrid coverstocks are meant to fall right between the frictional characteristics of solids and pearls. Hybrids aren't even really a unique formulation per se, but are instead just a mixture of the solid and pearl versions of the resin. Just as you could mix a cup of black paint with a cup of white paint to get grey, mixing solid with pearl gives you a "hybrid" of the two. When manufacturing hybrid balls, the solid and pearl are usually not even mixed together. Ordinarily one of the colors making up your hybrid ball's cover will be a pearl and the other color a solid, with the resulting swirled-together mass being deemed "hybrid." Look closely at the surface of a hybrid ball, and you will see that one of the colors has a silvery sheen while the other color does not. In a three-color ball you may have two colors of pearl and one solid, or two parts solid and one part pearl, giving the manufacturer further leeway in altering coverstock friction.

MAKING SENSE OF COVERSTOCK FRICTION

We have discussed three different aspects of ball manufacture which have an effect on the the ball's coefficient of friction. Coverstock surface finish affects the physical or "macro" friction between the ball and the lane. Coverstock chemistry influences both chemical friction and the portion of physical friction created by porosity. Coverstock modification via the addition of mica affects both chemical and physical friction. So which ball has a higher coefficient of friction; a top-shelf ball, a mid-tier, or a bottom shelf ball? A pearl, a solid, or a hybrid? A dull ball, a shiny ball, or a buffed ball? Unfortunately none of these distinctions is predictive on it's own. It is entirely possible to have a mid-tier ball with a higher coefficient of friction than a top-shelf ball, or a pearl with a higher coefficient of friction than a solid, or even a shiny ball with a higher coefficient of friction than a dull ball.

Ball selection would be simple if we could state categorically that top-shelf balls have a higher coefficient of friction than lower shelf balls, or that dull balls have higher friction than shiny balls, or that solids have higher friction than pearls. With other things being equal such statements would be valid, but with so many variables, things are never equal. Since we have three different factors affecting friction, each of which has three possible values, there are 27 possible combinations of coverstock chemistry, surface finish, and solid/hybrid/pearl additive, with each combination having its own unique frictional characteristics. Since bowling ball coefficient of friction numbers are never published, and possibly not even measured, we are left to try to figure out on our own where within this three-dimensional grid a particular ball falls.

It is this chaotic mess that makes questions such as "What's the strongest bowling ball made?", or "What's the best ball for a beginning or intermediate bowler?", relatively meaningless. The strongest ball, the most hooking ball, or the best ball depend on what we want the ball to do, the individual bowler's unique physical game characteristics, and the conditions on which the bowler will be competing. One person's "strongest ball I've ever owned" is another bowler's "worst ball ever made." With so many choices and so many variables, finding a well-qualified and highly knowledgeable pro shop operator is of the utmost importance. Anyone can drill holes in a ball or make a recommendation based on the manufacturer's marketing materials or a pro bowler's paid endorsement, but it takes study and dedication to go beyond such a simplistic approach and to make a truly informed recommendation.

Some bowlers like to do their own research and make their own equipment decisions, or do their own research but then bounce their ideas off of their pro shop operator. Others don't even want to be bothered with the "whats" and "whys," and would rather just tell the pro shop operator what they want the ball to do and then accept his or her advice. However you personally approach your purchase decisions, the following is intended as a very general set of coverstock guidelines to help you sort things out or to understand your driller's reasoning.

A higher end, chemically sticky coverstock will exhibit higher friction in the heavy oil, in the buffed area, and on the dry portion of the lane than will a lower end coverstock, other things being equal. Thus, a higher end ball will generally "read the lane" and start to hook sooner and in heavier oil than will a lower tier ball. A higher end ball will also generally hook more sharply on the drier portion of the lane, at least early in the set while there is still sufficient oil on the front part of lane. However, as the lanes dry out or if you bowl on lighter oil conditions, a lower tier ball can and often will hook more than will a top-shelf ball (more on this in later chapters, when we discuss "roll out"). As with so much within this sport, coverstock chemistry is not as simple as we might wish, and we cannot state categorically that a higher tier ball will out-hook a lower tier ball on all conditions.

A dull ball will exhibit higher friction in the "mid-lane"—the buffed area of the lane—but lower friction on the dry portion. A shiny ball will behave in the opposite manner, exhibiting lower friction in the buffed area, but higher friction on the dry portion of the lane. Surface finish seems not to have any material effect on friction on the heavily oiled beginning portion of the lane due to tribological considerations. Thus, a dull ball will tend to read the lane and start to hook sooner than will a shiny ball, but will also react more gently and gradually on the dry portion of the lane. The result of this early hook in the oil and lesser hook on the dry will be a more arc-shaped or so-called "controllable" or "continuous" ball path. A shiny ball will skid farther down the lane before starting to hook than will a dull ball, but will then grab onto the drier portion of the lane more aggressively and will hook more sharply. This longer skid and sharper hook tend to give shiny balls what appears to be a more "skid-flip" or "hockey stick" type of path. Be careful here, though. While *any given ball* with a dull finish will read earlier and have a more arc-shaped path than will *the same ball* with a shiny finish, we cannot necessarily make such a blanket statement when comparing one ball to another. It is entirely possible that a high-end ball with a shiny finish could read the lane and hook earlier than a lower tier ball with a dull finish due to the high-end ball's superior chemical friction. We believe that chemical composition will trump surface finish, and that bowlers should select the ball based on chemical friction and then use surface finish only as an adjustment to the basic level of friction provided by the coverstock. We were unable to locate any actual research in this regard, however, so consider this last statement to be our informed opinion.

In general, a solid coverstock will exhibit higher chemical and physical friction than will a hybrid, and a hybrid will exhibit higher friction than will a pearl. Here too, though, we must exercise caution. The above statement applies only to chemically identical coverstock formulations, where the only difference is whether or not mica was added. For example, if a ball company manufactures a solid, hybrid, and pearl version of *the same ball with the same coverstock formulation*, then the solid will hook earlier than the hybrid, and the hybrid earlier than the pearl. We cannot, however, extend this logic across different balls and state that solids are earlier and more arc-shaped than pearls. Just as with surface finish, it is entirely possible for a higher end pearl to hook earlier than a lower end solid. Indeed, the USBC Ball Motion Study concluded that solid/hybrid/pearl classification did not correlate in any way with hook. It is simply not predictive. As with surface finish, it is probably best to look at solid/hybrid/pearl options as a mere adjustment after selecting the ball based on other more important factors.

RG

While coverstock composition is by far the dominant ball-specific variable influencing hook, most of the balance of ball motion is attributable to the ball's radius of gyration (RG) characteristics. We have explored RG at length in previous chapters, so we won't rehash it all here. Recall from our earlier discussion that a higher RG ball is harder to rev up initially, but will hold on to those revs more tenaciously than will a lower RG ball. Because of this tendency, a higher RG ball will travel farther down the lane before hooking than will a lower RG ball, other things being equal. The lower RG ball will give up its initial rotational characteristics relatively easily, so tends to read the lane earlier and to complete its hook rather quickly, resulting in a more arc-shaped ball path. A higher RG ball, since it holds on to its rotational characteristics longer, will reach a drier portion of the lane before hooking, so will tend to hook more sharply. A higher RG ball is said to "retain energy," but what it is really retaining is its initial ball speed, rev rate, and axis rotation. The higher RG ball simply holds on to its initial launch characteristics longer before hooking, while the lower RG ball is much more willing to give up its initial launch characteristics and begin hooking earlier.

Bowling balls have two or three different RG numbers associated with them, but the one that matters here is the RG of the ball as it rotates about its pin, also called the *low RG axis*. This is the RG number most often quoted in bowling ball marketing literature. The USBC currently allows low RG axis values from 2.46 inches to 2.80 inches, though most balls made today fall well below the 2.80 inch maximum. We needn't be too specific about RG value when selecting a ball. It is enough to roughly divide them between low RG, medium RG, and high RG. While there are no industry standard categories, we generally consider balls in the 2.46 to 2.50 range to be low RG, those in the 2.51 to 2.55 range to be medium RG, and those at 2.56 inches and above to be high RG balls.

These ranges are useful in selecting a ball, but as soon as your driller punches the finger and thumb holes the RG will change, sometimes dramatically. If you look into the holes in your ball you will see white or sometimes blue material for most of the depth, but darker material in the bottom of the holes. The white is the lightweight polyester material that fills the gap between the heavy weight block and the coverstock. The darker color at the bottom of the holes is the weight block, and we can clearly see that the gripping holes removed some of this very dense and heavy material. It is the shape, size, and weight of the weight block which sets the ball's various RG values, but since we have now drilled out parts of it we have changed the shape, the weight, and the resulting RG characteristics.

Your ball driller uses to advantage the fact that the holes alter the shape of the weight block. By manipulating the placement and depth of the holes, he or she can control how the reshaping occurs. Through placement of the holes, your driller can either increase or decrease the RG of the ball from what it was before drilling. You may have noticed that some bowling balls are drilled with the pin above a line drawn through the finger holes. This is referred to as a "pin up" layout. Others have a pin placement below the finger holes, referred to as "pin down." In rare cases you may even see a ball with the pin so far below the finger holes that it is in the center of the grip. This specialty layout has a long history, but has recently come to be known as a "Rico" drilling. Each of these layouts, and the multitude of variations in between, result in the gripping holes removing material from different places on the weight block, resulting in differing alterations to the ball's original RG.

So how does hole placement affect the RG of the drilled ball? Recall that RG describes how concentrated toward the center or spread out toward the cover the ball's weight is. If the weight is concentrated toward the center of the ball it will have a lower RG value. If the weight is more spread out, the ball will have a higher RG. Figure 8.1, below, depicts a pin up and a pin down ball. Notice in the first image that when the ball is drilled pin up, the finger holes remove a small amount of material from the top of the core, but the much larger thumb hole removes material from the side of the core. Since more weight is removed from the center of the weight block, the remaining mass of the ball ends up being more spread out than it was before drilling, resulting in a higher RG.

In the pin down drilling the holes all remove material more or less from one end of the weight block. This results in leaving the weight more concentrated toward the center of the ball, which decreases the RG. A Rico drilling, with the pin in the center of the grip, results in the holes removing weight as close to the end of the core as possible, which leaves the weight concentrated more toward the center of the ball and therefore creates the lowest possible RG for that particular ball.

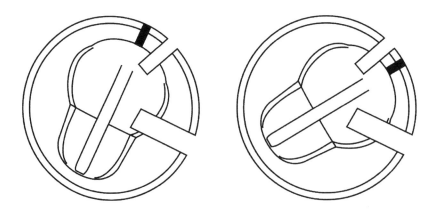

Figure 8.1: Weight removed from core, pin up and pin down ball.

You have likely also noticed that some bowling balls have a fourth hole drilled to the side of the gripping holes. This fourth hole is called a *balance hole* or a *weight hole*. It was originally intended as a way to make a ball legal if it had its weight offset too much to one side. Though balance holes are still primarily used for that purpose, ball drillers soon figured out that they could employ a balance hole as a way to further alter the ball's RG characteristics even if the hole was not required to correct an imbalance.

Look again at the drawings in Figure 8.1, and picture where the balance hole would intersect the weight block in each layout. We can see that for the pin up layout the balance hole would take additional weight out of the side of the core if it were drilled in the vicinity of the thumb hole. If it were instead drilled closer to the PAP, the weight would be removed more toward the top of the ball. This means that the balance hole on a pin up ball will tend to further increase the ball's RG if it is drilled near the thumb hole, but will tend to decrease the RG if drilled closer to the PAP. With a pin down layout, the balance hole will remove additional weight from near the end of the core pretty much wherever it is drilled, so will tend to decrease RG even further.

Since a pin up layout is intended to make the ball go longer down the lane and to hook harder due to the increased RG, a balance hole on a pin up ball drilled near the thumb hole will ordinarily serve to amplify this characteristic, while a hole closer to the PAP will decrease it. Since a pin down layout tends to make the ball read earlier and to hook more gently, a balance hole in a pin down ball will ordinarily enhance this characteristic no matter where it is placed. A weight hole can be viewed as a tweak to or an amplification of whatever you already did to the RG via layout.

All of this talk of weight holes will soon be rendered moot, however. At the time of this writing, the USBC has issued a new rule outlawing weight holes beginning in August of 2020. The rule change likely won't have much effect or be a game changer. While ball drillers will lose the fine control they had when they could locate the weight hole wherever they wished, they will still be able to make general RG changes by drilling the finger holes or especially the thumb hole deeper. Since weight holes really only serve as a minor tweak to the RG once a layout has been determined, the loss of fine control should not prove much of a detriment.

Just how much does the drilling layout change the RG of the ball? This is very difficult to determine. We do not possess equipment with which to measure a ball's RG, and published before-and-after measurements are scarce. We were only able to locate one paper from which we could infer this data, but even in this case there was not enough information provided to know with certainty where the pin was located.[39] After determining pin placement to the best of our ability from the limited information provided and comparing the reported as-drilled RG values to the balls' undrilled RGs, we saw RG increases in the pin up balls in the 0.01 to 0.02 range, and decreases in RG for the pin down balls ranging from about 0.01 for the more conventional layouts to a relatively huge 0.05 decrease for the Rico layout. While the decrease from the Rico drilling was significant, the changes from the more conventional layouts are small. When we discussed coverstocks we determined that chemistry was so much more important than was surface texture that we should consider surface texture to be only a "tweak" once we have selected a coverstock. Similarly, considering how small the effect of layout is on the as-designed RG of the ball, we should first select a ball that is naturally within our desired RG range, and then employ layout as a mere tweak to that natural RG.

Since the above numbers are based on very limited and incomplete data, they should definitely not be taken as gospel. In general, though, we can say that a pin up layout tends to increase the ball's RG while a pin down layout will decrease it, and that a balance hole will ordinarily amplify the increase or decrease. The chosen layout's effect on the shape of the ball path is a result of the layout altering the ball's RG characteristics.

SUMMING IT ALL UP

Let's sum up all of the ball-related factors affecting hook that we have covered thus far. The following should be considered only *very* general guidelines for allowing you to compare one ball to another:

Higher end balls hook earlier and more than do mid-tier, and mid-tier hook earlier and more than do bottom shelf balls.

A ball with a dull finish will hook earlier than will that same ball with a shiny finish, and will exhibit a more arc-shaped ball path. Shiny balls hook later and often more sharply than will the same ball with a dull finish.

Solid balls hook earlier than do hybrids, and hybrids hook earlier than do pearls, other things being equal. Solids tend toward more arc-shaped ball paths, and pearls toward sharper "skid/flip" ball paths.

Lower RG balls tend to hook earlier than do higher RG balls, and tend to have more of an arc shaped ball path. Higher RG balls tend to travel farther down lane before hooking than do lower RG balls, and tend to have more of a perceived "hockey stick" shaped ball path.

A ball with a pin down layout will have a lower RG than will the same ball with a pin up layout. A Rico layout will impart the lowest possible RG for that particular ball.

Though it is soon to be a moot point, a pin down ball with a conventionally placed balance hole will have a lower RG than the same ball without. A pin up ball with a conventionally placed balance hole will have a lower RG than the same ball without, but will have a higher RG if the hole is placed near the thumb hole.

ONE MORE FACTOR

There is one more ball-related factor that affects hook. It is a phenomenon called *track flare*. Track flare is the only other thing beside surface texture and RG that your pro shop operator attempts to influence when he or she lays out your ball. Track flare will be discussed in the next chapter.

CHAPTER 9

TRACK FLARE, OR MUCH ADO ABOUT NOTHING?

LOOK CLOSELY AT your bowling ball after a shot. Unless the lanes are very dry, you will see a bow tie-shaped pattern of oil rings on the surface of the ball, ordinarily just to the left of the gripping holes for right handers and to the right of the holes for lefties (Figure 9.1). The portion of the ball that contacts the lane is called the ball's track, and the spread out pattern of oil rings illustrates a concept called *track flare*. In actuality the oil rings aren't "rings" at all. They are actually successive overlapping loops in one long spiral. That, however, is a fine distinction that needn't concern us here. For our purposes we can continue to think of them as individual rings.

Figure 9.1: Track flare

In earlier chapters we briefly touched upon the concept of the Positive Axis Point, or PAP. Recall that the PAP is more properly referred to as the *initial spin axis*, and is defined as one end of the imaginary "axle" running through the ball that we spin the ball around as we release it. As the ball rotates on this imaginary axle, its contact point with the lane traces a path through the oil resulting in the first oil ring on the ball's surface. This first oil ring is easy to understand, but why don't all the subsequent rings just overlap into one big, greasy track?

A bicycle has its axle fixed in place, and the tire does indeed roll over the same strip of rubber over and over. If our bowling ball likewise spun around the PAP during its entire trip down the lane—that is, if the spin axis were fixed in place like the axle of the bicycle—it too would trace a single contact strip and display only a single oil ring. The fact that there are instead numerous oil rings traced onto the ball tells us conclusively that the ball in fact spins around a different axis with each revolution. Rather than remaining fixed in place, the ball's spin axis—the imaginary axle—moves or *migrates* away from the PAP as the ball travels down the lane. This *axis migration* causes a different portion of the ball's surface to contact the lane with each revolution. The movement or migration of the spin axis creates a phenomenon called *track flare*, since it causes the pattern of oil track rings to flare out over the ball's surface. A high-flaring ball is one that experiences a large degree of axis migration as it travels down the lane, and a low-flaring ball experiences very little migration of the spin axis.

So what causes track flare? What causes the ball's spin axis to migrate with each revolution rather than just staying in one place? A number of bowling blogs and discussion forums, and even websites aimed at teaching the physics of bowling, attribute track flare to a physical phenomenon called torque-induced *precession*.

When we twirl a toy spinning top it stands upright as it spins about its axis, which is an imaginary line extending through the stem and the pointed end of the top. As the top slows down due to friction with the table, it begins to wobble, rotating around in the same direction as the top is spinning. This wobbling is called precession. It is caused by friction-induced torque acting through the point of the spinning top, and is characterized by the entire top rotating while it spins (Figure 9.2).

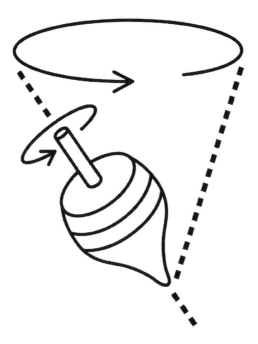

Figure 9.2: Precession (spin plus rotation)

If we roll a bowling ball down the lane with the PAP marked, the PAP will initially remain quite stable, but will soon begin to move in a circular fashion and become a blurred ring rather than a single point. Bowlers who hold to the precession idea liken this to the spinning top's stem initially being upright and stable, but then moving in a circle as the top begins to wobble. At least one physics website even states that precession causes the ball to rock back and forth as it travels down the lane, attributing the flared pattern of oil rings to this rocking motion.

The precession explanation of track flare sounds logical enough, but we have seen before that many logical-sounding ideas fail when we examine the evidence with a critical eye. In the case of axis migration, the evidence instead suggests that a bowling ball does not precess at all, and that the precession idea is simply a case of misdiagnosis.

The easiest way to disprove the precession idea is to simply observe a bowling ball as it travels down the lane. With some balls, especially those with swirls of contrasting color, we can often actually see the spin axis without it being marked. If bowling balls precessed, we would see this axis move away from us, downward, toward us, then upward. If the lane were long enough we would then see the spin axis move in this circular fashion over and over as the ball rolled down the lane. But this never happens. The spin axis remains stable, and merely moves smoothly to the side of the ball. While the lack of any visible wobble or circular motion should serve as enough of a rebuttal, it is the pattern of oil rings that truly puts the nail in the coffin and disproves the idea of precession.

If the bowling ball were to precess, the spin axis would not move or "migrate" along the surface of the ball at all. All spin would take place around the PAP over the ball's entire journey down the lane. The ball itself would instead wobble around to move the fixed PAP in a circle, just as the spinning top's spin axis always remains in place through the stem and the tip even as the entire top wobbles. Since precession does not alter the spin axis, and merely reorients the location of the constant spin axis in space, all of the oil rings would be concentric. They would simply form a spiral of smaller and smaller circles that never crossed one another, all sharing the same center point. Figure 9.3 is a photograph of a ball marked with simulated oil rings as they would appear under precession. The first oil ring is the one farthest from the gripping holes. Subsequent oil rings would flare toward and then over the holes.

Figure 9.3: Oil rings caused by precession

If our bowling ball isn't precessing in the true sense of the word, could the spin axis itself be migrating around in a circle? Figure 9.4 is a photograph of a bowling ball with axis migration marked out in an arc. We then drew in the simulated oil rings based on evenly spaced migrating axis points along this arc just as they would be formed on the lane. As you can see, there is again no characteristic bow tie pattern to the oil rings. Rather than two distinct crossing points shared by every ring to make up the bow ties, there is instead a strange pattern with each subsequent ring crossing the previous ring at seemingly random points. Nor are the rings "parallel" as they are on an actual bowling ball.[40] They instead take widely divergent paths over the ball's surface. If we were to carry out this hypothetical migration enough times around and around the circular path, eventually a complex, Spirograph-like pattern would emerge with our axis migration path at its center. This pattern, however, would not be anything like the simple and orderly bow tie pattern we find in real life.

Figure 9.4: Oil rings caused by pseudo-precession

So if the ball isn't precessing, and if the spin axis isn't migrating around in a circle, what is the ball doing that could account for the bow tie pattern of oil rings? Figure 9.5 is another photo of our bowling ball, but this time the simulated oil rings are laid out based on a straight axis migration path. We simply moved the PAP inward toward the center of the grip in the same even steps as in the previous example. This migration path yields a pattern of oil rings with constant spacing, "parallel" about the ball, and with constant and distinct crossing points displaying the characteristic bow tie pattern.

Figure 9.5: Oil rings caused by linear axis migration

Let's compare these three examples to the pattern formed by an actual bowling shot. The image on the left in Figure 9.6 is a photograph of our ball after a trip down lane. We traced over each resulting oil ring with a grease pencil. Just as we used an armadillo to determine the location of our PAP—our initial spin axis—from the first oil ring, we can locate each subsequent spin axis by performing the same procedure on the rest of the oil rings. The image on the right in Figure 9.6 is a photo of the same ball with each axis position marked out. We can clearly see that the spin axis did not migrate along a circular path, nor did it remain static as it would have had the ball precessed in any manner. Instead the migration path follows a fairly straight line from the PAP inward toward the center of the grip, with a slight curvature in the direction of the ball's pin—a path that is completely consistent with our observed converging oil rings.

Figure 9.6: Actual oil rings traced out, axis migration plotted

If axis migration and its resulting track flare are not caused by precession, what is the cause? Recall from our discussion in earlier chapters that a bowling ball possesses a number of different radii of gyration, or RGs, depending upon the axis chosen for measurement. The ball's lowest RG axis runs along the pin, through the center of the core. The ball's high RG axis runs more or less perpendicular to the low RG axis, through the side of the core. In a ball with an asymmetrical core, this point will be marked on the surface of the ball. For unknown reasons, this marked point is called the *preferred spin axis*, or PSA, though bowlers often refer to it as the *mass bias*. Once a ball is drilled, the high RG axis will ordinarily end up somewhere in the vicinity of the thumb hole regardless of where it was before the ball was drilled. The third RG axis we are concerned with is the one we release the ball on—the RG of our PAP. The RG about our PAP will ordinarily fall somewhere in between the ball's high and low RG.

Our bowling ball—or indeed most any rolling object—wants to roll such that its weight is in a stable position. If our bowling ball's weight were evenly distributed throughout, like a billiard ball or a basketball, it would be equally happy rolling on any possible axis. Since the weight in such a uniform ball is balanced no matter which way the ball is oriented, it simply doesn't care how it is rolling. Such a uniform ball possesses the same RG no matter how you position it.

Modern bowling balls, however, contain a core, also known as a weight block, which creates a rather dramatic imbalance in the ball's mass distribution. Think about your own body. It is stable when you are standing upright or laying down, and it is quite easy and effortless to maintain either posture. Now try leaning off to one side. You can do so to a very minor degree, but any meaningful offset causes you to either fall over or to catch yourself and stand back upright. Likewise, our bowling ball is happy and stable when it is spinning about its high RG axis (weight block standing up) or its low RG axis (weight block laying down), but it is not happy when the weight block is leaning off to the side (Figure 9.7)

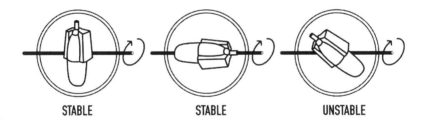

STABLE STABLE UNSTABLE

Figure 9.7: Ball spinning on stable and unstable RG axes

If we were to drill our bowling ball such that the low-RG pin were located right on our PAP, we would release the ball with the weight block laying down in a stable position. The ball would therefore already be "happy," so the spin axis would not migrate to any meaningful degree and our ball would not experience any meaningful track flare. Likewise if we were to drill the ball with the high-RG PSA on our PAP. Again, since the ball would already be stable with the core standing up, no meaningful track flare would result. For a variety of reasons, we do not typically lay out balls such that the weight block is in either of these stable positions nor even close to them. In pretty much every case, our bowling balls are drilled in such a way that the weight block is in an unstable position when the ball is released about our PAP. That is to say, the weight block is leaning off to one side when we release the ball, and the ball is not at all happy with this state of affairs.

While we have not conducted any controlled experiments nor worked through the rather daunting math, our research suggests that axis migration and its resulting track flare occurs as the ball attempts to seek a stable rolling posture. Since the weight is imbalanced when we initially spin the ball around our PAP, the ball attempts to make the weight block lay down. The ball's attempt to move the weight block from an unstable to a stable position causes it to shift its orientation as it rolls. This in turn causes the spin axis to be in a different position on the ball's surface with each revolution. The migration of the spin axis creates the track flare you see traced in the ball's oil rings.

If the ball's core is trying to lay down, why does its spin axis migrate more or less toward the center of the grip rather than toward the pin? Under certain theoretical circumstances, the spin axis would indeed migrate to one of the two stable positions, with the core either laying down on its low-RG axis, or standing up on its high-RG axis. There is a pro shop machine called a DeTerminator which spins a bowling ball with a constant applied torque. If you place a ball into the machine with your marked PAP centered in a sight window and turn on the motor, the rapidly spinning ball will shift its orientation until the PSA rather than the PAP is stable in that same sight window. If you don't want to spend many hundreds of dollars to purchase the device just to see this happen, there is even a down-and-dirty method of doing the same thing by balancing your ball atop the agitator in a top-loading washing machine![41]

In either case, under the constant torque provided by the DeTerminator or the washing machine, the spin axis does indeed migrate from the PAP to the PSA, with rotation going from an unstable position to a stable position on the ball's high-RG axis. This migration to the high-RG axis does not happen on the lanes though, because there is not a constant application of torque to keep the ball spinning. Even if there was constant torque, the average time a bowling ball takes to make the core "stand up" and reach the PSA on a DeTerminator seems to be on the order of five to 10 seconds even at the motor's extremely high RPM rate, but a bowling ball hits the pins only two or three seconds after release. There is simply not enough time for the core to "stand up" before the ball hits the pins even if it were under constant torque.

As to the spin axis migrating to the pin, we suspect that it would indeed do so as the ball slows down and loses energy to friction, if given enough time. Our understanding of the physics leads us to believe that the axis migration path would trace a spiral around the pin, tighter and tighter until eventually settling there. This is all moot, however, since the same time element precludes the spin axis ever migrating to the low-RG pin. The lane would have to be incredibly long, perhaps on the order of 300 or more feet, for the ball to have enough time for the core to "lay down" and for rotation to settle in around the low-RG pin.

Why does the spin axis instead merely trace a line from the PAP toward the center of the grip? Again, we have not worked through the incredibly complex math, but we suspect that as gravity attempts to make the core "fall over" onto its side, the spinning of the ball creates a torque against the lane surface which balances out this "falling" to one degree or another and pushes back up on the side of the ball. We believe that with these forces working in opposition to one another, the ball's spin axis instead migrates along an intermediate path between the pin and the PSA where the RG is essentially the same as whatever the RG of our PAP was. The ball then hits the pins long before anything else can happen in this regard.

DOES TRACK FLARE CREATE HOOK?

Now we know what track flare is and how it is created, but what does it actually do? Does track flare really create hook?

Since track flare is created by the ball's core trying to move from an unstable to a stable position, it follows that the amount of track flare would be a function of the initial degree of instability. Again, if the ball had a uniform construction it would have the same RG along every axis, and there would be no instability and hence no track flare. In real life there is a material difference between the ball's RG along the pin and the RG along its PSA, and this difference is called the *RG differential*, or just the *differential* for short. In general the larger the ball's differential, the greater its potential track flare. Note that there is a third measure called the *intermediate RG* on so-called asymmetric balls, but its influence is minimal and will be ignored for this discussion.[42]

The promotional materials from ball companies and retailers place a lot of emphasis on high-flaring cores and their ability to create hook. Indeed, the idea that high flare equates to high hook is quite prevalent. Bowlers search out high-flaring, high-differential bowling balls. Pro shops perform all sorts of manipulations of the pin position relative to the PAP, and lots of tweaking of the placement and size of balance holes in an effort to increase track flare and thereby increase hook. Bowlers marvel at the widely spaced oil rings on these high-flaring "hook monster" balls, as though the flare were a measure of the ball's power.

If the amount of track flare is a result of orienting the core of the ball in an unstable position, then we should be able to maximize flare by placing the core in the most unstable position possible relative to our PAP. We have already determined that placing the ball's pin right on the bowler's PAP puts the core in a stable low-RG position. Likewise, moving the pin 90 degrees away from the PAP again places the core at a stable high-RG position. Since a bowling ball has a circumference of 27 inches, this stable 90 degree high-RG position results in the pin being located one quarter of that circumference, or 6-3/4 inches from the PAP. Any position between these two will result in some instability. A position halfway between the two, with the pin located 3-3/8 inches from the PAP, will result in the core being tilted within the ball at a 45 degree angle relative to the PAP, which according to the theory results in the maximum instability and therefore the maximum track flare.

This flare-controlling pin-to-PAP distance is one of the three measurements your ball driller specifies when trying to tailor your ball's reaction. The other two measurements, the *core angle* (also called the *drilling angle*) and the *VAL* (*vertical axis line*) *angle* are employed to manipulate the ball's pin and PSA placement in order to alter the RG characteristics of the drilled ball, as we discussed in the previous chapter. The core angle and the VAL angle can have a secondary effect on track flare, as can any balance holes drilled into the ball, but they are not the primary tools for manipulating flare and we will not be discussing them here.

All of these tricks performed by the ball manufacturer in creating cores with large differentials and by ball drillers in enhancing these characteristics are indeed very effective in increasing track flare, and we have seen bowling balls where the oil rings are well over half an inch apart. In 2005 the USBC proposed a rule to outlaw balance holes in the belief that they increased flare too much, leading to too much hook, leading to too many "undeserved" honor scores, but the rule was not enacted at that time. At the time of this writing the USBC has just implemented a new rule banning weight holes, again aimed at limiting track flare. The new rule goes into effect in 2020. So does track flare really create or enhance hook? Much of the bowling world seems to think so, but unfortunately the physics say quite another thing.

THE EVIDENCE CONTRADICTS

It's not hard to figure out where the idea comes from that track flare creates or at least contributes to hook, and that higher track flare equates to greater hook. After all, in order to flare the ball has to be rotating to the side, and this rotation should help "pull" the ball to the side creating hook, right? This common interpretation is depicted in Figure 9.8.

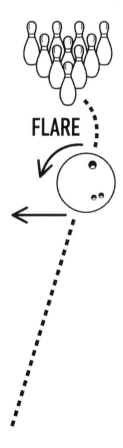

Figure 9.8: Common idea of how track flare creates hook

As with other tenets of common bowling folklore we have examined thus far, this interpretation seems quite logical on the surface but fails when we look closely at the details. Let's say for a moment that track flare really could help to pull the ball to the side. If so, the ball would of course have to be flaring in a counterclockwise direction as depicted above in order to be pulled to the left, and to quote Shakespeare, "there's the rub": A bowling ball flares in a clockwise direction for half of each revolution and in a counterclockwise direction for the other half as it travels down the lane. It is flaring in precisely the opposite direction required to somehow pull it to the left for half of each revolution.

Want proof? The photos in Figure 9.9 are of the same ball we marked out with simulated oil rings when we demonstrated axis migration. In the first image the ball is oriented with the first oil ring, the one closest to the finger and thumb holes, contacting the lane. For clarity, we have also placed a mark on the top of the ball at the twelve o'clock position. Watch what happens to this reference mark as the ball flares to consecutive oil rings. The second image shows the ball after it has flared to the third oil ring, and the third image after the ball has flared to the fifth oil ring. Which way did the ball rotate? As shown by our reference mark, the ball rotated to the right—in a clockwise fashion—as it flared, with our reference mark moving from the twelve o'clock position, to one o'clock, and then to two o'clock. As rolling continues over what would be the top half of the ball in the photos, flare moves in a counterclockwise direction. If track flare could somehow create hook, the ball is flaring in the wrong direction to do so for half of each revolution. It would instead make the ball wiggle back and forth rather than hook to the left, something the ball clearly does not do.

Figure 9.9: Rotation of the ball as it flares

In truth, flare is not "pulling" in either direction, and creates no side-to-side force at all. Indeed, it isn't even correct to say that the ball rotates in either direction or that it wobbles back and forth as it flares. Each revolution presents a nice, steady ring. The flaring ball merely changes the orientation of this steady ring.

So if track flare cannot pull the ball to the side, can it directly create or add to hook in some other manner? The simple answer is "no." The ball can only be deflected to the side, that is, can only hook, if some side-to-side force is applied, and track flare does not produce any side-to-side force. In fact, you can easily demonstrate for yourself that track flare does not create hook. Take your most hooking ball, and throw it straight by allowing your wrist to bend back just as you would if you had to use it to pick up a 10-pin. Now look at the oil rings, and you will see precisely the same flared pattern as when you throw the ball with a big hook. The ball flared just as much as it does when it hooks, yet it still managed to go straight. The track flare still exists, but it did not in any way cause the ball to hook.

Our determination that track flare cannot create hook is also supported by physics. Brunswick corporation released a video in 2005 in response to the USBC's proposed weight hole ban. In the video, Brunswick's Director of Research and Development specifically lists "Two common but *inaccurate* assumptions"; that "Track flare, by itself, causes the ball to hook," and that "More track flare always results in more hooking action and breakpoint angularity." He then goes on to demonstrate conclusively that track flare has no meaningful effect on the path of a bowling ball.

For the demonstration, Brunswick drilled three identical balls. One was laid out to develop minimal track flare, one to develop the maximum possible flare while still keeping the RG differential within legal limits, and a third ball with a massive amount of track flare, far beyond what the legal differential limits would allow. As a pro bowler threw the three balls, there was no difference at all in the path of the ball. Each ball hooked at the same point on the lane, and by the same amount. Changes in the amount of track flare did not alter hook in any way.[43]

Further corroboration is found in an article entitled "What makes bowling balls hook?", published in the *American Journal of Physics*.[44] The author of the paper, a professor of physics, concludes that a higher RG differential—the factor that creates track flare—does not always equate to more hook. If higher track flare does not always lead to greater hook, then track flare cannot possibly be causative and something else has to be at work. The author further states that where there *is* a correlation between higher RG differential and greater hook, the actual causative factor comes down to a secondary effect, and not directly to the RG differential or the track flare per se. We will discuss this secondary effect shortly.

The USBC's Ball Motion Study is also in agreement with our conclusion that RG differential—which causes track flare—has almost no effect on hook.[45] Of all of the factors they investigated in the study, they determined that RG differential, and hence track flare, accounted for only six percent of the ball's motion. Since we have already demonstrated that track flare has no direct effect on hook, this six percent influence likely derives from the same secondary effect cited in the American Journal of Physics paper. So what is this secondary effect? What does track flare actually contribute?

WHAT DOES TRACK FLARE ACTUALLY DO?

While track flare cannot create or even enhance hook, it does contribute to hook in a limited and indirect way. Let's go back to our bicycle example. As we ride our bicycle down the road, we encounter an overturned oil tanker which has spilled its load across the entire roadway. If we tried to ride through this oil slick, our tires would be nice and dry for their first revolution and would get a little bit of traction despite the oil. After this first revolution, though, our tire tread is now completely covered in oil that was picked up from the road. If we try to ride farther we will have an oily tire in contact with an oily road, with the resulting loss of even the little bit of traction we enjoyed during the first revolution. Suppose we somehow managed to stay upright through the entire oil slick, and have now cleared the oil and hit dry pavement. Even though the pavement is now dry our tires are still covered in oil. We still get little traction despite the dry road, and will not regain traction until all of the oil has worn off the tire.

The same thing would happen with our bowling ball if it did not flare. It would roll over and over the same track all through the oil, and would continue to roll over this same greasy ring even after the ball left the oil and encountered the dry part of the lane. Just like the bicycle tire, our ball would not get any meaningful traction until all of this accumulated oil wore off, and by then it would be far too late to obtain a useful amount of hook.

We think you can now see how track flare contributes to hook even though it cannot create it or directly influence it. Since the flaring ball presents a fresh band of clean coverstock to the lane with each revolution, it will be able to get at least some traction during its entire trip through the oil. More importantly, it continues flaring on the dry part of the lane even though we can no longer see evidence of it in the pattern of oil rings. The ball continues to present clean, fresh ball surface with every revolution, thereby maximizing friction.

That's really all that track flare does! Track flare's sole contribution is to present a fresh band of clean coverstock with each revolution, and this is precisely the secondary effect of high RG differential on hook referred to in the aforementioned paper and implied in the USBC study. The paper's author states that the track flare resulting from a higher RG differential adds to hook because it "leaves less oil on the ball surface at the point of contact with the lane and thus increases the friction when the ball reaches the unoiled part of the lane. This constantly 'clean' ball surface causes the ball to hook more."[46]

The clean band of coverstock creates higher friction with the lane surface than would an oil-soaked band of coverstock, and it is this increased friction that allows us to create hook. Note though, that friction alone does not *create* hook. It is instead merely a necessary condition for hook to be created. We can say, though, that other things being equal, higher friction equals more hook. That is, if we release two shots precisely the same way and on the same spot on a freshly oiled lane, and with two balls that are identical in every way except coverstock friction, the ball with the higher friction will hook more than will the lower friction shot. For the purposes of this discussion, though, let's be a little loose with our language and just say that more friction equals more hook.

If the fresh rings of coverstock presented to the lane by track flare allow for increased friction over that of a non-flaring ball, does it then follow that more track flare will equal more friction and therefore more hook? This does seem to be the prevailing thought, and it is easy to see why one might think this, but let's look at the science.

It is clear that as long as the oil rings are separated by *any* amount—as long as the ball isn't rolling over and over the same strip of coverstock—then clean surface is being presented to the lane with each revolution regardless of how far apart the rings are. Let's look a little deeper though. We have already demonstrated that the oil rings on our ball caused by track flare create a bow tie pattern in which the lines cross one another at two points on the ball's surface. At these two overlap points, our ball is rolling over an oily spot even if it is flaring to fresh coverstock over the remainder of each revolution. Figure 9.10 depicts one of the overlap areas created by closely spaced oil rings and widely spaced oil rings, equating to low track flare and high track flare. Notice the size of the oily spot at the crossing point in each image. The more closely spaced our oil rings, the larger the overlap spot. In our drawing, the overlap spot for the closely spaced rings is over twice as long as the spot produced by the widely spaced rings.

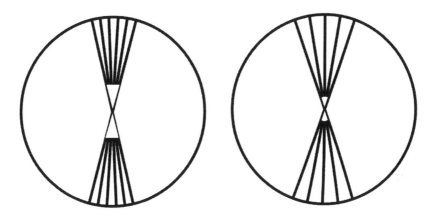

Figure 9.10: Oil ring overlap resulting from low and high track flare

When the ball is rolling over fresh coverstock, it will obtain the maximum amount of friction against the lane surface. When it hits the two overlap spots, however, it will be presenting an already oiled surface to the lane and so will have very little friction over these two segments of every revolution. It is obvious that the closely spaced rings will present less clean coverstock surface to the lane with each revolution than will the ball with the widely spaced rings. These drawings are exaggerated, however. In a more realistic example, will there be enough of a difference to have a material effect on hook?

For the photos in Figure 9.11, below, we laid out six simulated oil rings spaced five-eighths of an inch apart (center to center), three-eighths of an inch apart, and one-quarter of an inch apart. These spacings equate to an extremely high-flaring ball, an average, medium-flaring ball, and a low-flaring ball. Note the relative size of the three dark areas of overlap.

Figure 9.11: Oil ring overlap at track flare of 5/8, 3/8, and 1/4 inch

Just as in the drawing, the length of the overlapped area increases as track flare decreases. The overlap is 2 inches long on the high-flaring ball, 3-1/8 inches long on the medium-flaring ball, and 3-3/4 inches on the low-flaring ball. Let's figure out what effect this change in overlap might have on friction.

We know that a bowling ball has a circumference of 27 inches. Let's assign a revolution of the ball over completely oil-free coverstock an arbitrary friction value of 100. The high-flare ball has an overlap length of two inches, and there are two such overlaps for each revolution of the ball, for a total of four inches of oily surface for each revolution. The rest of the 27 inches of coverstock presented to the lane on each revolution is dry. Subtracting the four inches of oily cover from the total of 27 inches tells us that 23 inches of clean cover are presented to the lane over each revolution. 23 is 85 percent of 27, so our high-flaring ball will have a friction value of 85. Performing the same math for the other two balls gives us a friction value of 77 for the average ball, and 72 for the low-flaring ball. As track flare increases, the ball is clearly presenting more clean coverstock to the lane. While the physics paper stated that this increase in clean surface will increase hook, that conclusion is contradicted by the above referenced Brunswick video, which clearly demonstrated no material difference in hook between the normally-flaring ball, the high-flare ball, and the extreme-flare ball that was beyond the legal limits.

There is definitely a difference in "clean cover" friction between our high-flaring and normal-flaring balls in Figure 9.11, amounting to eight percentage points (85 minus 77). Assuming Brunswick's high and low flare example balls showed a similar difference in clean coverstock, their video demonstrates that this 8 percent decrease in clean cover is not enough to cause any noticeable change in hook from one ball to the other. Brunswick attributes this to what they call the "Limit of the Track Flare Effect." They state that while high track flare does indeed present more clean coverstock to the lane, there is no benefit to any flare beyond three-eighths inch. Stated another way, there was no benefit and no increase in hook from shortening the overlap area from 3-1/8 inches in the average flare ball to 2 inches in the high-flaring ball.

The unstated implication of Brunswick's Limit of the Track Flare Effect is that even though there is no increase in hook as track flare increases above three-eighths inch separation of the oil rings, there *would* be a loss of hook as track flare decreased below the three-eighths inch limit. The video did not demonstrate such a decrease, nor did it explain why this should be so.

We find this "limit" to be questionable. We absolutely agree with Brunswick that an increase in track flare above three-eighths inch cannot have any material effect on hook. The proof is right in the video, so there is no justification for doubt. We do not, however, accept the implication that there will be a decrease in hook if flare drops below three-eighths inch. If there was no perceivable decrease in hook when clean cover friction fell by eight percentage points from the high-flare ball to the medium ball, how then could a drop of only five percentage points from the medium-flare ball to the low-flare ball cause a decrease in hook?

Brunswick maintains that once the oil rings are separated by three-eighths of an inch, no more hook can be attained as a result of more track flare. Our own reasoning leads us to believe that the Limit of the Track Flare Effect is reached as soon as there is *any* separation between the oil rings. Clean cover is clean cover, whether the strips of coverstock are one-eighth inch apart or half an inch apart. While we lack the resources and the robot required to test our hypothesis, our research leads us to believe that as long as there is some minimal amount of track flare, additional flare will have no perceptible effect on hook.

If our measurements of the oil ring overlap areas from a few paragraphs ago clearly demonstrate that there will be at least some additional friction as track flare increases, even beyond Brunswick's three-eighths inch limit, how can there possibly be no increase in hook? Recall that the meaningful portion of our hook occurs once the lane oil has thinned out or the dry back ends have been reached. All of those oil rings on your ball were created on the oily part of the lane. If the lane is already coated in friction-reducing oil, how could two small spots of additional oil on the ball's surface possibly make any material difference? The ball is just sliding in the oil as it tries to dig in and get a grip on the lane. All that two slightly bigger spots of oil at the crossing points of the flare rings means is that the ball will be sliding as before, and trying only a tiny bit less to dig in. This tiny difference in friction on the oily, low-friction part of the lane just doesn't seem to matter much, and once the ball hits the drier part of the lane there is so much friction that, again, those tiny little spots of overlap won't have any noticeable effect. Our belief is that as long as there is at least some minimal separation between the oil rings, track flare has done all that it can do and any increase in track flare is largely meaningless.

So does track flare stop having an effect after three-eighths inch of oil ring separation, or does it stop as soon as the flare is perceptible, as we contend? Take your pick. Since pretty much every modern bowling ball, with the exception of polyester spare balls and perhaps a few extremely low end balls, is capable of obtaining three-eighths inch of separation between the oil rings, the point is moot. The ball manufacturers have designed their cores with the RG differential—and hence the track flare—that they felt was appropriate and sufficient in each case. You simply don't need to worry about track flare.

BOWLING BALL CORES (WEIGHT BLOCKS)

As the preceding discussion made clear, track flare is possible because the bowling ball has an RG differential, meaning that the ball's RG is not uniform across every axis. The ball's RG as measured about the pin is significantly lower than its RG as measured about the PSA . If the ball's core or weight block were a perfect sphere, or if it had no weight block at all, the ball would have no RG differential and hence no track flare, at least before drilling. Since lack of RG differential is not a desirable situation, ball manufacturers create a great variety of oddly shaped cores.

Bowling ball cores fall into two general categories which bowlers refer to as *symmetric* and *asymmetric*. A symmetric core is one which is symmetric about the pin. If we were to saw a symmetric core in half from top to bottom and examine the two-dimensional shape on the cut face, that shape would have the same amount of material on the right and left side of the pin. As long as the slice went along the pin, every slice would be the same no matter how we oriented the saw. We need to be a little careful here though. Symmetric cores do not necessarily need to have a visually even shape on every possible slicing plane. It is possible to create a core that has a somewhat odd shape, but where every possible slicing angle through the pin would still reveal a *mathematically* equivalent shape on each side of the pin even if they were not quite visually equal. This is a fine distinction though, and is not really relevant to the bowler. In either case, a symmetric core will have two distinct RG axes, the low-RG axis through the pin, and the high-RG axis at 90 degrees to the pin and running through any two opposing points on the core's equator.

An asymmetric core is one in which the weight is not evenly distributed about the pin. Such a core may have a big lump or a divot on one side, or a chunk of a heavier material hanging off to one side, or a structure looking a bit like poorly stacked building blocks. However the designer arrives at the asymmetry, the end result is a core in which the shape of a slice through the pin is different depending upon where the slice is made. Asymmetric cores, like their symmetric brethren, have their low-RG axis running through the pin. Because of the lump or divot or eccentricity in the core's construction, though, the high-RG axis, rather than being any random opposing points along the equator, will instead run through the heavy or light spot on the core. This high-RG axis will still be at roughly 90 degrees to the pin as with the symmetric core, but since there is one specific heavy or light spot on the core, the end point of the resulting high-RG axis will be marked on the ball's surface. As already discussed, this mark is called the PSA or the mass bias. Asymmetric cores also have a third *intermediate* RG axis which runs at 90 degrees to both the pin and the PSA, but as already discussed, its effect on the ball's path is minimal and will be ignored in this discussion.

We need to be a bit careful when describing a core as symmetric or asymmetric, because our bowling definitions are not the same as the definitions a physicist would use. We encountered a physics paper stating that asymmetric balls hook more than do symmetric balls.[47] A cursory reading would lead us to accept that statement on its face, since it comports with both common perception and bowling ball marketing. A closer reading, however, reveals the problem.

The paper's authors employed the terms "symmetric" and "asymmetric" in the physics sense and not in the bowling sense, and the two meanings are very different. They described a symmetric core as one like the perfect sphere we discussed earlier. In physics terms, a symmetric core has no RG differential at all, and hence no track flare. They described an asymmetric core as one possessing a low-RG pin as well as a high-RG PSA. From a physics standpoint the authors make no distinction at all between what we bowlers refer to as symmetric and asymmetric cores, and they simply lump both together under the scientifically correct umbrella term, "asymmetric." Thus, they are not saying that a bowling ball with an asymmetric core will hook more than will one with a symmetric core *as bowlers employ those terms*, but only that a ball with an RG differential will out-hook a ball with no RG differential. All they are saying is that a ball that flares will out-hook a ball that doesn't, which tells we bowlers absolutely nothing useful.

CORE SHAPE

Whether symmetric or asymmetric, bowling ball cores are manufactured in a wide variety of shapes, some simple, and some quite complex. Bowling ball marketing emphasizes the shape of the cores, even giving them names. A picture of the core features prominently in advertisements and on the "shelf talker" information card displayed beneath the balls at bowling pro shops. Bowlers will study the picture, and speak the name of the core in hushed tones. Arguments will ensue over which bowling ball line incorporated the best weight block ever, and marriages have ended over disagreements about the superiority of symmetric versus asymmetric cores.

Okay, maybe we've exaggerated just a bit, but the shape of the bowling ball core does seem to be a major consideration when bowlers select a new ball, and ball manufacturers put quite an effort into creating new shapes. With all of this emphasis placed on the shape of the core, does it really make a difference? Once more, the physics say "no," or at least not in any direct way.

A bowling ball core is just a dense hunk of plastic filled with rock dust. It doesn't possess any magical properties, it doesn't store energy, it doesn't really do anything other than sit there in the center of the ball. It's only real purpose it to make the ball lopsided from a physics standpoint even as the ball maintains its perfectly spherical outer shape. This lopsidedness is the RG differential. The only thing the weight block is really doing is setting the ball's high and low RG.

Physics doesn't care what shape the core is. All that matters in terms of ball motion is what the RG values are along the ball's pin and along the high-RG axis. The core designer isn't sitting down and saying "I think a weight block with a rectangular profile, but with a hemispherical lump on one side and the top left corner knocked off will provide the ball motion I'm looking for." Instead, he or she says, "I want a low RG value of X inches to match with this coverstock, and I'd like a differential of Y inches to get the track flare I desire. Now, what shape can I come up with that will get me those two values?" The shape chosen is only a means to an end, not an end in itself, and it is not the only possible shape that will yield the desired RG values. The laws of physics do not even "see" the core shape; they only see the RG values. In fact, two completely different core shapes that happen to possess the same high and low RG values would yield precisely the same ball motion.[48] This is why ball companies keep bringing back their "timeless" or "proven" tried-and-true weight blocks. Why reinvent the wheel when you've already got molds for a weight block with the RG characteristics you need?

How is it possible that two different weight block shapes will yield the same ball motion as long as their RG values are the same? Recall from earlier chapters that RG is a sort of averaging out of the mass and location of every particle making up the weight block. Picture it like taking off the bumps on the weight block and using them to fill the holes, leaving us with a smooth sphere of some new radius. Let's look at an example to make this more clear.

Imagine a greatly simplified two-dimensional weight block that contains only four molecules of weighted material. Let's place one of these molecules 1 inch from the weight block's center point, the next at 2 inches, the third at 3 inches, and the fourth at 4 inches, as depicted in the first drawing in Figure 9.12, below. This imaginary weight block has a very odd shape, but we can smooth it out mathematically. RG calculation does not employ a simple arithmetic average to smooth out the mass points, but rather uses a mathematical technique called *root mean square* (RMS). RMS is a way to average things out while giving more statistical weight to those mass points that are farther away from the center and less statistical weight to those closer in, reflecting their relative influence on the whole. Our imaginary weight block has an RMS of 2.74 inches, which is its RG. In the second weight block, each of the four mass points are 2.74 inches from the center, giving this core the same RG as the first oddly shaped example. Both of these cores would behave in precisely the same manner. While to our eyes these two weight blocks look very different from one another, in the eyes of the physical laws that govern motion they look exactly the same. In fact, once the core is molded into a ball, physics no longer even sees the core as a separate object. The mass distribution characteristics of the core get averaged in with that of the coverstock and filler material, and the laws of motion act only on the ball as a whole. As we said at the beginning of this section, all the core does is to make that "whole" lopsided.

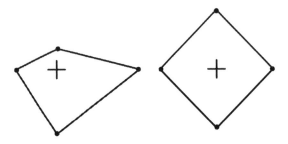

Figure 9.12: Equivalent RG, different shapes

The takeaway from all of this discussion is that core shape, RG differential, and track flare really don't make much of a difference in ball motion. Choose a ball with an RG suitable for the coverstock characteristics you have selected, your physical game parameters, and the conditions you intend to bowl on, and ignore the rest. Trust that the ball company's designer has determined an appropriate differential and resulting track flare, and has selected a core shape that let him or her achieve those desired numbers in a way that could be easily and economically manufactured. Core shape and differential will have very little influence on your game. Save your thought and concern for things that can have a far bigger effect.

CHAPTER 10

THE POCKET ISN'T THE POCKET...

...AND IT'S NOWHERE NEAR WHERE YOU THINK IT IS

"WHAT THE HECK was wrong with that shot? I smashed the pocket, and left the #@*%& ten pin!" ...or seven pin, or eight pin, or worse. We've all been there; a seemingly good pocket hit, yet a single back row pin or some nasty combination of back row pins remains. Watch most any PBA telecast and you will see the same. When a powerful shot leaves a ringing ten pin standing, the announcer will invariably attribute the failure to strike to bad luck. But as the gangster sang in Gershwin's *Porgy and Bess*, "It ain't necessarily so."

In almost all cases, when a "good" shot leaves pins standing, it wasn't bad luck at all. It was instead a lack of good luck, which is a far different thing. The fact is, a fair percentage of our "good pocket strikes" weren't actually very good at all, and carried due to little more than luck. When that luck fails us, back row pins result.

I began to think about the true causes of frustrating corner pin leaves as I suffered through a rather serious slump several years ago. I was consistently hitting the pocket, yet my strike percentage hovered at 30%. I threw shot after shot, all seemingly good, only to leave a corner pin or an 8- or 9-pin taunting me. Sometimes, just to keep my life interesting, the bowling gods would even leave a couple of them standing at the same time.

In bowling, everyone wants to help. Good bowler, mediocre bowler, high average, low average; everyone wants to troubleshoot your game and offer helpful advice. I received all of the usual diagnoses and suggestions for my lack of carry from well-meaning bowlers, coaches, and observers: You came in at the wrong angle. You came in too fast. Your ball rolled out. Hit it a little harder. Hit it a little softer. Move up a little on the approach. Move back a little. Just wait for the shot to come back to you.

Sometimes these tricks and tweaks would work, or at least would seem to, but never consistently and never for very long. One or two shots would carry, but the problem would inevitably return. Since none of the usual suggestions worked, I decided to go back to first principles and try to figure out exactly what was going on when the ball hit the pins.

Neither of us are engineers or physicists, but we knew we needed to start thinking about bowling in a more rigorous and scientific way. Collisions between multiple round objects, even in only two dimensions, are among the most complex interactions in classical physics, and impossible to model with any accuracy without resorting to large amounts of coding and a massive amount of computing power. As daunting as it is to model a two dimensional collision system, trying to model the unbelievably complex interaction between ten very oddly shaped pins and one very heavy ball, all bouncing off of both the walls and one another in three dimensions, would likely require a set of algorithms the size of an encyclopedia and a supercomputer to run it all. We're guessing the USBC won't be devoting such resources to our problem any time soon.

Even if we did manage to model the entire collision system, the fact that any or all of the pins can be set down by the pinsetter "off spot" in any direction renders any computation meaningless. Even if we could model the entire collision system in an idealized situation where every pin weighed precisely the same amount and was set precisely on spot, all of our computations would amount to nothing if even one pin varied in weight or position.

The vast number of variables means that each shot in bowling will be unique and unpredictable, but over a large number of shots general patterns will emerge. We can therefore take a "close enough" approach to the problem to get a good idea of what deflects where under various circumstances. Our "close enough" analysis can tell us both the cause and cure of pins left standing on seemingly good hits.

ON CAUSE AND EFFECT

Most of the time when we throw what we think is a good shot, but which leaves a pin or pins standing, it will be one or more of the back row pins; the 7-, 8-, 9-, and 10-pin. So what's really happening when our pocket shot fails to carry?

Our first clue toward determining the true cause of back row leaves on seemingly good pocket hits came from an observation shared with me by my coauthor, long before we began writing this book. He said that after years of coaching around the world, he noticed that every time a bowler he was working with left a corner pin, their ball exited the pin deck a bit right of center, more toward the 9-pin rather than from the center of the deck directly between the 8- and 9- (right-handed bowlers). I began watching carefully, both in my leagues and with the bowlers I worked with, and witnessed the same phenomenon.

The German philosopher of science, Hans Reichenbach, offered a framework for observation and problem solving that he called the *Common Cause Principle*. Simply stated, the Common Cause Principle says that where we find two events that occur together but where one cannot possibly be the cause of the other, we need to look for a common cause, some third factor that could have caused both of our observed events. Suppose you had a tropical fish tank with a heater and a thermometer. One day you noticed that the mercury in the thermometer was all the way to the top, and all of your fish were dead. Would you assume that mercury rising in the thermometer causes fish to die? Of course not, because there is no connection between the thermometer and the fish. But since they are both connected to the water, our logical assumption would be that a malfunctioning heater caused both the rising of the mercury and the death of the fish. The dying fish could not cause the mercury to rise, and the rising mercury could not cause the fish to die. Both observations share a *common cause*, which of course is the faulty heater.

Others have also noticed the ball's right-of-center finishing position on shots that leave corner pins, and have postulated all sorts of cause and effect relationships. The problem with this line of reasoning is that by the time the ball is exiting the pin deck, pretty much all of the primary collisions have already taken place. The ball's exit into the pit can no more cause a pin to remain standing than rising mercury inside a thermometer can cause a fish to die. Just as with our aquarium example, we need to look at both the ball's finish position and the standing pins as *symptoms of the same problem*, and to search for a common cause that can explain them both.

Given the chaotic and almost incomprehensible melee that occurs when our ball strikes the pins, most any explanation for back row pin leaves can sound plausible. However, when we add in that the hypothesis must also explain a right-of-center finishing position for the ball, most of these common ideas fail.

SEARCHING FOR A CAUSE

We've all heard confident statements as to why we leave 10-pins or 7-pins, what causes a 9-pin, the difference between a ringing and a flat 10-pin, and on and on. If the statement comes from a high average bowler, a PBA pro, or a well-known Internet pundit we tend to accept it unquestioningly. They couldn't possibly have such a high average if they didn't understand the physics, right? In fact, we are so quick to accept such reasonable-sounding explanations that we never even notice that in most cases the statements are based only on anecdote and are not backed up with any hard evidence. In accepting such common knowledge as fact, we all commit the classic reasoning error of *argument from authority*; Writer X is an expert on bowling, Writer X says such-and-such, therefore such-and-such is true.

We must understand that absent hard evidence or mathematical proof, all such unsupported ideas need to be regarded as opinions rather than facts until such time as they are proven. We are certainly free to act upon such opinions, but they still remain only opinions, and opinions should always be open to questioning and new evidence. The problem in bowling is that we all tend to state our beliefs as facts, without qualification. "You left a ringing 10-pin because your ball came in at the wrong angle…, or the wrong speed…, or because your hook had the wrong shape (whatever that means).

How many times have you heard similar statements? In most cases the truth of the matter is that the person making such a statement, though certainly well meaning, does not in fact *know* it to be true. He or she made an educated guess, or read it somewhere, or heard it somewhere. It sounded reasonable or authoritative, and they may even have convinced themselves that they saw evidence of it on the lane, but that is a far different thing than "knowing." If they said "I've *heard* that ringing 10-pins are caused my thus-and-so," or "I *believe* they are caused by such-and-such," all would be well. You, as the recipient of the information, would know that it may or may not be so, and that it is open to doubt and questioning. We rarely hear a qualification though. Instead, it is stated as incontrovertible fact.

The twelfth century French philosopher and logician Peter Abelard said that "By doubting, we come to inquiry, and by inquiry we arrive at truth." If we do not question our assumptions, we cannot move the sport of bowling forward. In this spirit we began thinking through the mechanical consequences of the commonly shared ideas as to what causes various standing pins on seemingly good pocket hits, and of the common prescriptions to remedy those problems. The more we examined these ideas, the more it became clear that they had to be incorrect, or at least incomplete. There just did not seem to be any way for the commonly stated reasons for leaving standing pins to actually produce that result, and even if the stated causes could somehow produce the result, the common "cures" didn't offer a viable way to fix it.

While there are almost unlimited ways to leave back row pins on bad hits due to random pin action, we are addressing here only pins left standing by seemingly good pocket hits. That is to say, bowling results of the "I was robbed!" variety. Before we delve into why we are leaving pins standing, we must first examine what happens during a classic or "textbook" strike, what the "pocket" really is, and what a pocket hit actually looks like from our vantage point on the approach.

THE POCKET ISN'T REALLY THE POCKET

"To get a strike, throw the ball into the 1-3 pocket." Every bowler has said it and every bowler has heard it, yet we believe this single piece of advice is at the root of all of our misconceptions concerning ringing 10-pins, stone 7s, 8-pins and 9-pins, and so-called pocket 7-10s and 8-10s. The idea that the pocket is the area between the headpin and the 3-pin is also the cause of our misconceptions regarding what really constitutes a "good pocket hit." Illustrations similar to Figure 10.1 abound, purporting to illustrate a "classic second arrow strike."

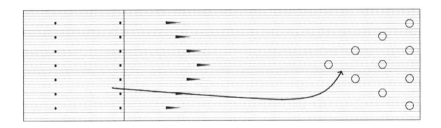

Figure 10.1: Supposed "classic second arrow strike"

These common illustrations all show the ball hitting between the 1-pin and the 3-pin, possibly even impacting both simultaneously. Such illustrations lead us to believe that when our ball hits in this zone we have thrown a good shot, and we therefore expect a good result. The reality, however, is that such a hit would most likely result in a horrible split. The rather shocking truth is that to have the greatest chance of achieving a strike, your target is nowhere near the 1-3 pocket.

What, then, does a textbook strike look like? Figure 10.2 illustrates the entire chain of events making up a textbook strike. The ball first contacts the headpin slightly to the right of center. It then deflects to the right, off of the headpin, striking the 3-pin somewhat left of center. The ball then deflects off of the 3-pin to the left, to strike the 5-pin slightly right of center. It once again deflects right off of the 5-pin to strike the 9-pin slightly to the left of its center. In this scenario, the ball actually follows a zigzag path through the pins, ultimately deflecting to the left off of the 9-pin and exiting the pin deck somewhere near the center of the lane. The 1-, 3-, 5-, and 9-pins are the only ones knocked down by the ball. The remaining pins are taken out by direct collisions from other pins. How does that work? The headpin is driven back and left into the 2-, which falls into the 4-, which falls into the 7- in one long chain reaction. The 5-pin, which was clipped by the ball, takes out the 8-pin, while the 3-pin, also clipped by the ball, takes out the 6-, which subsequently takes out the 10-, again in a chain reaction.

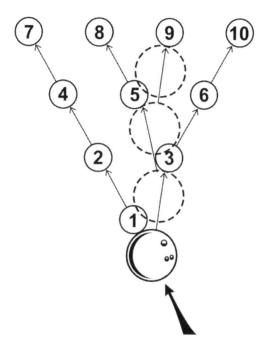

Figure 10.2: "Textbook Strike"

So let's look again at an actual 1-3 pocket hit. Figure 10.3 depicts a down-lane view of a ball hitting the 1-3 pocket; that is, hitting the headpin and the 3-pin simultaneously. We can clearly see from this photo that in order to hit both pins our ball must actually come in *behind* the headpin.

Figure 10.3: Actual 1-3 pocket hit

Let's now follow this actual 1-3 pocket hit to its logical conclusion. With the ball coming in behind the headpin, such a hit would result in the headpin flying out to the left wall without contacting any other pins. The ball, being almost directly in front of the 3-pin, would drive it straight back into the 9-. The ball then passes between the 5- and the 6-pins, clipping the 6-pin out to the right gutter without it ever contacting the 10-pin, leaving the 10-pin standing. Our headpin bypassed the 2-pin, leaving it standing. The 5-pin, being hit a bit more solidly than the 6-pin , drives left and back, hopefully hitting the 8-pin or the 4-pin. Absent luck, the 5-pin slides between the 8- and the 4-, taking out only the 7-pin, or merely continues off the back of the pin deck without hitting anything. The result? Likely a 2-10 split, or possibly a 2-8-10, a 2-4-8-10, or a 2-7-10. It is entirely possible that random bouncing and rolling pins will knock down some or even all of those left standing by the primary collisions, thus rendering the final leave either better or worse, but in any case what we experience following a 1-3 pocket hit will be very, very far from a textbook or classic strike.

IF THE POCKET ISN'T IN THE POCKET, WHERE IS IT?

If the pocket is not between the headpin and the 3-pin, where is it? Before we can discuss this, we must talk a bit about the layout of a regulation bowling lane. A standard bowling lane is 41-1/2 inches wide, plus or minus 1/2 inch. It is made up of 39 longitudinal boards. In days past these were actual wooden boards laminated together, and in many older centers they still are. Modern lanes are made of a synthetic plastic material, but are still imprinted with 39 wood-toned stripes to simulate the traditional boards. Dividing the 41-1/2 inch width of the lane by 39 boards, we find that each board is approximately 1-1/16 inches in width.

The lane boards, whether real or just printed, are numbered 1 through 39, beginning at the right gutter for right-handed bowlers and at the left gutter for left-handed bowlers. The headpin is in the center of the lane, on board 20. The targeting arrows on the lane are set at five board increments from the center board, as are the dots on the approach,and both correspond very roughly with the placement of the remaining pins. That is, the first arrow corresponds very roughly with the 10-pin, the second arrow with the 6-pin, the third arrow with the 3-pin, and so on. Each pin is set precisely 12 inches center to center in every direction from its immediate neighbors, in a 60 degree equilateral triangle. Thus, the 3-pin will be 6 inches, or a bit over 5-1/2 boards to the right of the headpin, or roughly on board 14-1/2, the 6-pin will be 6 inches to the right of the 3-pin, roughly on board 9, and the 10-pin is 6 inches to the right of the 6-pin, or roughly on board 3.

So where, then, is the actual pocket? There really isn't a pocket per se. The word "pocket," though universally used for our strike target, is actually a misnomer. In 2009 the USBC filmed over 200 high speed videos of what various industry experts classified as pocket hits, and then analyzed the resulting pin fall in order to determine strike percentages at various entry points relative to the pins.[49] This Pin Carry Study determined that the highest strike percentage entry point, regardless of the ball's angle of entry (the sharpness of the bowler's hook), occurred when the ball struck the pins on board 17-1/2—the seam between boards 17 and 18—which is just a bit over 2-1/2 inches to the right of dead center. The strike percentage was also very high in the areas half a board to the right or left of 17-1/2, so we can say that the high percentage strike target is from the center of board 17 to center of board 18, or a total width of a single board. Within this roughly one board wide zone we are almost guaranteed a strike regardless of our entry angle. In fact, the USBC Pin Carry Study puts the strike percentage for a hit on board 17-1/2 at just under 100 percent. Note that while a later study found a somewhat lower strike probability, even in that study board 17-1/2 had by far the highest strike percentage.

When we say "pocket" we really mean our target at the pins. Since this one board wide zone of high probability centered on board 17-1/2 is the one place on the lane where a strike is closest to a certainty regardless of entry angle, it make sense to refer to this point as "The Pocket." If our ball hits outside of this pocket, then a strike relies to a greater and greater extent upon random bouncing pins taking out the stragglers which were missed by the primary collisions. The farther away our ball is from this board 17-1/2 pocket the more luck will be required to clean up the missed pins, thus reducing our odds of obtaining a strike. These findings are depicted in Figure 10.4, below, which is adapted with permission from the USBC Pin Carry Study. It illustrates the strike percentage at three different angles of entry to the pins; 2 degrees (white graph), 4 degrees (grey), and 6 degrees (black).

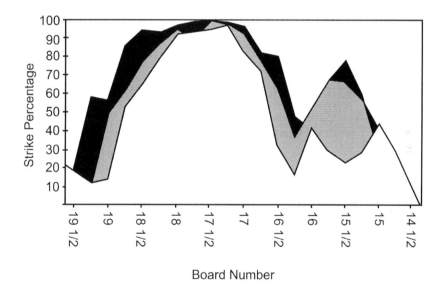

Figure 10.4: Strike percentage as a function of impact position and entry angle

Figure 10.4 shows us that if our ball hits the pins around board 16-1/2—just half a board or so light—our chances of striking drop precipitously, especially if we have only a modest hook. This is the beginning of the "corner pin zone," the hits that look good, but never seem to carry. Figure 10.4 also shows something a bit curious. For those with large 4 degree to 6 degree hooks, there is a small but significant secondary strike zone around board 15-1/2. This is sometimes referred to as the "swish zone," where so-called "mixer" strikes occur. Strikes of this sweeping "Hit 'em thin and watch 'em spin" variety—to use a term coined by the late, great Billy Welu—are easy to differentiate from good flush strikes. They sound different (weak), look different (pins moving sideways rather than back), and most often leave pins laying all over the deck. Such mixer strikes are far from "textbook," and should be considered *very* lucky breaks. So, hit the pins around board 17-1/2, get a strike. Come in a board light, leave back row pins. One board lighter still, maybe strike. Another board light, leave an ugly wash out or a bucket. Not much room for error, especially considering that our target is 60 feet away!

So now we know precisely where we need to hit the pins in order to strike consistently. We need to hit very close to board 17-1/2. But how do we know if we are actually doing so? During my aforementioned slump, I swore that I was pounding the pocket. Every hit looked good and sounded powerful, but most every shot left a corner pin or worse. The main problem here is that most of us, including very experienced bowlers, do not know what a true pocket hit looks like from our vantage point 60 feet down lane. What most of us would identify as a good pocket hit is in reality quite light, firmly in the corner pin zone, while a good, solid pocket hit actually looks very high from down lane.

Figure 10.5 depicts a true, "flush" pocket hit on board 17-1/2. Figure 10.6 shows a so-called "high flush" hit on board 18, while Figure 10.7 shows a light pocket hit on board 17. These three photos define the "pocket." Figure 10.8 is a composite view of all three shots. If your ball hits the pins anywhere else, you've missed the pocket.

Figure 10.5: True flush pocket hit

Figure 10.6: High flush pocket hit

Figure 10.7: Light pocket hit

Figure 10.8: Composite view of the entire pocket

Now admit it: You would have said that all three shots were very high hits! Don't feel bad, as you are not alone in this. We conducted a survey of nearly 300 bowlers of all levels of skill and knowledge, all the way from low average league bowlers to elite PBA touring pros. We had each participant self-rate their level of both skill and knowledge; either basic, intermediate, high, or expert. We then showed them photos, including those above, of a ball impacting the pins at various points, and asked them whether the shot was in the pocket, light (not catching enough of the headpin), or high (hitting too heavy on the headpin).

In the case of the ball entering the pins on board 17-1/2—the single highest percentage target on the lane—only nine percent of bowlers accurately identified the shot as being in the pocket. A full 91 percent said that the shot was too high. Even more shocking, there was an inverse relationship between self-rated knowledge level and having the correct answer. Only 4 percent of the bowlers rating their knowledge as "Expert" correctly identified the board 17-1/2 shot as being in the pocket. The figure was 8 percent correct for bowlers rating their knowledge as "High" and 10 percent correct for those rating their knowledge as "Intermediate." Curiously, 27 percent of those rating their knowledge as "Basic" correctly identified the shot as being in the pocket.

Now, in fairness, this doesn't mean our survey respondents did not know that board 17-1/2 is the pocket; it just means that even the experts don't necessarily know what a good pocket hit looks like. When we staged these photos, even we were surprised at how high the good pocket hits actually looked. All three "pocket" shots impact well to the front of the headpin and none are anywhere near the 1-3 pocket that we were all told was our target, yet this range represents the highest percentage strike shot we can make regardless of entry angle. What we all would have classified as high hits before reading this chapter, and might have even made an adjustment to correct, are in fact the actual pocket. While Figure 10.4 shows us that we have a decent chance of striking a bit to either side of this sweet spot, as our ball's impact point moves away from this board 17-1/2 true pocket, any strikes we get should be recognized as "lucky" to one degree or another.

While board 17-1/2 represents the highest strike percentage shot we can possibly make, it is also curious to note that an impact with the headpin at this point will *not* result in our previously discussed "textbook" or classic strike. Recall from our discussion of the textbook strike that the headpin is supposed to travel back and left at a 30 degree angle to the lane in order to squarely impact the 2-pin, which in turn hits the 4-pin, which itself then hits the 7-pin. We can clearly see from Figures 10.5, 10.6, and 10.7 that a true pocket hit is too high on the headpin to send it off at the required angle, and that the headpin would instead be driven too far back and not far enough out to the left to squarely impact the 2-pin. In fact, we can calculate that in order for the headpin to travel back and left at a 30 degree angle to the lane, the ball would have to impact the headpin on or near board 16-1/2, which we have already identified as a light hit with a much lower chance of striking. The USBC Pin Carry Study tells us that at a fairly high 4 degree entry angle, our strike percentage for a hit on board 16-1/2 is only about 60 percent. At a 2 degree entry angle our carry percentage on that same board 16-1/2 hit drops precipitously to a mere 30 percent. It makes you wonder, then, why we should characterize such a low percentage "lucky" strike as "textbook"?

KEEP YOUR EYE ON THE BALL

In order to correctly evaluate our shots, we must learn to recognize where our ball actually hit in relation to the pins. In the flush hit on board 17-1/2 in Figure 10.5, note that there is only about three-quarters of an inch of headpin visible to the left of our ball. In the high flush hit on board 18 in Figure 10.6, the left edge of our ball is actually even with the left edge of the headpin. In the lightest acceptable high-percentage hit on board 17 in Figure 10.7, there is just a bit over an inch of headpin showing to the left of our ball.

These three photos define what a "pocket" hit looks like from the foul line. We need to be very observant and very honest with ourselves if we wish to improve, and if we wish to address and avoid corner pins. Tripped pins, late falling pins, pins that fall forward or are tackled by another pin that bounced out of the pit, toppled pins left on the deck, and especially 10-pins taken out by a messenger flying across the deck are all signs that you missed the pocket but got a lucky break.

We often praise the power of a bowler who blasts a messenger off the wall to clobber the 10-pin. Yes, that messenger is indicative of a lot of power, but it is also indicative of a pretty bad miss to the right. If our ball hits higher or lighter than what is depicted in Figures 10.5, 10.6, and 10.7 and still results in a strike, we must be honest enough to acknowledge that we got a lucky break, and to recognize that we need to adjust now so that our lucky breaks don't give way to disaster. With this in mind, let's examine the likely result of various shots, from a high flush hit on board 18, all the way right to light hits in the 1-3 zone.

Five years or so after the Pin Carry study was completed, the USBC conducted a far more in-depth study of the results of hits on boards 15-1/2 through 18. They employed a ramp to keep the delivery consistent, and executed 1400 shots at various points of impact. As this study provides such rich results and seems rather rigorous, we will cite its findings in this part of our discussion rather than the more limited results of the Pin Carry Study.[50]

BOARD 18

Figure 10.9: Ball entering on board 18

Figure 10.9 again depicts a high flush hit on board 18, as viewed from the perspective of both a right hander and a left hander. All of the photos in this section will depict the ball position from a right-hander's perspective in the first image and the left-hander's perspective in the second image. So as not to bog this section down in excess verbiage, all descriptions of ball position will be from the right-hander's perspective. Lefties need only flip the pin positions in their head. If the right-hander's description says you will leave, say, a 4-9 split from a hit on board X, a lefty will instead leave a 6-8. If the righty description says you will leave a 2-pin, a lefty will instead leave a 3-pin.

Note that when the ball enters the pins on board 18, the left edge of the ball is almost perfectly flush with the left edge of the headpin and will be so regardless of the ball's entry angle or any other factor. Use this as your visual cue as your own ball enters the pins. If the left edge of your ball was flush with the left edge of the headpin, your ball entered the pins on board 18 for a "high flush" hit.

Board 18 is the third highest strike percentage shot, and is the heaviest hit that should be considered as being "in the pocket." A ball hitting the pins on board 18 has a 74 percent chance of striking and a 96 percent chance of a nine-count or better. Hit here, and at worst you leave yourself an easy spare. What will you most likely leave if you don't strike? According to USBC statistics you are most likely to leave a 4-pin, though the odds of that are only 10 percent. Other possible single pin leaves are a 7-pin (six percent chance), or a 9- or 10-pin (three percent chance each). If you are *very* unlucky on a board 18 hit, your most likely leave will be either a 4-9 or 4-10 split, though the odds of each are only a bit over one percent. As we mentioned earlier, almost any leave is possible due to off-spot pin placements, unlucky bounces, shifts in the space-time continuum, and other random factors, but these are the most likely results of a board 18 hit.

Clearly a hit on board 18 is a pretty darn good shot, and is definitely within our definition of "the pocket." Did our survey respondents agree with this assessment? No. Only one percent of respondents correctly identified this shot as being in the pocket. That's a grand total of three people out of nearly 300. Everyone else, including all of our experts, said the shot was too high. Though this shot has a 74 percent chance of striking, only two percent of our experts thought the shot would carry. Again, this doesn't mean they didn't know that a hit on board 18 is a good shot; it only means that they did not know what a good board-18 shot looks like. We have all, experts and beginners alike, been told that a good shot hits between the 1- and the 3-pin, and this errant proclamation is the root of most of our problems.

BOARD 17-1/2

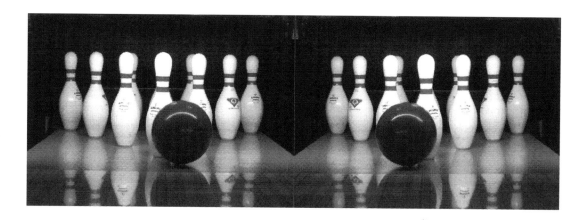

Figure 10.10: Ball entering on board 17-1/2

Board 17-1/2 is the highest percentage strike shot we can make, and should be the location we are talking about when discussing "the pocket." Your visual cue here is that there is only a thin slice of headpin visible next to the left edge of your ball, just over three-quarters of an inch.

If your ball hits the pins on board 17-1/2 you have an 85 percent chance of striking, and an almost 100 percent chance of getting a nine-count or better. If you don't strike, your most likely leave is a 9-pin at eight percent, followed by a 10-pin at five percent. Other possible but unlikely leaves are a 7- or 8-pin at one percent each.

So how do bowlers view this hit? As we said earlier in our discussion, only nine percent of respondents said this shot was in the pocket, and 91 percent said it was too high. Though this shot will result in a strike 85 percent of the time, only 22 percent of respondents thought it would do so, and again it was the beginners who got it right. Only seven percent of our experts thought the shot would strike. 21 percent of high knowledge bowlers and 23 percent of intermediate bowlers thought the shot would carry, while almost half of the beginners thought it would do so.

BOARD 17

Figure 10.11: Ball entering on board 17

Board 17 is the lightest hit that should still be classified as being "in the pocket." It carries a 76 percent chance of striking and a roughly 95 percent chance of a nine-count or better. Your visual cue for a board 17 hit is just over an inch of headpin visible to the left of your ball.

If your ball hits the pins on board 17 and fails to strike, your most likely leave is a 10-pin (10 percent) or a 9-pin (six percent). There is a one percent chance each for an 8-pin or a 5-pin, and a two percent chance of leaving both the 8- and the 5-. That's a 96 percent chance of a strike or an easy spare. Unfortunately though, the remaining roughly four percent is rather ugly. A hit on board 17, which is only about half an inch right of optimal, carries with it a one percent chance of a 5-10 split, a one percent chance of an 8-10 split, and a two percent chance of a 5-8-10 split.

Board 17 is also the point at which more bowlers started to recognize it as being a decent shot. Just over half of our respondents correctly identified this shot as being in the pocket, with the experts finally doing a little better than the beginners. A pretty decent 71 percent of respondents thought this shot would result in a strike, with the experts doing just a bit better than the high and intermediate bowlers, and the beginners doing just a bit worse. Note though that this hit is as far right as you can get and still be in the pocket, but it is only here that bowlers *begin* to see it as a good shot rather than one that is too high. Though it is as light as you can hit the pins and still have a good chance of a strike, almost half of our bowlers thought it was still too high.

BOARD 16-1/2

Figure 10.12: Ball entering on board 16-1/2

An entry position on board 16-1/2 certainly looks like a pretty good shot—right in the 1-3 pocket when viewed from down the lane—yet it is the beginning of the danger zone. This is the point of impact where really bad things start to happen. Note that on this hit roughly half of the headpin is visible beyond the left edge of the ball, and the right edge of the ball goes well beyond the 3-pin.

If we hit on board 16-1/2, only a half inch or so right of the pocket, our chance of striking plummets to around 58 percent. We have a 23 percent chance of getting a nine-count, and a nearly 20 percent chance of leaving something much worse.

If we fail to strike on a board 16-1/2 hit, our most likely outcome is a 10-pin, which has a 13 percent chance of occurring. This is followed by a 5-8 combination at 11 percent, a 5-pin at seven percent, an 8-pin at two percent, or a 9-pin at one percent. The rest of the possibilities are again rather ugly. There is a four percent chance of leaving an 8-10 split, a three percent chance of a 5-8-10 split, and a one percent chance of a 5-10 split.

Though a hit on board 16-1/2 is a fairly low percentage shot with a decent chance of a very ugly outcome, it was the shot most often identified by bowlers as being "the pocket." Fully 81 percent of respondents identified this light shot as being in the pocket. 11 percent of bowlers thought this hit was still too high, and only eight percent correctly identified it as being too light. Though this shot is a near 50-50 proposition in terms of its chance of striking, 91 percent of bowlers thought it would strike, with the numbers fairly constant across all self-rated knowledge levels.

BOARD 16

Figure 10.13: Ball entering on board 16

Board 16 still looks like a pretty good pocket hit, that is if we are still insisting that our target is the 1-3 pocket. In terms of visual cues, a hit on board 16 can be recognized by the right edge of the ball starting to overlap the left edge of the 6-pin.

A hit on board 16 has only a 51 percent chance of striking. Those are not terribly good odds, and any strike you get here should be considered the result of luck. This is where your ball is hitting on all of those shots where you insist that you hit the pocket, but left a 10-pin. In fact, you have a 21 percent chance of leaving a 10-pin on a board 16 shot. This is also where your ball is hitting when you can't figure out why you left the 5-pin or a 7-pin. The odds of leaving a 5-pin on a board 16 shot are 15 percent, and the odds of leaving a 7-pin are seven percent.

Other common leaves on a board 16 hit are the 5-8 (one percent), the 5-7 split (three percent), the 8-10 split (one percent), and the dreaded 7-10 split (one percent). This is also where you hit if you were unlucky enough to leave the much reviled 5-7-10 "sour apple" double split, though the odds of this split occurring are extremely low.

Though the odds of striking on a board 16 hit are rather low and the odds of leaving a 10-pin, a 7-pin, a 5-pin, or worse are so high, fully 78 percent of bowlers identify this shot as being in the pocket and 82 percent of bowlers expect a strike. Even worse, this misidentification of the pocket included over 70 percent of the bowlers who consider themselves to be experts.

BOARD 15-1/2

Figure 10.14: Ball entering on board 15-1/2

The hit on board 15-1/2 is the lightest shot that a majority of bowlers still identify as being in the pocket. Note that when this hit is viewed from down lane, the right edge of the ball solidly overlaps the left edge of the 6-pin.

A hit on board 15-1/2 has only a 49 percent chance of striking. Should you fail to strike, your most likely outcome is a 7-pin, at 21 percent odds. There is a 13 percent chance of leaving a 10-pin, and a six percent chance of a 5-pin. If you don't get lucky and leave one of those easy to cover spares, odds are you've left a bad split. A hit on board 15-1/2 carries a 5 percent chance of leaving a 5-7 split, a three percent chance of leaving a 4-5, and a three percent chance of leaving our old friend the 7-10.

Though the odds of a strike are even lower than with the board 16 hit and the odds of a really ugly split are even higher, 53 percent of bowlers still identify this shot as being in the pocket, and 70 percent expect a strike. 44 percent of experts, 51 percent of high knowledge bowlers, and 71 percent of intermediate bowlers thought this extremely light hit was "in the pocket," and 71 percent, 67 percent, and 71 percent respectively expect a strike. Curiously, while only 18 percent of the beginners thought this hit was in the pocket, 82 percent of them *still* expected it to strike.

While a few bowlers identified shots even farther right than this one as being in the pocket, the vast majority of bowlers correctly recognize them as being light, so we will stop our analysis here.

WHAT DOES IT MEAN?

The point of this exercise is not to show that bowlers, even expert bowlers, are wrong about the pocket. We are not pointing fingers nor making fun of anyone. Frankly, we would likely have answered similarly before we studied the issue of the pocket in depth. Our point is that we have all been mislead by the seemingly harmless yet insidious idea that the pocket is between the 1-pin and the 3-pin.

If we believe that the pocket is between the 1-pin and the 3-pin, then of course we will see such extremely light shots as being "in the pocket." If we think the pocket is between the 1- and the 3-pins, and we hit there only to leave a 10-pin or a 7-pin or the erroneously named "pocket 7-10," is it any wonder we get frustrated or think we were robbed? If we think that actual pocket hits on boards 17 through 18 were high, then it would be perfectly logical for us to move deeper inside following such shots, only to see our next shots come in light and leave pins standing.

Think of it this way: Suppose you had a baby, and every day of its life growing up you pointed to a dog but told him or her that it was a cow. Is it the child's fault when he falls asleep in school and tells the teacher that a cow kept him up all night with its barking, or when she doesn't turn in her homework and tells the teacher that the cow ate it? Most every bit of instruction and feedback we receive, either in writing or out on the lanes, tells us that shots striking in the vicinity of the 1- and 3-pins are "in the pocket," and that shots hitting higher on the headpin, in the very high percentage strike zone on boards 17 through 18, are "high." Given this, it is inevitable and perfectly logical that we would get frustrated when our 1-3 shots don't carry, and would think we were high and would move left when we were hitting the actual pocket. Even if we know intellectually that the true pocket is on board 17-1/2, when we look at our shots in the 1-3 area we think that such shots *are* on board 17-1/2.

The take away from this exercise is that our problem isn't so much in knowing what board the pocket is on, but rather in knowing when we are in fact hitting that board. If we wish to understand why we left what we left, if we wish to know factually when our shots are actually in the pocket and when they are high or light, if we wish to know what adjustments to our shot are needed or will be effective, then we must learn to recognize what it really looks like when our ball hits "the pocket."

Since we now understand that "the pocket" isn't really a pocket at all, and that it is nowhere near the area between the 1- and 3-pins, it would be very helpful if we could all stop using the word "pocket," and instead use a more descriptive term such as "target at the pins." We recognize, however, that this is never going to happen. The term "pocket" is simply too ingrained in the bowling psyche even though it is far from accurate or descriptive. The best we can hope for is that bowlers and coaches will at least stop referring to our target as "the 1-3 pocket" since it is nowhere near there, and to recognize that it is *much* higher on the headpin that we ever imagined.

The last thing we would like you to take away from this exercise is that the whole idea of being robbed—of leaving pins that you didn't deserve to leave—pretty much needs to go away. Barring bad luck, we now know that far from getting robbed, we probably got exactly what we deserved. If we left pins on what we thought was a good shot, we need to accept that the shot may not have been good at all, that it probably came in light, and that we need to make an adjustment—*now*. In the next chapter we will explore the actual causes of ringing and flat 10-pins, 7-, 8-, and 9-pins, and other common leaves. We cannot cure a problem unless we know what really caused it.

CHAPTER 11

I WAS ROBBED!

ONE DAY IN league, a friend on the next pair threw what he thought was a good shot, but left an ugly 8-10 split. He walked back toward the ball return with an absolutely shocked look on his face, and asked aloud, but of no one in particular, "What was wrong with *that* shot?" In truth there was a rather harsh expletive in the sentence too, but we left it out so as not to offend the tender sensibilities of we genteel bowlers. Though my friend's question was asked in a rhetorical sense, indicating his belief that there was in fact nothing at all wrong with his shot, I stunned him by answering. "Your shot came in a board-and-a-half light." He looked at me like I was from Mars. After completing his frame, he stomped around a bit as smoke blew from his ears. I explained to him that his shot had been coming in light for the last several frames, but he had been getting lucky breaks and either striking or leaving only a 10-pin. This time, his luck simply ran out and he paid the ultimate price. He argued a bit, insisting that the shot was perfect and in the pocket, but finally declared "I think it just came in with too much angle." Well, now we're getting somewhere! We've gone from nothing being wrong with the shot to at least *something* being wrong. Let's examine that something.

TOO MUCH ANGLE

The idea of too much angle or the wrong angle is a common one. We hear it quite frequently both in league and from the color commentators on bowling telecasts, often applied to 8-pins and so-called "ringing" 10-pins. The fallaciousness of this statement is fairly easy to demonstrate. The bowler described in the preceding paragraph rolls a relatively straight ball that hooks a few boards to the left as it nears the pins, a fairly typical "stroker" type of line. His ball typically enters the pin deck at about a 2 or 2-1/2 degree angle, perhaps 3 degrees when the lanes dry out. Suppose he happened to get an unusually big handful of the ball on this particular shot that left the 8-10 split, and managed to hook the ball into the pins at a 4 degree angle. If this extra angle were the cause of the 8-10 split, or the ringing 10-pin, or whatever other leave we might be addressing, why then does his teammate with a more powerful release—who *always* hits the pins at a 4 degree angle—not leave corner pins and splits on every one of his shots? If 4 degrees of entry angle causes splits or corner pins for one bowler, how could it not cause the same for all bowlers? If our 4 degree bowler likewise over-revs or over rotates his ball, entering the pins at 5 degrees and leaving a corner pin because of "too much angle," how then do power players such as Jason Belmonte or Tommy Jones, whose shots quite often enter the pins at large angles, ever strike? In fact, the USBC pocket study which we referenced in the previous chapter efficiently destroys the concept of "too much angle" by showing us conclusively that as angle to the pocket increases up to their stated ideal of 6 degrees, our strike percentage increases right along with it.

What if I am hooking the ball into the pins at greater than a 6 degree entry angle? Could that cause me to leave 8-pins or corner pins? The simple fact is, you almost certainly are not hooking at greater than a 6 degree angle. While 6 degrees doesn't sound like much, it is in fact huge. Very few bowlers release with a high enough rev rate-to-speed ratio to achieve even 6 degrees of entry angle, and even when they do possess enough power, the oil pattern most often precludes it. In order to hit the pocket at a 6 degree angle, and if we throw the ball way out to the 2-board with enough revs to bring it all the way back to the pocket from out there, basic trigonometry tells us that the ball would have to reach our breakpoint at about 47 feet down lane. If you tried to move inside and tighten up your line to the pocket, perhaps playing the 5-board or the 8-board at the breakpoint, your ball would have to travel even farther down lane before it hooked in order to achieve a 6 degree entry angle. The question now is, can a bowler get the ball that far down the lane before it hooks?

The common perception among bowlers is that the ball skids while in the oil, then completes the meaningful portion of its hook movement once it hits the dry portion of the lane somewhere past the end of the pattern. According to this model, the distance past the end of the pattern to your *breakpoint* where this major hooking occurs is called the push distance, or just push. The amount of push past the end of the oil pattern is thought to be a function of your rev rate, ball speed, axis tilt, and axis rotation, as well as the surface and coverstock of your ball.

In general terms, the stronger your release or the stronger your ball, the less your ball should push past the end of the pattern before digging in and hooking. Conversely, the higher your ball speed or the weaker your release or your ball, the longer your ball will push past the end of the oil pattern. According to what we have read on this hypothesis, average push past the oil pattern is thought to be in the range of three to seven feet.

If we subtract our push distance, say five feet, from the 47 foot breakpoint on the 2-board required to achieve a 6 degree entry angle, we find that the oil pattern would have to be about 42 feet long. Any shorter, and our ball would hook too soon to achieve the mathematically required 47 foot length. In reality, few bowlers would try to play the 2-board on a 42 foot shot. Suppose we moved a bit inside for a more reasonable line, say to a breakpoint on the 10-board rather than the 2-board. In this case trigonometry tells us that our ball would have to reach a point roughly 54 feet down lane before hooking in order to achieve a 6 degree entry angle. With five feet of push past the end of our 42 foot pattern, though, our ball would instead hook at only 47 feet down lane, which is seven feet too soon to achieve a 6 degree entry angle. If we wanted our breakpoint on the 10-board, the oil pattern would have to be a staggering 49 feet long or our ball would never get far enough down lane to hit the pocket at 6 degrees.

If we apply this hypothesis to a more real-world case of a 38 foot house shot and a breakpoint on the 7-board, and again assuming a bowler with five feet of push, our ball will hook at around 43 feet, giving us a maximum possible entry angle to the pocket of just over 3 degrees. If the bowler instead throws his or her ball out to the 5-board, the maximum angle to the pocket becomes a bit over 3-1/2 degrees. If our bowler is brave enough to throw the ball way out to the 2-board, and if he or she has enough revs to bring the ball all the way back to the pocket from way out there, it will enter the pocket at only just over 4-1/2 degrees. Figure 11.1, below, depicts the line your ball would have to take to the pocket to achieve a 0, 2, 4, or 6 degree entry angle. The photo shows us that for any given angle, as we move our breakpoint left to keep our line closer to the pocket, our ball will have to travel farther and farther down lane before hooking, a feat which the length of the oil pattern will not allow.

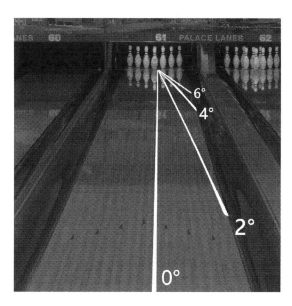

Figure 11.1: Entry angle to the pocket, 0, 2, 4, and 6 degrees, view from the foul line

Our discussion thus far demonstrates that under the "skid in the oil and hook on the dry" hypothesis, the oil pattern will almost never be long enough to achieve a high degree of entry angle. This is theory, however, and the reality is even worse. The mental picture created by this idea is that oil is applied to the lane out to some distance—this distance being the pattern length—and then the oil stops, leaving the rest of the lane dry. For example, Kegel's Dead Man's Curve sport oil pattern is listed as a 43 foot pattern. While there is indeed oil on the lane out to a distance of 43 feet, the actual picture is not quite so simple. A modern lane machine works by transferring measured amounts of oil onto a spinning brush while the brush is in contact with the lane. This brush "paints" the oil onto the lane. But if we look closely at the actual program used to create the Dead Man's Curve pattern, we would find that there is no oil being sprayed beyond 32 feet.[51] If no oil is sprayed beyond the 32 foot mark, how does the oil cover the rest of the distance out to 43 feet?

Though no oil is sprayed onto the brush past the 32 foot mark, the brush nonetheless remains in contact with the lane for the next 11 feet, spreading out the residual oil which was still on the bristles.[52] Suppose you wanted to paint a line down the center of your driveway. You dip the brush into the paint, touch it to the pavement, and start walking.

While the brush is saturated with paint the line will be heavy and solid. As you keep walking, however, the paint in the brush is used up, the brush dries out, and your line gets thinner and patchier until at some point the paint line tapers off to nothing. The same thing happens in the lane machine. The brush is nice and saturated for the first 32 feet, after which no more oil is applied. It then just spreads its residual oil thinner and thinner over the next 11 feet. This section of thinner and thinner oil is called the buff area, so named because this area contains only residual oil buffed onto the lane by the brush.

So while the idea that there is oil on the lane for 43 feet is true, the idea that our ball skids while there is oil and then hooks on the dry part of the lane is for the most part false. In truth, our ball will skid when it does not have enough friction between its coverstock and the lane surface, and it will begin to hook as soon as there is enough friction to allow it to grab even a little bit. A modern bowling ball does not need a completely dry lane in order to change direction.

Suppose your car is on a patch of curving road that has ice on the first part, then a section of snow, followed by a section that is simply wet from snow melt. When we turn the steering wheel on the icy part of the road we get no traction, and our car continues going straight despite the turned wheel. As the ice tapers off to snow our wheels begin to get a bit of traction, and the car slowly begins to turn. As the snow tapers off to water our wheels can get enough traction to turn the car more sharply. The same thing happens with our bowling ball. While in the heavy oil at the beginning of the pattern it cannot get any traction. The ball goes straight during this skid phase despite the fact that it is spinning toward the left. As it reaches the buff area where the oil gets thinner and thinner, the ball starts to hook. It reaches the point of maximum hook—the breakpoint—as soon as it has enough friction to sufficiently grab the lane. Soon after leaving the oil pattern and hitting dry lane surface the ball will complete its hook and enter into its roll phase. So rather than the push distance being the point after the end of the pattern where the ball makes the *major portion* of its change in direction, it is instead only the point at which it *completes* its change in direction. In most cases our ball will begin to hook while well within the oil pattern and can even reach its breakpoint before the end of the pattern if the oil is thin enough and the ball's coverstock is strong enough.

For a demonstration of this we can look to the USBC's 2005 Ball Motion Study.[53] For this study the USBC laid out an oil pattern which placed 30 units of oil onto the lane for the first eight feet and then buffed it out over the next 39 feet. This resulted in oil tapering off from 30 units at eight feet, to eight units at 32 feet, and down to only 5 units at 47 feet where the pattern ended. We do not need to understand precisely what this means in terms of actual oil volume; just know that the pattern had heavy oil for the first eight feet, tapering to medium oil in the middle part of the lane, and down to light oil out to the end of the 47 foot pattern.

Using the CATS system, investigators measured where the ball was changing direction. Despite the pattern being 47 feet long, the test shots—all thrown by a robot—began hooking at around the 20 to 25 foot mark. The shots reached their breakpoint, the major part of their hook, at an average distance of only around 35 feet. These shots all began to hook as soon as the oil tapered off enough to get some traction, and reached their breakpoint a dozen feet *before* the end of the oil pattern. Despite the 47 foot pattern length which should have been long enough to achieve a rather high degree of entry angle, the much shorter 35 foot breakpoint limits entry angle to only 2 or 3 degrees. This example isn't entirely representative, because the oil pattern used by the USBC had an unusually long buff area and had the heavier oil ending earlier than it would on a more typical shot. The point remains, though. While our ball will likely not hook quite as early as did the ball in the USBC example, it will still begin to hook, and possibly even reach its breakpoint, before the end of the oil pattern.

The preceding discussion assumed for the sake of simplicity that the breakpoint is just that—a point—and that the ball makes an instantaneous change of direction at that point. While this is a useful approximation, in reality the ball's hook takes on a somewhat hyperbolic path— starting its move gradually, increasingly tightening its turning radius as it approaches its vertex at the breakpoint, and then gradually straightening out again. Think of the ball's path as being straight from the foul line, then turning a little, then turning a lot, then straightening out a little, and finally going straight again as it exits the hook phase and starts rolling toward the pins. The fact that the ball's actual hook has a varying radius and occurs over the span of several feet means that it may not need to attain quite the distance we calculated in our discussion in order to "sneak into" any given degree of entry angle. Regardless, the distance required for a high angle of entry is still generally more than will be allowed by most oil patterns. In actual practice the folks on your league who are throwing the big hooks are likely only in the 4 degree entry angle range. The strokers playing near the track are likely in the 2 to 3 degree range, and the most a bowler throwing a straight ball can ever achieve is a paltry 1-3/4 degrees unless he or she lofts the ball over the gutter. The reality on the lanes is that even if "too much angle" could somehow be a liability, obtaining an excessively high entry angle is simply not a meaningful possibility.

A TRICK OF THE EYE

If too much entry angle isn't possible, why does it look like our ball is making a sharp and violent left turn far in excess of 6 degrees? If we could view the lane from above, we would see that the ball's motion, even when thrown in a big sweeping hook by a very high rev player, is actually a fairly gentle arc. The hook only looks sharp from our vantage point at the foul line due to an optical illusion called *foreshortening*.

Foreshortening is the illusion where objects closer to us appear larger than those farther away. Most of us learned about foreshortening in grade school art class, where the concept was called "perspective." We're sure you've seen drawings of a road or of railroad tracks where the road gets narrower and narrower as it stretches away from us, eventually diminishing to a point as it approaches the horizon. Perhaps you have observed a similar scene outdoors or when traveling on a highway. In such a situation, what happens to fence posts, mail boxes, guard rail posts, or utility poles that line the sides of the road? Though they are more or less equally spaced apart, as we look out into the distance they will not only appear shorter and shorter, but will also appear closer and closer together.

This same trick of the eye happens when we observe our ball path on the lane. Look again at Figure 11.1, the photo depicting entry angle lines. Just as in our perspective drawing example, the lane appears to narrow as it recedes into the distance. Now look closely at the apparent width of the lane at the pins, and at the 6 degree entry angle line. Though the 6 degree line touches the edge of the gutter at a point over 14 feet away from the pins, that 14 foot distance appears in the photo to be far shorter than the lane is wide. Since the lane is less than 3-1/2 feet wide, that entire 14 foot plus distance appears to be compressed down to less than two feet.

Even when thrown all the way out to the 2-board with a very large six degree hook, our ball only hooks back to the pocket about 16 inches, and this modest leftward movement occurs over a distance of almost 13 feet.[54] When this 13 feet of length at the end of the 60 foot lane is viewed from the foul line, the entire 13 feet appears compressed into just a foot-and-a-half. While 16 inches of hook over 13 feet is a gentle arc, that same 16 inches of hook over what looks like only a foot-and-a-half of distance will appear as a very sharp and violent move. This illusion of sharpness is the effect of foreshortening.

Look once more at how sharp the six degree hook line appears in Figure 11.1, which is a foreshortened view identical to what we would see from the foul line. As measured from the edge of the gutter, the 6 degree line appears to enter the pocket at close to a 40 degree angle. If measured from a line straight up the center of the lane our 6 degree line appears to enter the pocket at nearly a 60 degree angle. Compare this image with Figure 11.2 below, which is a scale drawing of that same 6 degree hook as viewed from above. Not so impressive anymore, is it? That "hockey stick," skid-flip hook you thought you saw is really nothing more than a gentle curve made to look sharp by a trick of the eye.

Figure 11.2: Bird's eye view of a 6 degree hook, drawn to scale

TOO LITTLE ANGLE

So if too much angle is not a possibility, what about too little angle? Could this be the culprit causing our back row splits and corner pins? Suppose our bowler had released his ball poorly on the shot that left his 8-10 split, managing only a 1-3/4 degree entry angle instead of his usual 2-1/2 degrees? The same logic that dismissed the idea of too much angle also casts doubt on the idea of too little angle. If 1-3/4 degrees of entry angle is the cause of the leave, how then could a bowler who throws a straight ball, who *always* enters the pins at 1-3/4 degrees, ever strike?

Not so many decades ago the PBA was dominated by bowlers who threw straight balls at low entry angles, and who still averaged in excess of 200 all while bowling with primitive equipment on lanes that were oiled with a bug sprayer and a dust mop. While the USBC pocket study does reveal a much narrower lucky strike zone for bowlers throwing a straighter line, their strike percentage is nonetheless almost exactly as high as that of the big-hook bowlers when they do hit the pocket.

It is certainly true that too little angle of entry can cause problems with carry. A straight shot has a very real chance of leaving pins standing following a decent hit, but the problem is not the result of low entry angle per se. Pins left by a straighter ball are a deflection problem, not one of geometry. In any case, shots that deflect too much typically leave the 5-pin or occasionally the 5-8 rather than the type of back row leaves we are discussing in this article.

Just as too much or too little angle can't really be blamed for back row pin leaves on decent shots, the same logic applies to arguments blaming too much or too little speed. Without belaboring the point, if too much or too little speed on a given shot caused back row pin leaves, then bowlers who *normally* bowl at those higher or lower speeds would never be able to strike. Since bowlers roll the ball and manage to strike consistently at a wide range of speeds, we must likewise dismiss speed arguments from consideration.

OK, IF IT WASN'T SPEED OR ANGLE, MAYBE IT WAS...

Beside too much or too little angle and too much or too little speed, the other common explanation for pins left standing is that there was something wrong with your hook. We hear statements such as "your ball was still hooking when it hit the pins," or that "it hooked right past the 9-pin," or that it "hit flat," or that the ball had "rolled out" and had stopped hooking. Let's examine these ideas.

STILL HOOKING?

There is a common misconception surrounding our mental picture of an object such as a bowling ball moving along a curved path. We tend to think that if the path is curved then the object wants to keep traveling along this curved path, that it has some sort of hooking or curving force guiding it. This is where the idea that the ball can somehow "hook past the 9-pin"—even after colliding with other pins—comes from. Following this mental picture of an imagined hooking force to its extreme would mean that if a high rev bowler threw a shot in the middle of a huge, flat floor with no obstacles rather than on a long, narrow bowling lane, the ball would continue to roll along a curved path and would eventually complete a big circle or spiral. This is obvious nonsense, as we know that at some point the ball would stop curving and would just roll straight in some direction. In fact, Newton's First Law tells us that all motion occurs in a straight line unless something acts on the object in question to cause its path to deviate from a straight line. Curved motion simply does not exist unless something acts on our object to force it to make constant course changes.

Suppose you tied a rock to a length of string, and swung it in a circle over your head. What happens when you let go of the string? Does the rock continue to move in a circle? No. As soon as you let go of the string the rock flies away from you in a perfectly straight line. The rock did not "want to" travel in a circle as you swung it over your head. It wanted to travel in a straight line all along, just as Newton's law demands, but your string prevented it from doing so. As the string constantly pulled the rock back in toward you, it forced the rock onto a curved path. Your string had constrained and altered the rock's motion, but as soon as you let go of the string the constraint is removed, Newton's law takes over, and the rock continues on in a straight line. The direction the rock travels on this straight line path, which is hopefully not toward your neighbor's window, will be along a tangent to the curve. The final direction is solely a function of where along the curve you removed the constraint by letting go of the string. In fact, physics doesn't even really recognize curved motion per se. It instead sees the curved path as being made up of an infinite number of straight paths, each in turn pulled in toward the center by the constraining string (Figure 11.3).

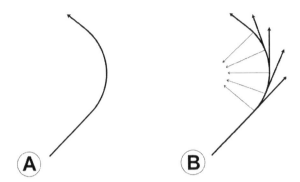

Figure 11.3: Curved path (A) made up of infinite number of straight paths (B)

Just as the rock did not possess any sort of curving motion even though it was moving along a curved path while tied to the string, your bowling ball does not possess any sort of curving motion. We know that the thing that forced the rock away from a straight path and into a curve was the piece of string pulling it constantly inward, but what causes a bowling ball to curve and hook? What pulls it off of a straight path?

As we discussed far more fully in Chapter 8, our bowling ball initially travels along a straight path when we release it. This is the portion of the ball's motion that the USBC calls the skid phase. During the skid phase, though the direction of travel is in a straight line down lane, the ball is spinning at an angle away from this path and pointed toward the left (right-handed bowler). As the ball reaches a point in the oil pattern where the oil has thinned out sufficiently to allow for some friction, this leftward spinning can start to grab the lane and pull the ball to the left. The ball's straight, down lane travel is just like what the rock wants to do, and the leftward pull of friction is like the string pulling the rock inward.

So now the leftward-angled spinning of the ball is pulling the ball's path toward the left. This is the portion of the ball's path that we call the *hook phase*. Does the ball keep turning left forever? No. Eventually the ball's path will be pulled so far leftward that it is now traveling in the same direction that the spinning ball is pointing. Once this happens, there is no more disparity between the ball's direction of travel and its direction of spin. Since the ball is now traveling in the same direction as it is spinning, there is no more leftward pull. Since there is no more leftward pull, the ball simply continues on in a straight line in its new leftward direction just as the rock did when you let go of the string.

This new, straight path is what we call the *roll phase* of the ball's motion. Just as the direction of the rock's new straight path was determined by where you released the string, the direction of the ball's new straight rolling path is determined by where the angle of the ball's spin could no longer pull the ball to the left. From the point where we release the ball onto the lane until the point where it hits the pins, the ball travels straight, then along a curve, then straight again as it skids, hooks, then rolls. This is of course a simplification of hook from our more complete discussion in Chapter 8, but the point holds. The ball does not possess any sort of curving force. It travels straight until acted on by a sideways force, it curves as the sideways force takes hold, and then it continues on along its new straight path when the sideways force inevitably ceases to act.

This description of skid, hook, and roll should change your perception of what is happening during the ball's curving path on the lane. We tend to think that our ball hooked from wherever our breakpoint was all the way left to the pocket. In fact, the ball hooked for only a very small portion of its time on the lane. The hook phase does indeed pull the ball to the left, but only briefly, and only over the span of a few boards. What the hook phase really does is to point the ball away from its down lane path and turn it leftward, toward the pocket. From this point on the ball simply rolls straight on its new leftward path, covering all of the remaining boards to the pocket.

Think of turning a corner in your car. You are traveling north on Main Street, but your destination is two blocks west of you on First Street. While on Main Street, your car is traveling in a straight line. This is equivalent to the skid phase of ball motion. As you approach First Street you turn the steering wheel to the left, gradually at first as your car approaches the intersection, more tightly as you round the corner, and then gradually straightening it out again as you exit the turn. This is the hook phase. Now your car is facing west rather than north, so you again drive in a straight line west until you reach your destination two blocks away. This new westward straight line travel is the roll phase. You would never say that your car turned left for two blocks to your destination. It turned only in the intersection, and after it was done turning it traveled straight to your destination on its new westward path. Similarly, it makes no sense to say that your ball hooked all the way to the pocket. Just as with your car, the ball hooked only out near the breakpoint, and then simply rolled straight again on its new angled path to its destination at the pocket.

BUT WHAT IF THE BALL WAS STILL HOOKING?

Since the ball possesses no "curving" motion, and since it completes its hook rather quickly and at some distance away from the pocket, the idea that the ball could still be hooking when it reaches the pocket or that it could hook past the 9-pin is rather far-fetched. Any supposed curving motion the ball had is long since gone, and the ball is almost certainly rolling in a straight line at an angle to the lane long before it impacts the pins. But what if it *was* still hooking? What if we threw a tight line very close to the pocket and on an oil pattern that was so long that the ball would still be in its hook phase when it struck the pins? Even in this unlikely situation the ball's hook would still have no effect, and the ball could not hook past the 9-pin.

As we learned in the chapter on deflection, when our bowling ball hits the headpin, the pin will fly away from the collision along a path defined by a straight line drawn from the center of the ball through the center of the pin. The ball will deflect away from the pin in a straight line on an angle away from the pin, and this deflection angle is dependent only on where upon the pin's surface the ball hit, the relative weight differential between the pin and the ball, and on the direction the ball was traveling *at the instant it hit the pin.* It does not matter what the ball had been doing before the collision, nor what path it might have followed if no collision had taken place.

We said that physics looks at a curved path as an infinite series of straight paths. Thus, even if our ball were traveling a curved path when it hit the headpin, physics sees the ball's direction of travel as a straight line tangent to that curve at the point where the ball struck the pin (Figure 11.4). Since the curved path of a hooking ball collapses into a straight line at the point of impact, even if the ball had possessed some imagined curving force, that force would disappear the instant the ball hit the pin and the ball would have no choice but to deflect away on a new straight path. No matter how we look at this, the idea of a bowling ball continuing to hook after it strikes the headpin is simply not in accord with reality. Your ball did not hook past the 9-pin.

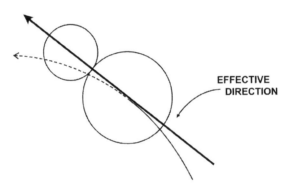

Figure 11.4: Effective direction of a curving ball

THE BALL HIT FLAT?

When a shot hits the pocket area but leaves pins standing, we often hear bowlers say that the ball "hit flat." Everyone will nod knowingly and the person who threw the shot will pretend he or she knows what that meant and what to do about it. So what does it mean when someone says your ball hit flat? According to all of our research, it doesn't mean anything.

The phrase "hit flat" seems to be merely a throw-away term with no definition whatsoever. Doctors sometimes use the term *idiopathic* when describing a condition. Suppose you wake up one morning, having done nothing out of the ordinary for several days, and see a lizard-man staring back at you from the mirror. After a thorough exam the doctor tells you that you are suffering from idiopathic dermatitis. What does that mean? It means only that the doctor knows you have a rash, but has no idea whatsoever what caused it. If the doctor had simply stated' "I have no idea why you have that rash," you would go away thinking, "then what did I just pay you all that money for?" By using the official-sounding "idiopathic" in place of "I don't know," you walk away thinking you've gotten your money's worth. The doctor can certainly give you some cream for the rash to make you feel better, but since the cause of the condition is unknown, how can he possibly tell you how to prevent it in the future?

Likewise, what the bowling commentator is really saying when he tells you that your shot "hit flat" is, *I thought it was a pretty good shot too, and I have no idea why it didn't strike.* Since the commentator has no idea why the shot didn't strike, how good can any advice be as to how to cure it? When a seemingly good shot fails to strike, there is always a reason. If you can find that reason, you can prevent it from happening again on the next shot. "Idiopathic," "hit flat," and "I don't know" are all synonymous terms. We guarantee you that "I don't know" was *not* the cause of your poor carry.

Sometimes we will hear that the ball lost too much energy which caused it to hit flat. Is that possible? While hitting flat isn't a real thing and so cannot be the cause of anything, losing energy is something real. Can losing too much energy cause our poor carry? Let's examine that idea.

Recall from our earlier chapters that the energy the ball hits the pins with, the energy that knocks the pins down, is kinetic energy. Kinetic energy is energy due to an object's motion. Recall also that kinetic energy is defined as one-half of the object's mass, multiplied by the square of the object's velocity ($1/2$ MV^2). There is no energy "stored" in the ball's core or anywhere else. Kinetic energy is just mass and velocity. Mass is just the ball's weight, which does not change as the ball rolls down the lane. Since mass cannot change, the only other factor that can possibly affect the ball's kinetic energy is velocity, which for our purposes is ball speed.

If the ball travels faster, it will possess more kinetic energy. Likewise, if it travels more slowly it will possess less kinetic energy. Therefore when we say that the ball "lost too much energy," the only thing we can possibly be saying is that it slowed down too much, and we've already spent several pages discussing why changes in ball speed, within reason, pretty much cannot be the cause of decreased carry. If you threw the ball at three miles per hour rather than your usual 15, then loss of energy may certainly have contributed to carry issues. If it only slowed down from 15 miles per hour to 14, you'd best look elsewhere for your explanation.

ROLL OUT

So we're left with one more hook-related explanation for our poor carry on what we thought was a pretty good shot: "Your ball rolled out." What does *roll out* mean? Recall our discussion of skid, hook, and roll. The *skid* phase is the ball's original path when we release it, which is most often not on a line directly toward the pocket. *Hook* is what turns our ball away from its original path and points it toward the pocket, and the ball then *rolls* along this new straight path until it hits the pins.

Suppose you are throwing a given bowling ball straight up the 7-board to a breakpoint at roughly 42 feet down lane, and that the ball hooks and then rolls on a 3 degree angle to hit the pocket for a strike. Things are going great and you are throwing strike after strike, but then the next shot, which you threw exactly the same way, leaves a 10-pin. It looked like a good pocket hit, so you stay put on the lane and keep throwing the same shot. Then you get another 10-pin, and another, then a 5-pin, then a 7-pin, then a 5-7 split, but this whole time your ball is reaching the 1-3 "pocket." Your helpful teammate tells you that your ball is rolling out. It's starting to hook just fine, but then seems to quit hooking too early and rolls in too straight. He said your ball "died" on the lane, or was "dead on arrival" when it hit the pocket.

So what is roll out? Recall from our discussion in Chapter 8 that it is friction between the ball and the lane which allows the ball to hook toward the left, and the more friction there is, the faster this hook phase is completed and the sooner the ball begins to simply roll on its new angled path. Let's look again at our driving example. We are driving north on Main Street. When we reach the intersection we turn the steering wheel to the left, and the angled wheels begin pulling our car to the left. We hold the wheels in this position for, say, five seconds as we round the corner, and then straighten them back out and begin to travel west on First Street. Now imagine what would happen if, as we were rounding the corner, the steering wheel slipped from our hands only three seconds into the turn and the car's front tires straightened out two seconds too early. Since we did not steer the car to the left for enough time to make the corner, the car will start to travel straight too soon. Because of the abbreviated turning time, our car was not pointed completely west when it starts to travel straight, and we drive up the curb on the northwest corner.

Roll out is a very similar phenomenon. In truth, most every shot we throw will roll out, in that the ball will complete its hook phase and then simply roll on an angle toward the pocket. When a bowler uses the term "roll out," however, he or she is not discussing roll out in this literal sense. Instead, he or she means that the ball completed its hook more quickly than it had been on that particular line, and so did not turn enough toward the left. They don't mean just that the ball rolled out, but rather that it rolled out too soon. The ball "died" in that it started to hook, but for some reason quit turning too soon. Just as our car failed to make the corner when we let go of the wheel too soon, our bowling ball fails to make a sharp enough turn when it rolls out too soon.

Roll out is caused by friction. If a given shot was reaching the pocket just fine but then after a few more frames it begins to roll out, then something happened to change the friction characteristics between the ball and the lane on the line you are throwing. We will discuss roll out more completely in later chapters, but for now we are only concerned with whether or not it can cause bad carry.

If our ball begins to roll out, then it is hitting increased friction. We know that the only real deleterious effect of friction is that it slows our ball down, and that a slower ball speed results in decreased kinetic energy. We have also learned, however, that as long as our ball hits the pocket, the slightly slower speed resulting from excess friction is not likely to cause enough of a drop in kinetic energy to affect our pin carry.

With friction pretty much eliminated as a cause of our bad carry, we are left with the only other possible aspect of roll out; the ball path did not turn far enough to the left. We have already determined that less hook in and of itself cannot affect pin carry. All it would do is decrease our entry angle, and we have already demonstrated that decreased entry angle does not cause back row pins to remain standing. It does, however, point us in the right direction on our quest to determine the cause of pins left standing on what we thought was a good hit.

When we discussed entry angle to the pocket, we determined that entry angle does not affect pin carry *so long as we are hitting the pocket.* That is, as long as the ball hits the true pocket—which is the area between boards 17 and 18—decreased entry angle will not be a significant cause of poor carry. In the case of roll out, since we have kept our breakpoint constant—in this case the 7-board at 42 feet down lane—a decrease in entry angle means that the ball is not pointed far enough to the left after hooking to reach the true pocket. Since the angle is decreased, our ball will hit the pins lighter and lighter— farther and farther to the right of the pocket (Figure 11.5).

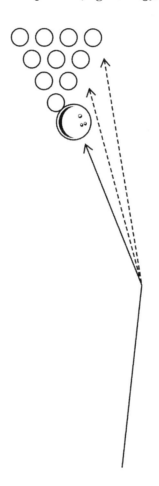

Figure 11.5: Ball finish position as entry angle decreases

With our breakpoint held constant, a decrease of just half of a degree in entry angle would cause the ball to hit the pins on board 16 rather than on board 17-1/2, or a board-and-a-half right of the true pocket. A further half degree decrease would cause the ball to impact the pins on the 14-board, or three-and-one-half boards right of the pocket. Though the ball will still hit in the 1-3 zone as entry angle decreases and will still look like a decent pocket hit, we now understand that this area is *not* the true pocket, and unless we get very lucky, will result in pins left standing.

So if entry angle decreases due to roll out but our breakpoint remains at the same 42 foot distance down lane, our ball will hit the pins too far to the right. It is possible, though, that the same increase in friction that caused the roll out will also cause our ball to hook a little earlier. Will this earlier hook make up for less angle and still get us to the pocket?

Let's suppose that in addition to hooking at only 2-1/2 degrees instead of 3 degrees, the ball also read the lane a foot earlier and hooked at 41 feet down lane rather than 42 feet. Doing the math, we find that in this case the ball will impact the headpin a fraction of an inch farther left, but still on board 16, which again is one-and-one-half boards right of the true pocket. If our entry angle further decreases to 2 degrees while the ball hooks another foot earlier, it will hit the pins on the 15-board, which is two-and-one-half boards too light. In fact, if roll out causes our ball to lose just half of a degree of entry angle, it would have to hook three feet earlier in order to still hit the pocket. Is this possible? In truth we do not know, but since your shot is leaving pins standing, the odds are exceptionally high that it is not. If your ball were still striking when it rolled out we would not be having this discussion!

Where does this analysis leave us? While roll out is real and can indeed cause a decrease in entry angle, the entry angle itself is not the cause of our poor carry. Instead, it is the light hit that results from the decreased entry angle that causes pins to remain standing, as we discussed more fully in the previous chapter. And it is not merely roll out that is the culprit here. *Any* shot that hits to the right or left of the true pocket has a good chance of leaving pins standing, with the odds for the most part increasing the farther away from the pocket you get. This statement is the key to the entire problem, the key to helping us ignore all of the false flags and will-o'-the-wisp solutions. If we reverse this key statement we arrive at what we call the BowlSmart Law:

"If you left pins standing on what you thought was a good shot, your ball did NOT hit the pocket!"

Even if you get nothing else from this entire book, engrave this law upon your brain. *If you left pins standing, you did NOT hit the pocket.* Stop being stubborn, stop trying to come up with reasons why you were "robbed," and by all means stop doing the same thing over and over while hoping for a different result. While a single shot does not define a trend and may just be an aberration, if you are consistently leaving pins standing, you are not hitting the pocket. In the next chapter we will examine what you left standing, and try to determine why you left it. If you don't know the true cause of pins left standing, how can you possibly come up with a real, meaningful way to fix the problem?

CHAPTER 12

SO WHY DID I LEAVE THAT?!?

We closed Chapter 11 with the BowlSmart Law: *If you left pins standing, you did NOT hit the pocket.* There are of course exceptions to every rule, but other than a few relatively rare cases which we will discuss, if your shot left pins standing you almost certainly did not hit the pocket.

In Chapter 10 we showed you what to look for as your ball hits the pins, and how to identify by sight whether your shot hit the pocket, or was too light or too heavy. As helpful as these photos and descriptions are, we need to consider just how quickly everything happens on the lane and how little time we have to make a good observation. Compounding the problem, bowlers tend to shift their attention away from the ball and onto the pins to watch their explosive strike if they think they've thrown a good shot. Both of these factors mean that very often we will not see clearly or in enough detail exactly where the ball hit in relation to the pocket. In fact, some bowlers we have worked with cannot even tell us where their ball crossed the arrows, let alone precisely where it impacted the headpin. It is hard to focus on so many things at once, especially considering how quickly they all happen.

Ideally, all bowlers would carefully and accurately observe precisely where their ball hit the headpin. Knowing that this isn't going to happen on every shot, we can instead use statistics and video to figure out where you likely hit based on which pins you left standing. To make these determinations, we analyzed video of several hundred fairly good pocket area shots, watching the result of each hit on a frame-by-frame basis to determine exactly where the ball and the pins were going and how they left what they left. For any given leave, there was an amazing amount of commonality among the videos. The same chain of events, with only minor variation, occurred over and over. We used this information combined with the statistical data revealed in the USBC's 2014 "I left what where" study of 1400 pocket shots to help us understand why our shot left what it left. We will reference this study throughout this section when quoting probabilities.[55]

In this chapter we will look at common leaves, describe the chain of events that cause them to remain standing, and tell you where your ball likely hit when you left it. If you know where you actually hit versus where you need to hit, you will be in a position to employ the tools we will discuss in later chapters to alter where your ball is impacting the pins, and return to striking.

JAMES FREEMAN and RON HATFIELD

THE 10-PIN

Perhaps the most common and frustrating leave on what we thought was a good shot is the 10-pin, or the 7-pin for the lefties. Based on the reaction we see from a great many bowlers, we should probably have called it the "@#$%! 10-pin"! Bowlers generally recognize two types of 10-pins. The "ringing" or "wrap 10" is characterized by the 6-pin flying rapidly and forcefully in front of the 10-pin, often bouncing off of the right kickback and wrapping or ringing around the 10-pin, which remains defiantly standing. The "flat 10" is similar, but in this case the 6-pin tumbles lazily into the gutter in front of the 10-pin, often just laying there until cleared by the sweep.

There is a common perception among bowlers that there is a material difference between the causes of a flat and a ringing 10-pin, and that a ringing 10-pin results from a better shot than does a flat 10-. We surveyed 135 bowlers who ranked their knowledge level as intermediate, high, or expert. The majority of bowlers, 56 percent, believe that a ringing 10-pin results from a bad break on a good pocket shot, while only 31 percent believe that a flat 10- results from a good shot. The most common reason given for leaving a ringing 10-pin was "bad entry angle," while the most common reason mentioned for a flat 10-pin was a weak shot or a "flat hit."

Of course we now understand that neither entry angle nor a weaker shot can cause pins to remain standing on a pocket shot. The truth is that there is very little difference between a ringing and a flat 10-pin, and both are caused by the same thing; a light hit that missed the true pocket to the right. In Chapter 10 we discussed where the pocket actually is, and the likely result if we stray from that true pocket. The aforementioned USBC study tells us that while it is possible to leave a 10-pin on a good pocket hit, the odds of doing so are quite low. In the rare instances when it does happen, it is likely the result of one or more off-spot pins, a bad bounce somewhere within the collision system, or some other unquantifiable chance occurrence.

Figure 12.1 depicts the probability of leaving a 10-pin based on the board upon which our ball enters the pins. The chart shows us that if you left a 10-pin, the likelihood is that your ball came in on boards 15-1/2 through 16-1/2, meaning that you missed the pocket to the right by a board or two. Unless you are very certain that your ball hit in the true pocket and you just got a bad break, if you leave a 10-pin—any kind of 10-pin—it is best to assume that you came in too light and that you need to adjust accordingly.

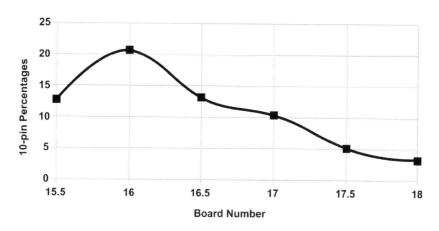

Figure 12.1: Odds of leaving a 10-pin, by board number

So why would a light hit cause the 10-pin to remain standing? Let's walk through the chain of events resulting from such a hit and try to determine what is happening. Figure 12.2-a, below, depicts the ball entering the pins on board 16. Look at the position of the ball relative to the pins. The ball hits the headpin way over on the right side, causing it to deflect away sharply to the left and across the front of the 2-pin, driving the 2-pin straight back into the 8- (Figure 12.2-b). The headpin continues left to sweep out the 4-pin, which then hits the 7-pin, thus clearing out the left side of the rack (Figure 12.2-c). Return now to Figure 12.2-a, and notice the position of the ball relative to the 3-pin. Recall from our discussion of the so-called textbook strike that the ball is supposed to drive the 3-pin into the 6-, which in turn is supposed to take out the 10-pin. In this board 16 shot the ball is clearly too far in front of the 3-pin to drive it to the right and into the 6-, and will instead drive it almost straight back, barely clipping the edge of the 6-pin (Figure 12.2-b). Since the 6-pin was only lightly clipped it will travel almost straight to the right, in front of the 10-pin, without possessing enough speed to bounce out of the gutter, and will just lay there. The 3-pin, being driven straight back, will hit the 9-pin, while the ball will deflect slightly to the left off of the 3-pin, hopefully catching enough of the 5-pin to knock it over (Figure 12.2-c). The end result of this chain reaction? A "flat" 10-pin.

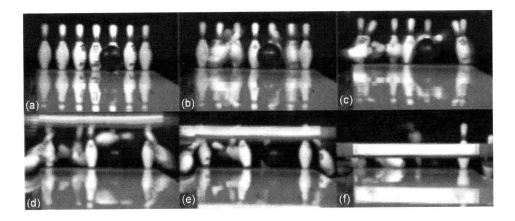

Figure 12.2: Collision system leading to a flat 10-pin

In the above analysis the 6-pin fell lazily into the gutter because it was barely clipped by the 3-pin as it was driven almost straight back by the ball. What would cause the 6-pin to instead fly powerfully to the right with enough velocity to bounce off the side kickback and "ring" around the 10-pin? Rather than the 3-pin just grazing the 6-pin, it needs to instead hit it just a bit more solidly. For this to happen, the ball needs to hit the 3-pin just a bit more to the left than it did for the flat 10-, by only half a board or so.

Figure 12.3, below, depicts a shot hitting the headpin on board 16-1/2, which is just half a board higher than our flat 10-pin shot, and still a board right of the pocket. The action on the left side of the rack is pretty much the same, with the headpin driving the 2-pin back into the 8- and the 4-, after which something in that tangle of pins trips the 7-pin (Figure 12.3-c). On the right, however, things are just a bit different. Rather than being driven straight back, the slightly higher hit causes the 3-pin to instead travel back and to the right, which causes it to impact the 6-pin just a little more solidly than it did on the flat 10-pin shot (Figure 12.3-b). The hit is not high enough to send the 6-pin into the 10-pin, but it does come closer to the 10-, and with much more velocity (Figure 12.3-d).

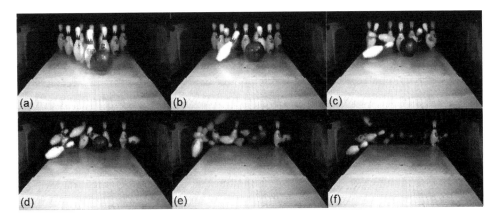

Figure 12.3: Collision system leading to a ringing 10-pin

Despite our common perception, there really isn't a material difference between a ringing and a flat 10-pin. Both are caused by precisely the same thing; a light hit that was right of the pocket. Now if you want to split hairs it would indeed be fair to say that the ringing 10-pin really did result from a better shot than did the flat 10-, that is if you want to claim that missing the pocket by a board is materially better than missing by a board-and-a-half!

Since both kinds of 10-pins are caused by a light hit, both can be cured by precisely the same thing; get your ball to hit just a tad higher. Since all we need to do is get the ball to hit a board or so higher, I think you can see the futility of most of the common prescriptions. How is moving up or back on the approach a few inches going to get your ball to hit higher? How is hitting a board-and-a-half light at 4 degrees better than hitting a board-and-a-half light at 3 degrees? Changing balls or changing lines may well cause your shot to hit a bit higher, but since you are so close to the pocket already why would you want to make such a drastic change and risk the guesswork that it entails? You can certainly try changing a bunch of fiddly details in your release to try to get the ball to come up just a bit higher, but again why introduce unknowns when there is a far simpler solution available to you.

Our advice? If you are absolutely certain that your ball hit the true pocket and that you just got a bad break, then do nothing. Stay put, and keep everything the same. While there is a roughly five percent chance of leaving a 10-pin on a good pocket shot due to various random factors, there is a 95 percent chance you won't do so again on the next shot, so staying put is a valid strategy. If you are not positive that you hit the pocket, assume you came in a board or two light. If everything about your approach and release seemed okay but your ball came in light, then just move your feet half a board or so to the right, keeping the same mark, the same ball, the same everything. Another simple option is to move both your feet and your mark one board to the right. Ockham's Razor tells us that when there is a simple and a complex solution to a given problem, the simple solution is to be preferred. There is nothing simpler or more effective than making a tiny move to the right and keeping everything else the same.[56]

DON'T SHOOT ME. I'M ONLY THE MESSENGER!

We've all seen PBA telecasts where a bowler throws a shot that demolishes the rack but leaves a 10-pin standing, but then another pin bounces off of the left wall and comes screaming across the deck to blast the 10-pin out for a strike. The announcers will invariably gush something along the lines of "That's POWER, folks!", and attribute the messenger to the bowler's incredible rev rate, or huge angle of entry, or other such measures of his or her superhuman abilities. The truth of the matter is far less impressive.

That powerful messenger, or "scout" as it's sometimes called, is usually the headpin. Where does your ball have to impact the headpin in order to bounce it off the left wall and back to the 10-pin spot? A little bit of trigonometry tells us that the headpin has to travel to the left at a roughly 68 degree angle to the lane in order to hit the wall in the right spot to bounce back to the 10-pin. In order for the headpin to travel at this angle, the ball must hit near board 14-1/2. Board 14-1/2 is an extremely light shot, three full boards to the right of the pocket, and carrying an equally low probability of striking.

We occasionally see a messenger cross the deck in front of the 10-pin, not traveling far enough back to hit it. This situation is usually caused by a slightly higher hit, somewhere in the vicinity of board 15-1/2. In this case the headpin, being hit just a bit more solidly, travels back just enough to catch the front of the 2-pin on its way to the left wall. Since it grazes the 2-pin, it deflects forward, causing it to hit the left wall a bit too far forward. Since the headpin bounces off the left wall forward from where it needs to be, its path back across the pin deck after bouncing will also be too far forward, causing it to pass in front of the 10-pin.

In either case, the lesson is the same. If a messenger took out your 10-pin, you threw a very light shot very hard, and it's nothing more complicated than that. Your messenger strike was almost pure luck, and you had best make an adjustment immediately. Luck is simply not a viable strategy no matter how hard you throw the ball.

THE 7-PIN

The 7-pin is another frustrating leave, usually happening on what most bowlers think was a good shot. There is a small possibility of leaving the 7-pin on a slightly high pocket shot, which we will discuss later in this section. Aside from this unlikely occurrence, 7-pins are instead caused by light shots that miss the pocket to the right, and the shots that cause them are usually a bit lighter than those that cause 10-pins.

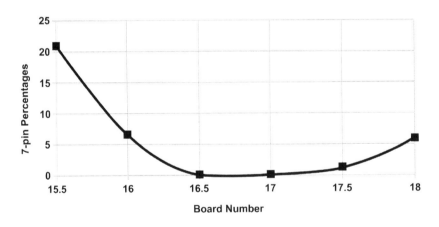

Figure 12.4: Odds of leaving a 7-pin, by board number

As Figure 12.4 illustrates, a hit in the vicinity of board 15-1/2 carries with it a very high probability of leaving a 7-pin, almost a 21 percent chance. A hit just half a board heavier, on board 16, has an almost seven percent chance of leaving a 7-pin. This area is therefore the danger zone for 7-pins. Though a board 15-1/2 or board 16 shot hits the pins in the 1-3 area, it is one-and-one-half or two boards right of the true pocket. Let's look at Figure 12.5, below, and see how a hit on board 15-1/2 causes a 7-pin.

Figure 12.5-a shows us that the ball is hitting way over on the right side of the headpin. This causes the headpin to deflect almost straight to the left, just catching the front of the 2-pin (Figure 12.5-b). The 2-pin travels straight back to take out the 8-pin, while the headpin bounces off of the left kick back and tackles the 4-, with everything completely missing the 7-pin (Figure 12.5-d). That takes care of the left side of the rack. Meanwhile on the right side, the ball, hitting the 3-pin much too squarely, sends it straight back between the 5- and 6-pins without hitting either (Figure 12.5-b), or occasionally with the 3-pin just barely nudging the 6-pin out to the side and into the gutter. The 3-pin hits the 9-pin, then bounces off to the right to knock over the 10-pin. The ball then splits the 5- and 6-pins, dropping each lazily to the sides (Figure 12.5-c). The end result? Pins laying everywhere, but the 7-pin still standing unscathed.

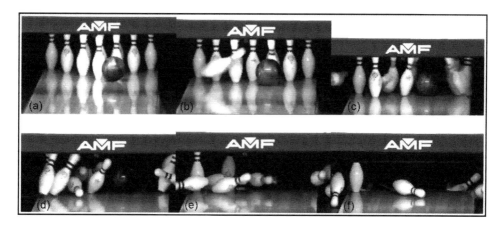

Figure 12.5: Collision system leading to a 7-pin

As the chart in Figure 12.4 showed us, the other way to leave a 7-pin is with a "high flush" hit on the left edge of the pocket, around board 18. A board 18 shot carries a 74 percent chance of striking. If such a shot does not strike, there is a six percent chance of leaving a 7-pin. Let's try to figure out why.

When the ball hits the pins on board 18, the headpin is driven more toward the back than it should be, causing it to just clip the 2-pin (Figure 12.6-b). Since the 2-pin was not hit solidly enough, rather than traveling back and left toward the 4-pin, it will instead send the 2-pin well to the left. Since it is traveling so far left, it only clips the front of the 4-pin (Figure 12.6-c). This light hit on the front of the 4-pin causes it to fall straight back, missing the 7-pin. The 2-pin continues left after clipping the 4-, thus also missing the 7-pin (Figure 12.6-e). The action on the right side of the rack is exactly as it should be, so everything falls except the 7-pin (Figure 12.6-f).

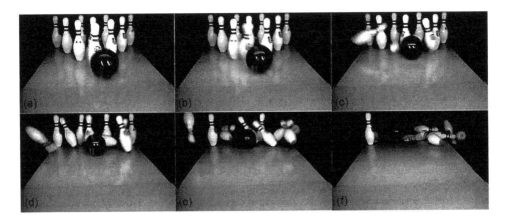

Figure 12.6: Collision system leading to a 7-pin on a high flush hit

Note that in the collision system resulting from a high flush hit on board 18, there are no pins traveling in the direction of the 7-pin, which is why it was left standing. How, then, do we strike so often on a high flush hit? Look at Figure 12.6-d. Note how close both the 4- and the 2-pins come to the 7-pin. It is easy to see that if either pin was turned toward the 7- pin as it traveled past, or if either takes a bounce after hitting the pin deck, the gutter, or any other pins in the pit, then the likelihood is high that the 7-pin will be toppled. As the strike statistics tell us, this in fact happens 74 percent of the time.

THE POCKET 7-10

This brings us to the dreaded 7-10 split. In Figure 12.7, below, we've overlaid our probability charts for both the 7-pin and the 10-pin. Since there is pretty much zero chance of leaving a 7-pin if we hit in the board 16-1/2 to board 17-1/2 zone, there is likewise pretty much no chance of leaving a 7-10 split. At the high edge of the pocket on board 18 there is a very small possibility of leaving either a 7- or a 10-pin, but the USBC study showed no occurrences of leaving both of them standing on such a hit. Likely one or the other pretty much always gets tripped by another pin on such a high flush hit. Since this zone covers the entire pocket area, and since there is pretty much a zero chance of leaving both the 7- and the 10-pins standing on a hit anywhere within this area, we can conclude that the entire notion of leaving a "pocket 7-10" is erroneous. That term needs to go away.

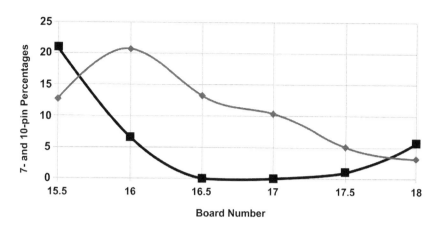

Figure 12.7: Odds of leaving a 7-pin (black line) and 10-pin (grey line), by board number

If we are not leaving a 7-10 split when we hit the true pocket, where are we likely hitting? Look at the left side of Figure 12.7. By far the highest probability for both the 7- and the 10-pin occurs in the zone between boards 15-1/2 and 16. Indeed, while the USBC study tells us that 7-10 splits are exceedingly rare, *if* they are going to occur it is almost always going to be in this zone. There is a three percent chance of leaving a 7-10 split on a board 15-1/2 hit, and a one percent chance on a board 16 hit. Every other hit, including a pocket hit, carries essentially no chance of leaving a so-called pocket 7-10 split. If you are unlucky enough to leave it, you can be certain that you did not hit the pocket. Your ball came in about two boards light, and you need to make an adjustment.

So how do we leave a 7-10 split on a light hit? Think back to our description earlier of how a light hit leaves a 7-pin. Recall also that on the right side of the rack, the 3-pin was driven straight back between the 5- and 6-pins, striking the 9-pin. The 3- then bounces off of the 9-pin to the right, and knocks over the 10-pin. Thus, the 10-pin was not hit by any of the primary collisions, and it was only a fortuitous bounce of the 3-pin off of the 9-pin that toppled it. What would have happened if the 3-pin had instead bounced to the left, or had been snowplowed straight back by the ball before it could even bounce? Had either occurred, there would have been nothing at all to hit the 10-pin, leaving a 7-10 split.

THE 5-PIN

As Figure 12.8, depicts, the odds of leaving a 5-pin rise dramatically in the same board 15-1/2 to board 16-1/2 zone that leads to 7-pins and 10-pins. You should be starting to see a pattern here. In this case, a hit on board 16 is the primary culprit, with a nearly 15 percent chance of leaving a 5-pin.

Probability of leaving a 5-pin

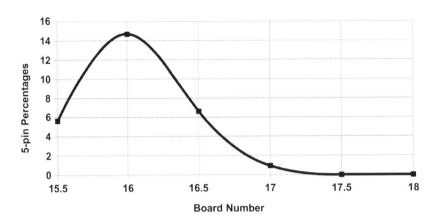

Figure 12.8: Probability of leaving a 5-pin, by board number

Let's trace out how a light hit on board 16 could lead to the 5-pin being missed. Just as with the light shots that left the 7-pin or the 10-pin, the ball's board 16 hit catches the headpin too far on its right edge, sending it too sharply across the pin deck. Since the headpin is traveling too sharply to the left, it again just grazes the front of the 2-pin before continuing off to the left gutter (Figure 12.9-b). The 2-pin travels straight back to hit the 8-, and then bounces forward off of the 8- to tackle the 4-pin from behind (Figure 12.9-d) before rolling left into the 7-pin (Figure 12.9-e). Not too pretty nor efficient, but this takes care of the left side of the rack.

On the right side, the light hit causes the ball to drive the 3-pin straight back between the 5- and the 6-, missing both (Figure 12.9-b). The ball clips the left edge of the 6-pin, toppling it into the gutter, but just misses the 5-pin (Figure 12.9-c). The ball then pushes the toppled 3-pin into the 9- and 10-pins (Figure 12.9-d). The 5-pin is never touched.

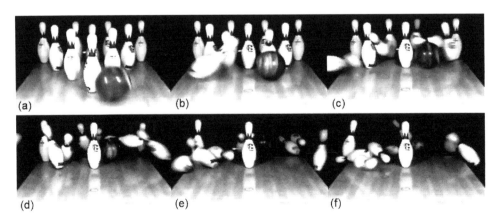

Figure 12.9: Collision system leading to a 5-pin

Note in the preceding description and in the accompanying photos that in the collision system leading to a 5-pin, the 4-, 7-, and 10-pins are all knocked down by secondary collisions with bouncing pins rather than being hit directly by the ball or a pin. In Figures 12.9 (c) and (d), we can see that those three pins are the last ones standing with the 5-, until they are tripped out by fortuitously bouncing and rolling pins. If any one of those fortunate breaks fails to materialize, any one of those pins, or any combination of them can be left with our 5-pin. Possible combinations include the 4-5 split (three percent chance), the 5-7 split (five percent chance), or the very low probability 4-5-7 split, 5-10 split, or the dreaded 5-7-10 "sour apple." In fact, if you've left any split that includes the 5-pin, it is almost certain that your ball missed the pocket and came in a board-and-a-half light, hitting on or about board 16.

THE 8-PIN AND THE 9-PIN

Bowlers use the term "tap" to refer to a shot that is solidly in the pocket but that somehow leaves a single pin standing. Bolstering this idea, in the recreational bowling variant format called "9 pin, no tap," any shot that leaves only a single pin standing is counted as a strike. Purists tend to say that this definition of a "tap" is overly broad, and that the 8-pin is the only "true tap" for a right-handed bowler. All other single pin leaves result from something being wrong with your shot, they insist, while only the 8-pin can result from a perfect pocket hit.

Why, then, have we grouped the 8- and the 9-pin together in this section? Because contrary to popular belief they both quite often result from almost identical shots. 8-pins are fortunately quite rare. 9-pins are more common, but both can be left on dead-flush pocket hits directly on board 17-1/2.

Let's look at the likelihood of leaving an 8-pin. As Figure 12.10 shows, there is indeed a roughly one percent chance of leaving an 8-pin on a dead flush pocket hit on board 17-1/2. There is an additional one percent chance of leaving an 8-pin on a board 17 hit on the right edge of the pocket, but essentially a zero chance of leaving it on a board 18 hit on the left edge of the pocket. Since it is indeed possible to leave an 8-pin on a solid pocket hit we seem to be justified in calling it a "tap," but as usual, things are not so simple. Note from the chart data that the odds of leaving an 8-pin on a board 16-1/2 hit—a board right of the pocket—is double that of leaving it on a pocket hit. To be fair, that doubling is only from a one percent chance to two percent, but the point remains. While it is possible to leave the 8-pin on a solid pocket shot, the odds are that if you left it your shot was just a little bit light. If an 8-pin is twice as likely to be left on a light hit as on a pocket hit, how can we possibly justify continuing to call an 8-pin leave a "true tap"?

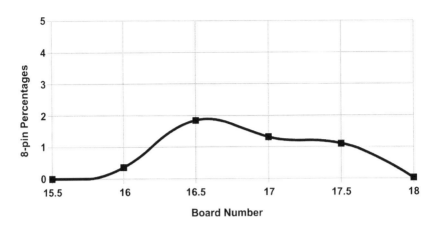

Figure 12.10: Odds of leaving an 8-pin, by board number

Figure 12.11,below, which depicts the odds of leaving a 9-pin, tells a far different story. Note that the highest probability of leaving a 9-pin, at over seven-and-one-half percent, is on a dead flush hit directly on board 17-1/2. You have a nearly three percent chance of leaving a 9-pin on a board 18 hit on the left edge of the pocket, and a six percent chance of leaving it on a board 17 hit on the right edge of the pocket. If you miss the pocket by only half a board to the right, on board 16-1/2, your odds of leaving a 9-pin drop to only one percent. Any lighter than that, and your odds are essentially zero.

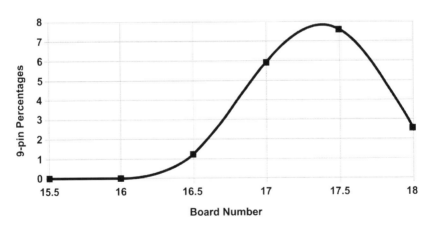

Figure 12.11: Odds of leaving a 9-pin, by board number

Do you see the problem with the idea that the 8-pin is the only "true tap" for a right-hander? If we left an 8-pin, the odds are almost twice as high that our shot was a board light than they are that it was in the pocket. If we left a 9-pin, the odds are that we hit dead flush in the pocket. Given that, wouldn't it be far more accurate to say that the 9-pin is the "true tap" for a right-hander? Curiously, bowlers seem to stay put when they leave an 8-pin, believing that it resulted from a bad break on a good pocket shot, yet they will make an adjustment when they leave a 9-pin, believing that a 9-pin results from a shot that was too high. Statistics say the opposite is likely true. While it is certainly possible to leave a 9-pin on a slightly high shot, as we will address in a moment, your 9-pin most likely resulted from a good, solid, pocket hit, while the 8-pin was more likely to have been the result of a light hit that missed the pocket to the right.

Splitting hairs and arguing over what is and what isn't a "true tap" is rather pointless. Though there are subtle differences, both 8-pins and 9-pins share the same root cause if the ball was in the pocket, and both pretty much come down to bad luck. Both are caused by the headpin interfering with the collision system after it has been knocked down by the ball. Let's look at some examples in detail, and you'll see what we mean.

THE 8-PIN

As we discussed in the previous section, if you left an 8-pin your ball was either in the pocket and you got a bad break, or was a board light. Let's first discuss the light version of the 8-pin. Recall our discussions of the chain of events occurring from light hits leading to 5-pins, 7-pins, and 10-pins. In all of those shots, the headpin was clipped on its right edge, sending it too sharply to the left to squarely impact the 2-pin. Since the headpin just catches the front of the 2-pin, it sends the 2- straight back and into the 8-pin. It is the 2-pin which knocks over the 8-, and nothing else comes anywhere near it. Given this, it is easy to see that should the 2-pin travel back on an angle rather than straight, or should it be pushed off to the side by the falling 5-pin before it can reach the 8-, then the 8-pin will remain standing. Note also that the same light hit that leaves an 8-pin also carries with it a 13 percent chance of leaving a 10-pin, and since either is possible, then both together are certainly possible. If you left an 8-10 split you can be almost certain that your ball missed the true pocket by a board or so to the right.

By now we should be getting better at recognizing light hits by sight, and at accepting that the cause of our leave was our less than perfect shot rather than bad luck. Harder to accept, though, is a shot that we know full well hit the pocket but that left an 8-pin anyway. How does this happen?

In Chapter 10 we discussed the so-called "textbook" strike, where the headpin travels back and left at a 30 degree angle in order to hit the 2-pin into the 4-pin into the 7-pin in a long chain reaction. As we calculated in that chapter, the pins only deflect on such a angle if we hit the pocket a board light, around board 16-1/2. By comparison, in a solid pocket hit around board 17-1/2, as depicted in Figure 12.12, below, the headpin is hit more squarely by the ball, driving it slightly more back than left (Figure 12.12-b).

Since the headpin is traveling toward the rear as it glances off of the 2-pin, it will bounce off of the 2-pin and deflect back toward the right, getting itself slightly in between the ball and the 5-pin. From this position, the headpin acts a barrier which prevents the ball from deflecting to the left off of the 3-pin, and also serves as a sort of ramp, directing and channeling the ball off to the right (Figure 12.12-c). The ball continues toward the right to take out the 9-pin, while the 3-pin hits the 6-, which hits the 10- (Figure 12.12-e). While this is happening, the fallen headpin, pushed to the left by the ball, topples the 5-pin (Figure 12.12-d). The ball pushes the toppled 5-pin off the back of the pin deck, while the headpin follows the 2-, 4-, and 7-pins to the left and into the gutter (Figure 12.12-e). In short, the headpin gets itself trapped between the ball and the 5-pin, where it channels the ball away from the 8-pin toward the right. Good shot; bad break!

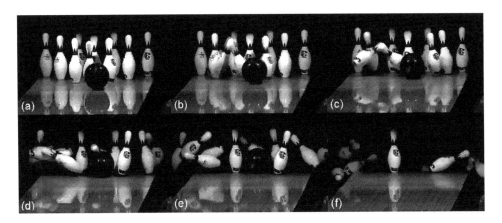

Figure 12.12: Collision system leading to an 8-pin, pocket hit

Since there are two ways to leave an 8-pin, one via a pocket shot and the other via a one board miss to the right, you will have to be very observant of the point where the ball hits the headpin in order to determine which version caused your problem. If you are very certain that your ball hit the true pocket—based on the pocket photos and on the fact that the 2-pin traveled back and left rather than straight back—then no change is required. You got a bad break on that one shot, but the odds are still dramatically in your favor that you will strike on the next. If, however, you hit a board right of the pocket, with the 2-pin traveling more toward the back than the left, then you need to make an adjustment.

THE 9-PIN

Like the 8-pin, there are two ways to leave a 9-pin. A very high hit around board 19, one-and-one-half boards left of the pocket, will often leave a 9-pin. This shot will be obviously heavy though, almost through the nose and with the left edge of the ball overlapping the left edge of the headpin by about an inch, so will be easy to differentiate from a pocket 9-pin. We will discuss this very high 9-pin shortly.

Right now we will concern ourselves with the true pocket 9-pin, which like the pocket 8-pin is caused by interference from the headpin. In Figure 12.13-a, below, we can clearly see that the ball indeed enters the pins flush in the true pocket, right on board 17-1/2. The headpin is pushed back into the rack (Figure 12.13-b), but instead of staying there safely out of the way, it takes a bad bounce off of the 2-pin and continues right, getting itself wedged firmly between the ball and the 5-pin (Figure 12.13-c).

Figure 12.13-c also shows us that the ball hits the 3-pin and deflects to the left as it should. Look closely at the headpin, however. Since it is so deep into the pin deck, the headpin actually knocks over the 5-pin before the ball can get to it (Figures 12.13-c and -d). Recall from our description of a textbook strike that the ball is supposed to deflect off of the 5-pin and back toward the right in order to hit the 9-pin. With the 5-pin already knocked over by the headpin there is nothing for the ball to deflect off of, so it continues on its leftward trajectory, pushing the toppled 5-pin into the 8-pin and missing the 9-pin entirely (Figure 12.13-e).

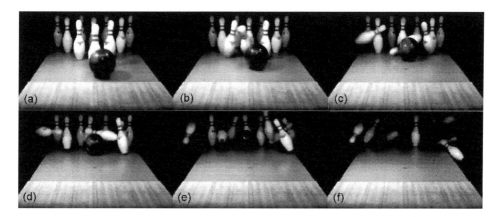

Figure 12.13: Collision system leading to an 9-pin, pocket hit

Our study of the collision systems leading to pocket 8-pins and pocket 9-pins demonstrates that both are caused by the headpin taking a bad bounce off of the 2- and getting itself wedged between the ball and the 5-pin. Figure 12.14 shows frame (c) from the 9-pin shot on the left and the 8-pin shot on the right. Note how much more the headpin interferes with the ball on the 9-pin shot than on the 8-pin shot. The only difference between the shot that left the 8-pin and the shot that left the 9-pin is the degree to which the headpin wedged itself in there.

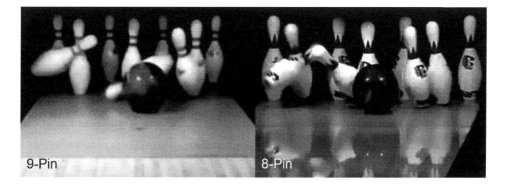

Figure 12.14: headpin interference, 9-pin versus 8-pin

Let's now take a look at the 9-pin left by a high shot that missed the pocket to the left. In Figure 12.15-a, below, we see the ball hit the headpin on board 19, which is one-and-one-half boards to the left of the pocket. Note that the left edge of the ball overlaps the left edge of the headpin by about an inch. This overlap is your visual cue that your ball hit too high.

Figure 12.15-b shows that just like the shots that left the pocket 8-pin and 9-pin, the high hit causes the headpin to travel back and get itself between the ball and the 5-pin. The difference here is that because the headpin was driven much more back than left, it deflects even more strongly to the right off of the 2-pin. The ball continues past the headpin and clips the 3-pin, sending it out to the right gutter. The headpin continues moving right through the deck and tackles the 6-pin, then bounces off of the 6-pin to hit the 10-pin (Figure 12.15-d).

On the left side of the rack, the 2-pin, being just barely hit by the headpin, travels too sharply to the left and misses the 4-pin (Figure 12.15-c). The 2-pin then leaves the pin deck, bounces off of the left kick back, and hits the 7-pin from the side (Figure 12.15-d). In Figure 12.15-e, we see that after hitting the 7-pin, the top of the 2-pin just barely taps the 4-pin, nudging it over. The end result of this chain of events is a 9-pin.

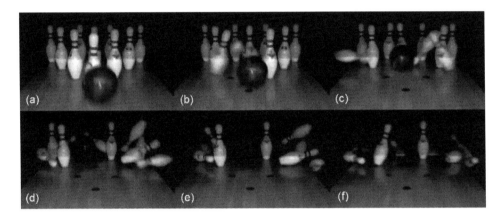

Figure 12.15: Collision system leading to an 9-pin, high hit

There are a few more important things to take away from this discussion of the high 9-pin. First, notice that the last pin to fall is the 4-pin. This should serve as another visual clue that your shot came in too high. If you notice the 4-pin falling late, you can be sure that you are hitting too high and that you need to make an adjustment. The second thing to notice is that in our example shot, the 4-pin was just barely touched by the 2-pin. If the 2-pin had bounced off the kick back head or tail first rather than sideways, it would have missed the 4-pin completely, resulting in a 4-9 split. In fact, every example of the 4-9 split in our video library happened in precisely this way.

The last important thing to note is that in this high, board 19 collision system, the 4-pin, the 7-pin, and the 10-pin were all toppled by what amount to lucky breaks. In fact, in Figure 12.15-d we can see that those three, along with the 9-pin, are the only pins standing after the primary collisions. Since toppling these three pins relies on fortuitous bounces, if any one of those bounces goes awry we can be left with a difficult split, including the 4-7-9, the 4-7-9-10, or the 9-10.

Our advice here is the same as for the 8-pin. If you know your ball hit high, make an adjustment. Your clues to a high hit are the left edge of the ball overlapping the left edge of the headpin, and the 4-pin falling late. If the ball hit the true pocket but left a 9-pin, stay put. You threw a good shot, but got a bad break.

LIBERATION!

When we thought that the pocket was in the 1-3 area, our shots that were solidly in this false pocket but left pins standing lead to frustration. If you are throwing shot after shot that you think are good pocket hits only to leave a corner pin or worse, how can you not become frustrated? Frustration leads to stress, stress leads to bad shots, and bad shots lead to more frustration. It's a death spiral, like a moth circling a flame.

We know three things now that we may not have known before reading these chapters. We now know where the true pocket actually is, and what it looks like down lane when our ball hits the pins at the proper point. We know and accept that if we left back row pins, we most likely did *not* hit the pocket. Lastly, we now know that if we are leaving back row pins we need to make meaningful changes that can alter *where* our ball hits the pins, not fiddly little tweaks to change *how* it hits the pins. In Chapter 13 we will explore all of the adjustments open to a bowler, including changes to our release, equipment, and lane play. We will also examine precisely what effect these changes will have on our ball's path to the pins. In Chapter 14 we will learn how to select and apply these changes in specific situations.

PART II

ADJUSTMENTS

WHAT DOES WORK.

CHAPTER 13

CREATE A BOWLER'S TOOL KIT

YOU'VE BEEN NAILING the pocket and racking up the strikes, but suddenly things start to feel different. Instead of blasting all ten pins into the pit, they begin to fall in a messy way, or worse yet they don't all fall. A few frames later your ball isn't even coming close to the pocket, either coming up short and leaving buckets or wash outs, or hooking too much and going right through the face leaving ugly splits. The lanes have changed, and you've run into what bowlers call *transition.*

As the night progresses and more and more balls roll down the lane, the oil gets pushed around, picked up by the ball on some portions of the lane, and often redeposited on others. It gets affected by heat and humidity, and generally "messed up" in any number of ways. The net result is that what started out as a nice, predictable oil pattern becomes much less so. We will discuss transition in far greater depth in later chapters, describing what can happen to the pattern, how to recognize what has happened, and what you can do about it. The "what you can do about it" part will always require you to change *something* about your shot in order to make your ball hit the pins in a different place. This chapter will describe all of the *somethings* available to you, and explain what each does to the shape of your shot.

TOOLS

A mechanic doesn't attempt to repair your car with only a screwdriver. Mechanics own a whole chest full of tools. Some tools only perform one job. Others are more versatile, performing one job really well, and able to perform others in a pinch. Even with an entire box of tools, the mechanic will still occasionally run into unique situations where none of their tools are ideal for the job, and improvisation and creativity are required.

So too, a bowler needs to develop a tool kit; a collection of techniques that can be employed when the shape of the shot needs to be changed. There are eight different things a bowler can alter in order to modify the shape of the shot, and all of these things will change where the ball impacts the pins. These eight changes comprise a bowler's tool kit. Just as a mechanic does not always own the right tool for a given job, not every bowler will gain the skill and agility to employ every one of the eight tools, but every bowler will be able to employ at least some of them. Just like the mechanic, the more complete your tool kit, the easier it will be for you to get the job done.

The eight tools available to the bowler are:

Ball Surface Alteration
Ball Change
Line Change
Ball Speed
Axis Rotation
Axis Tilt
Loft
Rev Rate Alteration

This chapter will discuss each of these tools. We will describe what each is, what it does, and how to use it. The next three chapters will help you recognize when a change is required and what that change needs to do to the path of the ball, but the choice of which tool to employ will ultimately depend on which of the tools you own and which you are comfortable using.

DISTANCE

A young friend of ours once asked Chris Barnes for advice on arsenal selection. Mr. Barnes replied that he should "think north-south, not east-west." What he meant was, think about how far the ball gets down the lane before hooking, not about how much it hooks. Success in bowling comes down to controlling distance, and this is what every one of our tools ultimately affects. Your ability to assess the lane conditions and then get your ball to skid the proper distance down the lane before hooking will determine your chance of success. The appropriate distance will vary from house to house, lane to lane, and even frame to frame, and will depend on factors such as oil pattern, lane surface type, topography, and many others.

Distance is everything in our sport. Hook is secondary. Figure 13.1 illustrates this sequence of priorities. Everyone wants to hook the ball more. Many bowlers who approach us for coaching believe their problem is not enough hook. But what good is a big hook if you can't control where on the lane it occurs?

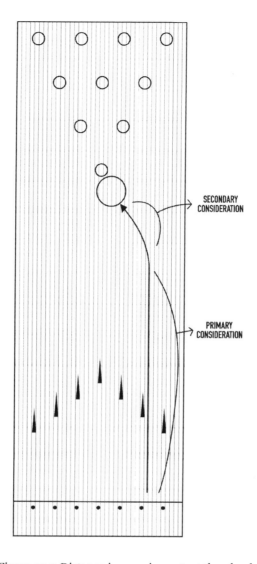

Figure 13.1: Distance is more important than hook

Most bowlers we observe mistakenly think that a shot that missed the pocket either hooked too much or too little. The truth is that it hooked too soon or too late. Too much or too little hook is easy to adjust for; just move your line or change its angle a bit and you're back in the pocket. If your ball is hooking too soon or too late, though, you will have a much more challenging time trying to find something that works.

When having trouble on the lanes, bowlers are often advised to "use a ball with a different shape." This seems like an odd statement given that all bowling balls are spherical. What they mean is to choose a ball that displays a differently shaped path on the lane, one that displays a more arc-shaped, gentle and continuous curve, or one that has a more "skid-flip" path. In fact, bowling balls are often marketed as skid-flip balls or as continuous balls. This is looking at the problem a bit backward though. The shape of the ball path is not something intrinsic to the ball. Ball path shape is simply the result of how early or late the ball begins and ends its hook.

A ball that starts to hook early *has to* trace out an arc-shaped path if it is to hit the pocket. Since it is hooking early, it makes its move on the oilier parts of the lane, and the reduced friction caused by the oil prohibits a sharp movement. By the time such a ball hits the dry portion of the lane it has already given up so much of its axis rotation that there is not enough left to cause a sharp break. In contrast, a ball that travels well down the lane before hooking will make its move on the drier portion of the lane, so its movement toward the pocket will be sharper. The shape of the ball's path is a byproduct of where it began to hook relative to the lane oil. That is, shape is a byproduct of distance.

Since distance, not hook, is the primary factor affecting how our ball hits the pins, our adjustments should be chosen on the basis of distance. Let's look at all of our available tools and examine what each does to our ball's path.

ADJUSTMENT 1: BOWLING BALL SURFACE ALTERATION

In Chapter 8 we discussed in depth how surface texture affects the path of the ball, so in this chapter we will cover the practical applications rather than the technical issues. Though your ball came from the factory with a certain finish, you are under no obligation to keep it that way. You are free to alter it in any way you wish, from a dull, coarse, sanded finish all the way up to a high polish, and these surface alterations will have a strong effect on distance and ball motion. Unlike our other adjustment tools which can be employed at any time, in most competitive situations surface finish cannot be altered once play has begun.

During sanctioned league or tournament play, surface adjustments can only be made before the first ball is thrown in competition. This leaves you only a very small window of time between when practice starts and when competition begins. There are a few exceptions to this rule. Current World Tenpin Bowling Association (WTBA) competition rules allow surface changes between games, but only if done in designated areas so the sanding dust does not contaminate the approaches or bowlers' shoes. The USBC also allows league and tournament directors to completely prohibit surface changes if they so choose, even during the practice session. The majority of USBC leagues and tournaments make no such restriction, however, and allow surface changes (performed by hand) up until the time the first ball of competition is thrown.

The ability to alter the ball's surface based on the reaction you saw during practice is one of the most underused freedoms that bowlers have. If none of the balls you brought to league or the tournament seem to match up to the lane conditions, a tweak to the ball's surface texture in practice can make the difference between winning and losing.

Bowling ball surface adjustments can be made with a variety of abrasives, from 3M Scotch-Brite scouring pads and common woodworking sandpaper on the coarse end of the spectrum, through extremely fine sanding pads, and on to rubbing and polishing compounds capable of leaving a soft sheen or a high gloss. The most commonly used abrasives for altering the surface of bowling balls are Abralon pads, manufactured by Mirka Ltd. in Finland, and siaair pads, pronounced "sea-ah air," and made in Switzerland by sia Abrasives (Yes, the proper names of the pads and the company are indeed lower case!). Similar pads are also made by the German firm JÖST Abrasives (pronounced sort of like a cross between "Yost" and "Yust"), though they are less common, at least in the U.S.

These sanding pads are not made specifically for bowling balls. They are something we borrowed from industry. In fact, their primary uses are in metal finishing and automotive paint preparation. Though they are available through bowling suppliers, they can be purchased for significantly less money from woodworking tool suppliers and industrial supply houses.

Sanding pads are available in a wide variety of grits. While your pro shop will use many different grits when professionally resurfacing a ball, you only need to carry four in your bag, 500, 1000, 2000, and 4000. These numbers refer to the coarseness of the sanding pad. The lower the grit number, the coarser the pad. Bowlers need to be a little careful here, though, especially those in the United States. Since the sanding pads we use for ball resurfacing are manufactured in Europe, the grit sizes are on a different scale than what we are used to in the US. European abrasives are graded according to the FEPA P scale (Federation of European Producers of Abrasives). The sanding pads and papers ordinarily sold in the U.S. are graded using a scale called CAMI (Coated Abrasive Manufacturers Institute), and the two scales are very different. For example, a 500 grit Abralon pad would be equivalent to roughly 350 grit on the U.S. scale. If you decide to use pads other than Abralon, siaair, or JÖST, make sure you use the proper equivalent grit. The closest U.S. grit to a 500 pad would be 360. U.S. 600 grit is just a little finer than a 1000 pad. A 2000 grit pad is equivalent to 1000 grit on the U.S. scale, and a 4000 pad is equivalent to U.S. 1500 grit.

Since lower grit numbers are more coarse, the lower the number, the earlier your ball will hook. The higher the number, the finer the grit and the later your ball will hook. If you threw a ball with a 4000 grit surface, and then re-sanded it to 500 grit and threw it again, the 500 grit will hook much earlier than will the 4000. It will not necessarily hook more, but it will hook sooner.

Altering the ball's finish is done by rubbing the pad evenly and randomly all over its surface using firm pressure. This is not the method used by your pro shop when they professionally resurface a ball, but it works well enough for our purposes. You can alter the ball's surface in a matter of 10 or 15 seconds, and materially change the distance it travels down the lane before hooking. A caveat needs to be pointed out here though. If you choose to alter the surface of a bowling ball in practice, USBC rules demand that you alter the entire surface, not just parts of it. You can't just sand the track area on your ball and call it good.

Devote one of your upcoming practice sessions to getting more comfortable using these surface adjustment pads, and to noting the result of surface changes on your ball's path. Don't change any other variables. Start with a ball sanded to 4000 grit, which produces nearly as fine a surface as polish. Get yourself lined up and then throw half a dozen shots, paying close attention to where the ball hooks and where it hits the headpin. Now move down a pad, sanding the ball to 2000 grit. Stand in the same place on the lane and target the same arrow as before, and throw another half dozen shots. Repeat this process with the 1000 grit pad and the 500 grit pad, keeping everything else the same, and watching the ball path very carefully. Compare how far the ball travels down the lane before hooking, and where it enters the pins. As you go from 4000 all the way down to 500, you should observe a significant difference in ball motion.

What you learn about ball motion from this practice session will pay off immensely, giving you the confidence and knowledge to make a sound surface adjustment decision. Next time you compete, when you see your ball hook a little too soon or a little too late during practice, a quick alteration of your ball's surface will dial in the reaction you need. Remember, success is all about controlling distance.

ADJUSTMENT 2: BALL CHANGE

The rest of the adjustments in our bowler's tool kit can be applied at any time during league or competition, and one of the most important tools is the ability to change balls. A golfer could certainly play an entire round with only one club, but scores aren't likely to be very good. A driver can get you out of a sand trap, eventually, but it's certainly not the best tool for the job. You can make a putt with a wedge, but you'd be much more effective with a club designed specifically for that task. The same holds true for bowling balls. You can make do with any ball if you have enough physical skills, but life is so much easier when you have the right tool for the job.

We all understand why a golfer needs a whole bag full of clubs. Golfers are constantly faced with different conditions; sending the ball short distances over closely cropped turf, driving it tremendous distances over ponds and obstacles, or punching it through or around trees. But why does a bowler need more than one ball? Don't bowlers just roll the ball down the same smooth lane, over and over?

Like golfers, bowlers are faced with a great variety of lane conditions. The difference is that ours are invisible. A golfer can see the trees, the sand, and the rough areas. Bowlers don't know there is a sand trap until after they hit it, when they watch their ball do something entirely unexpected. Just as a golfer will select a different club based on the shot he or she has to make, a bowler should have the ability to select a different ball that is better suited to the changed conditions.

Golf has settled in on a standardized set of clubs that most golfers carry. We have no such standardization in bowling, and the set of balls that individual bowlers carry—their "arsenal"—varies widely. Some arsenals are meticulously assembled and make sense, while others are random collections of all the "latest and greatest" balls, full of duplication of motion and big gaps. We'd like to propose our own ideas on standardized arsenals based on the bowler's competitive level.

The main thing to keep in mind when selecting an arsenal is diversity of ball motion. Just as it would be pointless for a golfer to carry two 9-irons, there is no point in a bowler carrying two different balls that display the same or nearly the same motion on the lane. We believe that every bowler, even those who only bowl on noncompetitive recreational leagues, needs to carry a plastic spare ball. This ball is your "putter," and as we shall discuss in depth in Chapter 17, it should be used for almost every spare. Beyond the spare ball, bowlers of differing abilities, desires, and levels of tournament participation will carry some number of "strike balls." When we discuss arsenals in the following paragraphs, we are talking about the number of strike balls you will carry in addition to your spare ball. That is, a one-ball arsenal means one strike ball plus a spare ball, a three-ball arsenal means three strike balls plus a spare ball, and so on.

Bowlers often ask their pro shop operator for "the best ball out there." This is an almost meaningless question, and if you do receive a specific answer you may wish to find a new pro shop. The truth is, every bowling ball made is a great ball, and every ball made is a terrible ball. It all depends on what you need the ball to do. Ask a golfer "what's the best golf club made," and the response will be, "for what shot?" A wedge is a great club if you have to get out of a sand trap. It's a terrible club if you have to make a 250 yard drive. Bowlers need to think about their equipment in the same way. A top-shelf, dull "hook monster" is a great ball if you are playing on an oil-flooded sport shot. It's probably a bad ball on a house shot, and almost always a terrible ball if the pattern is short and the lanes are dry.

The number of possible variations in ball motion is infinite. Elite-level pros may need balls that are so close in motion that the difference amounts to splitting hairs, but for the rest of us such subtlety is completely unnecessary. Indeed, most of us would not even notice the difference, and trying to cover every eventuality would result in an arsenal so large that the number of choices offered start to work against you. For all but elite players, we have distilled useful ball motions down to only six. Even for elite players, start with these six, and then split hairs where necessary.

The first five of our ball motion categories are based initially on distance; early read, mid-lane read, and late read. Within each length category, we then specify the aggressiveness of the hook; strongly hooking, or moderate. Our first five ball motions are therefore:

Early read / Strong hook (Early/Strong)
Mid-lane read / Strong hook (Mid/Strong)
Mid-lane read / Moderate hook (Mid/Moderate)
Late read / Strong hook (Late/Strong)
Late read / Moderate hook (Late/Moderate)

You've surely noticed that we left out one possible combination; Early/Moderate. This was intentional, as we have not been able to come up with a reasonable use for such a ball motion even if it were possible to achieve.

An Early/Strong ball will typically be a top-shelf, high-end ball with a dull, solid coverstock. Such balls almost always have very low RG weight blocks, but the RG is typically decreased even further via a pin down drilling. Such a ball is primarily intended only for very heavy oil sport shots.

For mid-lane balls, think "middle of the road." We refer to them as benchmark balls. Such balls represent a happy medium, displaying no extremes of either length or motion. These will ordinarily be middle shelf balls, right in the middle of the manufacturer's price scale, though there are a few such intermediate balls that are marketed as top-shelf and priced accordingly. These mid-level balls will have moderately aggressive coverstocks, and an RG in the medium range. They will ordinarily have solid or hybrid coverstock chemistry, though there are certainly exceptions. The Mid/Strong balls will often have a slightly lower RG and a slightly stronger coverstock than the Mid/Moderate, but the distinction is somewhat subjective. With mid-lane balls, the drilling layout should be used as a tweak to adjust the ball's RG based on the individual bowler's release characteristics.

The Late/Strong balls are typically top-shelf "hook monsters," but with a pearlized coverstock and a very fine grit or polished surface. Such balls are often just pearlized versions of Early/Strong balls, so tend to have a very low RG which, while suited to an early ball, is not ideal for a late ball. Drilling layouts therefore tend to be well into pin up territory in order to raise the RG and get the ball farther down the lane.

Late/Moderate balls are usually bottom shelf balls, most often marketed as "entry level." Such balls most often have low friction coverstock chemistry combined with high RGs, both of which help the ball get far down the lane. Since a high RG is desirable in this category, drilling layouts are typically pin up, though variation is certainly possible based on the ball selected and upon the bowler's release characteristics.

We originally called our sixth and final ball motion "control," but a better description might be "Smooth Arc." This is a motion that is not so much a hook as it is a small and gentle curve. Smooth Arc is the motion most bowlers obtain with a modern urethane ball rather than more aggressive reactive resin. There is also at least one ball on the market at the time of this writing that has a coverstock that is a hybrid of urethane and reactive resin, which could be a good choice for a bowler with only moderate revs but who still desires a very controlled, smooth, gentle ball motion. The undrilled RG of modern urethane balls varies widely, so the drilling layout will again depend on the particular ball selected and on the bowler's release characteristics.

A similar motion can be obtained from a middle shelf ball with a weaker cover, but drilled with a specialized ultra-low RG layout. This drilling, which has come to be called a "Rico" layout, places the ball's pin directly in the center of the grip, and results in the lowest possible drilled RG for any given ball. A Rico ball may still be too strong for a very high rev player if conditions are very dry, but it can work well for those with low revs.

Smooth Arc balls are very useful at the competitive level, especially on short oil patterns or when the lanes are extremely dried out from long blocks. Very high rev "crankers" and no-thumb bowlers also find Smooth Arc equipment useful when they need to tame their otherwise extreme ball motion, or when conditions simply call for playing more toward the outside of the lane.

Now that we've defined our six basic ball motions, we can make informed arsenal decisions to provide you with the widest possible variety, subject to the number of strike balls you can afford or the number you are willing to schlep around. Remember, each of these recommendations is for strike balls. We still expect you to carry a plastic spare ball.

ONE BALL ARSENAL

If you will only carry one strike ball, we suggest choosing one in the Mid/Moderate, benchmark range. Bowlers with a one ball arsenal are typically only bowling in a house shot league, and a Mid/Moderate ball is a good middle of the road choice. Such a ball will have a predictable reaction and ball path, allowing you to more easily find a good strike line somewhere around the track area of the lane. A ball from the other categories could work, but you might encounter trouble when the lane starts to transition. A Mid/

Moderate ball will give you enough versatility to manage the changing lane conditions over a three game block.

TWO BALL ARSENAL

If you carry two balls, your first ball should still be a Mid/Moderate benchmark ball. We suggest the second ball be in the Long/Strong category. The benchmark ball will give you the predictable motion you need to begin your league session. When the lanes change and your Mid/Moderate is hooking too early, the Long/Strong will allow you to move toward the inside part of the lane where there is more oil. The Long/Strong ball will get you the added distance you need, and since the deeper line means you are angling the ball a little more away from the pocket, the strong reaction of the top-shelf coverstock will help the ball recover from the later breakpoint.

When the time comes to change from the Mid/Moderate to the Long/Strong ball, you will often be able to stay in roughly the same part of the lane. It all depends on how aggressive your Long/Strong ball's hook is. The best way to learn if an adjustment is needed when switching balls is to practice with them. Find a strike line with your benchmark ball on a given part of the lane, and then switch to your Long/Strong ball, shoot the same line, and see where the ball goes. Repeat this process in other parts of the lane. The information you gain will let you make an informed decision when a ball change is required instead of making a random guess and wasting a frame or two as you dial in the new shot.

THREE BALL ARSENAL

If you can add a third ball to your arsenal, we suggest the same Mid/Moderate and Long/Strong as in the two ball arsenal, plus a Long/Moderate ball. Say you start off the night with your Mid/Moderate benchmark ball, but it starts hooking too early. You try your Long/Strong ball in the same general zone on the lane, but it hooks too sharply and hits too high. You try moving left with the Long/Strong ball, but there is too much oil on that part of the lane, and the ball goes too long and can't turn the corner sharply enough to get back to the pocket. What to do? Switching to your Long/Moderate ball should allow you to stay in the track area and get the necessary distance down the lane without over-hooking.

Bowlers who carry a three ball arsenal are often at a level where they are bowling in some tournaments with more difficult conditions than the typical house shot, and possibly even competing occasionally on sport patterns. These three shapes will give you the variety and options you need to play various target lines and tougher patterns, but a word of caution is in order. If you are going to be playing on a heavy oil sport pattern, you may find it beneficial to dull your Mid/Moderate benchmark ball to get it to read early enough in the beginning of the tournament.

FOUR BALL ARSENAL

In addition to the ball motions covered by the three ball arsenal, we suggest your next addition be an Early/Strong ball. If you are at the stage in your development as a bowler where you are lugging around four balls plus a spare ball, you are almost certainly bowling in tournaments. Since the heavy oil conditions you will be encountering in competitive tournaments don't yield much friction, you will need an Early/Strong ball to begin the block with. On such heavy oil conditions, the other balls in your arsenal will likely go too long and prevent you from obtaining a useful amount of entry angle, at least until the pattern starts to break down and transition.

For most bowlers, the Early/Strong ball would not be a good choice for a house shot. It will tend to "burn up" and roll out too soon, yielding low entry angles and loss of kinetic energy. We don't even bring our Early/Strong balls to house shot leagues and tournaments, but we don't want to state that as a hard and fast rule since conditions at your home center and your unique characteristics as a bowler may suggest otherwise.

FIVE BALL ARSENAL

At five balls, we are getting into the advanced bowler range. Start with the same ball motions as in the four ball arsenal. We have two different suggestions for your fifth ball, based on the type of bowling you typically do.

If you are primarily a league bowler, maybe competing in local tournaments, we suggest adding a Mid/Strong ball to your arsenal. Sometimes your Mid/Moderate benchmark ball is just not aggressive enough to make it back to the pocket even though you may be very happy with its distance. Having another mid-lane ball that gives you a stronger benchmark motion will round out your arsenal, ensuring that you have something that will match up with most of the conditions you are likely to encounter. Remember, these benchmark balls present a smoother, "softer" ball motion than do your more aggressive balls, giving you more control and predictability. Tournament conditions can often be such that predictability will be more valuable than "flip," and until the pattern transitions enough to call for more angle and flip, you can manage the pocket more successfully with your more moderate mid-lane equipment.

If you are a competitive bowler who participates in more serious, longer format tournaments or you bowl in a sport shot league, we suggest that your fifth ball be a Smooth Arc, and for most bowlers we suggest that this ball be a urethane. With today's dull balls and high rev rates, the lane oil is being depleted faster than ever. There will often come a point where you've gone through all of your ball changes and physical tools, but nothing seems to be working. In such situations a good course of action is to stop struggling with trying to match up to the conditions, and instead just take the lane conditions out of play. Solution: Urethane.

Urethane balls are very tame and mild, and will not do anything surprising. We often say that urethane seems to ignore the oil, and mostly just does what it does regardless of the lane conditions. Switching to a urethane ball will let you reduce your angles through the front part of the lane, and will smooth out your ball reaction. Sometimes the lanes become extremely dry or exceedingly difficult or unpredictable due to transition from bowlers playing too many target lines and angles. At other times the lanes might be fine, but your own game is off and you just can't seem to match up to the conditions. Urethane will allow you to manage such situations better, letting you play straighter angles within the track area, or let you move to the outside part of the lane where traffic has been lighter.

SIX BALL ARSENAL

The six ball arsenal is easy. Since there are six basic ball motions, you just need to select one from each column. With six choices in your bag, you will always have something at least close to ideal for any given condition you may face, and can then make fine adjustments to the ball reaction by employing one or more of your other tools. And don't forget the one tool that is often the most effective—surface changes. A surface change can fine tune your ball's motion and take it from "close" to "wow!" in just a few seconds.

FINAL ARSENAL CONSIDERATIONS

A couple of final notes are in order on arsenal selection. First, you don't need to lug every ball you own to every event. If you are heading to your house shot league, you almost certainly won't have a need for your Early/Strong ball. If you will be on conditions that you know very well, you may only need to bring a couple of balls and still be certain you have things covered. If you are heading to unfamiliar lanes or unknown conditions, you might want to bring everything you've got. Otherwise, it's pretty safe to leave the specialized equipment at home.

Second, recognize that your arsenal will change over time. As balls get older and oil-soaked, they will start to go longer and to hook less. Your Mid/Strong ball could easily become a Late/Moderate ball as the games pile up. When a particular ball stops displaying the motion you bought it for, replace it. Move the old ball out of your arsenal or into a new, lower position. As things change, be vigilant in assuring that you've still covered the ball motions you need and that you are not carrying balls that started out different once upon a time, but are now duplicates.

Also, make sure you always know which ball is your current benchmark. As we've already discussed, your benchmark ball is your moderate hooking, mid-lane-reading ball, right in the middle of your arsenal. This should be the ball you start with during the practice period before competition. The reasons for starting out with your benchmark ball are as much mental as they are physical.

By starting with your benchmark ball, you can get a good read of the lane environment in your first couple of shots. You know this ball well, because it is the one you use the most. You know what it *should* do, so any odd behavior in practice will give you valuable information about the lanes. You can then move to more or less aggressive equipment as necessary, based on what your benchmark ball shows you. By starting out with your benchmark ball every time, your practice period stays informative and meaningful.

Using your benchmark ball to start out the practice period before competition can also help you mentally. Suppose you instead start out with your strongest ball in practice, but there is so much oil on the lane that it doesn't hook. Panic sets in immediately. "If my strongest ball won't hook, then everything else I brought is useless!" You feel trapped already, and you've convinced yourself that you're out of options before the tournament even begins.

If you start practice as you always do, with your benchmark ball, it's obviously not going to hook either, but that's okay; you've got options. "My benchmark isn't strong enough, so I'll just throw my dull hook monster on my next shot." You are calm rather than stressed, because you see a path out of the danger. That path may or may not work, but you are primed to think about adjustments rather than locked in blind panic. Now, when your second shot with your strongest ball doesn't hook either, no problem. "My first adjustment didn't work, so what else can I do differently?" You are in the same situation, but in the first instance you start out in a panic, while in the second you start out calmly thinking about options. Your mind stays clear, and you continue to make different shots and gather information. Which is a better position to be in?

ADJUSTMENT 3: LINE CHANGE

Changing target lines is probably the most common adjustment. All bowlers, regardless of skill level, are capable of changing lines, even those bowlers who only own one strike ball. There will be rare nights when you will never have to move, but in most cases, especially if you play near the track area, lane transition will force you to make an adjustment to your line.

As the part of the lane you are playing starts to dry out, both from your own traffic and that of your teammates and competitors, your ball will start to hook earlier and earlier. You will notice your ball hitting higher on the headpin, and you will see the telltale late-falling 4-pin or an exit position closer to the 8-pin than to the center of the lane. Your ball is telling you to make a change *now*, before that late 4-pin becomes a standing 4-pin, or a 4-9, or an even bigger split. If your ball is hooking early because your line is getting drier, an obvious adjustment is to move to a part of the lane that still has oil. That is, change your target line.

Changing target lines entails either changing where you stand on the lane, changing where you target at the arrows, or both. Bowlers describe such changes in terms of "feet," and "eyes," plus a specified direction. Moving "2 left with your feet" means to move your feet two boards to the left of where you had been starting. If you had been standing on board 18, you will now stand on board 20, keeping everything else the same. "Move 1 right with your eyes" means to move your target one board to the right at the arrows, but to keep everything else the same. If you had been targeting the second arrow, which is board 10, move your target to the 9-board.

Most of the time, moving only your feet or only your eyes, which we call *simple* moves, won't work very well. Since you are trying to get away from a dry streak in the area where your ball is supposed to be skidding, such moves often result only in your ball hitting that dry spot even sooner. Most of your moves need to be *compound*, with both your feet and eyes moving. Compound moves are also described by numbers and direction. In such cases, the first number always refers to your feet and the second number to your eyes. If you are advised to move "2-and-1 left," that means to stand two boards farther left, and to target one board farther left at the arrows.

Compound moves are divided into two types, *parallel*, and *angular*. A parallel move is when your feet and eyes move the same number of boards and in the same direction, resulting in a new ball path that is parallel to the old one but shifted a bit to the right or left. If you move only your feet or only your eyes, or if you move them in opposite directions or by a different number of boards, your new ball path will be both in a different place on the lane and on a different angle than you were playing. Since all such uneven moves result in the ball traveling on a different angle, they are called angular moves. "2-and-2 left" is a parallel move. "2-and-1 left" is an angular move (Figure 13.2).

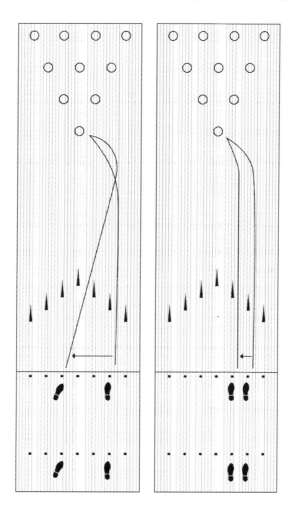

Figure 13.2: Angular (left) and parallel (right) moves

Which type of move should you employ? Simple? Parallel? Angular? Like everything else we've discussed so far, it comes back to watching your ball motion closely and trusting what it tells you. On typical house patterns, moving target lines toward the outside—to the right for right handers and to the left for left handers—will get the ball into the higher friction part of the lane and cause it to hook a little earlier. Moving target lines to the inside—to the left for right handers and to the right for left handers—will get the ball into the oilier part of the lane and cause it to hook a little later. When bowling on a house shot, these moves, perhaps coupled with a ball change at some point, are usually all that you will need to keep scoring well over the course of three or four games.

Tournament shots present a few more challenges, and will require you to be fearless and creative with your target lines. Parallel adjustments are often best at the beginning of the block to keep your launch angle straighter and not give up the pocket while lane friction is still relatively low. As you move deeper, parallel moves would bring your breakpoint too close to the headpin, so angular moves start to be required.

CHANGING ZONES

How far right or left will you need to move your target lines? This is limited only by what your ball tells you to do, and by your own "comfort zone." Most bowlers have a fairly narrow comfort zone, and they tend to play in that zone even if the ball reaction there is less than ideal. Beginning and even intermediate bowlers often target exclusively near the second arrow, moving a board or two here or there to try to make it work. This is a very limiting strategy. Sometimes there is simply no good line in your comfort zone, especially once transition begins, and some sport or tournament shots may require you to play far from your usual house shot line even at the start of the block. By expanding your comfort zone, you increase your chances of finding a good line and of keeping up with transition.

We recommend working to expand your comfort zone, and the only way to do that is to practice throwing along unfamiliar lines. With practice, we believe that most bowlers can become comfortable targeting anywhere from first to third arrow. This sounds like a lot of area and may even look like a lot. In reality it is less than a third of the lane. There will be occasional house shots that are better played outside of first arrow or inside of the third arrow, but on most league house shots, that zone will be more than enough. On sport and tournament shots, or even on house shots after a lot of transition, you may be forced to play almost anywhere on the lane, so the bigger your comfort zone, the greater your chances of finding a shot.

There is no magic wand to wave that will make you more comfortable all over the lane. It takes repetitive practice to gain that comfort, confidence, and competence. We often use a drill we call the *arrow race* to help bowlers increase their comfort zone.

The arrow race works best when practicing with another person, but can certainly be done alone. The object of the race is simple. Each bowler needs to throw a good strike over every arrow from first to fifth, and then back down to first. Each bowler starts at first arrow. They keep throwing shots until they get a good, solid strike. Slop doesn't count. Once you've thrown a good strike over first arrow, move on to the second, then third, fourth, and fifth. After fifth arrow, start moving back down. The first person to make it back down to first arrow and to throw another good strike there wins.

You will of course have to make adjustments to your shot as you change your line. If you want to make the game easier, allow ball changes. If you want to make the drill tougher you can limit yourself to only one ball, which forces you to work on the finer physical adjustments that we will discuss in the remainder of this chapter.

Comfort zone practice does not even need to be about striking and scoring. If you go to practice one day and the lanes are not conducive to playing far outside or far inside, you can still work on comfort zone enlargement. Even if your ball won't make it back to the headpin on a given part of the lane, you can still practice there. You are increasing your versatility by increasing how much of the lane you are comfortable playing. You could miss the headpin all day and it could still be a good practice session if you have developed more comfort, confidence, and competence playing a part of the lane where you were never comfortable before.

A NOTE ABOUT LINE AND ZONE CHANGES

When changing lines, and especially when making big moves and changing zones, you need to pay attention to two aspects of your approach—body angle, and drift. Body angle refers to how you orient your body relative to the lane while in your stance. Drift refers to the direction you walk as you move from stance to delivery. Errors in drift or body angle can easily negate the effect of moving to a new line.

BODY ANGLE

On every shot you make, but especially if you've moved to a different part of the lane to pick up a spare or to adjust your strike shot, you have to pay attention to your body angle. It is crucial for shot accuracy and repeatability that you align your feet, your hips, and most importantly your shoulders with your intended target line.

Though our shoulder joint is capable of movement through an incredible range, in bowling we attempt to use it as a simple pivot. As a pivot, we want it to swing forward in a straight line along the side of our body, without any extraneous movement side to side or at an angle. The better we are at maintaining this simple back and forth pivot motion, the simpler it becomes to consistently hit our mark and repeat shots. Since you want your arm to swing in a straight line, it is imperative that your shoulders are aligned square to your ball path. Any deviation would require you to pull your swing off of its natural path and realign it toward your intended target during your approach, or to swing the ball on an unnatural path out to the side or across the front of your body. Attempting to alter and control your swing plane pretty much guarantees variability from shot to shot. Best to keep it neutral.

The easiest way to attain the proper body angle in your stance is by first setting your feet parallel to the intended launch angle of the ball. First, place your feet side by side, a board or so apart, and pointed in the direction of your intended target line, which will not necessarily be straight up the lane. Once your feet are aligned with your target line you need to orient your feet in relation to one another depending on the direction you intend to throw the ball. If you are throwing the ball toward the right, move your right foot back a few inches so the toe of your right shoe is about half a shoe length behind the toe of your left shoe. If you are throwing toward the left, reverse the feet, moving the left toe half a shoe length behind the right toe. If you are throwing the ball straight up the boards you should keep your feet more or less side by side. You're bowling-side foot should still be a little bit behind your slide foot for stability in your stance, but not nearly to the same degree as when you move to deeper lines (Figure 13.3).

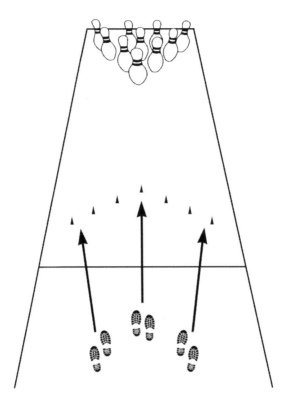

Figure 13.3: Feet aligned with intended ball path

If you properly set your feet, the rest of your body tends to fall naturally into place. For example, moving your right foot a little to the rear will cause your hips to also align themselves toward the right. With your hips squared toward the right, your shoulders will follow. You've now got your entire body naturally and comfortably aligned, feet opened toward the right, hips angled to the right, and shoulders squared toward the right. Aligning your feet and letting the rest of your body fall in line is much easier than trying to twist only your upper body into place. Assuming good swing fundamentals, by simply changing the angle and orientation of your feet and body you automatically realign your swing to match your chosen launch angle. Think of your shot in terms of three lines; target line, body alignment, and swing plane. By squaring yourself to your target line rather than to the lane, you have all three of these lines pointing in the same direction. It is much easier to maintain accuracy and consistency when these lines are not crisscrossing one another (Figure 13.4).

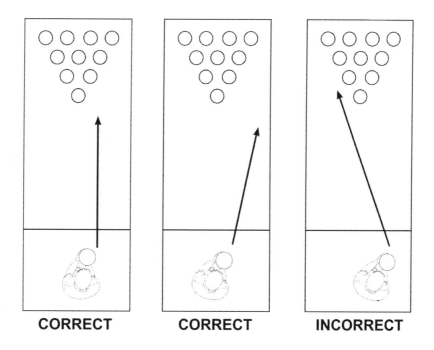

CORRECT   **CORRECT**   **INCORRECT**

Figure 13.4: Body Angle aligned with target line

Bowlers use the terms *open* and *closed* when referring to their stance. An open stance is where your feet, hips, and shoulders are angled away from the center of the lane, toward the right for righties and toward the left for lefties. A closed stance is the opposite; feet, hips, and shoulders angled toward the left for righties and toward the right for lefties. A neutral stance is where the bowler is squared up to the foul line, angled neither right nor left (Figure 13.5). A lot of bowlers habitually set up in their "usual" comfortable stance, and then use that same stance for every shot regardless of where they are on the lane. If your comfortable stance is slightly open, then you are lined up nicely for a hooking strike shot that you want to throw toward the right. The problem is that if you keep that same comfortable stance when shooting at a 7-pin, everything is angled in precisely the wrong direction. This forces you to realign your body during your approach, or worse yet, to swing the ball across your body.

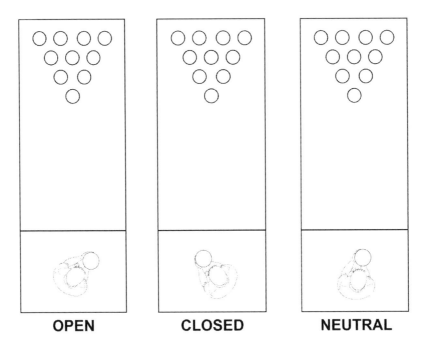

Figure 13.5: Open, closed, and neutral stance (right hander, highly exaggerated for clarity)

The body angle you choose for your setup is the same angle your body should end up on at the foul line, and both are determined by squaring up to your chosen ball path. Most bowlers understand this, but what you may not realize is that as you move your starting position on the lane, whether to pick up a spare or to adjust your strike line, your body angle has to change too. Body angle must always match the current intended target line. Because the lane is very long but not very wide, you do not need to change your body angle very much to stay properly aligned (Figure 13.6).

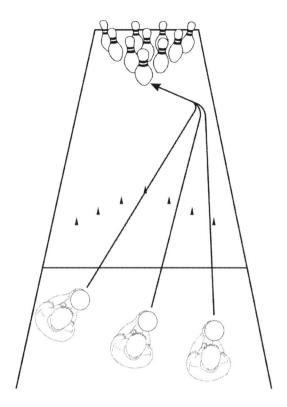

Figure 13.6: Keeping body angle square to launch angle

The key point to remember when employing body angle is to walk straight up the boards, and not in the direction your feet are pointing. Your body stays angled towards your target as you walk, but your approach remains straight. This does require something of a side-stepping motion, but it is actually very subtle and not nearly as hard to do as it might sound. Unless your body angle is extremely exaggerated it will be almost unnoticeable in feel, but it keeps all of your important lines parallel—body angle, swing plane, and launch angle.

DRIFT

Changing your body angle comes with a huge caveat. When you angle your body toward the right or left, there seems to be a subconscious tendency to then walk in that direction rather than straight up the boards. Other than those rare bowlers who need to play left of the ball return, there is just no good reason to walk diagonally on your approach and plenty of reasons against it.

Sometimes an angled approach is carried to extremes. We watched a gentleman at a recent county tournament who stood right up against the ball return on the right lane. He then ran diagonally across the entire approach, sliding on the 10-board as he released his ball. We see the same thing fairly often in league bowlers too, but usually to a lesser degree. It is not unusual to see a bowler standing on board 20 or 25, but then walk diagonally, sliding somewhere around board 15 and sending the ball straight up the second arrow. We sometimes call this phenomenon *imaginary hook syndrome*. The sufferer greatly overestimates the degree of their hook, so stands too far left. The subconscious mind sees the exaggerated angle, knows that it is too great, so sends the body back to the right during the approach to end up in a more reasonable position. Even looking beyond the wasted movement in an angled approach, with such a huge diagonal movement the odds of ending up on the proper board at release are pretty slim. There is just too much chance for variability, and it is very easy to wander several boards right or left of your desired finish position on any given shot. As you move deeper on the lane, your likelihood of walking diagonally increases right along with the increased angle to your breakpoint. Our advice is to start on the board you wish to end on, and walk straight up the approach regardless of where you are playing on the lane.

While a straight up the boards approach is the ideal, few bowlers actually walk in a perfectly straight line every time. Small variations right or left are called *drift*. Drift is not the same thing as a diagonal approach. While a diagonal approach is either intentional or caused by an intentional decision, drift is an entirely unconscious act.

Very few bowlers have zero drift. A small amount of drift is normal, however it should be minimal and consistent. If you drift a board or two in the same direction every shot, there is nothing to worry about. If you drift more than three or four boards, or if you drift a different number of boards or in a different direction on each shot, the variability will cause you great inconsistency from shot to shot and will make effective line changes all but impossible to execute (Figure 13.7). What good is a two board move left with your feet if you're going to randomly drift two extra boards back to the right? If you do experience excessive or inconsistent drift, we advise you to seek help from a qualified coach who can diagnose the cause of the drift and suggest potential cures.

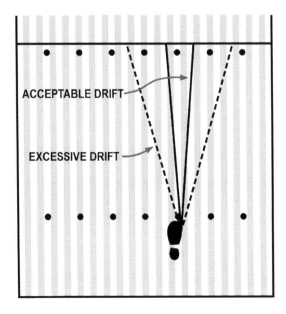

Figure 13.7: Acceptable and excessive drift

ADJUSTMENT 4: SPEED CHANGES

Raise your hand if you have ever been told to slow down while bowling. Wow, that's a lot of hands! Although well-intentioned, it's really not good advice. As we learned in Chapter 2, ball speed is a good thing. The laws of physics tell us that ball speed is kinetic energy, and kinetic energy is what knocks down pins. We want as much ball speed as we can develop without losing control of the shot or overpowering our revs.

A lot of bowlers try to adjust ball speed by changing the amount of muscular force they put into their arm swing. This is a bad way to approach the problem. While putting more or less force into your swing will certainly change your ball speed, it can also cause a number of negative side effects. Trying to increase speed by throwing the ball harder will often cause the bowler to inadvertently "grab" the ball, leading to an inconsistent release. Because muscles and joints tend to work in kinetic chains, putting more arm force into the swing can cause upper body movement, leading to movement of the eyes away from the target. All of these side effects also lead to "pulling" the ball—yanking it across the chest and missing toward the opposite side of the lane.

There is another school of thought that advocates adjusting ball speed by changing the height of your backswing, making it higher for more speed, and lowering it for less speed. Advocates of this school say that you change the height of your backswing by changing how high or low you hold the ball in your stance. Without even arguing about whether or not changing stance height will alter backswing height, we can also dismiss this idea as another bad approach to the problem. Why try to alter something that is a natural and unconscious part of your game? Any time you substitute control in place of muscle memory, the consistency of your shot will suffer. More importantly, even if you manage to develop the ability to effortlessly adjust your backswing height, its effect on ball speed would be negligible.

So how do you properly adjust ball speed? The simplest method of adjusting ball speed is to speed up or slow down the tempo of your entire delivery—your approach, your swing, and your release. By changing the tempo of every part of your delivery, you keep your timing intact, you keep your swing in line, and you keep your grip pressure the same. Nothing changes except your ball speed. The simplest way to adjust the tempo of your entire delivery is to move your starting position on the approach.

By moving forward on the approach by 12 to 18 inches, you compress everything down. You will walk more slowly and swing the ball more slowly as your brain subconsciously adjusts everything to fit the shorter approach distance. It will feel like you are moving at a crawl, but you are not. The change is actually subtle. It only feels drastic because you are not used to it.

The opposite happens when you move back on the approach by 12 to 18 inches. Everything stretches out. Your feet will move faster, your swing will move faster, and your ball will roll faster, but your release and your timing will be unaffected. You will feel like you are almost running, but again, this is only a mental illusion (Figure 13.8).

TEMPO CHANGE - MECHANICS STAY THE SAME

Analogy - The "movie" of you needs to be the same- same actors, same script, same ending-

Just press fast forward on the remote.

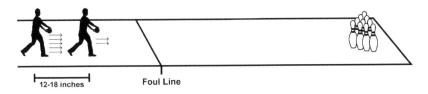

Figure 13.8: Changing ball speed by changing delivery speed

Spend some time in practice working on speed changes. Move forward and back from your normal stance, and watch your speed on the monitors. Most bowlers we have worked with will have a three or four mile per hour speed range just from moving forward or back, and speed changes of this magnitude are enough to have a material effect on ball motion. You will find yourself mastering this skill very quickly. You will also find that regardless of where you start on the approach, you will end up the same distance from the foul line when you release the ball. As long as you don't consciously think about the distance, your brain will make all the proper adjustments.

Slowing down your ball speed will make the ball hook sooner and hook more, but it does so at the cost of kinetic energy. Recall that kinetic energy is one half of ball weight multiplied by the square of your ball speed ($1/2 \times MV^2$), so even a small decrease in ball speed will result in a meaningful drop in kinetic energy. Since kinetic energy is what knocks down pins, decreasing ball speed should be one of the last tools you use. There are other ways to alter ball motion that don't come at such a high kinetic energy cost.

Increasing ball speed will help your ball get farther down the lane before hooking, and at the same time delivers a substantial kinetic energy increase. Your ball will hook a bit less than it did at slower speeds, but that is an easy thing to adjust for, and the kinetic energy boost is definitely worth the trade off. Because it comes with an increase in kinetic energy, increasing ball speed should be one of the first tools you reach for when you need to get more length out of your shot.

ADJUSTMENT 5: AXIS ROTATION

Axis rotation is a much simpler concept than bowlers make it out to be. It is the functional equivalent of turning the front wheels on your car in order to make it turn a corner. As your ball travels down the lane, it is spinning on an imaginary axis that runs through the ball. When you hear "axis," think "axle." Our tire spins on its axle; our ball spins on its axis. If we want our car to turn left, we have to turn the front axles toward the left. If we want our ball to curve to the left, we have to rotate the ball's axis toward the left. The amount we turn the car's axle determines how sharply the car moves left. The amount we rotate the ball's axis determines how sharply the ball moves left.

The analogy between the car's axle and the ball's axis runs even deeper. Think about approaching a left turn in your car. If you don't turn the wheels enough, your car goes too far into the intersection, does not turn enough to make the corner, and you run up on the opposite curb. If you turn the wheels too sharply your car will skid too far through the intersection on the sides of the front tires, and then when it slows down enough, the tires will stop sliding and suddenly grab the road, jerking the car violently to the left. Too little rotation of the axle makes the car go too far through the intersection and turn too little. Too much rotation of the axle also makes the car go too far through the intersection and then turn too sharply. But if you turn the axle just the right amount based on your speed, the car turns smoothly and controllably.

Your ball works in precisely the same manner. If you don't rotate its spin axis enough—that is, if you don't turn the steering wheel enough—the ball goes too long and doesn't hook enough to make it back to the pocket. If you rotate its spin axis too much the ball goes too long and then hooks too violently. Rotate the ball's axis just the right amount, and it travels a reasonable distance and makes a nice, controllable curve.

What bowlers refer to as axis rotation is what a physicist would call *slip angle*. On a car, slip angle is simply the difference between where the front wheels are pointing and the direction the car is traveling. In bowling, slip angle (axis rotation) is the difference between the angle our ball is pointing as it spins and the direction it is skidding down the oily part of the lane (Figure 13.9).

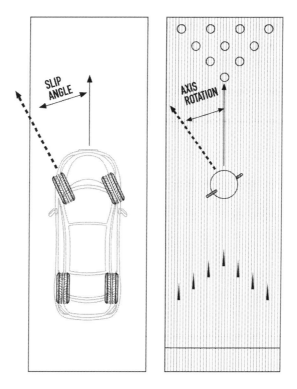

Figure 13.9: Slip Angle and Axis Rotation

So how do we know how much axis rotation is optimal? If we set maximizing hook as our goal, then a branch of physics called *dynamics* provides a way to calculate optimal axis rotation based on your ball speed and rev rate. The derivation of the formula is way beyond our mathematical skills, but the application of it is quite simple. For those with a mathematical bent, optimal axis rotation is the arcsine of rev rate times the radius of the ball, divided by ball speed ($\sin^{-1} \omega r/v$), where rev rate is in radians per second, ball radius is in meters, and ball speed is in meters per second.[57] For the rest of us, the formula shows us an interesting relationship even if we don't delve deeply into the math.

Since the radius of the ball never changes, let's just ignore it and say that optimal axis rotation is a function of rev rate divided by ball speed, or revs/speed. This simple relationship tells us that as rev rate goes up, optimal axis rotation goes up. The effect of ball speed is the opposite; higher ball speed calls for a *lower* optimal axis rotation. The higher your rev rate, the higher your axis rotation should be. The higher your ball speed, the lower your axis rotation should be. This relationship is not intuitive at all, but it is fact.

To save you a lot of trouble, we have calculated the optimal axis rotation for various rev rates and ball speeds, and the results are presented in Table 13.1. Just trace across from your rev rate and down from your ball speed, and your optimal axis rotation is in the box where those two lines intersect. The calculations reveal that for combinations where revs and ball speed are in balance—that is, not rev dominant nor speed dominant— optimal axis rotation falls within a band between roughly 25 and 35 degrees. Figure 13.10 shows us what 0, 20, 40, 60, and 80 degrees of axis rotation looks like from the foul line. The large dot on the ball represents your PAP. As you can see in the photos, the 25 to 35 degree optimal range is not very much rotation at all.

Optimal Axis Rotation

Rev Rate (RPM)	12 MPH 5.36 M/s	13 MPH 5.81 M/s	14 MPH 6.26 M/s	15 MPH 6.71 M/s	16 MPH 7.15 M/s	17 MPH 7.6 M/s	18 MPH 8.05 M/s	19 MPH 8.49 M/s	20 MPH 8.94 M/s
180	23°	21°	19°	18°	17°	16°	15°	14°	13°
200	25°	23°	21°	20°	19°	18°	17°	16°	15°
220	28°	26°	24°	22°	21°	19°	18°	17°	16°
240	31°	28°	26°	24°	23°	21°	20°	19°	18°
260	34°	31°	28°	26°	25°	23°	22°	20°	19°
280	37°	33°	31°	29°	27°	25°	23°	22°	21°
300	40°	36°	33°	31°	29°	27°	25°	24°	23°
320	43°	39°	36°	33°	31°	29°	27°	26°	24°
340	46°	42°	38°	35°	33°	31°	29°	27°	26°
360	50°	45°	41°	38°	35°	33°	31°	29°	27°
380	54°	48°	44°	40°	37°	35°	33°	31°	29°
400	59°	52°	47°	43°	40°	37°	35°	33°	31°
420	64°	56°	50°	46°	42°	39°	37°	34°	32°
440	70°	60°	54°	49°	45°	41°	39°	36°	34°
460	79°	65°	57°	52°	47°	44°	41°	38°	36°
480	90°	71°	61°	55°	50°	46°	43°	40°	38°
500	90°	80°	66°	59°	53°	49°	45°	42°	40°

Table 13.1: Optimal axis rotation

Figure 13.10: Axis rotation, 0, 20, 40, 60, and 80 degrees

WHAT AXIS ROTATION DOES

Dynamics tells us that as axis rotation increases from zero degrees up to our optimal slip angle, hook will steadily increase. However once we go beyond the optimal value, hook starts going back down again. This means that the relationship between axis rotation and hook is not linear in the "more equals more," or "more equals less" sense. Let's explore this relationship in practical terms so we can figure out how axis rotation will affect our own shot.

If you don't turn your car's wheels at all, the car will obviously go straight through the intersection. The same is true of our ball at zero degrees of axis rotation. Zero degrees of rotation means the ball has all forward roll and no side roll, so it goes very long and never hooks. In fact, bowlers who don't own a plastic ball use this to their advantage when they throw their strike ball straight at a corner pin spare.

As we increase our axis rotation, that is, as we turn the ball toward the left just as we would turn our car's wheels to the left, the ball hooks more and more and also earlier and earlier. This increase in hook and decrease in distance continues all the way up to our optimal axis rotation value, at which point hook is maximized and distance is minimized. As we continue to increase axis rotation past this optimal value, a curious thing happens. Our ball starts to go longer again, and though the total amount of hook also decreases, the hook we do get becomes sharper and more violent (Figure 13.11).

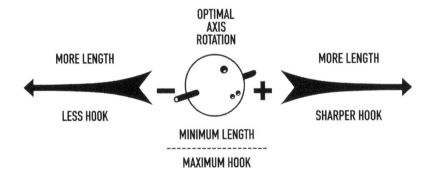

Figure 13.11: Distance and hook as axis rotation increases and decreases

As we get up to very high levels of axis rotation, our ball will go very far down the lane and then jump sharply to the left. Though the actual hook phase will not cover as many boards, it will turn the corner more sharply, and the sharper angle will still give the ball a chance to make it back to the pocket (Figure 13.12).

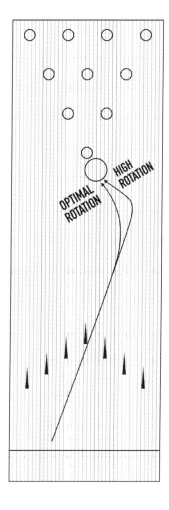

Figure 13.12: Entry angle as axis rotation increases

Figuring out how to apply axis rotation adjustments would be very easy if we all released our "normal" shot at our optimal level of rotation. If we did start at our optimal level, decreasing rotation would make the ball go longer and hook less sharply and increasing rotation would make the ball go longer and hook more sharply. The problem is that very few bowlers release at their optimal rotation. The vast majority of bowlers we observe have "normal" axis rotation that is higher than optimal, sometimes significantly so. We aren't being judgmental here, just making an observation, and in fact both of us have "normal" axis rotation that is higher than the optimal level too.

     Starting with more than the optimal degree of axis rotation just means that rotation adjustments are a little more complex than they otherwise would be. If you release with higher than optimal rotation, then you are starting out somewhere along the right half of the spectrum in Figure 13.11. Your ball is going longer and hooking a bit more sharply than it would if you started at your optimal rotation. If you increase your axis rotation above your "normal" level your ball will go longer and will hook more sharply. Decreasing your axis rotation from your normal level is not so straightforward though, and becomes a two-stage process. Since you started out with higher than optimal axis rotation, as you start to decrease from your normal rotation you are actually moving toward your optimal level. Your ball will therefore hook earlier and more, though a bit less sharply. This gives your ball more of an arc or "continuous" motion, and less of a skid/flip reaction. This will continue all the way down to your optimal rotation level. As your rotation drops below your optimal level, your ball will then start to go longer and straighter.

We know this sounds a little confusing, so let's simplify it. Assuming that you—like most bowlers we have seen—have higher than optimal axis rotation as your normal release, then we can sum it up as follows: Increasing your axis rotation will make your ball go longer and have a sharper hook. Decreasing axis rotation will make your ball hook earlier and in a more continuous fashion. Decrease it too far, though, and your ball starts to go longer and straighter. Decrease it all the way to zero, and your ball goes straight.

HOW TO ALTER AXIS ROTATION

Now we know what axis rotation is and what it does, but how do we physically alter our ball's axis rotation? The amount of axis rotation you impart to the ball is a function of where your hand is in relation to the ball during your release. If your hand is directly behind the ball at the point of release you will get all forward roll and zero degrees of axis rotation. The ball's spin axis will be perpendicular to its path, just like the axle on a bicycle wheel. As you "turn the wheel" to the left by moving your hand more and more toward the side of the ball, axis rotation increases. If your hand is completely on the side of the ball at the point of release, your axis rotation will be 90 degrees, or all side roll and no forward roll. Figure 13.13 shows the hand positions required for zero through 90 degrees of axis rotation. Note the change in location of the bowler's PAP, marked with a square of white tape, as his hand moves to the side of the ball.

Figure 13.13: Hand position as axis rotation increases from zero to 90 degrees

Being able to manipulate axis rotation via different hand positions at release is paramount to success in bowling at the highest level, and is an important skill for the rest of us when competing on sport conditions. Changing the amount of axis rotation alters not only distance, but also the resultant shape of the overall ball motion. Being able to affect these changes is critical to properly adjusting to lane transition, especially when competing on tough conditions. When we use the term "matching up" in bowling, we are referring to finding the right combination of factors that allow you to fine tune your ball motion so you can score at a high level, not only at the beginning of the block when the oil pattern is fresh, but also throughout the entire competition. Axis rotation is a very powerful tool, and mastery of it will help you match up to the lanes for much longer periods before having to move or change balls.

Getting your hand into the proper position to set your axis rotation can be done either statically or dynamically. Most bowlers employ static rotation. In static rotation, the bowler's hand turns to the side of the ball very early in the downswing and is sometimes even preset there in the stance. The hand then stays in that position through the rest of the swing and release. Since the fingers are already on the side of the ball when the thumb releases, a relatively high degree of axis rotation is achieved. There is nothing intrinsically wrong with static rotation, and it is the most common release we see in league bowlers. The limitation is that most bowlers we have talked to who employ static rotation don't even know that their hand is on the side of the ball at release, so changing rotation becomes difficult.

Most high-level bowlers adjust their axis rotation dynamically. Their hand does not turn during their swing, and they enter their release zone with their hand mostly behind the ball. Just prior to release, they turn their hand to their desired position toward the side of the ball, release with their thumb, and spin the ball with their fingers just as we described in Chapter 5. They regulate axis rotation by controlling how far their hand turns toward the side of the ball. They can keep their hand behind the ball for zero degrees of rotation, turn it all the way to the side for 90 degrees, or stop at any point in between.

If you adjust axis rotation dynamically, you are already used to moving your hand around the ball prior to release. Making adjustments becomes simply a matter of learning how to control how far your hand rotates. Of course, a bowler could statically set any degree of hand rotation prior to release too, but since they aren't rotating their hand around the ball consciously, learning to make these adjustments is a bit more difficult.

Axis rotation is actually a rather easy thing to adjust, though you will have to really concentrate during practice in order to override your old muscle memory. Adding this skill to your game opens up new ways to attack a tournament condition. Gaining the ability to alter your axis rotation will be well worth the effort it takes to master it, as it will allow you to match up to the lane more consistently and to tweak your shot to get your ball back in the true pocket for better carry.

ADJUSTMENT 6: AXIS TILT

Changing axis tilt is a less common adjustment than axis rotation, but it shouldn't be. There are many reasons why tilt is neglected. Most bowlers we talk to don't completely understand what axis tilt is or what it does to ball motion. They don't know how to alter it, and they believe it is a difficult skill to master. Tilt is in fact no harder to master than is axis rotation, but learning how to do it properly will require a fair bit of practice and repetition.

While axis rotation describes which way the ball's "axle" is turned toward the left or right, axis tilt describes the degree to which the ball's "axle" is tipped from horizontal (Figure 13.14). The effect that axis tilt has on your ball's path is far simpler than axis rotation. As we increase axis tilt, our ball will go farther down the lane before hooking and will hook less and less. If we were to increase axis tilt all the way to 90 degrees, our PAP would be right on top of the ball and the ball would go perfectly straight. The reason that axis tilt increases length while decreasing hook is a little bit complex, but it ultimately comes down to geometry and friction.

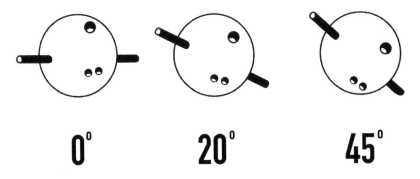

Figure 13.14: Axis tilt

To understand why axis tilt increases length and decreases hook, we need to look at our ball's *track*, which is the strip of coverstock that contacts the lane during one revolution. Bowling balls have a diameter of just over 8-1/2 inches, which means they have a circumference—the distance around the ball—of roughly 27 inches. If our axis tilt is zero degrees, that is, if our ball's "axle" is completely horizontal, then the ball's track will wrap around the full circumference of the ball, as in the first drawing in Figure 13.15, below. In geometry, this full-circumference path is called the *great circle*. It is like the Earth's equator, and is the longest possible circular path around the ball. As the axis is tilted higher the path no longer traces out a great circle. As we see in Figure 13.15, as axis tilt increases, the diameter and circumference of the track become progressively smaller. When the axis it tilted at 20 degrees the circumference of the ball track shrinks from 27 inches down to 21 inches. At 45 degrees of tilt the track has a circumference of only 14 inches, or about half of what it had at zero degrees of tilt.

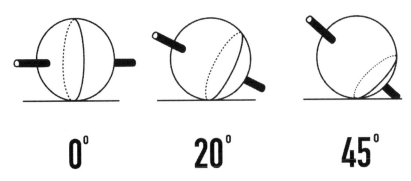

Figure 13.15: Ball track circumference as a function of axis tilt

So geometry dictates that as axis tilt increases, the size of the ball's track decreases, but how does that affect distance and hook? Recall that hook, in terms of both magnitude and distance, is a function of friction, where more friction equates to more and earlier hook. Let's perform a little experiment. Place a rubber pencil eraser and a basketball shoe on a table, and try to slide them toward you. Which object requires more force to slide? Obviously the basketball shoe requires more force because it has a large amount of frictional surface grabbing the table, while the eraser's tiny frictional footprint is relatively easy to overcome. The same thing happens with a bowling ball as we increase axis tilt.

If your axis tilt is zero degrees your ball is tracking on its great circle, so each revolution of the ball presents 27 inches of clean frictional surface to the lane as it tries to get a grip and move the ball to the left. If we increase our axis tilt to 20 degrees, each revolution of our ball presents only 21 inches of clean cover. This small increase in tilt caused a 22 percent decrease in friction between the ball and the lane. Since friction has been reduced, the ball skids farther down the lane before hooking, and hooks less. If we increase our axis tilt to 45 degrees we have reduced total friction by a whopping 48 percent. No wonder, then, that such a "spinner" ball skids extremely far down the lane and hooks only a little bit.

CREATING AXIS TILT

Axis tilt is created by bending the wrist sideways, in toward the body. This wrist position is called ulnar deviation, because the wrist is bent toward the ulna bone in the forearm. The photos in Figure 13.16 show how ulnar deviation tilts the bowler's PAP—marked with a square of white tape—up toward the top of the ball. The more you deviate your wrist inward, the greater will be your resulting axis tilt.

Figure 13.16: Axis tilt created by ulnar deviation

While axis rotation is best created "on the fly" during the release, the best way to increase axis tilt is to set up in your stance with your wrist deviated to the proper position, and then to simply maintain it there throughout the entire swing and release (Figure 13.17). Holding your wrist in this deviated position throughout your release is fairly difficult to do at first, and you need to guard against subconsciously relaxing the wrist into your normal position during your swing. After some practice, it will become more natural and easier to do.

Figure 13.17: Setup: normal release (left), axis tilt (right)

The effect that changes in axis tilt have on your bowling ball's path and reaction can be substantial. Tilt and loft, which we will discuss next, were rarely talked about in days past. Very few bowlers used them, because conditions in those days simply didn't require them. Today, porous bowling ball coverstocks and generally higher rev rates are "burning up," or stripping the oil from the heads and mid lanes, often very early in a block. As a result, tilt and loft have both become necessary tools for getting the ball through the burnt parts of the lane.

The increasing use of axis tilt as an adjustment tool is a great example of how the evolution of bowling ball technology and playing styles has forced a change in the way we approach our physical game. As bowlers look for advantages over their opponents in varying situations, they need to find ways to change their ball reactions by controlling distance. Axis tilt is a very useful tool when your ball starts to lose distance and hook in the mid lane. Increasing your axis tilt will get the ball to "push" a little farther down the lane before hooking, and gives you another option if moving your target line left or right isn't the best choice.

ADJUSTMENT 7: LOFT

Like axis tilt, loft was rarely used as an adjustment tool until recently. Loft is the rather poetic name we give to the act of throwing the ball farther down the lane. Most bowlers we have measured loft the ball two or three feet beyond the foul line. We consider this to be "normal," so when we talk about loft we are referring to greater distances; often much greater.

Loft is another tool we can use when our ball is hooking too early and we need to get a little more length. It is especially useful when the early hook is caused by "burnt heads." This condition is not as gruesome as it sounds. "Heads" refers to the first third or so of the lane, where the oil is supposed to be the heaviest. "Burnt" is bowler slang meaning that the oil that is supposed to be on the heads is gone, either carried away by high-end bowling balls, carried down toward the end of the lane by plastic balls or ancient urethane equipment, or just soaked into old wood lanes through cracks and failing varnish.

Burnt heads create excessive friction very early in the ball's path. This causes the ball to lose speed and axis rotation far too soon, resulting in an early and muted hook, a fairly straight ball path, and a weak hit because of the excessive loss of ball speed. Our other tools increased length by manipulating the amount of friction between the ball and the lane. Loft is far cruder. Loft increases length by effectively making the lane shorter.

Suppose our normal loft distance is two feet. This means that the ball will encounter friction along the remaining 58 feet to the headpin. If we were to loft our ball six feet out onto the lane, it will only encounter friction over the last 54 feet. We have effectively skipped over some of the excessive friction on the heads, allowing our ball to hang onto its speed and axis rotation a bit longer.

CREATING LOFT

We create loft in a manner similar to how we alter speed—by using our body and not our arm. Many bowlers make the mistake of using their bowling arm to literally throw the ball farther out onto the lane when they want to increase loft. In our discussion of altering ball speed, we talked about the many reasons why using arm swing to increase or decrease speed was such a bad idea, and the same admonitions apply to using the arm to increase loft. While using arm strength to throw the ball farther down the lane will certainly increase loft, doing so tends to cause the bowler to "grab" the ball, leading to an inconsistent release and an unpredictable ball path.

To keep our arm swing and release more "quiet" and natural, loft has to come from the lower body, specifically the hips. As bowlers advance on the approach from the stance to the foul line, they gradually lower their hips four to six inches as they move from a fairly upright posture to a deep knee bend. It helps to picture this motion like an airplane coming in for a landing—a gradual descent with a smooth, tapered finish on the tarmac. To increase loft, you glide in for your landing as usual, but then you rise back up part way just before release, as if the plane decided to take off again without landing. As you are going into your slide and your swing is nearing the release zone, straighten the knee of your slide leg just a little, bringing your hips back up. This action will cause you to release the ball from a slightly higher position, which changes the trajectory and results in a longer "glide path" before the ball touches down on the lane.

By varying the degree to which you rise back up before release, you can control how far you loft the ball. The higher you rise back up, the farther the ball will go before touching down on the lane (Figure 13.18). Using your lower body to gain loft allows the upper body and bowling arm to stay relaxed, keeping your swing, release, and timing consistent from shot to shot.

Figure 13.18: Varying loft by varying finish position

We have worked with hundreds of bowlers as they learned to control loft using their legs rather than their arm, and the great majority of them were able to very quickly add this valuable tool to their tool kit. If you don't already use loft as an adjustment tool, put it into your upcoming practice plans. Start paying attention to the better players when you watch or compete in tournaments. You will see loft being employed far more often than you may have imagined, especially later in the block. Loft is rapidly becoming a necessary adjustment tool.

ADJUSTMENT 8: REV RATE

Rev rate has traditionally been the hardest thing for bowlers to vary, so it rarely figured into most bowlers' adjustment tool kit. Even where a bowler had the skill to do so, they still rarely employed it as an adjustment. In today's game, oil patterns seem designed to reward high revs, so bowlers tend to want their rev rate maximized at all times. Cutting down on revs will make your ball go longer and hook less, but we have already discussed easier ways to do the same thing without requiring you to back off on a skill you have worked hard to develop.

For bowlers who want to add rev rate adjustment as a tool, there is a method available that will allow you to do it rather easily. Recall our discussion in Chapter 5 of the three types of releases; passive, static, and active. The highest possible rev rate for a conventional, one-hand bowler results from using an active release. If your normal release is active, you can cut your revs quite a bit by switching to a static release, and with practice may even be able to create a release halfway between the two by maintaining the forward flexing of the wrist from the active release, but without the extension beforehand. Of course there would be nothing stopping you from decreasing revs even further by going to a passive release, though it does not seem to us to be a terribly productive option. Again, there are other tools available to increase distance and cut hook without altering the powerful release you've been working so hard to create.

Many bowlers and coaches teach that rev rate can be altered by varying the placement of the index finger and pinkie finger of your bowling hand in your setup. The standard line is that by sticking your pinkie out you will cut your revs, and pulling your pinkie in and sticking your index finger out will increase revs. Revs can be maximized, so the idea goes, by simultaneously sticking your index finger out while tucking your pinkie finger under such that the knuckle of your pinkie finger rather than the tip contacts the ball—often painfully so.

The idea behind the finger position theory is that the index and pinkie finger somehow create extra drag or extra spin against the surface of the ball during release. There's a big problem with that idea, though. Look closely at Figure 13.19, which is a frame capture from a video of PBA bowler Brad Angelo's release. We can clearly see that once his thumb exits and he begins to rev the ball forward, the only fingers still in contact with the ball are the two that are in the finger holes, and it is these two fingers that spin the ball. Since his index and pinkie fingers are not touching the ball at all, how can they possibly affect his revs? The obvious answer is that they can't.

Figure 13.19: Index and pinkie fingers during release

We did not cherry pick Mr. Angelo's release to demonstrate this point. Look again at the various release photos in Chapter 5, and you will see the same thing. Every bowler we looked at, whether amateur or professional, does precisely this. As soon as a bowler begins to release his or her ball, it immediately starts to fall away from their hand, leaving the middle two fingers as the only point of contact. Since your index and pinkie fingers are not in contact with the ball during your release, go ahead put them wherever they feel most comfortable or wherever you need to make the ball sit in your hand the way you want it to. We don't see any way that they can affect your rev rate.

ASSESSING YOUR TOOL KIT

The more adjustment tools you have available to you, the easier it will be to keep your ball in the pocket and keep striking. We have now studied the eight possible adjustments available to bowlers. We have described the effect each will have on distance, and therefore on the shape of the ball path, and we have learned the basics of their execution. That was the easy part. There are two more steps involved before you can assemble your adjustment tools into an effective tool kit, and before you can become confident and competent in their application.

You need to devote a number of practice sessions to developing and evaluating each of the eight adjustment tools. Find a line to the pocket using your standard delivery and release. Once you have it dialed in, try out one of the eight tools without changing any other shot variable. Carefully observe what the tool does to the distance and shape of the shot. Practice each tool over and over until making the change becomes natural, and predicting what it will do to the shot becomes second nature.

You may find that some of the tools are simply unavailable to you. You may have physical limitations that prevent you from using a tool, or may simply not yet have enough knowledge or experience to be able to coach yourself. That's fine. Eliminate the tools that you are physically unable to use, and seek qualified coaching to help you develop those you are having trouble with. Some of these changes are very technical in nature, so a truly qualified coach may prove essential. Don't just ask the high average bowler with the insane rev rate for help, because he may not be doing these things correctly either!

Once you have decided which tools belong in your tool kit and have practiced them until you are very comfortable in their execution, you need to prioritize them, deciding which will be your "go to" tools and which will be your last resorts. Base your decision on which you are most comfortable with using, which you have practiced the most, and which work best for you given your own unique physical and mental game and the conditions you are bowling on.

You've now assembled your bowler's tool kit. You know what each tool is and what it does, and you have developed at least a basic comfort level with using each of them. Now comes the hardest part of all—learning when to apply them and which to use in a given situation.

Unfortunately, there is no shortcut to this process. The time required to learn the adjustments is not exceedingly long, but the time it takes to gain the experience necessary to make effective in-game decisions is a process; a journey. Think about our sport at the highest levels. You still see a great many bowlers succeeding who are 35 or more years old. In most sports, that is past retirement age, but in bowling, you are just hitting your prime. Longevity in the sport is the secret to gaining experience, and there is no substitute for putting yourself out there and competing in tournaments and on tougher conditions.

There are more and more young players making a splash at elite levels now. Don't let their tender years trick you into thinking they managed to win without experience. Chances are they have already gained years of experience beginning at a very early age. At the risk of sounding self-serving, a big reason they were able to gain that experience early is because of the availability of better coaching. Many of today's top players have had the benefit of private coaching as youth bowlers, and then went on to train and compete in high school and in a great college program. They continue to work with their coach as they make their mark in professional and amateur competition. If you aren't currently working with a certified, knowledgeable coach, we urge you to do so. A coach can help you develop a practice plan for acquiring the skills discussed in this chapter, and can help you learn when to apply them on varying lane conditions. You can certainly do all of this by yourself, but the journey is always shorter and easier with an experienced guide.

Throwing a bowling ball better and more consistently is only a small part of being a great bowler. Bowling is easy when you are striking and everything is going your way, but on most days you are going to have to work for it. The following chapters will help you recognize and understand what is happening on the lane when strikes become harder to find, and will help you to fearlessly put your newfound adjustment skills into action and get back into the game.

CHAPTER 14

APPLYING YOUR TOOLS

IN THE PREVIOUS chapter we described the adjustments we can use to alter ball reaction and maximize scoring as the lanes transition. Hopefully you will find time to experiment with all of them, determine which ones you are able to perform, and note what each does to your own ball path. All of these adjustments are intended to do one thing; alter where your ball hits the headpin. But how do you know when an adjustment is required? How do you decide which one to apply?

The information we need to make these decisions is usually right in front of us, but we often fail to see it. You may not know what to look for or how to interpret what you see. You may see and understand what's happening but not know what to do about it. Even worse, if you've been throwing shot after shot that you think are good but that fail to strike, frustration sets in, blinding you to what the lane, the pins, and the ball are trying to tell you.

There is a lot going on out on the lane all at once, far more than most bowlers are even aware of. Bowling is a very complex game with a lot of ever-changing variables, and most of them are out of our control. All of these variables play into how your ball is reacting now, and how it is likely to react next frame. We can't directly see these variables, but we can often figure them out by watching how the ball reacts and how the pins fall. In this chapter we will talk about what these variables are, how to recognize and interpret the clues they provide, and how to decide which of your adjustment tools to apply to help you adapt to them.

SETTING THE STAGE

Lane transition occurs when the lane oil gets pushed around, depleted in high traffic areas, and sometimes even redeposited by the ball onto parts of the lane that are supposed to be dry. The outcome is that the shot changes, and what had been working fine gradually stops working, requiring you to make a change. Lane transition is a fact of life. It's going to happen, and there is nothing we can do about it. If we are observant, though, there are plenty of clues available before competition even starts that will help us anticipate not only the conditions we are likely to see, but also when, how, and how much these conditions are likely to change.

There is no way to know with certainty how or when the lanes will transition. The best you can do is make an educated guess, but an educated guess is still better than no plan at all. You may have to alter or completely abandon your initial assessment, but even if you've guessed wrong, planning for change keeps you engaged with what is happening.

Since you know that *something* is going to change, you will be more attentive and will not become complacent, missing clues or failing to act on them. It's not always the physical game that wins tournaments. Sometimes winning comes down to paying attention to all of the invisible information that is molding how the lanes play and transition, and then choosing your best combination of adjustments to stay matched up. Let's look at some of the preliminary clues and what they might tell us.

TYPE AND AGE OF LANE SURFACE

The type of lane surface you bowl on will have a large effect on ball motion, both initially and after transition. There are three different lane surface types; wood, synthetic, and synthetic overlay (Lane Shield and Guardian). Wood lanes are made from laminated strips of wood, much like a butcher block or cutting board. Hard maple is used in the front part of the lane to resist the abuse caused by the heavy ball, and the back portion is made of much softer pine. Wood lanes are coated with a polyurethane varnish or a waterborne finish. Synthetic lanes are made up of panels of resin-impregnated paper laminate. They can be thought of as giant sheets of Formica like we might find on kitchen countertops or laminate flooring. Synthetic overlay is essentially a huge translucent sticker that is placed over the surface of old, worn out wood lanes in an effort to squeeze a few more years of life out of them.

These three lane surfaces differ from one another in many ways, but the most important difference to the bowler is surface hardness. Surface hardness translates directly into friction—the softer the surface, the higher the friction. There are a number of ways to measure surface hardness, but for bowling lanes we use a system called Sward hardness, which involves measuring how long it takes a weighted rocker to stop rocking when placed atop a surface sample. Lower hardness numbers equate to a softer surface.

Synthetic overlays are the softest and therefore highest friction lane surfaces. They have a Sward hardness of around 20. Wood lanes come next in line, with a hardness of about 30. Wood lanes are very easy to identify. A close look reveals that they are individual strips of wood, often with visible cracks between some of the boards. Overlays will look like what they are; wood lanes with a clear plastic film over the top. Wood lanes and wood/overlay lanes are still found in many older and smaller bowling centers.

Synthetic lane surfaces are far harder than either wood or overlay. There are many different synthetic lane surfaces on the market, but the most common, at least in the United States, are HPL and SPL, made by QubicaAMF, and Pro Lane and Anvilane, made by Brunswick. Of the four, HPL is the softest at 50–60 Sward, but it is still almost twice as hard as wood. SPL is just a bit harder than HPL, at 60–70 Sward. AMF lane surfaces can be identified by their very realistic natural maple wood look, with randomly placed darker and lighter boards, though they are also sometimes found in crazy colors in "entertainment center" type bowling centers.

Brunswick Pro Lane and Anvilane are the hardest commonly found lane surfaces. At 75–90 Sward, they are almost three times as hard as wood. Brunswick surfaces can be recognized by some trademarked features. Anvilane has natural looking wood coloration, with a dark outline between every board. Pro Lane has alternating darker and lighter boards, with outlines around every fifth board corresponding to the locations of the dots and arrows. Pro Lane also has four unique dark marker boards located about two-thirds of the way down the lane.

Another factor affecting lane friction is the age of the surface. Lanes wear down over time, causing friction to increase. This will be especially pronounced in what is know as the track area, which is a swath of lane in the vicinity of the second arrow where the majority of league and recreational bowlers play. The older the lane surface, the more we can expect wear and the resulting friction. The age of the surface is sometimes difficult to obtain. The lane maintenance tech may know, if you can find him or her. If the owner or manager is working the front desk, they will likely know too. If you can't get an answer, the best you can do is just guess based on appearance and condition whether it's older, newer, or somewhere in between.

We've now assessed the type and condition of the lane surface, but what clues does this give us about how the lanes might play? On softer lane surfaces you can expect your ball to hook earlier than on harder surfaces. The harder the surface, the longer your ball will skid before hooking. On softer surfaces the ball will slow down and lose energy more quickly than on harder surfaces. Once you've made your friction assessment based on surface type, you can then adjust for age. The older the surface, the earlier you can expect your ball to hook.

Information on lane type and condition can help you select the right bowling ball. In general, on higher friction conditions you will want a ball with a higher RG and a weaker coverstock to help it get farther down the lane before hooking. On lower friction conditions a stronger ball will be in order, with a lower RG and a higher end coverstock. Think of this as trying to strike a balance. On higher friction lanes, you'll want a lower friction ball. On lower friction conditions, you'll want a higher friction ball. The specific ball selected will depend on your individual delivery and release characteristics, but these general rules will at least keep you in the proper part of your arsenal.

Understanding the lane surface we are bowling on will also help in predicting lane transition. It has been our experience that wood lanes transition faster, more often, and more severely than do synthetics. We have not noticed any real difference in transition between the various synthetic surfaces. This is all just anecdotal, though, based on observation rather than science. Your own experience may differ, and there is always the possibility of anomalous conditions at any given bowling center. What is actually happening on your lanes always trumps what you expected to happen.

TYPE OF LANE OIL

The type of oil applied to the lanes—called *conditioner* in professional jargon— has a profound effect on lane friction. *Viscosity* describes the flow characteristics of a liquid. Think of it as a measure of how runny or thick the liquid is. There are a number of ways to measure viscosity, but the most common unit is *centipoise*. We don't need to know what centipoise is; we just need to know that the higher the value, the thicker the liquid. The lane oils we looked at had viscosity values in the range of 30 to 50 centipoise. A good way to visualize what these numbers mean is to compare the lane conditioner viscosity to common liquids you are already familiar with. Water has a viscosity of 1 centipoise, and pancake syrup is around 200. The corn oil in your kitchen cupboard has a viscosity of about 30, which is at the low end of the lane oil spectrum. Olive oil measures roughly 40. Cream has a viscosity of around 50, which is equal to the heavier lane oils.

In Chapter 8 we discussed hydrodynamic friction, which describes the conditions on the oily front part of the lane. Under hydrodynamic conditions, any friction our ball is able to get will be between the ball and the oil rather than between the ball and the lane surface. Under such conditions, the more viscous (thicker) the oil, the higher will be the friction. The ball will both grab a little earlier and slow down a little more when higher viscosity lane oil is used. Higher viscosity oils will also tend to stay in place longer, decreasing the amount of transition we are likely to experience.

We mention lane oil type because it is definitely a factor affecting both playing conditions and transition, but it is unfortunately a factor that is likely to remain invisible to us. The lane maintenance person certainly knows which specific oil was used, but even if they told you what it was, it would take a lot of research to get anything meaningful from it. There are currently 146 different lane oils from 19 different manufacturers approved for use. Some manufacturers publish viscosity figures, and some do not. Some quote viscosity in centipoise, and some use other units that would need to be converted. About the best you are going to do is to hope the lane tech can tell you if the oil is high or low viscosity.

LANE TOPOGRAPHY

Topography is, without question, the lane variable that has the biggest effect but gets the least respect. When a lane behaves in a way we did not expect, we are quick to blame the oil, but in a great many cases it is actually lane topography that caused the problem. So what is topography?

Topography describes "the lay of the land." It is a description of the three-dimensional surface of a piece of land, or in our case a bowling lane, including the hills, valleys, slopes, and other variations. We tend to view bowling lanes as being flat, but none of them are. Not even close. Worse yet, the topography—the bumps and dips and swales—differs from lane to lane. The USBC currently allows variations from true flatness of up to 40 thousandths of an inch, or 0.04 inches over each 41-1/2 inches of lane. Just how big of a hill or valley is that? 40 thousandths of an inch is 1 millimeter. This is roughly the thickness of nine pages in this book, or almost as thick as a U.S. dime.

Now one millimeter certainly does not seem like much of a variation, especially when spread over 41-1/2 inches of width or length, but it is enough to have a meaningful effect on ball motion. Kegel, a manufacturer of lane dressing machines and other bowling products, set up a pair of test lanes. One lane was flat, or at least as flat as it was humanly possible to get it. The other had variations in topography, but all well within legal limits. They asked three professional bowlers to play on them, without telling them what they had done. Hall of Fame bowler Pete Weber experienced a ten board difference in how he had to play the two lanes, despite the fact that they were oiled precisely the same. Weber said of the lanes, "I was blown away when they told me the lanes were oiled the same, but sloped differently... and [that] they were still legal."[58]

A golfer squats down low and sights across a green to try to see the subtle variations in topography that will influence the path of their putt. We do not have that ability in bowling. Our hills and valleys are too small to see. Kegel invented a machine capable of measuring these slight variations from flatness and printing out an easy to read lane map displaying the results graphically. If graphs of topography were available every time you bowled, bowling would be much easier. Because you could "see" the topography on which you were bowling, you would know exactly where to play on each lane to avoid detrimental topographic features and to take advantage of beneficial ones. The reality, though, is that you will almost always bowl without the benefit of topography graphs.

Though we can't see the hills and valleys directly or in most cases even view them on a map, we can still see their effects very clearly as we watch our ball go down the lane. If you know you've released your ball well and hit your mark but your ball does something different on the left lane than on it did on the right lane, you can safely chalk it up to differences in topography. Instead of trying to play these two lanes the same, make an adjustment on the bad lane to counteract the unfavorable topography. Bowlers often assume that both lanes on their pair should play the same, and they will make adjustments on one lane based on their ball motion on the other. This is often the cause of those nights where you just feel lost and can't seem to ever find the pocket. There will be many times when you will need to play your two lanes differently from one another, and this is largely due to differences in topography.

TEMPERATURE AND HUMIDITY IN THE BOWLING CENTER

The temperature and humidity in the bowling center can play a big part in how the lanes play. Temperature affects the viscosity of the lane oil. When temperatures go down, the viscosity of the lane oil goes up. When temperatures go up, the viscosity of the oil decreases. Lane oils typically change viscosity between one-half and two centipoise units for each degree of change in ambient temperature. If the temperature in the bowling center is low, lane oils will thicken considerably, resulting in increased resistance and increased friction. Your ball will slow down sooner and hook a little earlier. Additionally, the colder, more viscous oil doesn't move around as much, so transition is reduced. Carry down is also decreased, and the back ends stay dryer and stronger for a longer period of time. Cooler conditions in the bowling center therefore suggest using a weaker ball with a higher RG or a less aggressive coverstock, or a more open, or angled ball path. The reverse is true when the bowling center is warm. Warm conditions cause oil viscosity to decrease, making conditions far more slippery. Your ball will go longer before hooking, and the oil will be pushed around sooner and to a greater degree. Warm conditions may therefore call for a stronger ball or a straighter and more direct line.

Humidity in the bowling center can have a big impact on your game by changing the lane topography. Many synthetic lanes are installed over pre-existing wood lanes. In climates with high humidity in the summer, moisture in the air finds its way between the boards on the old wood lane. The moisture causes the wood to swell and bow beneath the synthetic panels, causing the lane to crown in the middle and slope downhill toward the gutters. Any ball thrown too far toward the outside of the lane will have to actually climb a hill in order to hook back to the headpin, so you will have much less miss room to the outside. In the winter, when humidity is lower, the panels sink and create a dish-like effect. The outsides now slope downhill toward the center of the lane, so shots tend to hook more and miss room toward the outside of the lane increases. If a perfectly legal 0.040 inch crown in the lane was enough to make Pete Weber have to play the lanes 10 boards differently, imagine what a humidity-induced bow or cup in the lane surface will do!

Since high humidity can cause crowning of the lane surface, you may have to play closer to the inside part of the lane to avoid the downhill slope toward the gutter. If you choose to play an outside line out near the gutter, the crowned lane will force you to use a straighter ball path. You will also want to use a ball with a stronger cover that can get some friction a little earlier so that it doesn't have to make the entire uphill climb only on the back part of the lane.

Cupping of the lanes when humidity decreases gives you "free hook" on the outside part of the lane. The downhill slope toward the headpin makes your ball hook harder and earlier than it otherwise would have. To get maximum benefit from this effect, move your breakpoint farther right and use a ball with a weaker cover so that it won't hook as early when it hits the slope on the outside of the lane.

THE OTHER BOWLERS ON YOUR PAIR

Another great source of information available to you before competition even begins comes from the other bowlers playing on your pair. Too many of us bowl in a vacuum and don't watch what is going on around us. Being observant is one of the most underutilized skills a bowler can possess. Watch where others are playing, watch what type of balls they are using, and see what surface finish those balls have.

Are most of the balls on the ball return shiny, or are they dull? Dull balls tend to pick up more oil than do shiny balls. Your ball is definitely going to hook earlier and earlier as the session wears on, but if you see a lot of dull balls you can expect the early hook to happen sooner than if you see mostly shiny balls.

If most everyone is playing the same part of the lane, you can expect that part of the lane to show early hook sooner rather than later. If you've started the set playing outside of them, you can anticipate running into a mess if you try to move toward the center of the lane later in the block. If you are fortunate enough to possess a high rev rate, you might consider playing a deeper line, bouncing your ball off of the dry track they will inevitably create.

These are just examples of clues you can get from watching other bowlers. Your own style and capabilities will dictate the strategy you choose to deal with the expected changes, but the important point is to *have a strategy*. This information is out there, waiting for you to use it. Your lane play decisions should come not only from what you see your own ball doing, but also from where others are playing, the balls they are using, and how their shot is reacting on the lane.

We can also gain insight by observing the characteristics of the bowlers on our pair. The most important variable to note is their rev rates. If you are bowling with high rev players, you can expect to see the lane "burn up" sooner than if you were bowling with lower rev rate players. Higher rev rates deplete the lane oil more quickly, making everyone's ball hook much earlier. If you are bowling with high rev players and your ball starts hitting high, assume that the oil is being depleted and make your adjustment accordingly. If you are bowling in a recreational league with a lot of people using plastic balls or rolling ancient, oil-soaked equipment in an end over end manner, you can expect carry down. If you have been striking but your next shot comes in light, assume you've hit a puddle of oil tracked down to the dry part of the lane and adjust accordingly. Careful observation of the other bowlers on your pair will help you quickly accept that a bad result was the fault of the lane, not you. Quicker acceptance leads to quicker adjustments instead of wasting frames trying to tweak your shot.

LOCATION OF YOUR LANES RELATIVE TO THE FRONT DESK

We've already discussed how topography can make one lane or one pair play differently from another, but the location of the lanes within the bowling center can also play a big part. In many centers, the lanes that are closer to the control counter get more play than do those out toward the ends of the house. Bowling center personnel like to keep bowlers in view, especially inexperienced recreational bowlers, so they tend to give them the lanes closer to the counter. Because these lanes get far more play, they often develop more friction than those toward the ends due to increased wear and tear. These high traffic lanes may hook a little earlier or break down a little sooner than the lanes farther from the control counter. This is not true of every bowling center, but it is a common practice and could help you anticipate and explain differences in ball reaction and lane transition.

WATCH FOR CLUES

So we've developed our preliminary assessment based on all of the information available to us before play begins. We know that the lanes will change, and we've made our best guess as to how and when this will happen. But this is all just theory at this point, and as soon as competition begins, theory has to take a back seat to what is actually transpiring. We've got to start watching for real-time clues.

In Chapter 13 we explored why the distance your ball skids down the lane before hooking is far more important than how much it hooks. Skid distance is an easy enough concept to understand, but it is not always easy to see. In an earlier chapter we discussed the trick of the eye called foreshortening. This is the optical illusion that makes objects at a distance from us appear much smaller than they are, and is also what makes our rather gentle and gradual ball path appear to be a sharp, hockey stick–shaped break to the pocket. Foreshortening pertains to our current discussion because it also makes it very difficult for us to judge distances.

Suppose you are throwing your ball out to a breakpoint on the 5-board at a point 45 feet down lane. Everything is going fine, but after a few more shots your ball is hooking a foot earlier. Will you notice this distance change? In all likelihood, you won't. Judging distance on a bowling lane is very difficult anyway because of the lack of reference marks.

Sure, the little box containing the electric eyes is out there on the gutter cap somewhere, and if you are bowling on Brunswick Pro Lane surfaces you get the three-foot-long dark bars on board 10 at 40 feet and board 15 at 34 feet, but that's not much to go on. The real problem, though, comes from foreshortening. From our vantage point at the foul line, if our ball hooks a full foot earlier, the optical illusion created by foreshortening makes that foot of length look like only just over an inch. Are you really observant enough to detect an apparent inch of difference way down the lane? You also probably won't notice that the earlier hook caused your ball to hit the headpin a full board higher than it did on previous shots. It will still almost certainly strike, and that is all most bowlers will see.

A few shots later the ball hooks another foot earlier. Will you notice this? Again, probably not. The two foot decrease in length will appear to be only about 2-1/2 inches. It's tough to see a 2-1/2 inch difference from 43 feet away. But this shot will hit the headpin noticeably higher—on board 19-1/2—which is two full boards left of the pocket, and a strike here is unlikely. Several more shots go by, and now the ball is hooking another foot early, three full feet from where we started. Surely you'll notice this huge change, right? Maybe not. That three foot decrease in length will appear to be less than 4 inches, or about the length of your index finger. What you *will* notice is the ball going right through the nose—dead center on board 20—and you'll certainly notice the huge, ugly split staring back at you. If a change in your ball's distance on a given shot is large enough for you to see, you are already well behind the transition. Since foreshortening makes a foot look like an inch, if the decrease in distance is enough to easily notice then it's actually huge. If we can't detect a decrease in distance that is large enough to affect our shot, how will we ever know what's happening?

The lane is actually transitioning constantly, but transition is very hard to see before its effects become disastrous. There will be times when everything is going along well, but then on the next shot your ball goes crashing through the center of the headpin or even tears off all the way to the Brooklyn side. This doesn't mean the lane changed that much in one shot; it just means that you didn't see it coming. Don't stress. Even the best players can't always pick up on transition and make the needed adjustments before something bad happens. While the lanes won't wave a flag or shout, "Hey, we're transitioning!", there are still plenty of clues that can tip you off before a major distance change becomes visible, and well before disaster strikes.

CLUES FROM TEAMMATES AND OPPONENTS

What other clues are out there? Remember that there are other bowlers on your pair who are fighting the same battle. There will be times when they pick up on the clues faster than you do. Pay attention to the bowlers you trust and watch what they are doing. It can either validate what you are thinking or show you something you may be missing. Watching another bowler's ball motion can give you as much information as your own, so don't bowl in a vacuum. In addition to watching other bowlers' shots, a smart bowler also watches for the one language we all speak—body language. If you are observant, and if you put your clues together, you may learn that it's time for an adjustment without having to suffer a bad frame yourself.

We always advise the competitive bowlers we coach to keep their emotions hidden after a bad shot. You would never tell your opponent that the lanes had changed, because that information would give him or her a competitive advantage. Let them figure it out for themselves the hard way! The problem is, while you remain verbally silent, your body language can still reveal volumes.

The two most useful body language clues are expressions of anger and of surprise. Suppose your opponent throws a shot that goes right through the nose. Watch their body language after the shot. A nonverbal expression of anger will often indicate that the bowler executed a bad shot. Were they shaking their head as they walked back to the ball return? Were they cursing, smacking the ball return, grumbling or snarling? A reaction that signals anger at themselves is a strong indication that they simply threw a bad shot, which means that the lane probably hasn't changed and you don't need to make an adjustment.

Displays of surprise are even more helpful than displays of anger. Surprise is usually the result of the bowler throwing a pretty good shot, but which resulted in a ball reaction that was not at all what they anticipated. These are the shots to really pay attention to. Your opponent's surprise is signaling that the lanes have changed, and fortunately you weren't the poor sap who had to bear the brunt of it. Don't ignore what you saw in that bowler's ball reaction. If you are playing on the same part of the lane, make a decision now on how to adjust your next shot. There is no reason to share their fate.

CLUES FROM THE PINS

We gathered clues before competition began, and used them to formulate a plan. We've been picking up clues as we watch other bowlers, and using them to anticipate changes before we get up there to roll the ball. Now it's our turn to bowl, and if we are observant, the strongest and most direct clues will present themselves. These clues come from the pins, both those left standing after our shot and those that fall late or in an odd way.

This probably doesn't need repeating at this point, but let's do it anyway. The pocket is a very narrow area on the lane, a board or so in width, and centered on board 17-1/2. If pins are left standing or fall late, accept that you've missed the board 17-1/2 pocket. Those remaining or late falling pins are telling you with near certainty that you've missed, even if the shot looked good to you. They are also telling you everything you need to know for your next shot on that lane, if you are willing to listen. The pins are trying to give you critical information, often well before your ball does.

Corner pins left standing after decent shots are almost always telling you that your ball came in light, missing the true pocket a bit to the right (left, for left handers). 4-pins and 4-9 splits for right handers or 6-pins and 6-8s for left handers tell you that your ball hit too high. 9-pins for righties and 8-pins for lefties are sometimes telling you the same thing. Don't argue with the pins, don't grumble that you were robbed, and don't futz around with minutia trying to "get your ball to come in at a different angle," or some other fiddly little thing. Pick up your spare, accept what the pins just told you even if you think you threw a good shot, and use the information to decide on an adjustment before your next shot on that lane. Why "before your next shot *on that lane*" rather than just "before your next shot"? Because the two lanes on your pair can, and usually do, play differently from one another. The clues you pick up on one lane don't necessarily apply to the other lane. Play them as they are—two completely independent environments.

We have learned that if our ball doesn't hit the true pocket but the shot results in a strike anyway, we got lucky. No problem; we will gratefully accept that lucky break, perform our best fist pump, and move on. But we can't move on successfully without accepting that luck carried our strike and that our ball did not hit the pocket. We must apply the information provided by the pins to our next shot. If you saw your ball hit high or light, great! But even if you misjudge the hit or fail to truly see it, a pin will almost always fall at least a little late and provide you with the same information. The information a late-falling pin is giving you is the same as if it remained standing. If that 4-pin falls late, or the 10-pin is taken out by a messenger, or the 2-pin falls forward, celebrate the strike briefly, and then get to work mentally and figure out what you can do to make sure it falls more convincingly next time you are on that lane.

WATCH THE BALL THROUGH THE PINS

Everything we have talked about so far in this chapter has been focused toward one goal; to gather clues about what is happening to the lane. The most direct evidence comes from watching our ball's actual path. The change in path is caused by a change in the distance our ball travels before hooking, but we've learned that this change is extremely difficult to see due mostly to the optical illusion caused by foreshortening.

Our next best evidence comes from seeing where the ball impacts the headpin. In Chapter 10 we learned to recognize what it looks like when our ball enters the pins on various boards. This is easy to see in photos, but much tougher in real life. We are talking about mere inches, or even fractions of inches, viewed from 60 feet away, and in the midst of a bunch of distractions. Unless we are really paying attention, this is pretty hard to do.

If we didn't pick up on the evidence provided by our ball's path and by its impact point on the headpin, we learned how the pins can still provide us with the same information. Pins fly around very quickly, though, and often we get tunnel vision and only see our hook and hear the KABOOM! as the rack explodes. Don't despair. Even if you've missed the first three sources of information, your ball will provide you with another chance to figure out what is happening, and this one is even easier to see.

When scientists are searching for subatomic particles, there is no way to observe them directly. A single photon, for example, is just too small and too fast for any of our instruments to see. What we can see, however, is the streak it leaves on a photographic plate as it passes by. We have the same situation in bowling. Just as the photon leaves a very visible streak of light based on where it hit the photographic plate, our ball will exit the back of the pin deck in a position based on where it hit the headpin. By observing and analyzing this exit position, we can still figure out where the ball hit the headpin even if we missed all of the chances for more direct observation. There is a direct correlation—a cause and effect relationship—between where the ball impacts the headpin and where it exits the lane off the back of the pin deck.

Barring any pins set down off spot by the pinsetter, a ball impacting the headpin in the pocket—board 17-1/2—will almost always exit the lane on or very near board 20, which is right in the center of the lane. The ball will seem to split the 8- and 9-pins, often sending them off to the sides. Such a "flush" or pocket hit will result in a strike nearly every time. Thus, if we see our ball exit between the 8- and 9-pin, we know that it was in the pocket even if we never even saw it hit the headpin.

A ball hitting the headpin "light," on board 17, 16-1/2, 16, or 15-1/2, will not exit the lane on board 20. Since it hit light, it will exit the pin deck light, to the right of board 20 and closer to the 9-pin for right handers, and to the left of board 20 and closer to the 8-pin for left handers. Why should this be? Let's look at a right hander's shot. If the ball hits too far to the right of the pocket, it will hit the 3-pin too squarely. Since it hits too high on the 3-pin, the ball will not deflect enough back toward the 5-pin. The ensuing light hit on the 5-pin then causes the ball to deflect too much toward the right, so instead of exiting from the center of the pin deck, it travels too far in the direction of the 9-pin. If we see our ball exit the pin deck right of center for right handers or left of center for lefties, we can be almost certain that our shot came in light even if we never saw where it hit the headpin.

A ball hitting the headpin "high," on board 18, 18-1/2, or 19, will likewise not exit the lane on board 20. Just as the light hit caused the ball to exit light, the high hit will cause it to exit high, toward the 8-pin for right handers and toward the 9-pin for left handers. If we trace through a right hander's high hit, we see that by hitting the headpin too squarely, the ball will not deflect enough toward the 3-pin. The resulting light hit on the 3-pin will cause the ball to deflect too much toward the 5-pin. The too solid hit on the 5-pin will result in the ball not deflecting enough back toward the right, causing the ball to exit the pin deck too far toward the left. If our ball exits the pin deck toward the 8-pin for right handers or toward the 9-pin for lefties, we can be almost certain that we hit too high even if we never saw the ball hit the pins.

For many bowlers, seeing where the ball exits the lane is much easier than seeing exactly which board it was on when it hit the headpin. And because there is a direct cause and effect relationship between where the ball hits and where it exits, even if you don't clearly see the ball's entry point you can still infer it based on the exit point. In the absence of a reliable direct observation, this inference will still guide you to the right adjustment. Use the gap between the 8- and 9-pins as your reference point.

Deducing where you hit the headpin by watching the ball's exit position is unfortunately not a 100 percent proposition. As we learned in Chapter 12, there is a small chance that the headpin or the 5-pin will get tangled up in the center of the pin deck and channel the ball off to the left or right, altering its exit position regardless of where it hit. For the most part, though, for both left and right handers, if your ball exits the pin deck right of center, you missed the pocket to the right. If your ball exits left of center, you missed left. Accept it, make your adjustment, and get back to striking.

It might be easier to learn to watch the ball travel through the pins by watching another bowler's shot instead of your own. After you note where their ball hits the headpin, watch where it exits the pin deck and see which pins are left standing or which fell late. You will soon start to see how all of these clues relate. Everything that happens to the ball and the pins after impact is the result of where your ball hit the headpin. You will soon learn to accept that most of your shots that leave pins standing were not really good pocket hits after all, and the two great insights that come from this realization are critically important. First, you start to take ownership of your game instead of attributing poor results to bad luck or to imaginary things you can't control anyway such as wrong entry angle or the ball "going through the pins wrong." Second, since you now accept responsibility for poor results, you start to make quicker and more confident adjustments, because you understand that you have the ability to change things for the better.

YOUR ADJUSTMENTS MAKE ALL THE DIFFERENCE

You've watched your ball's path, and noted where the ball impacted the headpin. You watched for standing or late falling pins, and saw where your ball left the back of the pin deck. Based on these clues, you now have a pretty good idea that your ball is not hitting the true pocket, and is instead hitting a little high or a little light. You know you have to change something about your shot to get it back in the pocket and get back to striking, but what adjustment should you make?

Most often when a bowler's shot starts to hit too high, we hear them state that their ball started hooking too much. This is almost certainly not the case. The amount your ball hooks—that is, the sharpness and duration of its change in direction at the breakpoint—is a function of two things; your release characteristics, and the ball's coefficient of friction. The ball's coefficient of friction can change over the course of months or years, especially if you aren't in the habit of wiping off the lane oil between shots and cleaning it after each set, but it does not change to any noticeable degree from shot to shot. If the coefficient of friction didn't change and your release didn't change, your ball did not hook more than it was before.

If your ball didn't hook any more than it had been, how did the shot miss the pocket to the left and come up high? In most cases it happened because the ball hooked *earlier*, not more. Figure 14.1 shows a representative strike line. If the ball travels the proper distance, its hook takes it right into the pocket. If the shot goes too long before hooking, the identical amount of hook will be insufficient and the shot will come up light. If the ball hooks earlier than it was supposed to, the same hook leads to a miss to the left. Note that all three shots displayed the same amount of hook. The thing that changed was not hook, but rather distance. What we are trying to accomplish when we make an adjustment to our shot is to control that distance.

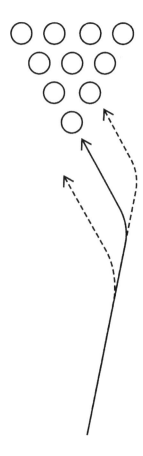

Figure 14.1: How distance affects entry point

While a high hit is almost always the result of the ball hooking too early, a light hit needs to be analyzed a little more deeply. When our ball hits too light in the pocket, too far to the right for righties and too far to the left for lefties, the cause may come down to either distance or hook. While there is nothing we can think of that can make your ball suddenly hook more, there is something that can make it start hooking less; a phenomenon called *roll out*. When your ball starts coming in lighter and lighter, it is likely hooking less than it was before, and roll out is the usual culprit. Roll out is a situation where your ball completes its hook motion much too quickly. It is caused by excessive friction, and most often occurs when using too strong of a coverstock or too much surface texture for lane the conditions.

Your ball can also hit light if it skids farther down the lane than it had been before hooking. This happens much less often than does roll out. When it does, it is the result of *carry down*, which is when oil from the front part of the lane is picked up by a ball and redeposited on the portion of the lane that is supposed to be dry. Carry down is usually caused by recreational or relatively unskilled league bowlers throwing plastic balls, which tend not to flare. The ball acts something like a paint roller, picking up oil from the front of the lane, and then rolling it back out on the dry part of the lane. Carry down is also often attributed to urethane balls. This was probably true "way back in the day" when balls did not flare very much, and can still happen when bowlers roll ancient urethane equipment. Modern urethane balls all possess enough RG differential to flare. Since track flare presents a clean strip of ball cover to the lane with each revolution, it seems unlikely that a flaring, modern urethane ball will cause carry down.

Both roll out and carry down will cause a ball to hit light, but they have opposite causes and opposite cures. It can be very difficult to distinguish between the two, so we will cover both in greater depth in Chapter 16.

When we miss the true pocket, whether right or left, we are usually talking about a matter of mere inches and in some cases only fractions of inches. The pins are 60 feet from the foul line, and this game often comes down to getting your ball to finish only an inch or so more to the left or right over this huge distance. All the adjustments we discussed in Chapter 13 are intended to do just that. By employing these adjustments to control your ball's distance, you are altering the board upon which your ball will impact the headpin. If your adjustment shifts your ball from board 16-1/2 to board 17-1/2 when it hits the headpin, that one inch difference takes you from leaving a corner pin on what *looked like* a good shot to getting a strike on what *was without question* a good shot. Putting your ball in the general area of the pocket and hoping for the best is not a great strategy. Making that distance adjustment to make the ball finish a half inch farther left or right, and continuing to make adjustments as the lanes transition, will put you in a position to win.

HOW DO I KNOW WHAT TO APPLY AND WHEN TO APPLY IT?

Your "tools" are the adjustments we discussed in Chapter 13. Some adjustments will have a bigger effect than others. Different bowlers can experience different results from a similar adjustment because of differences in release characteristics. As you work through learning the adjustments and applying them in different situations, you learn which work best for you and what their effects are on your ball path. Knowing what each tool does to your shot is critical information when you need to make a distance change to alter where your ball impacts the headpin.

The other big consideration in selecting a tool is comfort and confidence. You may be uncomfortable using a tool or may not have practiced it enough to be confident in your execution. Some tools may even be completely missing from your tool box. You will be using these adjustments in the heat of battle based on an educated guess, with no opportunity to test them out beforehand. You may have one or two adjustments you feel equally good about. You will need to trust your gut, and go with what you feel most comfortable with and most competent in executing.

After practicing all of the tools, most bowlers are going to have a short list of "go to" adjustments, and another short list of adjustments they hope they don't have to use but that are available when needed. Go with your favorites first, because you have a better chance of executing them well. If those tools don't work, then it's on to Plan B, and Plan C, and Plan D. You have practiced them all, and though you may not have the same level of comfort and confidence in your secondary tools, it is game time, and you have to do what you have to do.

Making adjustments really comes down to answering three simple questions:

>1: What does my ball need to do differently?
>2: What adjustment tools do I possess that can make that change?
>3: Which specific tool should I select for this situation?

How do you make these decisions? If you're doing odd jobs around your house, some tasks will require only little tweaks with sandpaper or a screwdriver. Others require a sledgehammer or a chainsaw. When trying to solve a bowling problem it is usually best to start out with the finest tools in your tool kit before bringing out the big guns. Don't jump right in there with a chainsaw when a pocket knife can do the job. If your pocket hits have turned into slightly off–pocket hits with late falling pins or loss of carry, a small change will usually do the trick.

When selecting an adjustment, it is best to employ a tool that keeps you in the same general place on the lane, without moving very far left or right. If the line you've been playing has been working, why abandon it without first trying something that will let you stay there? Sometimes, though, your "sweet spot" on the lane completely disappears. You try to tweak the shot with your smaller, finer adjustments, but every little change takes you from too high to too light, and you just can't find a way to get back in the pocket. The lane is telling you that it is time to abandon that target line and try some other path. No fine adjustment will help you if oil has been carried down to your breakpoint or if your line has gotten so dry that your ball is hooking halfway down the lane, so it's time to bring out the bigger guns, perhaps even moving to a different part of the lane.

Whenever you change your target line, be prepared to add in a secondary adjustment or a ball change, especially if you've made a big move. Once you find a new line that seems like it will work, you can then fine tune your ball's reaction with adjustments to rotation, speed, or another of your precision tools. Let's look at a few common scenarios to get an idea of how this might play out.

SCENARIO 1

You've been throwing strikes, but on the next shot you see a late falling 4-pin and your ball exited the pin deck a bit toward the 8-pin. Putting your clues together, you quickly determine that your ball is hitting too high, meaning that it is most likely hooking too soon. Now you need to look in your toolbox and see what tools you have that can get the ball a bit farther down the lane.

Since your ball is just beginning to drift high, there is no need for drastic action yet. Try some adjustments that will leave your feet and eyes on the same boards. An increase in ball speed is about the simplest move. Move your feet back about a foot or so on the approach so your delivery becomes quicker and you roll the ball faster. More speed will get the ball farther down the lane before hooking, and the later hook will cause the ball to finish just a bit farther right than it had been, putting you right back in the pocket. As you'll recall from earlier chapters, another bonus from increased speed is increased kinetic energy, which will improve your pin carry should the ball still hit just left or right of the pocket.

Other physical adjustments that will give your ball the extra distance it needs are increased axis tilt, increased loft, and decreased revs. Another option that requires no physical change to your game is to switch to a ball that has a weaker cover, a higher RG, or both. A weaker chemical composition, shinier surface finish, or higher RG will all get the ball farther down the lane, and get it to finish in the pocket rather than going too far left.

Perhaps the most common adjustment bowlers make when their shot starts to drift high is to move to a deeper line by moving their feet and target toward the center of the lane. While this is certainly a viable option, it's not the best. Since your current line has been working so well for you, avoid the temptation to abandon it by moving deeper on the lane. Moving deeper takes you out of the "sweet spot" you found, so it's better to exhaust other options first before moving left or right.

If you do need to make a lateral move, your goal is to find a line with less friction so your ball will stop hooking too early. If you are bowling on a house shot, moving left for right handers and right for left handers will get your ball away from the line that has started to dry out, and into more oil, which will help your ball get farther down the lane. Start with a parallel move of 1-and-1, or an angular move of 2-and-1 toward the center of the lane. This means that right handers will move either one or two boards left with their feet and one board left with their eyes.

On sport patterns, especially when the shot is fresh, your lateral move may have to be in the opposite direction. Because the oil on the lane is "flatter," to get the ball to hit farther right at headpin impact you may need to move your feet and eyes to the right as well. Parallel moves in this direction usually work best on sport shots because they let you keep your angles straighter, without opening them up too much. A move of 1-and-1 or 2-and-2 will usually be enough to get you back in the pocket.

SCENARIO 2

On your last couple of strikes the pins seemed to "fall funny." Then you left a 10-pin, then a 5-8, and then the dreaded 2-4-5-8 "bucket." You hit your mark just fine and released the ball well. It started hooking, but then just seemed to quit, and the ball hit like a pillow.

Though the results are quite different, this situation shares a similarity with the one above. In both cases your ball is seeing friction too early and hooking too soon. In the first scenario the ball grabbed onto this early friction and hooked hard. In this scenario, the early friction caused the ball to *roll out*.

Roll out is a far more severe case of early friction than is early hook. In roll out, the ball saw so much friction, so early and continuously, that it very quickly gave up its speed and axis rotation and pretty much just ran out of gas. Unlike early hook, roll out is usually caused by using a ball that is too strong for the conditions. This could be caused by trying to use a high-end dull, solid, low RG "hook monster" ball on conditions where there was just barely enough oil even at the start of the block, or by using a ball that had been working just fine, but staying in the same place for far too long after the oil is depleted.

If you are experiencing roll out, the conditions where you are playing the lane have gotten so bad that the adjustments you might have tried under normal circumstances probably won't have enough effect. You could certainly try staying in the same spot by using more speed, more tilt, or more loft, but most of the time these adjustments will not be enough, and you're going to have to move.

If you've been trying to use your super-high-end dull ball on a house shot and it quit working after a few frames, there is probably still enough oil there to allow you to ball down to something a bit more suitable from the middle of your arsenal and be just fine. But that's just a case of making a bad initial ball decision, and is not really the kind of roll out we are discussing here. If it's later in the block and your ball had been working well until now, you're going to have to move. Not a little 1-and-1 type move either. Roll out is usually going to involve a large move to a different part of the lane.

If you're experiencing early friction and roll out, it is probably the result of many bowlers, not just you, playing the same part of the lane and depleting the oil. By making a big move to another zone, perhaps 5-and-5 or more, you will sidestep that dried out strip of lane, find more oil, and return to getting sufficient distance from your ball. Sometimes moving to a deeper zone will result in too much distance, with your ball skidding too far and not being able to get back to the pocket. If this happens, try "balling up," switching to a stronger ball that will either hook just a bit earlier or turn the corner harder or both. This is not an uncommon situation. Large moves to combat roll out often also require switching to a stronger ball because of a greater oil volume than in your previous zone.

SCENARIO 3

Everything was going fine during practice and the first few frames of game one, but on your next shot the ball just keeps on skidding. You can see it spinning and spinning, but it doesn't seem to want to grab the lane. It slides right through the 3-pin, leaving you with a big, ugly wash out.

Such a scenario describes a condition called *carry down*. As discussed earlier, carry down is a condition where bowling balls pick up the oil from the front part of the lane and redeposit it on the back ends where the lanes are supposed to be dry. This down-lane oil effectively increases the length of the oil pattern, causing your ball to start skidding more than it had been.

Carry down is much less of an issue than it used to be, but it can still occur and affect ball motion. However, on most of the occasions when we have heard bowlers complaining about carry down, the actual cause of the light hit was either roll out or a topography issue with the lane. If your lanes have had a lot of traffic from recreational bowlers rolling plastic balls or oil-soaked antiques in a helter-skelter manner all over the lane, you may very well see carry down, but the odds of it developing when playing with more serious bowlers are slim.

Most of the time any carry down you experience will be minor, and will occur during your practice time before the first frame or during the early part of game one. If you are seeing carry down on a house pattern right after practice, the most effective adjustment is to simply make a parallel move of 1-and-1 toward the outside of the lane. This will put your ball on a fresher part of the lane that doesn't have the carried down oil on the back ends, and it does so without changing your angles.

Another effective adjustment could be to stay in the same place on the lane, but to switch to a stronger ball that will read the lane just a little sooner. While a ball change can certainly work, if the ball you were using in practice was working well, why change it? Make the parallel move to the outside and stay with the ball that had been working.

Other possible solutions to a minor carry down issue include less axis tilt, less axis rotation, less loft, and more revs. Of course these are going to involve physical changes, which are always harder to implement than just moving to the outside or changing balls. We intentionally didn't mention decreasing ball speed as an effective adjustment—*effective* being the key word. Decreased speed will certainly make your ball hook earlier, before hitting the carry down. Unfortunately, it will also decrease your ball's kinetic energy and your resulting pin carry on slight off-pocket hits, so it's simply not worth the trade off. There are far better ways to get the job done.

These scenarios are of course just examples. Bowling is a complex game when you get to this level, and your own experience may well be different. Remember that your first job as a competitive bowler is to be a detective, analyzing the clues to figure out what is causing the problem with your shot. Once you have a good idea, you need to become a mechanic, sorting through your tool kit to find the best tool or combination of tools to get the job done. Then become a scientist, implementing your adjustments and observing the results. Rinse, lather, and repeat!

PART III

BUILDING A
COMPETITIVE GAME

PUTTING IT ALL TOGETHER.

CHAPTER 15

LANE PLAY

WHAT MAKES THE pros so good? Are they so deadly accurate that they can split hairs on the lane? Are they that much better than the rest of us at precisely repeating their shots? No, not really. They are not superhuman, but they are way better than the rest of us at one important thing. They are really, really good at finding the part of the lane that gives them the most room for error.

Bowling is not a game of perfection. The key to bowling at a competitive level isn't throwing nothing but perfect shots, it is finding a line to play where your less than perfect shots will still carry. Bowling is a game of making the right decisions and adjustments to maximize your room for error. Find a place on the lane where you can miss a little left or right and still get the ball back to the pocket, and you maximize your potential for great results.

We've all been in the situation where someone on our pair has a world of area, spraying the ball all over the lane and still striking, while we have to hit a gnat square in the tail to strike. When this happens, instead of getting mad, become more observant. If you don't have the same amount of area they do, pay attention, because they are doing something that you aren't. Something they are doing differently in their game is allowing them to match up better to that particular lane environment. Sometimes the factors creating the difference in area are subtle and sometimes they are obvious, but they are definitely there. Don't let your anger or frustration cloud your decision making and keep you from finding the same miss room that everyone else is enjoying.

Every oil pattern has at least the potential for miss area, or room for error. Some of the variables that can affect the miss area are the same things we discussed in Chapter 14; lane topography, lane surface type, age of the lane surface, type of oil being used, how bowlers on your pair are playing the lanes, the equipment they are using, ball surface preparation, and so much more. The thing that makes bowling challenging isn't the pins or the lane. The challenge is all of the information we need to take in and process in order to find the right combination of factors to allow us to "match up" to conditions and to create the most room for error possible.

YOU'VE FOUND SOME MISS ROOM

You've done your job, and found a line where you have some miss room. Now you throw a less than perfect shot, pitching it out a board or two toward the gutter or pulling the shot to the inside, but the ball still finds its way to the headpin and you get a sloppy strike. This happens to all of us, and our first inclination is to apologize to our opponents or to shake our head in shame. Why?

If our job as bowlers is to find a place on the lanes where we have some miss room, why should we apologize for using it? If you have done your job and found some area, and you hit within that area, how is that a miss? Not only are you apologizing for doing a good job and being a good bowler, you are also giving your opponent a mental advantage. While we don't condone bad sportsmanship or rubbing a lucky shot in your opponent's face, we also don't condone apologizing for creating room for error and then using it. That is what bowlers are supposed to do.

When you walk in the front door of the bowling center, your one goal should be, "I am going to find the most area I can, and then use every bit of it." Bowling is full of perfectionists. Perfectionism is both an asset and a liability. *Striving* for perfection in practice is a positive, but trying to *be* perfect in competition will severely work against you. We tend to evaluate our shots based on both accuracy and results. We view our target as one specific board at one specific distance. We'll say, "I'm playing third arrow," or "I'm targeting the 8-board." If the ball rolls over the board next to the intended target, perfectionism makes us see it as a miss. If we do hit our target but the shot doesn't strike, perfectionism tells us that we threw a bad shot. Both of these assertions are not only incorrect, they are harmful.

There isn't an oil pattern on earth that limits you to only one board of area if you've done your due diligence and found the right line to play. There is often a fair amount of miss room right and left of your target at the arrows. The miss room may only be a board or so in total on a sport shot, but it's sometimes up to two boards on either side of your target on a walled-up house shot, especially for those bowlers who have a fairly high rev rate. So perfectionists, you can relax when you have room for error that you purposely and consciously discovered. A miss of one board is not really a miss if it still plays into the room for error that you found. This is a more realistic way to look at targeting. You would be hard-pressed to find a bowler, even at the professional level, who can hit the same board at the arrows ten shots in a row. If you find a little bit of wiggle room and then throw your ball within that wiggle room, you've hit your target.

One very important point needs to be made here. Finding and using that miss room at the arrows and getting your ball into the pocket zone doesn't guarantee a strike, it just guarantees a chance to strike. As we learned in Chapter 10, the true pocket is a finite spot on the headpin. But we are counting on some good luck once in a while too, and getting your ball at least close to the pocket will increase your chances of getting "lucky" strikes. If you've found a spot where, for example, you can hit anywhere from board 8 to 11 at the arrows and still get the ball back to the general area of the pocket, some of the resulting less than perfect shots will still strike. Even when you don't get the lucky break, you'll most likely leave just an easy single pin spare. So save your perfectionism for practice. Relax, and throw the ball toward your mark. Celebrate the solid strikes, happily accept the well-deserved lucky breaks, and pick up the easy spares when luck isn't in your favor. Now you're scoring and bowling at a higher level.

HOW DO I MAXIMIZE MY ROOM FOR ERROR?

The most important time in any bowling competition is the practice period prior to the first frame of the first game. This is when you gather critical information on how the lanes are reacting, enabling you to make your best educated guess about where to play and what ball to use to give you the most room for error. Instead of simply observing and accepting what the lane tells us about where to play, too many bowlers and coaches rely on lane oil graphs. They decide before they even throw a ball how they must attack the lanes and where they need to play based on nothing more than a picture of the oil pattern (Figure 15.1).

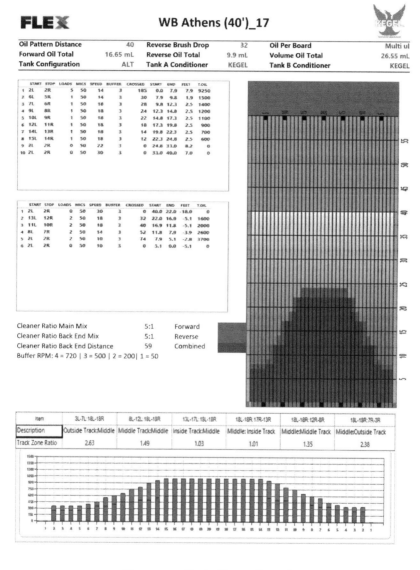

Figure 15.1: Typical lane oil graph

Copyright Kegel LLC and World Bowling. Used with permission

The lane oil graph only reveals a small piece of the lane environment puzzle, and many other factors combine to actually determine how you need to attack the lanes. Lane oil graphs tend to create tunnel vision and prevent bowlers from formulating a Plan B or Plan C. Lane oil graphs are great as a guideline to start from in practice, but bowlers need to explore more areas of the lane than the graph might suggest.

There is a huge amount of critical information that is simply not found on the lane oil graph, but which nonetheless affects how the lanes play. The missing information includes many of the factors discussed in the previous chapter. The most important variable, invisible to the naked eye and found nowhere on the lane oil graph, but having a profound effect on ball motion, is related to gravity. The invisible and almost universally overlooked gravitational variable stems from lane topography, which we explored in depth in Chapter 14.

No lane in the world is perfectly flat or even close to flat, and those little peaks and valleys on the lane will have a direct effect on your ball's motion down the lane. Figure 15.2 is a topographic map of a pair of lanes created using Kegel's LaneMapper system. The various shaded patches in the image correspond to high and low spots on the lane, similar to the topographic maps used to highlight a geographic area's hills and valleys. If a lane oil graph tells you to play the 7-board at the breakpoint, but your lane slopes even imperceptibly toward the gutter at that point, gravity will force you to play somewhere else no matter how loudly the lane oil graph protests.

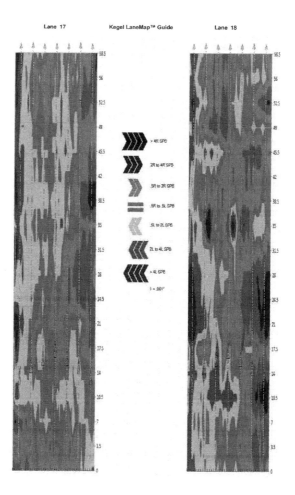

Figure 15.2: Lane topography, as revealed by Kegel LaneMapper

Copyright Kegel LLC. Adapted with permission

If you rely on the lane oil graph to tell you where to play without exploring other areas of the lane during practice, you may miss finding the "sweet spot." It is completely fine to start practice playing where the lane oil graph suggests, or even in your "usual" comfort zone, but you should quickly move left and right of that spot, and experiment with different balls, in order to gather as much information as you can with the limited number of practice shots you are allotted.

If you repeat the same shot twice in practice, you are wasting time, energy, and opportunity. If you throw a shot that resulted in a beautiful pocket hit and strike, there is no need to throw the same line again, at least not on that lane. Not only do you fail to learn anything new, you are also tipping your hand to your opponents. Move around, try different balls, and do something a little differently on each shot. Even if your test shot did not go precisely where you intended, don't turn away in disgust. Watch it closely anyway and consider it an unintentional experiment.

When practice ends you can put all of this information together and come up with your best Plan A with which to start the match. As soon as Plan A fails you—and it almost certainly will at some point as the lanes transition—you will have a confident Plan B waiting to be implemented, because you've already gathered all the required data during practice.

If you are nearing the end of practice and you've found one or two promising target line options, see if you can expand those good lines into good area. Purposely miss a little left and a little right to see how much area you can create and still get the ball back to the pocket zone. On typical house shots, you should have at least a little miss room both right and left. If not, try something different, because you have not maximized your room for error. If you can't miss a board right or a board left and still hit the pocket area, try a different zone, a different ball, or both.

When you have found a line to play where you can miss a little at the arrows and still hit the pocket zone, get ready to enjoy bowling. These are the days we hope for, but they don't have to be just wishful thinking. Such days can become your new normal by doing what you are supposed to do as a bowler; purposely and consciously, through strategic and open-minded shot making in practice, find the largest margin for error on the lane, where your errant shots still hit the pocket zone.

We demonstrated in Chapter 1 that most of the luck in bowling is good luck, not bad. Then let's do something to make that good luck happen more often. Lucky strikes—those strikes that occur from hitting the headpin anywhere other than board 17-1/2—can become more frequent if you do your homework during the practice period before the match begins.

Throwing strikes in practice is not important, nor should it be your primary goal. Most of us can recall nights when we couldn't miss in practice, but as soon as the lights came on and competition began everything went to pot and strikes were nowhere to be found. Chances are you were striking in practice because you found a good line and ball choice early, and just kept repeating the shot. What did you learn? Unfortunately, you learned very early in the first game that you didn't learn enough in practice. Now that Plan A has failed you, what is your Plan B? Without a previously developed fallback plan, it's now wild guess time. Not a good place to be.

On the flip side, recall those nights when you couldn't strike at all in practice, but you somehow start the first game with five or six in a row. You may not have consciously done so, but while you were floundering in practice you were forced to move around the lane and to try different balls precisely *because* you weren't striking. You were in emergency survival mode. You needed to find something before the first frame, so you tried everything, hoping to stumble on something that worked. Despite yourself, you collected valuable data by trying something different on each practice shot. Learn from this! You need to apply this strategy to all practice sessions, survival mode or not. When you start out striking in practice, store that information and then move on and try something else so you can gather new information and formulate a backup plan.

While "survival mode" practice is pretty brutal from a stress perspective, it is made even worse if you waste time trying to pick up the spares you leave. Spare practice is for actual practice sessions and training time, not for competition. When you are in practice just before competition or league and are limited to perhaps only six or eight shots, you need all of those shots to gather information on strike target lines and ball choices. Don't waste a shot on a spare that you should already know how to cover. Even if there is nothing but the 10-pin left standing, throw a different strike shot with the next ball and watch it as closely as if there were a full rack. Even without the pins, you will get all the information you need.

At this point, we haven't even discussed how much the lanes are going to change and transition in just the first 10 or 15 minutes of practice. By the end of practice the lanes will already have changed quite a bit. If you experimented with different variables in practice, you will be able to stay caught up with the transition. Many bowlers make the mistake of not accounting for how the oil is moving around in practice, and then when their ball starts to hit light or even misses the pocket zone completely, they are bewildered. Being a great bowler means making constant adjustments to account for how the lanes are changing. The important thing is to trust your ball motion and accept what it tells you.

WHAT IS MY BOWLING BALL TELLING ME?

Your ball is telling you the truth. We see bowlers every day who watch their ball do something unexpected, and then disregard it. Or they rationalize it away, convincing themselves that "I must not have seen it right," "There is no way it just did that," "It must be a fluke," or "It must have been a bad release."

We must learn to accept that our ball is *always* telling us the truth. A bowling ball is an inanimate, non-feeling, non-thinking object. It doesn't have the means nor the desire to lie to you. Simply watch your ball, trust what it is telling you about the lanes, and make the proper adjustments. You may not stumble upon the right adjustment on your first try, but doing something is better than doing nothing at all. As you gain experience, your correct guesses will come earlier and more often.

Even at the highest levels of our sport—in competing, in coaching, and in ball selection, layout, and drilling—everything still comes down to making educated guesses. We never have complete information. We make the best guess we can given the information available to us, and then hope for the best. But our educated guesses will be right far more often if we trust what we see, and stop concocting arguments for why it can't be so. The best bowlers in the world are the best guessers. They take in all the information they can and make the best educated guess they can, letting experience be their guide.

Don't doubt what your eyes are telling you. Absorb the information your ball motion is trying to communicate, and make your best guess about what your next adjustment should be. Execute that adjustment, observe the result, and then reassess. If it worked, stay with it until further information tells you to adjust again. If it didn't work, don't dwell on it or beat yourself up. Make another decision, and move on. Whatever you do, don't be stubborn and try to force a bad decision to work when your ball clearly shows you that it won't. Guessing wrong is not a crime, but stubbornly sticking with a bad guess is.

HOW DO I APPLY WHAT MY BOWLING BALL IS TELLING ME?

Watching ball motion is easy, but knowing what to do with that visual information takes a little more work. It really isn't very complicated, though. Say you throw a good shot and hit your mark, but the ball hits light. Or maybe it hits heavy. On a house shot the general adjustment rule is to *move in the same direction as the miss*, but what does that mean?

Suppose you are a right hander and your shot hits the pocket zone light and leaves a 2-pin. Since your ball missed the pocket to the right, you need to move to the right to compensate. You could move your feet a board or two right, your eyes (target board) a board or two right, or both. Moving only your feet to the right shifts your shot to the left, making it more directional toward the pocket and resulting in a heavier hit. Moving only your eyes or your feet and eyes to the right shifts your shot in the opposite direction, more toward the gutter. House shots display increasing friction the closer you get to the outside of the lane. Moving your ball path to the right will put the ball more deeply into the high friction area, so it will hook earlier and finish farther left at headpin impact. If your adjustment results in the ball now going too far to the left, a change to a weaker ball might get you just a bit more length and get your shot back in the pocket.

Suppose instead that your ball hits the pocket zone high and leaves a 4-pin on a well executed shot. The ball missed the pocket left, so you need to move left. You might try a parallel 1-and-1 move, shifting both your feet and eyes one board to the left, or maybe an angular adjustment of 2-and-1 or 3-and-2. How big the adjustment needs to be depends on both the extent of your miss and on a number of shot-specific considerations. These include the ball you are using, the amount of lane surface friction, how quickly the lanes are transitioning, and a host of others. Only experience will guide you to the best option. Again, make the best decision you can with the information available, confidently implement your decision, reassess, and repeat.

A common question is whether it is best to move your feet and eyes or to change balls. The answer is, "yes." Both are effective adjustments, and the best choice will depend on the situation you find yourself in at the time. We wish we were able to write a book that gave the correct adjustment for every bowler in every situation in every bowling center in the world. Even if it were possible, it would be the largest book ever written. There are just too many variables at work, and it would not be possible to anticipate and catalog every potential situation.

You have to bowl in the here and now; in the present. You have studied and practiced your tools. You have carefully watched your ball and the pins. All you can do is put it all together and go with your best educated guess, at this moment, in this situation. And if your first guess doesn't work as you'd hoped, no worries. Make a different decision, and move forward. If you guessed wrong and moved when a ball change might have been best, all you've lost is a frame or two. If you choose to ignore the information and do nothing, you will lose a lot more.

We have all had nights plagued by bad carry. We are now well aware that it is not bad luck at play; it is just the inevitable result of the ball not hitting the right point on the headpin. If corner pins are the issue, your ball is coming in just a touch light. If you're bowling on a house shot and it's early in the block, the simplest adjustment is a slight move to the outside—right for right handers and left for left handers. Usually just a board or so move to the outside with your feet or eyes or both will be enough to get the ball back to board 17-1/2 at headpin impact. Our usual first adjustment is a 1-and-1 move to the right for righties or left for lefties. If one or two such moves don't get you back to striking, then make a ball change. Something just isn't quite right with how you are playing the lane, and if a little tweak doesn't work, make a more meaningful change.

If it is later in the block, the little moves to the outside probably won't work. If there has been a lot of traffic on the lanes and you've gone from striking to leaving corner pins without anything else changing, it's likely the result of roll out. On house patterns many people play the same part of the lane, the area around the second arrow called the *track*. All these repeated shots over the same area rapidly deplete the oil from the front part of the lane. The increased early friction causes your ball to "burn up," losing speed and rotation too early on the lane and not being able to make a strong enough move on the back end to get back to the pocket. You need to find more oil to get more distance out of your ball motion, so we suggest a parallel 1-and-1 move to the inside—left for right handers and right for left handers—or an angular move of 2-and-1 or 3-and-2.

These are just some general guidelines. Choose your adjustments based on what you see happening on the lane, which tools you have in your tool kit, and your prior experience in similar situations. Any adjustment is better than no adjustment at all. Doing nothing and expecting the corner pins to suddenly start falling again is definitely not the best strategy. When the ball is not hitting the true pocket and when your off-hits are not resulting in lucky strikes, do something different. Take control of the pocket and of your pin carry. No fear. Take chances. Be aggressive in your decision making.

PLAYING SPORT CONDITIONS

Lane play considerations on sport oil patterns are generally the same as for a house shot, though there will be far less miss room on these more challenging conditions. While shots thrown a bit wide or pulled a bit toward the inside on a house shot will usually find their way back to the headpin, on a sport shot you need much greater accuracy. Your ball will go pretty much wherever you throw it, and you can't expect as much help from the lane technician on bad shots.

The reason sport shots are so much less forgiving than house shots lies in how the oil is spread over the lane. The relationship between the oil volume in the center of the lane versus the oil volume toward the outside of the lane is referred to as the *oil ratio*. The oil ratio on a house pattern is very different from that of a sport pattern.

House patterns typically have a very high oil ratio, sometimes 10-to-1 or more. This means there is 10 times as much oil in the middle of the lane as there is on the outside of the lane. These drastic differences create the relatively large amount of miss room both to the right and left. If you throw your ball too far toward the outside of the lane the dry boards out there will make the ball hook earlier and harder, helping it back toward the pocket. If you pull a shot, throwing it too far toward the center of the lane, that flood of oil up the middle will prevent your ball from hooking as hard, and will help it to stay on line and skid toward the pocket. The miss room on a house shot isn't advertised or marked out for you. You still have to do your due diligence in practice to find it and maximize it, but it's definitely there.

Sport patterns are much "flatter" than house shots, with far less difference in oil volume between the outside and inside boards. Currently, sport patterns are required to have an oil ratio of 3-to-1 or less. The lower the oil ratio, the less miss room you will enjoy. Figure 15.3 shows the difference between a house shot on the left and a tough sport pattern on the right. Darker areas indicate heavier oil.

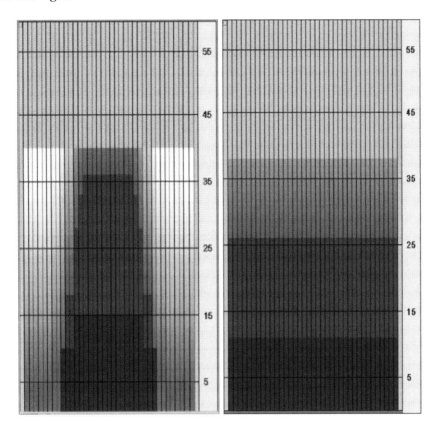

Figure 15.3: House shot versus sport pattern
Copyright Kegel LLC. Adapted with permission

When playing on a sport pattern, though you go through the same information gathering routine as on a house pattern, don't expect to find as much miss room. Since the sport pattern does not give you the very dry outside boards or the flood of oil in the middle, missing right or left even a little can take the ball completely out of the pocket zone. Don't misunderstand—there is still miss room to be had on sport patterns. It just won't be as much as you enjoy on a house shot. If you ever feel like you have to "thread the needle" to hit the pocket on a sport pattern, rest assured you have not found the sweet spot yet. There is area out there somewhere, waiting to be discovered. You may be playing in the wrong zone, using the wrong ball, or both. Or it could be that you have not tapped into your versatility skills—your ability to alter the shape of your shot using the tools you learned in Chapters 13 and 14.

When a sport pattern is fresh, it is important to remember three suggestions that will help you manage your ball motion and room for error. The first is to "keep your angles in front of you." This means that you should play straighter, more direct lines of attack than you might use on a house shot. Don't try to play big angles and a huge, sweeping hook, swinging the ball way out toward the gutter through the front part of the lane. Because of the lower oil ratio on the sport pattern, you don't have as much high friction area to the outside as you do on a house shot. Big angles toward the outside through the front part of the lane will take the ball too far away from the pocket and there won't be enough friction to bring it back. Once the lanes transition and more friction develops, you will be able to move deeper and create bigger angles of attack.

Our second suggestion is to use less axis rotation. Keep your hand more behind the ball rather than around the side. As described in Chapter 13, less axis rotation keeps your hook more subtle and gradual, thereby making your ball reaction more predictable. If you start with lots of axis rotation when the back ends are fairly fresh, your ball will experience too sharp of a change of direction down lane. Such a sharp reaction will be harder to control on a sport pattern's lower oil ratio. As play progresses and the heavy oil starts to deplete, the lanes will "open up," and you can start to increase your launch angles and your axis rotation.

Note, though, that "opening up the lanes" and increasing your launch angle could be problematic if there are others on your pair who don't play the lane similarly to you. You are not bowling alone, and what others are doing with their lines and ball choices may prevent you from playing the lanes the way you might prefer. For example, if a lot of extremely low-flaring balls are being used, there is a possibility of oil carry down and a loss of down-lane friction. If bowlers are using very high-end balls with dull surfaces you may very well experience earlier "burn," or oil depletion, both in the heads and in the mid lane. Either of these friction problems will make it challenging to open up your angles. Even when bowlers are not using such equipment, if they are playing a variety of criss-crossing lines to get to the pocket, this spiderweb of ball paths is not going to carve out a very consistent "bounce" area on the lane. If these or other unique situations cause your pair to break down in a less than orderly fashion, it will be best to keep playing the lane in a more direct manner and avoid the possible pitfalls presented by increased launch angles across messy conditions.

Our last suggestion is to start your sport shot session with a dull or matte bowling ball. A polished ball typically changes direction more sharply than does a dull or matte ball, which again makes your shot harder to control. A polished ball can trick you with its more violent reaction. One shot will look really good as it goes into the pocket and blasts the pins back, but because of the sharper change of direction and the inconsistency this can yield with fresh back ends on a sport pattern, the next shot could miss the pocket completely even though it felt exactly the same off your hand.

If the lane is transitioning in an orderly and consistent manner, and you have a good "look" with some room for error, you should try to play that same general area on the lane as long as possible. If you need an adjustment, try a small parallel move first. Since your line has been good so far, a small parallel move inside, perhaps 1-and-1 or 2-and-2, will keep your angles the same while putting your ball in a slightly different part of the lane. Other alternatives for your first adjustment could be a ball change, a speed change, or any of your other tools that will keep you in the "sweet spot."

Consider this scenario: You start a sport pattern tournament with a 240 and a 230 game. Things are going well but now you see the lanes starting to change, with everyone's shot beginning to drift a little high. Rather than moving in toward the center of the lane along with pretty much everyone else, try making some adjustments that will let you stay "camped out" right where you are. If you select your adjustments wisely you can stay in the same zone that has been working so well while everyone else is chasing the shot inward.

Every decision we make in bowling comes down to managing distance—how far your ball skids before it hooks. If you effectively manage distance by using the versatility provided by your adjustment tools, and stay in the same sweet spot longer than your opponents are able to, the situation will definitely be in your favor.

Most bowlers who consistently chase the shot inward do so because they don't have the versatility to stay outside longer. "Moving left" is pretty much their only trick. But wouldn't staying put and simply changing balls to one that will go longer be easier than trying to find a new line? Increasing your ball speed is another option to increase distance and let you stay put. Or increase your axis rotation, or your axis tilt, or your loft. Or decrease your rev rate. All of these things will increase your ball's distance and let you keep playing the same part of the lane. Using these adjustments individually or in combination can allow you to camp out for much longer—maybe even for the entire block—on that sweet spot on the lane that has been working so well.

The true pocket is the same whether you are on a house shot or a sport pattern. Trying to maximize your room for error should still be your foremost goal. Though your room for error will be less on a sport pattern than it will on a house shot, it will still be there somewhere. Find that miss room, throw a lot of strikes, and even when luck fails you, you will still leave easy spares.

In many sport pattern tournaments, those who pick up their spares and fill their frames are the ones who come out on top. Spares aren't glamorous, but they have always been the most important part of the game. That has never changed, and it isn't likely to. Maximizing your miss room gives you more chances to hit the pocket for a good, solid strike, or to at least get close for a lucky strike. Maximizing miss room increases the odds of leaving yourself a make-able spare when the lucky strike doesn't happen. Staying in the zone that gives you some miss room for as long as possible gives you the best chance of success every time you compete.

On house patterns, a ball change or a small move with your feet and eyes are usually all that you need to keep your ball near the pocket. On sport patterns, you need to be more open-minded and creative with your adjustments. When bowling on sport conditions, be prepared to dig a little deeper and to use your versatility skills, adjusting your speed, rotation, tilt, loft, and revs. No one said being great was easy, but there is also no reason to make the game more complicated than it has to be. Learn the necessary skills, and gain experience in applying them. Watch your ball motion and let it tell you everything you need to know. You may not guess right the first time every time, but with experience you will guess right most of the time. Don't overthink it. Watch your ball, adjust, bowl. Watch your ball, adjust, bowl. Watch your ball, adjust, bowl...

CHAPTER 16

ADVANCED CONSIDERATIONS

BOWLING IS A very challenging sport because our playing field is always changing. Every ball that goes down the lane is doing something to change the environment within which you are competing, and every day the lanes will break down and transition differently. That is why adjustment recommendations can never be a "one size fits all" proposition. The adjustment that worked perfectly yesterday probably isn't going to be the right one today.

There are many variables that influence your adjustment decisions in any given situation, and we have already discussed these at various points in this book. While it would be impossible to formulate hard and fast rules about which adjustment to apply when, there are nevertheless certain issues that are fairly common and that you are almost sure to run into from time to time. This chapter will provide you with some strategies you can employ when these inevitable situations arise.

ROLL OUT VS. CARRY DOWN

We talked about roll out and carry down in Chapter 14. Recall that both conditions cause a shot that had been striking to start coming in light. Though both roll out and carry down result in similar light hits, their causes—and more importantly their cures—are quite different. If roll out and carry down both result in the ball hitting too light in the pocket, how can we tell which one we are experiencing?

We've been imploring you throughout the last several chapters to be very observant, not just of where your ball hits the pins, but also of the path it took to get there. Observing your ball path is critical when trying to differentiate roll out from carry down, and without doing so you will not know which is the culprit.

Roll out is fairly easy to see. As you watch your ball from the foul line, you can see its path straighten out very early, well before it hits the pins. The ball usually makes it at least to the general area of the pocket, but the hit often looks and even sounds weak. When experiencing roll out, your ball will hook, but it loses its axis rotation and quits hooking too early.

Carry down has the opposite effect on your ball path. When carry down is the culprit, your ball seems to just skid forever. You will see your ball spinning and spinning, but it's just not able to get a grip on the lane. Once it skids past the carried down lane oil, it will grab hard on the dry part of the back end. It will make a quick hook, but this usually happens much too late, and the ball can't make it all the way back to the pocket.

Based on these visual clues, our differentiation rule is that if the ball hooks, but quits early, it's roll out. If it skids too far and only hooks at the last minute, it's carry down. Watching your ball path tells you what the impact with the pins won't. Once you know which of these two issues caused your light hit, you can select the right adjustment tools to cure the problem.

CURING ROLL OUT

Recall that roll out is caused by excess friction on a part of the lane where friction should be low. The lane oil has been depleted on the front part of the lane, so the ball grabs and hooks where it should still be skidding. The increased friction will make the ball roll early and hook less, and will reduce its entry angle into the pins. The decreased entry angle will cause the ball to start coming in too light (Figure 16.1).

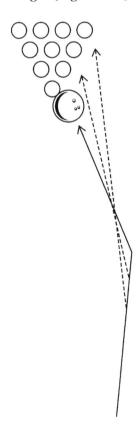

Figure 16.1: Roll out causing light hit

Since our ball is no longer making it back to the pocket, some type of adjustment is definitely necessary. The crux of the problem is too much friction before our desired breakpoint. The possible solutions are many, some being better choices than others. The usual cause of the excess friction is a dried out area on the lane where too many bowlers have been playing. We therefore need to either play that part of the lane differently, or play a different part of the lane.

Your versatility skills such as tilt, rotation, rev rate, speed, and loft will all change your shot in some way, but while they will increase the ball's distance, their effect may not be enough to get the ball past the dried out area on the lane. If friction has increased severely enough to cause roll out, there is likely just too much friction for these fine adjustments to overcome.

Since our precision tools aren't up to the task, we need to bring out the bigger guns—a ball change, a line change, or both. The most obvious answer to roll out is to simply move, and play a different part of the lane. In most situations a move toward the inside is your best option, as it puts your line back into the heavier oil nearer the center of the lane. Finding oil toward the center of the lane will give you back the length your shot needs. It may also create some miss room to the right, as the same high friction area you had to move away from becomes your "bounce" area, helping your ball get back to the pocket.

As we discussed in Chapter 13, while an angular move often works best on a typical house shot, a parallel move is your best option if you are bowling on difficult lane conditions or on a sport pattern. After your first few parallel moves inward, you will reach a point where further parallel moves would bring your line too close to the pocket. From that point on, you will have to start making angular moves to keep your breakpoint at a reasonable distance from the headpin. When you need to get away from a dried out area that is causing roll out, be prepared to make much larger moves than you do for ordinary adjustments. Moves of 1-and-1 or 2-and-1 aren't going to do it. You need to get your ball into a completely different zone on the lane, so think about moves on the order of 5-and-5, 5-and-3, or 6-and-4.

When you move to a new zone to get away from the roll out, you may find that the increased oil volume in the middle of the lane is too much for the ball you had been using. Very often, a zone change will also require you to "ball up." Switching to a ball with a stronger coverstock will give you additional friction, allowing you to overcome the increased oil volume. We know this advice doesn't sound right. When you think back to times you had to move inside due to too much friction you likely either stayed with the same ball or even "balled down" to one with a weaker coverstock. That is conventional thinking, and not necessarily wrong, especially when the moves are small. However, when the situation calls for a big lateral move or a zone change, you may well end up in a place with much more oil than expected. Don't let your more common small moves lock you into thinking that a move to the inside of the lane either won't require a ball change or will require a change to a weaker ball. When making large moves, think outside the box (if you'll pardon the cliché), and go with a stronger ball. You will be surprised how often you will be rewarded for that decision.

There is another way to adjust for roll out on sport patterns that is not available to us on house shots. House shots are typically fairly dry on the outside part of the lane, so there is inherently more friction there. The extra friction precludes moving to the outside to get around the roll out area, because our ball would just hit the dry outside boards and give us the same problem. On sport patterns, however, moving to the outside is often a viable option. Since oil ratios are lower on sport shots and the patterns flatter, moving to the outside can get you away from the roll out without hitting inherently dry boards.

Every situation is different, and what worked last week may not work this week, but if you are on sport conditions be sure to consider moving your line to the outside when your original line stops working. Depending on the pattern and the topography, you might find a better line of attack to the outside of the roll out zone rather than to the inside.

CARRY DOWN

Carry down is a divisive topic today. Most bowlers contend that carry down doesn't exist anymore, while others disagree. Our own belief is that carry down is still a problem today at least to some degree, though it manifests itself in a different way than it did a decade or two ago.

If you have a fresh 40 foot pattern, then the last 20 foot section before the pins is supposed to be completely dry. If the management of your bowling center ever offers you the opportunity, go down lane and see what that last 20 feet looks like when fresh. Then, after 15 minutes of play or practice, go look at it again. If you get your eyes close to the lane surface, the reflected light will let you see oil on the lane where there was none before play began.

Several decades ago you would have seen long stripes of oil carried down to the dry part of the lane. Bowling balls back then did not flare as much as they do now. They rolled over and over the same general part of the ball. Non-flaring balls acted like a paint roller, picking up oil from the front part of the lane and then rolling it back out on the dry area.

Today's bowling balls exhibit dramatically increased track flare. Because modern balls roll over a fresh ring of coverstock with every revolution, we no longer see long stripes of carried down oil. Instead, we get short patches of oil that are far less obvious.

Even though carry down is different today, its effect is similar though not as severe. Bowling balls that encounter carry down will skid a little farther down the lane before hooking. Sometimes the increased skid will be so small that the ball hits the pocket zone just a board or so light, leaving a corner pin. Sometimes it is severe enough that the ball never properly grabs the lane, and misses the headpin completely (Figure 16.2).

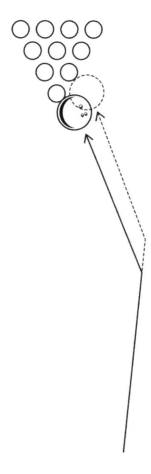

Figure 16.2: Carry down causing light hit

Since most bowlers play near the track area on typical house patterns, the carried down oil will usually end up somewhere around the 10-board down lane. If your ball starts skidding too far where it had been hooking, you are probably hitting this carried down oil. The most effective adjustment for carry down when playing on a house shot is to make a parallel move with your feet and eyes, one or two boards toward the outside of the lane. For a right hander, this is a 1-and-1 or 2-and-2 move to the right. Such a parallel move shifts your entire line, enabling your ball to hit cleaner lane surface at the breakpoint and go around the area affected by carry down. Your ball will start hooking back to the pocket like it did when you threw your first couple of shots in practice before the carry down problems began. If your new line starts to go away, you will have to migrate back in toward the center of the lane. There is a good chance that the carry down that forced you to move has by now been eliminated by other bowlers' traffic, allowing you to move back to your original line. If the carry down is still there, make another move to jump to the inside of the problem area.

On sport patterns, moving to the outside to get around carry down often doesn't work. Sport oil patterns are much flatter than house shots, often with heavier oil toward the outside of the lane that prevents your ball from recovering sufficiently to hit the pocket. If your line in practice looked really good but now your ball is skidding too far, try staying in the same place but switching to a stronger ball with more surface and a lower RG so it hooks earlier. If the tournament rules permit it, you can also try putting a little more surface on the ball before practice ends.

Another idea to combat carry down is to increase your rev rate. Increasing your rev rate will make your ball hook a little sooner, but since most bowlers start out at their maximum rev rate anyway, this is often not an option. Another possibility is to decrease your ball speed just a little. Remember though that any decrease in ball speed comes with a drop in kinetic energy at the pins, and this will negatively affect your carry.

Of all the available options, changing balls or adding surface to your ball at the end of practice are the simplest answers to carry down encountered on a sport shot. A ball change doesn't require any physical changes to your game, but if you are confident in your ability to alter speed or revs, don't hesitate to use these tools. The worst thing you can do is nothing, just hoping the carry down will go away.

You are almost certain to run into roll out or carry down during league and tournament play. While they both look the same at the pins—a light hit—they look very different going down the lane. Another clue as to which one is causing your problems is that carry down often occurs very early in the league night or tournament, while roll out occurs later in the block after a lot of traffic has burned up the oil.

As roll out or carry down cause your ball to hit lighter and lighter, you may still luck into a strike. Eventually, though, you will start leaving back row pins, and buckets and wash outs won't be far behind. Don't let a few lucky strikes lull you into complacency. Believe what the pins are telling you, and make an adjustment. If the first adjustment doesn't work, make another one. Now, not after disaster strikes.

TOO MANY BOWLING BALLS, NOT ENOUGH TIME…

The equipment available to athletes definitely makes a difference, whatever the sport. If golfers in the 1920s had the clubs we use today, they would certainly have hit longer drives. Sports achievement is not just about talent; it is talent plus tools that give rise to success. Equipment can't make up for inferior skills, but the right tools in a talented athlete's hands is a winning combination.

The same holds true in bowling. A great bowler using old school, low tech bowling balls might have quite a fight on his or her hands trying to beat a merely good bowler who has the latest and greatest equipment. But a great bowler who not only has the latest and greatest bowling ball technology, but also the experience and skill to make the right decisions about when and how to use them, will always be near the top of the leader board.

Owning an array of modern bowling balls does not guarantee success. In fact, it is quite often more of a detriment. Having too many bowling balls leads to complacency in physical game and skill development. If you have several bags full of balls to choose from, you can get locked into a mindset focused on trying to select just the right ball instead of learning the physical skills necessary to make any given ball roll in a different way.

When your game is centered around owning a ball for every possible situation, your adjustments in competition end up limited only to line changes and ball changes. Such a ball-centric approach to the game may serve you well enough in house shot leagues, but in tournaments some degree of physical game versatility is required if you want to be consistently competitive. No matter how many balls you own, the perfect ball for the shot you are playing will be the one you left at home. It is much better to be able to change your game enough to make a ball that is "close enough" do the job than it is to constantly chase after the perfect ball.

Having too many bowling balls also leads to confusion. If you need to make a ball change but have too many choices, you are guaranteed to be overwhelmed, especially with the added stress of trying to get lined up again. World renowned coach Fred Borden once told us, "If a bowler walks in the building with only two balls in his bag, I know I can beat him because he doesn't have enough tools. If a bowler comes in with 14 balls, I know I can beat him because he doesn't have any versatility."

What is the optimal number of bowling balls for an arsenal? This is not a simple question, and there are several possible answers based on the bowler and the situation. We talked extensively about arsenal choices in Chapter 13, and all of that general advice applies. That was just a starting point, though, and other factors can influence your decision.

Some tournaments make the decision for you by limiting the number of balls you can check in. In many of today's tournaments, bowlers are limited to only five or six balls. For a tournament arsenal, six balls is a good number, perhaps eight at the high end. For house shot leagues, a three or four ball arsenal should be plenty. It is much easier to anticipate the conditions you will run into on a house shot, and you will rarely need equipment at either extreme of ball motion. No matter how many balls you choose to bring, we implore you to make one of them a plastic spare ball. The reasons why a plastic spare ball is so important will be discussed fully in Chapter 17.

We have heard of bowlers, even PBA pros, hauling 20 or more bowling balls to a competition. How then can a six ball arsenal, one of which is plastic, possibly provide enough options over the course of an entire tournament? The answer lies in surface changes and in your own versatility. When you have the ability to change loft, or ball speed, or axis rotation, or axis tilt, you change not only the ball's length before hooking, but also the shape and even the degree of its hook. If you throw a ball at normal speed and then throw it at a faster speed, you have created two different ball path shapes with just one bowling ball. Add to your physical versatility the ability to change ball surfaces during practice, and you can turn a five ball arsenal into an arsenal of 20 or more ball path shapes, each subtly different. One of those shapes is going to be the right one to get you matched up to the lane environment and to help you stay lined up throughout.

If hauling a truckload of bowling balls to a tournament will cause mental overload from too many choices, won't 20 different ball paths from a five ball arsenal cause the same stress? Maybe, but usually not. Most bowlers will not perfect all of the adjustment tools we explored in Chapter 13. In fact, we often advise bowlers we work with to pick their best two, or three, or even four adjustment tools depending on the level at which they compete, and to then prioritize them. Even if you do master all of the tools, if you've spent the necessary time working on and perfecting your surface changes and versatility skills, you will have a very good idea of what each will do to your ball path. Ball selection then comes down to simply picking the ball that is closest to your desired path, and then applying the right adjustment to dial it in to current lane conditions.

If a bowler brings 10 or 15 or 20 balls to a tournament, even if he or she knows them very well, it is entirely possible that the ball path shape you need today will fall in between two of those balls. A bowler who has no versatility or surface management skills, but brings 14 balls to a tournament, is going to have larger gaps between ball motions and a decreased ability to match up to conditions than will a bowler who brings six balls but can alter surfaces and change their ball path through physical versatility. When you have versatility skills, the gaps are much smaller and you can fine tune your ball path according to conditions. The bowler who lacks versatility and instead relies on a large number of balls has to hope that one of those balls will just happen to match up.

CHANGE BALLS, OR MOVE?

One of the most common questions we get from bowlers we work with is, "How do I know when to move or when to change balls?" This is a valid question, but there is no absolute answer. There are so many variables in bowling that the answer will be different from bowler to bowler, week to week, and even lane to lane. Lane topography, temperature and humidity, where the other bowlers are playing, what balls and what surface textures other bowlers are using, and many other variables will affect how you need to play and adjust to the lanes. Since you can't control these variables, and in some cases can't even see them, how can you possibly know what to do?

Effective decision making always comes back to the same thing—watch your ball. Your ball cannot lie to you, so watch it and accept what it tells you with unconditional trust. If you were lined up well and were throwing lots of strikes, but your ball or the pins start to give you clues that something is about to change, listen to them even though you are still striking. Make a slight change. Let your experience help you decide if it should be a parallel move or an angular move of your line, or even a tweak with one of your physical skills. Don't make a drastic step like a ball change your first option. Why abandon the ball that has been working so well when a small move might do the trick? Try taking a toy away from a baby who is having a great time with it. Now try simply moving that baby to a slightly different location but letting it keep the same toy. Which way involves less crying?

Many times such small moves will work. Sometimes they won't. A good general rule of thumb is to give it two moves. If you made the first move because pins are falling late or your carry has gone away and this move did not yield better results, try one more move. If the second move gives the same results, it's time for a ball change. Sometimes your first move will take you from bad to worse. You make the first move because you are leaving 10-pins. Your move is only a board or two, but now you leave a 4-pin. If things are that touchy, don't waste time with a second move—it is time to change balls.

There will be times when you just can't seem to get lined up. You can't find a good shot, and you feel trapped. It seems like you need to throw an absolutely perfect shot in order to hit the pocket, with no miss room at all. In these situations, a ball change is a better choice than a move. A young man we work with was participating in a Junior Gold youth bowling clinic, and PBA great Tommy Jones was one of the teachers. Our young friend wasn't doing terribly well, and told Mr. Jones that everything he was doing was wrong. Tommy's reply was, "If you're doing everything wrong, try doing it wrong with a different ball." Getting yourself into a different ball can reduce the feeling of helplessness, of being trapped. To shake things up, maybe you change balls and move at the same time. You weren't striking consistently anyway, so what do you have to lose? Give yourself a mental fresh start.

Always be aggressive in your decision making. This doesn't necessarily mean to always make big moves or big changes. It just means to always stay proactive. Act, don't react. Watch your ball and make a decision before something really bad happens. Make a change when a pin falls late. Don't wait for a big split that can ruin a game—and that split could well be coming on your next shot. It doesn't take much for a 4-pin to turn into a 4-9. Keep up with lane transition by making smaller adjustments more frequently. The lane environment is changing more quickly than ever before, so you have to make your adjustments quickly if you want to stay matched up over the course of a league night or tournament.

SO, WHICH BALL?

You need to make a ball change, but how do you know which ball to choose? Unfortunately it will always be a guess, but by taking careful note of the motion characteristics of all of your equipment you can make it a highly educated guess rather than a shot in the dark. In an earlier chapter we advised you to spend a practice session finding a good strike line with your benchmark, middle of your arsenal ball, and to then throw each of your other balls over the same line and note the difference in length and hook. Knowing what each of your balls does relative to the others is key to making smart decisions in competition.

Some bowlers are able to keep all of this information in their head, but for the rest of us we advise writing out a simple spreadsheet containing all of the pertinent data on your arsenal. At a minimum, you should list each ball's RG and RG differential, the manufacturer's "out of box" original surface, the current surface texture, and the ball's layout, which you can obtain from your pro shop operator. If the actual layout isn't available, a notation on whether it is pin up or pin down will suffice. We also suggest writing out a few sentences describing the ball's path in terms of length and hook, and where it fits in your arsenal with reference to the general ball motions we discussed in Chapter 13.

Even if two bowlers own the same ball with the same layout, their comments about the ball may be quite different. Player A and Player B have different physical games, different skills, different experiences, and bowl on different conditions, so their results will almost certainly be different even when using the same ball. The comments that you write about each ball will help to trigger memories from when you recently used the ball, and when it worked well and when it didn't. A quick glance at this valuable piece of paper will help lead you to the right ball change, and can also give you confidence in your decision because you've based it on real data instead of resorting to the somewhat less reliable "eenie meenie miney mo" method.

STRATEGIES FOR LESS THAN IDEAL CONDITIONS

The conditions under which we compete are often less than perfect. We've all experienced those nights or tournaments where the lanes just didn't play right. That doesn't make the conditions bad—just challenging. When we call conditions "bad," we are likely to feel a loss of control which leads us to make excuses. When we look at something as challenging, we know we have a fighting chance and just need to look for and find the right solution.

Less than ideal conditions are certainly challenging. Let's look for solutions and dispense with the excuses. Challenging conditions include lanes with burnt heads, lanes that are playing wet/dry or over/under, a flood of oil, challenging topography, and many others. It is helpful to keep in mind that if you are experiencing any of these, then so is everyone else on your pair. The lane technician is not picking on you, and the playing field is still level. The deciding factor becomes who is going to keep a cool head and figure out the best course of action to maximize scoring in spite of the challenging conditions.

Sometimes the best solution is to go into damage control mode, keeping your lines of attack straighter and keeping your ball close to the pocket. You may not rack up scores of 240 or 250, but neither will anyone else. Sometimes just staying clean is enough to win, so smart choices to minimize bad results become paramount to success. With this in mind, let's look at some of the challenging conditions you are likely to encounter.

WHO FRIED THESE HEADS?

The heads, or the first 15 feet of the lane, are critical to attaining optimal ball reaction. The heads are where an important part of the skid phase of ball motion occurs, and they play a big part in determining the ball's distance before hooking. As play progresses and the oil starts to dry up you may have difficulty getting your ball to clear the heads as cleanly as you would like, and it starts to *read the lane*, or hook, too early. Excessive friction on the front part of the lane is rather gruesomely referred to as *fried heads* or *burnt heads*.

Burnt heads are a common experience when bowling on wood lanes. Wood lanes naturally have more inherent surface friction than do synthetics, and this problem is made worse by the fact that wood lanes are typically quite old. No one has built a wood lane bowling center in a very long time, so any wood lanes you encounter have developed even more friction due to prolonged wear and tear. Even a fresh oil pattern applied to wood lanes may not be enough to overcome the extreme friction these lanes can develop. Wood lanes, especially those in poor condition, quickly absorb the lane oil through the cracks between the boards and the inevitable flaws in the lane finish. The oil absorption is especially pronounced in the heads where wear is concentrated. Older synthetic lanes can also start to develop burnt heads due to excessive wear, though usually not as severely. Even when synthetic lanes are in good condition, tournaments with long formats that do not re-oil between blocks can cause burn and early hook in the heads. In the modern game, porous coverstocks and high rev rates are making the problem of burnt heads even more commonplace.

Burnt heads cause your ball to start hooking earlier and earlier. Your ball hits higher and higher, and you have trouble keeping it on the proper side of the headpin. You may start to think that you have begun to *pull* your shots toward the center of the lane, but the truth is that your ball is just reading the lane and hooking far too soon. As soon as you see dry heads start to negatively affect your ball's distance and motion, make an immediate adjustment.

Choices we make as bowlers have a profound influence on how severely we are affected by dry heads, and we exacerbate the problem if we make choices that lead to early hook on their own. Things that make the problem worse include selecting a bowling ball with too strong of a coverstock or too much surface, using a ball with a very low RG, not throwing the ball with enough speed, not using enough axis tilt, not using enough axis rotation, having too many revs, or laying the ball down too early on the lane. When the heads are fried, we need to make choices that will increase our ball's distance by reversing the variables listed above. We need to change to a ball that has a weaker cover or a higher RG, increase speed, increase axis tilt or rotation, decrease revs, or loft the ball farther out onto the lane.

Some adjustments will be more effective than others. If you were bowling poorly even before the heads became burnt, consider combining several changes. The most obvious thing to try is moving away from the burnt part of the lane. It wasn't working well anyway, so you lose nothing by abandoning it. If you find that the heads are still burnt on the new part of the lane, you are going to need to change something else. Our next move would be to switch to a ball with a weaker cover and a higher RG. Choose a ball from a lower tier, and with a shinier surface than the one you had been using. Select a pearl if you had been using a solid or a hybrid. If the ball change doesn't fix the problem, consider more ball speed, more tilt, more rotation, or lower revs if you have developed the skill to change these factors. One of these changes, or some combination of them, will get your ball's distance back to where it needs to be, getting you back in the pocket and back to striking.

If you had been bowling well before the heads started to burn up and your line started to go away, we suggest that you stay where you are on the lane and just try to address the increased friction. We have one adjustment in our tool kit that might let you do so without having to change any of the factors that had been serving you well to this point. That tool is loft.

Since our lanes dry out more quickly and completely than in the past, loft is more necessary as a versatility skill today than ever before. It wasn't very long ago that most players didn't know how to loft their ball, and didn't even need to worry about it. Now it is much more common to see bowlers using loft during tournaments.

Loft lets us bypass at least some of the excessive friction on the front part of the lane by simply throwing the ball over it. Bowlers who loft the ball correctly will often inadvertently increase their ball speed at the same time. Though unintentional, this is actually an advantage. Not only will the added ball speed help the ball skid a little farther through the burnt area, it also adds a little more to our kinetic energy at the pins.

If you haven't practiced loft yet, please do so. You are bound to run into conditions where no matter where you move on the lane, your ball seems to hook as soon as you lay it down. Without loft, you have no way of getting your ball far enough down the lane to get you back in the pocket. Lane surfaces are getting older, bowling balls are getting stronger, and rev rates are getting higher, all of which only increase the likelihood of encountering burnt heads. If you can't beat 'em, just go over 'em! Loft is a great tool to have in your tool kit should you ever need it. And at some point, you surely will.

LIVIN' ON THE EDGE

See if this sounds familiar: You miss your mark by one board to the outside, and your ball hooks early and hits too high on the headpin. On your next shot you miss by a board to the inside, and your ball goes forever without hooking, missing the headpin completely. Sometimes a pattern will be deliberately designed to play this tightly, but most of the time such conditions arise through lane transition. When the lanes play this way, we call it a wet/dry or over/under condition.

Over/under conditions can be very frustrating and confusing. Those of you who always play near the second arrow will experience over/under conditions way more than you need to. With typical house patterns, the bulk of the oil is located toward the center of the lane, between the right-hand and left-hand second arrows. Think of it as like a bell curve, with the low spots on either end representing the lower volume of oil outside of the second arrows (Figure 16.3).

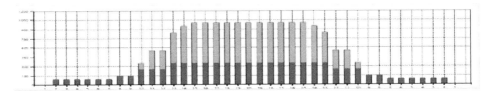

Figure 16.3: Oil placement on a house shot
Copyright Kegel, LLC. Adapted with permission

If your house pattern's oil drop-off occurs where you are playing, you are bowling right along the edge of that cliff. Miss a little right, and your ball hits the drier boards and hooks too much. Miss a little left, and you hit the heavier oil and your ball just skids. On one side of the cliff the lane is too wet, and on the other side it is too dry. On one side your ball overreacts, on the other it underreacts, hence wet/dry or over/under conditions (Figure 16.4).

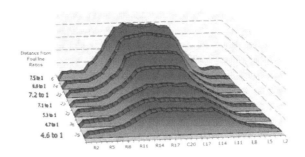

Figure 16.4: Wet/Dry cliff
Copyright Kegel, LLC. Adapted with permission

In bowling, as in real life, it's not safe to play on the edge of a cliff. If you are experiencing over/under conditions where you are playing, try playing somewhere else. Moving your line a little to the outside, shifting both your eyes and feet by a board or two, can help eliminate those over/under ball reactions. A move to the outside on a house shot will put your ball in a less oily part of the lane, so if it hooks too early, switch to a ball with less surface, a weaker coverstock, or a higher RG to help you match up to the increased friction.

Even on sport shots, wet/dry conditions are fairly commonplace. If this situation causes unpredictable results, just make a move out of that zone. The lane isn't wet/dry everywhere. Either move outside toward the dry with a weaker ball and more ball speed, or move into the wet with a stronger ball, straighter launch angles, and less axis rotation. If conditions force you to play near the wet/dry cliff, you can help "smooth it out" through effective ball selection. A ball with a duller surface, a stronger coverstock, and a lower RG will generally yield a smoother, more predictable reaction. Be careful though not to go to so strong a ball that you risk roll out. Stay with a predictable and boring ball motion. In most cases, a medium ball with a little surface—2000 grit, give or take—will do the trick. You have many other options, but this is a good starting point.

There is another over/under condition that you may encounter on *any* oil pattern, and it is not related to a wet/dry situation. Wet/dry causes your ball to hook too much if you miss outside and too little if you miss inside. From time to time, though, you will experience the opposite effect; a miss to the outside causes your ball to skid forever, while a miss to the inside results in going right through the nose for a split. This over/under condition is caused by bad lane topography.

While a wet/dry reaction results from trying to ride the crest of a figurative cliff, bad topography can cause you to ride a literal cliff. If the lane is raised up even a little right in the area of your breakpoint, a miss to the outside means that your ball has to literally climb a hill to get back to the pocket. You see your ball spin and spin, but it just can't seem to grab the lane. Miss a little to the inside, and your ball rolls down the hill toward the center of the lane, hooking too soon and too much. While your best option on wet/dry is to move away from the figurative cliff, moving away is your *only* option if the cliff is real. You can't fight gravity with a ball change!

SLIP SLIDIN' AWAY

Bowling on heavy oil is just plain tough. It can make you long for the ease and simplicity of dealing with burnt heads. Heavy oil can be an intentional part of the oil pattern, or it can be the result of a lane machine malfunction. Regardless of the reason for the flood of oil, you still have to shoe up and bowl on it. As difficult as it may be, you are not facing it alone. Everyone on your pair is in the same boat. High oil volume is very humbling. Bowlers who are used to hooking half the lane will feel like they have completely lost their strong release.

Heavy oil is not bad, just challenging. It is not unlike other challenging conditions you may encounter, it just requires a different set of answers. You may need these answers only temporarily if the lanes transition very quickly, or you may be stuck with them for the whole night.

One of the most obvious solutions to heavy oil is to use a very high-end ball with a low RG and lots of surface. If there are a number of high rev bowlers on your pair using strong, dull balls, the excess oil may deplete rather quickly no matter how heavy it was at the start, so be ready not only for quick lane transitions, but also for major adjustments as the block progresses.

Beyond selecting a dull, porous, high-end ball with a low RG, what else can we do to cope with a heavy oil condition? Most dull balls have a surface finished with 1000 or 2000 grit. While this is all the surface you will ever need under ordinary conditions, don't hesitate to go down to 500 grit or even lower when faced with extremely heavy oil. Since most of the high-end balls have a very low RG to begin with, we also suggest selecting one with a pin-down layout in order to bring the RG down even further and get the ball hooking and rolling sooner.

You will not see a lot of hook on heavy oil conditions, so it is best to play the lanes more direct, with straighter launch angles. Our advice is, "Don't give up the pocket." You need to keep your line closer to the pocket since you can't count on a lot of recovery if your ball gets out too wide. Another useful adjustment to your "normal" game is to use less axis rotation. Release the ball a little more "up the back" so that it hooks and rolls sooner instead of trying for a big change of direction down lane. A decrease in axis rotation will result in a smoother and more subtle ball reaction that will be easier to control. Ball choice, launch angle, and axis rotation are the big three adjustments when facing heavy oil. Other adjustments to consider adding to the mix are less loft, less axis tilt, and increased revs, but in most cases, ball selection, appropriate launch angle, and suitable axis rotation will give you everything you need.

SHOULD I STAY OR SHOULD I GO?

You will not be the only bowler trying to fight the heavy oil and making these same decisions. At some point, maybe sooner than you imagine, the lanes will change fairly dramatically. All of those strong balls will start to "carve out" the oil on the lane, drying it up in the areas where most of the play is taking place. When this happens, you will face another decision: Do you stay where you are and employ your adjustment tools to compensate for the increasing friction, or do you move away from there and again contend with the heavy oil on a fresher part of the lane?

The decision to move or stay depends on a great many things, including what the other bowlers on your pair are doing. Other players' ball choices and lane play decisions can affect the options open to you. Your most important consideration, though, is how well you had been doing up to this point. If you were bowling well on the heavy oil and making good adjustments, then why change your strategy now? Move to another zone on the lane where the heavy oil has not been depleted, and keep doing what has been working for you. Why stay put and try to dial in a completely new strategy to contend with the newfound friction?

If you were struggling on the heavy oil and couldn't find a consistent shot that worked, then the transition will come as a relief. With the heavy oil depleted and higher friction prevailing, you can stay put and change to a more conventional game, opening up the lanes a little and letting the friction be your ally. The simplest adjustment to the higher friction is switching to a pearl or polished ball with a higher RG, which will naturally get farther down the lane before hooking. Other helpful adjustments are to increase ball speed, increase loft, or increase axis rotation or axis tilt. You probably won't need to make all of these adjustments, but it's good to keep them in mind. Most of the time a weaker ball and more speed will get you where you want to go.

HOW DO I BEAT GRAVITY?

The simple answer is that you can't. But you can certainly work with it. Lane topography is an invisible variable, but it has a strong effect on your ball reaction because you are dealing with the force of gravity. When the lane is not completely flat—and there is not a completely flat lane on the planet—your ball will react to all of those little hills and valleys, and it doesn't take much of a rise or dip to take your ball off line.

At the time of this writing, the legal limit on how much a lane can be out of level is 40 thousandths of an inch. That's thinner than a US dime, and you will not see it with the naked eye. While 40 thousandths of an inch does not seem like much of a hill or valley, it is more than enough to make your ball react in unanticipated ways. Since you can't see the topography, you will have to rely on your ball motion to tell you where it is and what it's doing. There are of course other variables that can cause unusual or unexpected ball motion—lane surface type and age, lane friction due to pattern and bowlers, and so on—but topography will trump all the others.

How many times have you bowled on a freshly oiled pair, but the two lanes played completely differently from one another? Topography. Have you ever had to play a pattern *very* differently from how you are *supposed to* play it based on the lane oil graph? Topography. Ever had a night when you threw nothing but strikes on one lane but couldn't buy a strike on the other? Topography again.

Most bowlers don't know enough about topography and how it affects ball reaction. Others are aware of it, but don't give it the respect it deserves. In either case, you are setting yourself up for a frustrating battle, one that you are always going to lose. There are various types of topographic maps that reveal the lane's hills and valleys, such as the those created by Kegel's LaneMapper system (Figure 16.5). These maps are occasionally provided by tournament venues, but the vast majority of the time you are going to have to trust your ball motion to tell you what is happening and how you need to play the lane.

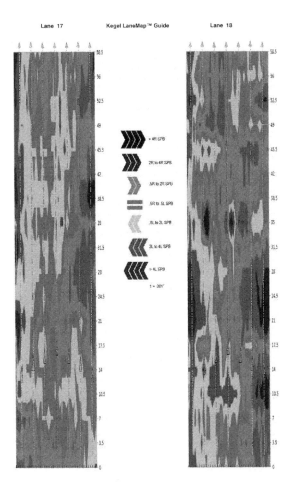

Figure 16.5: Lane topography, as revealed by Kegel LaneMapper

Copyright Kegel LLC. Adapted with permission

Lane topography is not always a negative. Many times, you will bowl on topographic conditions that actually help you increase your room for error. If the lane is depressed toward the center—higher on the outsides and lower to the inside—it creates a funnel effect, channeling your errant shots right back into the middle of the lane. Such conditions benefit players on both sides of the lane, leading to higher scores since there is no "out of bounds" area on the outsides. No matter how far you miss, the dished lane brings your ball back into play.

There are also plenty of situations where one side of the lane is favored by a ramp effect and the other side is not, while still remaining within the legal 40 thousandths limit. We have all bowled on lanes that seem to favor either the right or left handers. Again, this is topography at work. If the lefties have all the miss room in the world while the righties struggle to hit the pocket, don't blame the bowlers. It is just the product of the environment in which you are competing that day. Some days the gravitational force will be with you, and other days it works against you. Making excuses or giving up will never lead to winning. Accepting what you can't control and working at finding the best solution can lead to winning even in the face of gravitational adversity.

When you encounter a pair of lanes where one plays very differently from the other, don't immediately blame the lane machine. Most often, the differences in play are due to differences in topography. Rather than fighting gravity and trying to force the same ball and line to work on both lanes, accept what your ball motion is telling you. Make an adjustment to compensate for the difference in topography. It may only require using a different ball or a slightly different line on each lane. Simple adjustments such as speed or axis rotation may do the trick, or it could require something more drastic like moving to a completely different zone on one of the lanes.

If the right lane seems to hook less down lane than the left, there is probably a little more slope toward the gutter on the outside of the right lane or a slope toward the center on the left. You won't see it with your eye, but your ball will see it and alert you to what is going on if you are willing to observe its motion and listen to what it's telling you. On the lane that is hooking less, move your feet, move your eyes, change balls, or use some other tool or combination of tools. The extent of your miss down lane will clue you in to the degree of adjustment you need to make. The quicker you recognize topography at work, the quicker you can dial in the right combination of adjustments to match up on each of your lanes.

When facing a new oil pattern, many bowlers will try to figure out in advance how best to play it. Some use simplistic rules of thumb such as the Rule of 31—more of a very general suggestion than a rule—which states that if we subtract 31 from the length of the oil pattern, the resulting number tells us what board our breakpoint should be on. While the arguments in support of the Rule of 31 aren't terribly sound or compelling, it nonetheless yields fairly reasonable results, though all it is really saying is to play more outside on short patterns and more inside on longer patterns.

With our rules of thumb failing to provide specific advice, the more sophisticated among us turn to the lane oil graphs. We stare intently at the colored bars and stripes, and we nod knowingly as we pore over the cryptic numbers atop the printed sheet. We go online, searching for videos and forum posts telling us how best to play Pattern X. We formulate our strategy, throw a shot, and... it doesn't work. Not even close.

When the pattern doesn't play anywhere close to where it *should* play, a number of factors are probably at work, but one of the biggest is topography. Lane oil graphs give us a few clues about how the lanes should play, but topography dictates how they *will* play. Topography is greatly affected by climate. Not just differences in climate from one geographic area to another, but also from season to season within the same bowling center. Topographic changes from summer to winter can be drastic, so the same pattern will often play quite differently from one season to the next. If you bowl on a given pattern in a northern state during winter and then on the same pattern in humid central Florida, it's pretty much a guarantee that they will play differently. Even if you stick to one bowling center during one season, the building will shift and settle over time, changing the lane topography.

If all of these shifts and variations are within the legal limits but still affect game play to such a large degree, is *legal* good enough? If gravity has such a profound effect on ball motion, is a 40 thousandths of an inch legal variance too much? If bowling's governing body ever decides to tighten up the allowance, will flatter lanes even be technically possible and economically feasible, or will it just drive more bowling centers out of business or force them to drop their sanctioned leagues and tournaments? Whatever the case, until extremely flat lanes become the norm, gravity needs to be acknowledged, respected, and trusted. As you learn more about topography and its effects, and as you observe your ball motion more closely, your adjustment decisions will be more confident, more rapid, and more effective.

CHAPTER 17

SPARE CHANGE

PRACTICE YOUR SPARES—PRACTICE your spares—practice your spares.... Every bowling coach repeats this to their bowlers until they are sick of hearing it. Every bowler tells themselves that they "really need to practice spares more," usually saying so just after missing their third 10-pin in a row. Why do coaches emphasize spare shooting so much? In today's big-hooking and high-scoring environment, are spares still as important as they used to be?

We can all cite examples of tournaments, both professional and amateur, that have been lost by missing too many spares along the way. How many times have you missed making match play in a tournament or lost your point in league play because of one or two missed easy spares? Those occasional open frames seem harmless enough at the time. "I'll just make it up by putting a few strikes together," we tell ourselves, but the damage caused by those open frames just keeps adding up. When all is told, those missed spares are often the difference between making the cut and going home empty handed.

The math doesn't lie, and the record books reveal just how much damage an open frame or two can do. In 2004, a gentleman in Ohio rolled nine strikes in a single game, but ended up with a score of 176! He had three open frames, and if he had converted those spares he would have posted an impressive 230 for the game. In 2002 a gentleman from Indiana rolled 10 strikes during a game, but his two open frames left him with a score of only 205. Had he converted those two spares, he would have had a great game with a score of 251.[59] Indeed, this happens at all levels of our sport, from the casual once per week league bowler all the way up to the PBA. On the flip side, many tournaments have been won because of effective spare shooting. Some days the shot will simply not be there and strikes will be very hard to come by, but one bowler will manage to grind out more frames than did their opponents. Everyone can strike. It really isn't that impressive. But show us bowlers who can systematically make all of their spares—now you have our attention.

REVIVING A LOST ART

In some ways, spare shooting is becoming a lost art. In today's game, strikes are more plentiful, and it seems as though every bowler with a high rev rate carries an average of 210, or 220, or 230. We marvel at the league bowlers who can throw their shot seemingly anywhere on the lane, even missing their mark and their breakpoint by many boards, yet every shot comes screaming back to the pocket. Many factors have contributed to this phenomenon, from high-tech lane surfaces, to computer-controlled lane machines capable of laying out a consistent and repeatable shot, to oil patterns purposely designed to give extra hook to shots thrown too far out toward the gutter and to cut down the hook of shots thrown too far toward the center of the lane. Add to this our modern engineered lane oil, and high-tech balls capable of taking advantage of forgiving house shots, and you have a recipe for higher overall scores than we saw a decade or two ago. The advances in lane maintenance technology that allow these very forgiving lane conditions to be created have lead to far more strikes, and have bred complacency with spare shooting for many bowlers. We've even heard bowlers excuse an open frame with a flippant, "No one ever shot a 300 by making their spares"! Such complacency will come back to haunt you. You may strike a lot on a given day or at a given house, and maybe even shoot an honor score, but those missed spares will add up (or more correctly, not add up) and cost you games, matches, and titles. When you lose a game and you look back at it frame by frame, do you think about the strikes you threw, or do those missed spares and open frames jump out at you? We feel confident it is the latter.

PRACTICE, PRACTICE, PRACTICE!

How many times have you spent an entire training session working only on spares? We have watched a lot of bowlers over the years but we rarely see anyone practicing their spares, and the reasons are simple; spare practice is not exciting, and it is not glamorous. Spending an entire game shooting only 10-pins and 7-pins doesn't lead to good scores on the computer monitor, which can feel a bit humiliating when all of those strangers see it as they walk past your lane. We admit, this feeling is hard to overcome, and it takes a lot of willpower to do so. One day last year, I was working on a spare drill suggested by Norm Duke; trying to pick off just the 10-pin and the 7-pin from a full rack every frame. Partway through the game, a league bowler walked up, looked at the monitor and exclaimed, "39 in the 8th??? And you call yourself a coach?" Another time, a league bowler from the next pair looked at my pathetic score resulting from a game of spare practice, and said consolingly, "Well, I guess even coaches have bad games now and then." Any good bowler will understand exactly what you are doing and will know that the score is not representative of your skill. Yet the judgmental looks from strangers make it very hard to continue, and even harder to fight the urge to go back to throwing strike balls.

Such reasons for avoiding spare practice just don't cut it. We understand that spare shooting is not necessarily fun or exciting. It is, however, a major part of the bowling success formula. You can strike all day in practice and impress all of those strangers, but what have you done to improve your game? If you do strike all day in practice and score really well on the monitors, what does it get you? Other than providing false confidence, high scores in practice mean pretty much nothing. Practice is not about score, or at least it shouldn't be. It is about skill development. If your mind is on scoring in practice, you are not really practicing.

While spare shooting may not be exciting, it is without question an important part of what makes a true champion. If being a champion were easy, everyone would do it. The famous modern artist Chuck Close said, "Inspiration is for amateurs—the rest of us just show up and get to work." It is precisely those few individuals who put in the work—who devote all the necessary effort, time, and energy—that have a chance of seeing the top of the mountain. Champions and potential champions don't make excuses for not having time to practice or not wanting to practice things they don't enjoy. They just do it, and they do it without hesitation and without question. They "show up and get to work." That is why we don't see champions everywhere we look. Most bowlers don't have the drive and discipline to do what it takes. If you are one of the few who do, the few who truly want to reach their own potential, we sincerely hope you will take a lot from this book to help you on your journey, and we implore you to make this chapter on spare shooting a priority on that journey toward greatness.

A SPARE SYSTEM IS BORN

Many years ago, long before we even thought about writing this book, I began to experience a lot of trouble with my spare game. While I was always far from perfect when shooting 10-pins, my shot seemed to have deteriorated dramatically, and I began to miss almost all of them to the left. In fact, I couldn't seem to cover any right-side spare with any consistency. While working with my coauthor on some other aspects of my game, I mentioned my 10-pin problem. He watched as I threw a few shots, then told me I was standing too far left. This made no sense to me at the time. I am a right-hander. If I were standing too far left, I should be missing right and throwing every shot into the gutter. Instead I was routinely missing left, sometimes by a little, sometimes by an embarrassing amount.

My coauthor explained that even though I thought I was standing in the right place, my subconscious mind knew better. It saw that the ball would go in the gutter if thrown from where I was standing, so I subconsciously adjusted my swing off line and "pulled" the shot left to compensate. If I pulled the shot just right, I hit my pin. If I pulled it too much, I would miss left. In either case, my swing was no longer free and in line, resulting in irregular ball placement from shot to shot. He asked how I had come to stand where I was. I replied that I had been taught the common "3-6-9" spare system, and that is what I used. I found where to stand for targeting the 10-pin via trial and error, and then adjusted 3, 6, and 9 boards from there. He replied that my "trial and error" was more error than trial, and he moved me several boards to the right.

During the three hour drive home from that coaching session, I had plenty of time to think about both what he said, and about the efficacy of the 3-6-9 spare system in general.

THE 3-6-9 SPARE SYSTEM

The 3-6-9 system is the most commonly touted system for targeting spares. It is based on making adjustments to your strike shot in order to pick up spares, and is accomplished by moving your feet left or right on the approach while maintaining the the same target arrow.

The 3-6-9 system dictates that for each pin position to the left of the headpin that you wish to target, you move your feet three boards to the right from your strike stance and then throw the ball over your strike mark at the arrows. Thus to hit the 2- or 8-pin, which are both one pin position to the left of the headpin, you move your feet three boards to the right and hit your strike mark at the arrows. Another three boards to the right, or six in total, lines you up to shoot the 4-pin over your strike mark, and a further three board move, or nine boards in total, lines you up for the 7-pin. For right-side spares you reverse the procedure, moving your feet three boards to the left and targeting your strike mark in order to hit the 3-pin or the 9-pin, with subsequent three board moves to the left to hit the 6-pin and finally the 10-pin.

The idea behind the 3-6-9 system is both clever and fairly logical, but as with so many simple systems or ideas, "the devil is in the details." The 3-6-9 system is based on lane geometry and a simple ratio. A bowling lane is 60 feet long. The arrows are (very) roughly 15 feet from the foul line, leaving 45 feet from the arrows to the pins. The system further assumes a breakpoint 45 feet down lane.

Think of this initial 45 foot portion of the ball path from the foul line to the breakpoint as being attached to your strike mark by a pivot. Assume that you are all lined up for your strike shot. You have discovered where to stand so that your shot crosses your target arrow and then continues on to hit the headpin. If you now need to hit a pin that is to the left of the headpin, say the 2-pin, you just move your starting position to the right. Since your ball will be crossing the same target arrow as it did for your strike shot, the ball path will pivot to the left of where your strike ball hit. Similarly, to hit a pin to the right of the headpin, you can pivot your ball path to the right by moving your feet to the left (Figure 17.1).

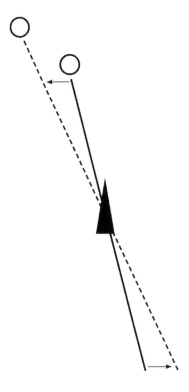

Figure 17.1: Moving feet to the right to pivot the ball path to the left

Let's walk through an example to see how the geometry works when targeting the 2-pin. The 3-6-9 system says that you need to move your feet three boards to the right. Doing so will obviously make your ball start out three boards to the right at the foul line. Since the ball still crosses the same mark you targeted for your strike shot, your three board move to the right with your feet makes the ball end up three boards left of your strike line at a point halfway down the lane. It will continue traveling left over the next 15 feet to your breakpoint, where it will now be a total of six boards left of your strike line. At this point, 45 feet down lane, the ball hooks (Figure 17.2). Since the pins are roughly six boards apart, the six board move in the ball path caused by the three board move with your feet should put the ball in a position to hit the 2-pin. Each subsequent three board move with your feet adds another six boards at the breakpoint, ostensibly sending the ball toward the next pin over.

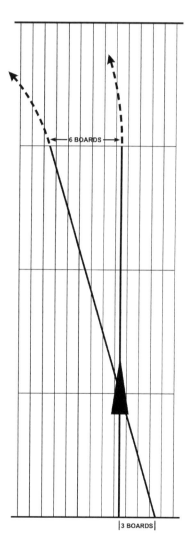

Figure 17.2: Three boards right at foul line = six boards left at breakpoint

DOES THE 3-6-9 SYSTEM WORK?

The assumptions required to make the 3-6-9 system work even just in theory are fairly significant, and the problems with trying to make it actually work on the lanes are legion. First, the 3-6-9 system absolutely requires that you hook the ball, and your hook has to be rather large. To see why, let's follow the logic surrounding the three board move to the right from your strike position in order to target the 2-pin, and apply it to a straight ball.

Just as with the hook, the straight ball will start out three boards farther right of the strike line, cross the arrow, move three boards farther left at a point 15 feet past the arrow, and another three boards over the next 15 feet, or six boards in total at a point 45 feet down lane. The straight ball, however, has another 15 feet of straight travel toward the left before it hits the pins. Because its path does not change, the ball will move *another* three boards left during this last 15 feet of travel, for a total of nine boards to the left (Figure 17.3). Since the pins are only about six boards apart, the three board move with our feet causes us to miss the center of our target pin by over three inches.

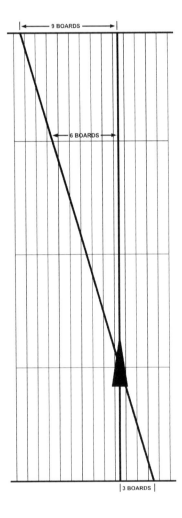

Figure 17.3: Three boards right at foul line = nine boards left at the pins

Rather than hitting the intended 2-pin squarely, the first three board move from our strike line will instead hit between the 2- and 4-pins. The prescribed six board move to hit the 4-pin will instead hit the 7-pin spot, and the nine board move to hit the 7-pin will instead put the ball solidly in the left gutter. If our bowler throws a straight or relatively straight ball, he or she will probably get away with the first three board move, will miss the target pin following the second three board move, and will miss horribly with the third.

Since a straight ball misses the target pin to the left when following the 3-6-9 system, wouldn't a hook shot miss by even more? While the straight ball traveled to the left by three boards too many during the last 15 feet, the hook ball, since it is also moving left on its own, should miss by the same three boards as did the straight ball, plus an additional number of boards depending upon the magnitude of its hook. Let's test this idea visually.

Suppose for this example that we throw our strike shot straight up the boards over the second arrow. Let's assume that the ball travels 45 feet down lane, hooks over the next 10 feet, then rolls the last five feet, entering the pocket on board 17-1/2 at a 4 degree angle. A bit of math tells us that on such a path the ball hooks roughly 3-1/2 boards to the left, then rolls on its new angled path to cross the final four boards before hitting the headpin.

Figure 17.4, below, is a scale drawing of a bowling lane. We removed the center section of the drawing to make it fit on the page. The black line illustrates our strike shot. The dark grey ball path results from a three board move to the right with the feet. It is precisely the same ball motion as in the strike shot, but pivoted over the second arrow by three boards at the foul line, just as the 3-6-9 system dictates. This ball will exhibit the same degree of hook, but will have a slightly longer roll phase before reaching the pins. The other two lighter grey ball paths are also identical ball motion, but shifted by subsequent three board moves, or 3-6-9 in total.

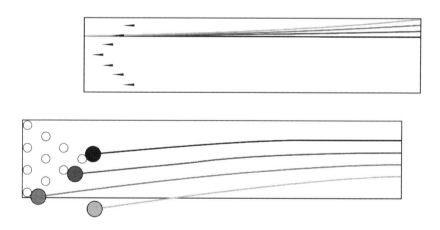

Figure 17.4: Adjustments of 3, 6, and 9 boards, hook shot targeting second arrow

We can see that, as predicted, each ball began its hook phase roughly six boards to the left of the previous shot (the right edge of the bottom drawing), but since the ball is also hooking, the miss at the pins is even greater than it was with a straight ball. Just as with a straight ball, mathematics dictates that the first three board move hits the 2-pin left of center. The next three board move that was supposed to hit the 4-pin instead barely catches the 7-pin before falling into the gutter. The final three board move, nine boards in total, rather than hitting the 7-pin as the system claims, will instead drop the ball into the left gutter long before reaching the pin deck. Mathematically speaking, on the left-hand side of the lane each step of the 3-6-9 system moves the ball too far, whether we throw a straight ball or a hook.

3-6-9 SYSTEM ON RIGHT-SIDE SPARES

It is equally easy to demonstrate that the 3-6-9 system moves the ball too far for the right-side spares too. Figure 17.5 depicts three, six, and nine board moves to the left with the feet in order to target the 3-, 6-, and 10-pins on the right-hand side of the lane. Again, the black line depicts our bowler's strike shot over second arrow. The dark grey line is the ball path resulting from the first three board move to the left. As can be seen, rather than hitting the 3-pin squarely, the ball just catches it on the right edge. The subsequent three board moves with the feet produce the other two depicted ball paths. These last two shots are no longer visible in the bottom drawing because in both cases the ball ended up in the right gutter about halfway down the lane.

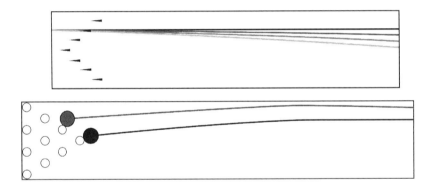

Figure 17.5: 3-6-9 system, second arrow, right-side spares

3-6-9 SYSTEM: VARIATION FOR RIGHT-SIDE SPARES

The reason that the last two shots went in the gutter is because our strike mark is too far to the right to serve as an effective target for right-side spares. Since we were targeting our strike shot over the second arrow, our first three-board move to the left with our feet projected our ball path perilously close to the gutter, leaving no more room on the lane for subsequent moves. Since moving our feet to the left and targeting our strike mark pretty much can't work for the common strike targets which tend to cluster around the second arrow, a variation on the 3-6-9 system was developed for covering right-side spares. The variation requires us to shoot the right-side spares over a more appropriate target, typically near the fourth arrow.

To employ the variation on the 3-6-9 system for right side spares, we first need to find where to stand for shooting the 10-pin over our chosen target arrow, and we do this through trial-and-error. Once we've found a suitable starting position for shooting the 10-pin, we then simply move our feet three boards to the right for each subsequent pin. For example, if you hit the 10-pin by standing on the 35-board and throwing your ball over the center arrow, then to hit the 6-pin you would move your feet three boards to the right of your 10-pin spot—board 32 in this case—and hit the same target arrow. Likewise, to hit the 3-pin you would move your feet three more boards to the right, or a total of six boards from your 10-pin spot, and again hit the same target arrow. Three more boards, nine in total, should put your ball on the headpin.

While this variation on the 3-6-9 system for right side spares makes far more sense than does the original formulation since it keeps the ball farther from the gutter, the three board adjustments with the feet still bring about the same problem on the right side of the lane as they did on the left. The three board move to the right with your feet again produces a six board shift at the breakpoint, but since the ball has a further 15 feet of travel it should end up at a point far to the left of our intended target pin which is only six boards over from its neighbor, and our subsequent three-board moves merely amplify the error.

BACK TO THE DRAWING BOARD

So, the 3-6-9 spare system is problematic at best. What, then, to do? As I continued the long drive home from my lesson, I pondered this problem. I thought there had to be a better way than trial-and-error to find my 10-pin line, and a better way in general to target spares. As I gazed out through the car's windshield and watched the yellow and white lines on the road converge to a point in the distance, the answer struck me: Spare targeting is nothing but simple trigonometry. We realize that the words "simple" and "trigonometry" probably shouldn't appear in the same sentence, but if you throw a straight ball at your spares rather than trying to hook at them, or if you possess only a small hook to begin with, then the problem of targeting spares really does become simple, even trivial.

Calculating a mathematically sound spare system first requires us to select an appropriate target arrow for the pin we wish to hit. Let's use the example of a right-handed bowler targeting everyone's favorite spare, the 10-pin, over the fourth or center arrow. If we were to draw a straight line from the 10-pin, across the center arrow, and on to the foul line, it would show us the precise path our ball must take if it is to cross the center arrow and hit that pin. A straight line is a straight line, and there is no other possible straight path over the center arrow that will hit the 10-pin.

If we can figure out exactly where our straight line crosses the foul line, we will know where our ball has to cross the foul line in order to make our spare. The USBC specifies the exact dimensions of a bowling lane and precisely where each pin must be set. They also specify the side to side placement of the targeting arrows, and the various lane manufacturers can tell us how far from the foul line—and therefore how far from each pin—each arrow is located. We can use these standardized dimensions to calculate exactly where our straight line drawn from the 10-pin over the center arrow would cross the foul line (Figure 17.6).

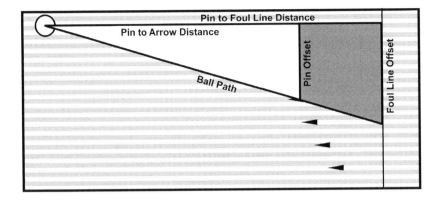

Figure 17.6: Calculating ball path for targeting the 10-pin over fourth arrow

CALCULATING BALL POSITION

The math required to calculate where our straight shot needs to cross the foul line is not terribly difficult, but the explanation of where all of our numbers come from is a bit tedious. Since we don't want to risk losing readers by bogging you down in minutiae, we will follow the same approach as we employed in the deflection chapter, relegating all of the fiddly bits to Appendix B and just providing you with the answers. We absolutely encourage you to read Appendix B so that you understand how we arrived at our numbers, and to assure yourself that we didn't pull them out of thin air.

The results of all of our computations are presented in Table 17.1. This table lists the board your ball *has to be on* when it crosses the foul line in order to hit any given pin when targeted over the third, fourth, or fifth arrow, and for both right- and left-handed bowlers. For example, for a right hander to shoot the 6-pin over fourth arrow, the table tells us that ball must cross the foul line on board 24. To shoot the 7-pin over fourth arrow, the ball must cross at board 14-1/2, which is the seam between boards 14 and 15.

Pin		Lay-down Board at Foul Line		
Right hander	**Left hander**	**3rd Arrow**	**4th Arrow**	**5th Arrow**
10	7	19	25.5	32
6	4	17	24	30.5
3 or 9	2 or 8	15	22	28.5
1 or 5	1 or 5	13.5	20	26.5
2 or 8	3 or 9	11.5	18	25
4	6	9.5	16	23
7	10	8	14.5	21

Table 17.1: Spare shot lay down board when targeting the arrows

To verify our math and to prove that the lay down boards in Table 17.1 are correct, we ran actual tape lines on a bowling lane running from the pins to the foul line, correlating to every shot denoted in the table. As examples, Figure 17.7 depicts the 10-pin and the 7-pin, both targeted over fourth arrow. In both cases you can see that the physical lines agree completely with the calculated foul line positions in Table 17.1—board 25-1/2 for the 10-pin and board 14-1/2 for the 7-pin for righties, and the opposite for lefties.

Figure 17.7: 10-pin, fourth arrow, and 7-pin, fourth arrow

Before anyone points it out and objects, we call your attention to the third and fifth arrow columns in Table 17.1, which reveal what seems to be an error. Take the case of a left hander shooting the 7-pin over third arrow. This is precisely the same line that a right hander's ball must travel if it is to hit the 7-pin over his or her fifth arrow. The two lines have to be the same because the right-hander's fifth arrow *is* the left-hander's third arrow. Why, then, does our table say the left-hander must lay the ball down on board 19, but the right-hander must place it on board 21?

This confusing state of affairs arises because while the pins possess absolute numbers regardless of which hand the bowler uses, the boards and arrows do not. Instead, the boards and arrows are numbered relative to the side of the lane closest to the bowler's bowling hand. Thus, a right hander's board 39, as counted from the right gutter, is the same physical strip of wood as the left hander's board 1 as counted from the left gutter. The table tells us that our left hander's ball must cross his or her board 19, which is one board to the left of the center board. That same physical board, one left of the center board, is the 21st board when counted by the right hander from the right gutter. The table, then, is not in error. The discrepancy between the numbers results only from differing frames of reference, and any pair of corresponding numbers, though different, both refer to the same physical board.

CALCULATING WHERE TO STAND

Table 17.1 tells us where our ball must cross the foul line to hit any given pin, but how do we know where to stand in order to accomplish this? To determine where we need to stand on the approach, we must introduce a concept called *lay down distance*.

We swing our bowling ball from our shoulder, which necessarily places the ball some distance away from the center of our body. Additionally, many bowlers, especially power players and two-handers, tilt their body to the side to some degree, which places the ball even farther from the body's center line. These two factors combine to cause us to place the ball onto the lane some distance away from our slide foot. This distance, from the instep edge of our slide foot to the center of the ball, is called our lay down distance, which is sometimes shortened to lay down.

Determining your lay down distance is a simple matter, requiring only an observer with either a keen eye or a camera. Station your observer behind you on the approach as you deliver your ball onto the lane. Make certain to post up your shot, and observe which board the instep edge of the sole of your slide shoe came to rest on at the foul line. Subtracting the board on which your observer said your ball crossed the foul line from the board upon which your slide concluded yields your personal lay down distance (Figure 17.8). For example, if your slide foot ended up with the instep edge of the sole on board 20 and the center of your ball crossed board 14 at the foul line, your lay down distance is six boards—20 minus 14. It is best to repeat this process a few times to verify the results. If your results are consistent, you now know your lay down distance. If your results varied, you should average the distances, and should also consider consulting a qualified coach to help you determine what is causing your inconsistency.

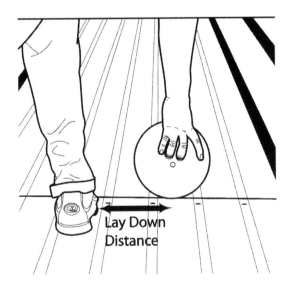

Figure 17.8: Lay down distance

Most bowlers we have observed possess a lay down distance in the range of five to six boards as measured from the instep edge of the sole of the slide shoe. Since a bowling ball has a radius of roughly 4-1/4 inches, if your lay down is less than 4-1/2 boards you've likely just smacked yourself in the ankle with the ball! If your lay down is much greater than six boards, it may be indicative of a problem in your delivery for which you should seek help from a qualified coach.[60]

Once you've determined your personal lay down distance, all you have to do to determine where to stand on the approach is add this distance to whatever board your ball needs to be on at the foul line. By way of example, suppose your lay down distance is five boards. If you are shooting the 10-pin over fourth arrow, Table 17.1 tells you that you need to place your ball on board 25-1/2 at the foul line. Since you lay your ball down five boards away from your instep, you need to stand with your instep five boards to the left of 25-1/2, or board 30-1/2. To cover any spare, just take the appropriate lay down board from Table 17.1, add your lay down distance to this board to find your starting position, and then stand with the instep of your slide foot on the edge of that starting board.

DRIFT

The starting position we calculated above—lay down position from Figure 17.1 plus your personal lay down distance—assumes that you walk straight up the boards during your approach. Many bowlers, however, will on a fairly consistent basis end up some small number of boards left or right of their starting position once they reach the foul line. This variation in your approach is called *drift*, and it must be taken into account when determining where to stand.

As we discussed in Chapter 13, drift is not the same thing as intentionally walking diagonally across the approach toward your target. Drift is an unintentional act, often the result of physical factors such as the first or last step in the bowler's approach being out of line, or psychological influences such as fear of the gutter. Since drift is unintentional and is performed at the subconscious level, it tends to be fairly consistent from shot to shot. As long as your drift is reasonably consistent and is not excessive in degree it will not adversely affect your shot, but you do need to adjust for it when determining where to stand when shooting your spares.[61]

In the above example of targeting the 10-pin over the center arrow, you determined that you needed to stand on board 30-1/2 so that your five board lay down distance would put your ball right on board 25-1/2 to make the spare. Suppose, however, that you routinely drift two boards to the left. If you start on board 30-1/2 but drift two boards left, you end up on board 32-1/2 at the foul line. From this position, your five board lay down distance puts your ball on board 27-1/2 at the foul line, two boards left of where it needs to be, and you miss your spare to the right.

If you do consistently experience drift, you must compensate for it. If you consistently end up left of your starting position, farther away from your target pin, you must subtract these drift boards from your calculated starting position (move right) in order to end up on the proper board at the foul line. Likewise, if you drift to the right, toward your target pin, you must add these drift boards to your calculated starting position (move left). Some bowlers will drift by differing amounts or in a different direction on one side of the lane versus the other. Again, this is not harmful so long as the drift is not excessive.

If you do drift by differing amounts or in a different direction when shooting left side and right side spares, you will need to make separate adjustments to your starting position on each side of the lane. Note too that the drift adjustments we just described apply to right handers. Lefties need only reverse the procedure, subtracting boards for rightward drift, and adding boards if drift is to the left.

That's it! Look up the foul line position in Table 17.1, add your lay down distance, add or subtract any consistent drift to the right or left, and you will know where to stand on the approach. From that position, if you are accurate enough to hit your mark, mathematics dictates that your ball must impact the target pin dead center.

CREATING YOUR OWN CALCULATED SPARE SYSTEM

Spare targeting really is that simple. All that *any* bowler has to do is add his or her unique lay down distance to the board numbers in Table 17.1, then adjust for any consistent drift. The result tells you which board to stand on for any possible spare. While the starting board for any given spare shot may differ from bowler to bowler depending on lay down distance and drift, the board the ball must cross at the foul line *is the same for everyone.*

So let's move from theory to practice and construct a system. Suppose you are a right-handed bowler who has a six board lay down distance and you wish to shoot all spares over the center arrow, which is the spare target arrow that we generally recommend. The table tells us that to hit the 10-pin your ball must cross board 25-1/2—the line between boards 25 and 26—at the foul line. To hit the 6-pin the ball must cross board 24, and to hit the 3-pin the ball must cross board 22. Adding your six board lay down distance to each of those positions, you determine that you need to stand on board 31-1/2 to shoot the 10-pin (board 25-1/2 plus your six board lay down distance). A 1-1/2 board move to the right to board 30 lines you up to hit the 6-pin, and an additional two boards right, to board 28, will let you target the 3-pin.

The system for left side spares is constructed in similar fashion. The Table tells us that when shooting the 7-pin over the 4th arrow, your ball needs to cross board 14-1/2 at the foul line. The Table further tells us that the lay down point is board 16 to hit the 4-pin, and board 18 to hit the 2-pin. Again, just add your six board lay down distance to each point. You therefore need to stand on board 20-1/2 to shoot the 7-pin (14-1/2 plus 6), and then move 1-1/2 boards and two boards to the left in order to shoot the 4-pin and 2-pin respectively. Make minor simplifications or tweaks to your spare system as necessary to fit your own game and conditions, and you're set![62] You will never miss a spare again. Well, at least not because you were standing in the wrong place!

We realize that this can sound a bit complicated as you read through it, but it's actually quite simple to design your spare system. To make it even easier, we have provided worksheets for both right-handed and left-handed bowlers in Appendix C at the end of this book. Simply photocopy the appropriate form, fill it in with your own choice of target arrow or arrows (you don't have to use the same arrow for both sides of the lane). Next write in your lay down distance and drift, and then create your own table of starting positions for every spare. To help you understand the form, Figure 17.9 is a sample worksheet for a right-handed bowler with a six board lay down distance and two boards of consistent leftward drift.

BowlSmart Spare System Worksheet: Right-hander

My lay down distance is __6__ boards.   My drift is __2__ boards R/L (circle one)

Pin	Lay-Down Board at Foul Line		
Pin	3rd Arrow	4th Arrow	5th Arrow
10	19	25.5	32
6	17	24	30.5
3 or 9	15	22	28.5
1 or 5	13.5	20	26.5
2 or 8	11.5	18	25
4	9.5	16	23
7	8	14.5	21

Pin	Target Arrow	Foul Line Board	+ Lay Down Distance	+ Drift Right (boards)	– Drift Left (boards)	Stand On Board
10	4TH	25½	6		2	29½
6		24	6		2	28
3 or 9		22	6		2	26
1 or 5		20	6		2	24
2 or 8		18	6		2	22
4		16	6		2	20
7		14½	6		2	18½

Figure 17.9: Sample Personal Spare System worksheet

A WORD ABOUT COMPOUND SPARES

We now have our starting positions on the approach in order to target any single pin spare, but what if we leave more than one pin? Simply split the difference between the two pins. Let's use the spare system worked out in Figure 17.9, above. Suppose our bowler left both the 2- and the 4-pin. The spare system says to stand on board 20 for the 4-pin and board 22 for the 2-pin, so splitting the difference and standing on board 21 will put the ball right in between them, covering both. Since a one and a half or two board move with your feet moves your ball all the way to the next pin over, splitting the difference with a one board move in either direction from any stated pin position will instead make your ball hit two adjacent pins, allowing you to easily convert multi-pin spares.

BUT IT WORKS FOR ME

Whenever we present our Calculated Spare System to a group, someone will invariably say that they use the trusty old 3-6-9 system in their league and it works just fine. Here's the odd thing regarding the 3-6-9 system: Mathematically, the 3-6-9 system for targeting spares should not work. Nevertheless, on the left side of the lane, and on a very forgiving, "easy" house shot, the 3-6-9 system does in fact often work, at least to an extent, as does the variation on the 3-6-9 system for the right-hand spares. Since the math seems to preclude the system from working at all, how can this be?

The key factor that allows the 3-6-9 system to at least have a chance of working lies in the structure of a *typical house shot*. On a competitive or sport oil pattern such as we often encounter in a tournament situation, the oil is dispersed in a more or less flat manner, or at least far flatter than on a house shot. "Flat" means that the oil is fairly evenly spread side to side across the lane. On sport shots there is also typically a greater volume of oil than one finds on a house shot, and there is far less "shape" to the shot, meaning that your ball will react in a similar fashion regardless of where you throw it on the lane. Certainly there can be differences from zone to zone on the lane depending upon the specific oil pattern employed, but the differences in the shape of our ball path as we make small adjustments with our feet will be small when bowling on sport conditions. On such competitive oil patterns, the 3-6-9 system tends not to work at all, with results resembling those depicted previously in Figures 17.4 and 17.5.

A typical house shot such as we encounter in league or open bowling situations is far different than a sport shot. While a sport shot is designed to be "fair," meaning that your ball will go pretty much where you throw it, a house shot is designed to create high scores by helping your ball find the pocket even on less than ideal deliveries. A house shot tends to have a wall of dry boards on the outside of the lane, moderate oil in the so-called track area around the second arrow, and a big, heavy wall of oil in a more or less triangular area up the center of the lane. The outside wall of dry boards helps your ball recover and still hook back to the pocket even if you miss your mark to the right, while the heavy wall of oil in the center helps stop your ball from hooking and instead hold its line if you miss toward the center of the lane, allowing your errant shot to slide into the pocket rather than crossing over or going "through the nose" for a split.

This walled up feature of the house shot is what allows the 3-6-9 system to work, and without these walls, it fails. Figure 17.10 illustrates the difference between a typical house shot and a tough sport shot. The darker colors indicate areas of higher oil concentration, while the lighter colors indicate drier areas.

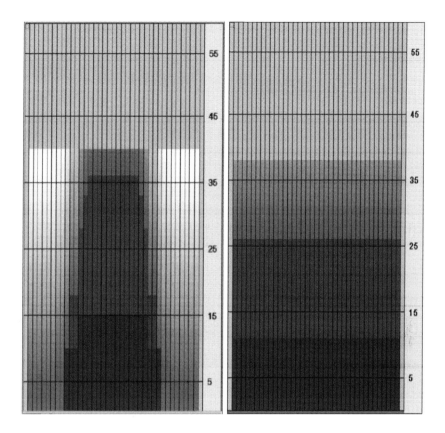

Figure 17.10: Typical house shot versus flat sport shot

Copyright Kegel, LLC, Kegel Pattern Library. Adapted with permission

On a house shot, a bowler's strike shot breakpoint—the part of the lane where the ball makes the meaningful portion of its hook—tends to be in the area of the drier boards. The ball therefore hooks relatively sharply in order to reach the pocket. When we move our feet to the right by three boards on a house shot while still targeting our strike mark, the ball enters an area of heavier oil as its path moves more toward the center of the lane. The heavier oil causes the ball to skid a bit longer and hook a bit less than it did on the strike shot, and this longer skid and lesser hook allows the ball to "hold line" and hit the 2-pin rather than hooking past it as it would on a sport shot. The next three board move right with our feet puts the ball into heavier oil still, thus killing the hook sufficiently to allow the ball to hit the 4-pin. The last three board move with our feet puts the ball path squarely into the heaviest oil in the center of the lane, allowing the ball enough skid and decreased hook to have a chance of hitting the 7-pin rather than hooking into the gutter.

A similar situation occurs on the right-hand side of the lane. The 10-pin shot travels out to the dry boards near the gutter, hooking quite a bit in order to stay on the lane and hit the pin. As we move to the right with our feet the ball encounters more oil, so skids farther and hooks less. Again, it is this progressively increased skid and decreased hook provided by the shape of the house shot that gives the ball any chance at all to hit the intended pin rather than hooking past it. This required variable hooking condition exists to a much lesser extent or not at all on tougher sport shots, and without it, the 3-6-9 can't work.

SO WHICH SPARE SYSTEM SHOULD I EMPLOY?

First, let us state that moves of 3, 6, and 9 boards when throwing a hook at spares are not set in stone, and many bowlers will make slight adjustments based on their own ball path and the precise conditions they bowl on. For example, at my usual bowling center, and with my release characteristics, my first move to the right to shift from my strike line to the 2-pin needs to be four boards, and the standard three board move would fall short. Therefore when we use the term "3-6-9 system" from this point in the discussion forward, we refer to *any* consistent system that involves hooking the ball at spares by moving your feet and keeping your mark constant, regardless of the actual number of boards moved.

The primary shortcoming of the 3-6-9 system is that it requires a fairly easy house shot and a fairly decent hook, and it simply cannot work if the bowler shoots straight at spares or even if he or she possesses only a moderate hook. A major problem with teaching or suggesting the 3-6-9 system to bowlers is that these two facts are almost universally omitted from the discussion, possibly because the limitations are unknown even to the teacher. Another problem is that the 3-6-9 system is often taught to beginners who have either no hook or only a very limited hook, and these are precisely the people for whom the system cannot work at all.

Why does 3-6-9 sort of work with a bigger hook, but not with a smaller one? Say you throw a fairly decent hook, and your strike ball hits board 7 at the breakpoint before hooking. That means your ball covers roughly 10 boards on its way to the pocket. If you move your feet three boards right, math says your ball will travel nine more boards to the left before hitting the pins (plus a bit more because of the hook). The problem is, the 2-pin is less than six boards to the left. If your ball happens to cover 1/3 fewer boards because of hitting the heavier oil toward the center of the lane, you can still hit your pin. To target the 4-pin, your next three board move, or six in total from your strike shot, puts your ball 18 boards left, but the 4-pin is only just over 11 boards away. If your ball can give up another three plus boards of hook to the even heavier oil it now encounters, it too can hit the pin. For the 7-pin, your next three board move would put your ball a total of 27 boards left of the headpin, but the 7-pin is only 17 boards away. If your ball gives up all of the hook it still has left, all 10 of its original boards of leftward travel, you can still hit your pin. That's a lot of "ifs," but it's at least theoretically possible.

Now let's look at a more modest hook. Say you play a directional line over second arrow, hitting board 14 at the breakpoint, with the ball hooking the last 3 boards to the headpin. Your first three board move to the right to target the 2-pin will put your ball nine boards left, but again the 2-pin is less than six boards away. Your ball therefore has to give up *all* of its hook in the heavier oil in order to hit the pin. In reality, your ball will not give up all of its hook from this first move, but for the sake of discussion, let's assume that it did. You now move three more boards right in order to target the 4-pin, or six boards in total. Your ball now wants to end up 18 boards left, but the 4-pin is only 11 boards away. Since you've already given up all of your hook to hit the 2-pin, there is nothing left to give up, and you miss the 4-pin to the left. In fact, the best you can do is miss it by four boards. Note that this is from the center of the ball to the center of the pin, so you still might just catch the very left edge of the 4-pin, but this is an iffy proposition at best. Let's now try to hit the 7-pin. Moving three more boards to the right, or nine boards in total, wants to move your ball 27 boards left, but the 7-pin is only 17 boards away. Again, even if all of your hook goes away in the heavier oil, you've still missed by seven boards, which puts your ball solidly in the left gutter.

In short, the 3-6-9 system requires that you possess at least ten boards of hook (or more accurately, ten boards of hook plus leftward roll), and that your ball gives up a little over three boards of that hook with each move to the right or left. If your ball hooks less than ten boards to begin with, or if it does not give up a consistent three plus boards of hook with each move, the 3-6-9 has to fail.

Since the 3-6-9 system relies on very soft and forgiving lane conditions, the actual application of the system can vary from house to house. It may work well at a bowler's home center, but may not work without modification at another bowling center even if that house also has a forgiving shot. While you can certainly make adjustments to compensate for the variation, doing so may well cost you open frames until you figure out the required changes. The 3-6-9 system also fails to a greater and greater degree as we move to flatter oil patterns, and fails almost completely on tougher sport shots. The system can also begin to fail even on a house shot as the lanes break down and the oil dries up or gets moved around.

In contrast to hooking the ball at spares, the straight ball path employed in the Calculated Spare System never changes. It works precisely the same regardless of oil pattern. A straight path to the pins is always a straight path, and remains so from house to house, game to game, and oil pattern to oil pattern. In short, it always works.

The straight ball path of the Calculated Spare System even takes the bowler's release out of the equation. If you are hooking the ball at spares as in the 3-6-9 system, the ball path is dependent not only on the oil pattern, but also upon how well you release the ball. Release weakly, and the ball may not hook enough to make it to your target pin, and if you happen to really get a handful of the ball, the shot is likely to hook right past the target pin. With a straight shot, in contrast, the bowler's release does not really matter. Straight is straight, regardless of how much hand the bowler gets on the ball.

The 3-6-9 system does present one potential advantage over a straight shot. For those who do possess a reasonable hook, it can be argued that the same soft lane conditions that allow the 3-6-9 system to work at all can also provide a bit more miss room when shooting at spares. Just as with a strike shot, if you hook at spares with the 3-6-9 system, a small miss to the right may put the ball into a drier area of the lane, allowing it to recover and still hit the pin, while a small miss to the left may hit heavier oil and hold line.

This potential advantage offered by the 3-6-9 system involves a lot of "maybe," and we need to weigh this "maybe" advantage against the consistency of the straight spare game. Additionally, even if the slight additional miss room from the 3-6-9 system is real, how much room do you actually need? When shooting straight at a single pin, the ball need only be within a 12 board area in order to hit the pin (Figure 17.11). That's almost a third of the lane, and translates to more than a three board wide area of miss room at the arrows. This means that you can miss your mark by over a board-and-a-half on either side of your target and still hit your pin. While hooking at spares on a soft house shot *may* provide a bit more miss room than does a straight ball, we would offer that if you consistently miss a target mark that is only 15 or 16 feet away by more than a board-and-a-half on either side, then your primary problem is probably not with your spare system!

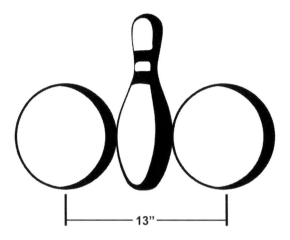

Figure 17.11: Miss room at the pins

THE CHOICE IS CLEAR

We have already demonstrated that the 3-6-9 system, or any spare system involving a hook ball, will be problematic at best and completely ineffective at worst on sport shots or tougher lane conditions. Such tougher oil patterns pretty much require straight shots at spares. On the PBA tour, we occasionally see a top level competitor throw a hook at a 2-pin or a 3-pin, especially once the shot "opens up," but even this is rare, and it is rarer still to see them hook at spares that are even farther from the headpin. Except for so-called "double wood" or "sleeper" shots—the 2-8 for righties or the 3-9 for lefties—the pros will almost without exception throw a straight ball at their spares.

You may argue that since the 3-6-9 system offers the possibility of some additional miss room when bowling on a soft house shot, then the smart course of action is to hook at spares when on league or recreational bowling conditions in order to capitalize on the increased area, while shooting straight at spares when bowling on a competitive shot. While this seems logical enough, we do not recommend it for a couple of reasons. First, recall that the increased miss room, if it even exists, carries with it a fair amount of increased variability as the shot breaks down and as you change balls or bowl at different venues, so at best it represents a trade off rather than a pure advantage even on a house shot. If a bowler hooks the ball at spares, they must accept increased variability from shot to shot in exchange for the possible added miss room. In bowling, as in life, you just can't get something for nothing.

An even more important argument against hooking at spares even on a soft house shot has to do with practice. Most everyone will agree that performance improves with practice, and that the more we repeat a movement, the more accurate and consistent our execution becomes. Outside of the top players on the PBA tour, it is safe to say that most bowlers roll far more games on soft house shots than they do on competitive sport shots. Even bowlers who enter tournaments with some regularity still likely bowl at least 90 percent of their games on house conditions. They would therefore spend at least 90 percent of their time hooking at spares. When such bowlers get to a tournament and need to throw straight at spares, they will now be playing their "B" game. They have spent almost all of their time dialing in their hook spare game, so now, when it really counts, they have to execute shots that they almost never use and never practice. If we instead always throw a straight ball at spares, even when on a soft house shot, then the straight shot becomes our "A" game. Now, when we compete in a tournament, we are throwing our best and most practiced shots at precisely the time when it matters most.

STRAIGHTER IS GREATER

If you are strictly a recreational bowler who bowls almost exclusively at a center with a consistent and forgiving house shot, and you never bowl competitive tournaments, then go ahead and hook at your spares if that is more comfortable for you. You'll be able to figure out some sort of variation on the 3-6-9 system that will work well enough, and the only serious problem you will likely have will be with the 10-pin if you are right-handed or the 7-pin if you are a lefty.

If you compete in tournaments, bowl on a sport league, have aspirations of being a competitive bowler at the high school, collegiate, or professional level, or simply want to develop your game to the highest possible level, you must learn to shoot straight at spares. Throwing straight at spares means every spare, not just the corner pins. We recognize only a couple of cases where hooking at a spare is a better option, where the loss of accuracy is worth the gain from increased angle.

For right-handed bowlers, there is a higher likelihood of converting the 2-8 "sleeper" or "double wood" with a hook ball than with a straight ball. Likewise for the 3-9 for left-handed bowlers. If a right hander throws straight at the 2-8, he or she must hit the 2-pin pretty much dead center in order to drive it back into the 8-pin. If the ball hits more than a tiny bit off center the 2-pin will deflect off to one side and the ball to the other, with both missing the 8-pin. By throwing a hook at the 2-8 you can cover it by hitting the 2-pin dead center or even a bit to the right. The slightly-light hook shot that hits right of center has a chance of carrying because the ball, which is traveling at a greater angle toward the left than had it been thrown straight, will deflect less off of the 2-pin, so has a greater chance of continuing on to hit the 8-pin rather than deflecting away. The same argument holds for left handers shooting the 3-9.

The case of a right hander throwing a hook at the 3-9 and a left hander at the 2-8 is more of a 50-50 proposition. Let's again examine this from the perspective of the right-hander. When our righty threw a hook at the 2-8, the ball traveled at a fairly high angle *toward* the spare, allowing it a chance to continue on its path to the 8-pin should the shot hit the 2-pin right of center. With the 3-9, however, the shot is moving across the lane *away* from the pins, and has to hook back into them. Since the ball has such a short distance to travel during this abbreviated hook it may not obtain enough angle back toward the pins, so will be unable to overcome deflection enough to carry a slightly right of center hit. Both the straight and the hook ball must therefore hit the 3-pin pretty much dead center in order to carry the 9-pin. Since the straight and the hook ball have an equal chance of covering the spare, you might argue that is doesn't matter which method you chose. This argument seems logical on the surface, but when we consider our previous discussion about how a straight path is always straight while a hook path can change and vary, the straight shot again wins out. While the straight shot at the 3-9 is technically the better option, it is a close enough call that we won't argue with you if you chose to hook at it.

Another possible exception to the "throw straight at all spares" rule arises in the case of the 1-2-4 or 1-2-4-7 for right-handers and the 1-3-6 or 1-3-6-10 for lefties, the so-called "clothesline" or "picket fence" spares. When bowling on a sport shot, these spares should be covered with a straight ball for all of the reasons mentioned previously. A hook ball can hit your mark but hook a little too much or push down lane a little too far, either missing the headpin, or hitting it too heavily and leaving the corner pin. With a straight ball, if you hit your mark, you cover your spare.

Probably the easiest ways to cover the 1-2-4 or 1-2-4-7 for a righty is to either throw a straight shot directly up board 25 (fifth arrow) or a touch to the right of it, or to line up as you would to shoot the 2-pin cross lane with a straight ball, but then move one extra board left with your feet. Note too that both of these approaches will also cover the 1-2-10, 1-2-4-10, or 1-2-8-10 "wash out," with the straight up the boards shot likely having a higher carry percentage than the cross lane shot.

When shooting these clothesline or picket fence spares on a league or recreational house shot, we are somewhat ambivalent as to which approach you take. A straight shot is undoubtedly a better and more accurate choice, and the one which both of us employ in pressure situations even when playing on a very easy house shot. Having said that, we both also admit to occasionally getting lazy and just moving three or four boards to the right, hitting our respective strike marks, and carrying the spare with a Brooklyn (wrong side of the headpin) strike shot. While the problem of the ball hooking a bit too much or too little still exists, a house shot is often forgiving enough in that area of the lane to render the Brooklyn shot a fairly high percentage endeavor. Having said that, our objection about practicing the straight shots you will need on tough conditions rather than practicing the hook shots that will almost certainly fail you again tips the balance firmly toward the "shoot straight at all spares" side of the equation. Note also that in the case of the 1-2-4-10, 1-2-8-10 or 1-2-10 wash out, a straight ball will have a greater chance of covering the spare than will a hook, even on a house shot. Since the hook is traveling toward the left to a far greater degree than is the straight ball, it will be more difficult for the ball to hit far enough on the left side of the headpin to send it on a sufficiently rightward path to hit the 10-pin.

STRAIGHT SHOOTER

By far the easiest way to throw straight at spares is to use a plastic ball. As we discussed in earlier chapters, plastic balls—sold by almost every ball manufacturer—are made with a very hard and low-friction polyester coverstock and the most rudimentary of weight blocks. They are designed specifically *not* to hook. This feature allows you to employ your ordinary strike release, and the ball will still go straight, or at lease mostly so.

Most intermediate to high caliber bowlers already own a plastic spare ball, but other than 10-pin shots (7-pin for lefties), it pretty much sits in their bag collecting dust. If you do not own a plastic spare ball, buy one. If you do own one, take it out of your bag and use it. If shooting straight allows you to make just one extra spare per game, your average will go up by 10 pins. How many corner pins, or 8-pins, or 9s have you missed lately? How many combination spares have you chopped? At less than $100 drilled at the time of this writing, a plastic spare ball is the cheapest and easiest way for a bowler to raise their average.

There are a few PBA bowlers who do not use a plastic ball for spares, and instead have learned to throw their strike ball straight. These players allow their wrist to bend backward, or "break" during release. This wrist position causes them to lead with their thumb rather than the palm of their hand, and causes their fingers and thumb to exit the ball at more or less the same time. This action both eliminates most of their side roll and drastically cuts their rev rate, thus "flattening out" the shot.

Elite players typically take a "best of both worlds" approach to shooting straight. They use a plastic ball *and* they also allow their wrist to break back, much like wearing both a belt and suspenders. With the high rev rates of many elite professional bowlers, even a plastic ball can hook a board or two. By using a plastic ball and allowing their wrist to break, there is pretty much no chance of the shot diverging from a straight line.

For intermediate level bowlers and for those just learning to throw a plastic ball, we recommend employing your ordinary strike release. Bowlers at this level are often still trying to perfect their release. By not varying it between strike and spare shots they will get more practice and repetition, and will dial their release into muscle memory that much faster. Such bowlers also typically possess rev rates low enough that, unless they have exceedingly low ball speed, the plastic ball will not hook to any meaningful degree no matter how they release it.

For more advanced bowlers and for those with very high rev rates (or very low ball speed) we recommend taking the approach of the elite bowlers, throwing a plastic ball *and* flattening out the shot by allowing your wrist to break backward. For those bowlers employing a two-handed or other no-thumb delivery, a plastic ball is pretty much a necessity since manipulating the wrist to flatten out the shot during release is much more difficult. Two handers can also learn to reduce their axis rotation to near zero, further reducing the chance that their ball will hook. In all cases, nowhere is the bowling adage "straighter is greater" more applicable than when applied to spare shooting.

SO, WHAT ABOUT THE DOTS?

All of our discussion thus far has revolved around targeting the arrows for our strike and spare shots. While the arrows are by far the most commonly employed targets on the lane, others do exist. Many people new to bowling target the pins rather than the arrows. While we do not at all condone targeting the pins, it does render spare shooting rather simple; stand wherever you want, aim at your pin, and throw the ball!

There is another set of targeting marks on the lane in addition to the arrows, one which most bowlers ignore and many have not even noticed. Located between the arrows and the foul line are a row of small dots. There are ordinarily ten of these dots, five on each side of the lane. They are arranged in a straight line across the lane, roughly seven feet from the foul line. While the arrows are spaced evenly across the lane at five board intervals, and the pins are spaced evenly at roughly six board intervals, the dots are oddly spaced and fall on seemingly random boards, and there are no dots at all in the center portion of the lane. Unlike the pin and the arrow spacing, the USBC does not specify how many dots there are nor how they are spaced. In fact, they do not even require the dots at all. USBC regulations state only that *if* the dots do exist, there can be no more than ten of them and they must fall within a band across the lane a minimum of six feet and a maximum of eight feet from the foul line. Everything else about their placement is left to the lane manufacturer.

No one we have spoken to, including some manufacturers of synthetic bowling lanes, has any idea what these dots are for or why they are where they are on the lane. Left to speculate, we originally thought that perhaps the dots fell on a line drawn from various pins through various arrows such that they could be used as supplemental targets when shooting spares cross lane, but working through the trigonometry disproved that idea. Our next thought was that they might line up with the headpin targeted with a straight ball over various arrows, but again trigonometry threw that idea out the window. Since there are no dots in the middle of the lane, they probably weren't intended for targeting strikes either.

Our best educated guess is that the dots were originally intended for targeting spares straight up the boards, a holdover from back in the days when no one had much of a hook, and perhaps didn't know that you have a bit more miss room when shooting spares cross lane. Despite the lack of a USBC standard, Brunswick and several other synthetic lane manufacturers we looked at place ten dots on the lane in two groups of five. In these instances the dots are on boards 3, 5, 8, 11, and 14 on the right side of the lane, and boards 26, 29, 32, 35, and 37 on the left-hand side, and they all place the dots 84 inches from the foul line. Since these manufacturers account for a sizable percentage of synthetic lane installations, at least in the United States, we will accept their placement as standard for the purposes of this discussion even though no true standard exists (Figure 17.12).

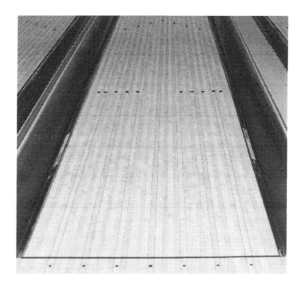

Figure 17.12: Mysterious target dots

Let's look at the right-hand set of dots. According to USBC specifications, the 10-pin is 2-3/4 inches from the gutter. This places it close to the center of board 3, which corresponds to the first dot. The 6-pin is 8-3/4 inches from the gutter, placing it near the seam between board 8 and 9, which is at least in the neighborhood of the third dot on board 8. The dot in between those two is very close to halfway in between the 6-pin and the 10-pin positions, so could be used to target the 6-10 with a straight shot parallel to the lane boards. Likewise, the 3-pin, which is 14-3/4 inches from the gutter, is on the far left edge of board 14, so it lines up reasonably well with the fifth dot. Again, the fourth dot is pretty much in between the 3-pin and the 6-pin, so could be used to target the 3-6 straight up the boards. While the dots line up reasonably well with the pins, their location at seven feet from the foul line seems to be random and meaningless.

If our speculation is correct—that the dots were originally intended as targets for shooting at spares straight up the boards—then they are superfluous. The arrows, while not truly lining up with the pins, are nonetheless close enough to be well within the margin of error for targeting spares. You could simply throw your ball straight up the boards over the first, second, and third arrows, and hit the 10-, 6-, and 3-pins respectively.

Despite the fact that no one seems to know what the dots are for, and despite the absence of dots in the center portion of the lane, a small percentage of bowlers use them as targets for their strike shots. We recommend against targeting the dots for *any* shot for a number of reasons, some of which will become apparent during the ensuing discussion. Having said that, if you do target the dots for strikes, and if you do not wish to switch to the arrows, then so be it. For spare shooting, however, we strongly advise against targeting the dots, and implore you to instead use the arrows at least for these shots.

WHY NOT TARGET THE DOTS?

The most important argument against targeting the dots, for spares or otherwise, has to do with a fact of geometry we call *lane leverage*. Lane leverage refers to how many boards the ball's finish position will shift for each board of movement with our feet. Since the dots are so close to the foul line, the lane leverage is tremendous. While a one board move with the feet will result in a roughly three board shift in the ball's finish position when targeting the arrows, that same one board move with the feet will result in an almost eight board shift in the ball's finish position when targeting the dots (Figure 17.13).

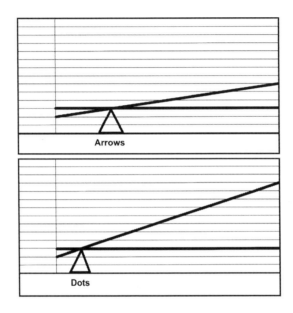

Figure 17.13: Lane leverage when targeting the dots versus the arrows

Since the lane leverage is so great when targeting the dots, the moves with the feet required to shift our shot from pin to pin are minuscule, on the order of half a board for each successive pin. Most bowlers do not possess enough consistency in their drift or in the direction of their swing plane to achieve this level of accuracy, and any little inconsistency will result in a very large deviation at the pins. Since the dots are so close to the foul line, they produce too much lane leverage to be effective spare targets. Note that the dots are not effective strike targets for the same reason, but when throwing a hook on a forgiving house shot there may be enough miss room at the breakpoint to compensate for the decreased accuracy and consistency.

Another potential problem with targeting the dots is that there is not necessarily any uniformity as to their placement on the lane. While both Brunswick and two other manufacturers we looked at place their dots 84 inches from the foul line, the USBC does not mandate this. They only require that the dots fall somewhere between six and eight feet from the foul line. Should you ever bowl on lanes where the dot position varies from what you are used to, the required moves with your feet to shift your spare shot from pin to pin could be significantly different. For example, if the dots are six feet from the foul line at your home center, a one board move with your feet will produce roughly a nine board shift at the pins. If the dots are eight feet from the foul line at your tournament, a one board move with your feet will produce less than a seven board shift at the pins. We do not know if all 21 manufacturers of synthetic lane surfaces and all past installers of wood lanes adhere to the 84 inch Brunswick standard, and neither did anyone else we talked to. To the extent that they do not, this will become an adverse issue. In fairness this issue could also exist when targeting the arrows since like the dots, the USBC does not set a firm standard on how far they must be from the foul line, but because they are over twice as far away as the dots, the effect will be much smaller.

Another possible problem with targeting the dots is that, unlike the arrows, there is not necessarily any uniformity as to how many dots there are or where, side to side, they are placed on the lane. The USBC only specifies that there be a maximum of ten dots, with almost everything else about them left up to the individual lane surface manufacturers or installers. Again, Brunswick and the two other manufacturers we checked all provide ten dots and all place them on the same boards. The dots were also on these same boards at a nearby bowling center with old wood lanes, so this may not be an issue at all. Since there are no specifications, however, it is possible that the fifth dot in one house may not correspond to the placement of the fifth dot in another house. Since the moves required to shift the shot over by one pin are only on the order of half a board, if your target dot in the house where you are bowling your tournament is placed only one board over from its position at your home house, then even if you hit the dot perfectly you've missed your target pin by almost two full pin positions.

If, after all of this discussion, you still insist on targeting the dots, the following table presents the required moves with your feet to hit each pin, targeting the fifth and sixth dots (the two dots closest to the center of the lane), and for both right and left handers. The calculations are based on the Brunswick "standard" of the fifth dot being on board 14, the sixth dot on board 26, and both being 84 inches down lane from the foul line. If your dots are on different boards than these or at a different distance from the foul line, you'll have to experiment a little to adjust the lay down point for your given conditions. These board positions have been rounded to the nearest 1/4 board. Note too that since the moves from pin to pin are so minuscule, in actuality roughly 5/8 of a board, the miss room at the dots is essentially zero. Missing your target dot by more than a fraction of a board or drifting more than a fraction of a board will result in a complete miss at the pins.

Pin		Lay-down Board at Foul Line	
Right-hander	Left-hander	5th Dot	6th Dot
10	7	15 1/4	29
6	4	14 3/4	28 1/4
3 or 9	2 or 8	14	27 1/2
1 or 5	1 or 5	13 1/4	26 3/4
2 or 8	3 or 9	12 1/2	26
4	6	11 3/4	25 1/4
7	10	11	24 1/2

Table 17.2: Spare shot lay down board when targeting dots

CHAPTER 18

CONCLUSION

"If a man will begin with certainties, he shall end in doubts; but if he will be content to begin with doubts, he shall end in certainties."

–Francis Bacon, *The Advancement of Learning* (1605)

FAMED INVESTOR HUMPHREY B. Neill wrote in his 1931 book, *Tape Reading and Market Tactics*, "Doubt all before you believe anything." Counter-culture icon Dr. Timothy Leary taught a generation of hippies to "question authority." As children we are taught the adage, "Don't believe anything you hear, and only half of what you see." Yet all of that good, healthy doubt goes right out the window when it comes to bowling. Bowlers are a trusting lot, and we tend to blindly accept any pronouncement made by anyone we find credible. One of the goals of this book is to break that trust.

19th Century humorist Henry Wheeler Shaw, writing as Josh Billings, shared many versions of what became his signature line; "It ain't so much the things we don't know that get us into trouble. It's the things we know that just ain't so." Much of the bowling advice we hold as divine writ "just ain't so." If we want our sport to progress, we must break free of supposition and speculation and start looking for fact and reason. We want bowlers to "question authority," even if you've heard the advice for years, even if you've heard it from a great bowler, even if you've heard it from us. We want you to "doubt all" until you are presented with real evidence and a real explanation that comports with physical law. We have backed up everything we've said with facts and evidence. Examine our evidence and our reasoning for yourself. If you find a hole in it, then patch that hole with real data and follow it where it leads. If we've stopped short, then take what we have started, and run even farther. Bowling can only grow if we abandon blind acceptance and start demanding evidence.

Our second goal for this book is to push you to build your knowledge base, build your skill set, and improve your decision making. For some time now this game has been about little more than high revs. As lane conditions became softer and more consistent, those blessed with fast wrists started to dominate. Seeing this, many of us with slower wrists figured out that if we didn't put our thumb in the ball we could get as many revs as those who had won the genetic lottery. This is all great, and we celebrate the diversity of styles that have sprung up, but we want to show that there is another way. We want you to "Bowl Smart."

We have tried to provide you with all of the knowledge you will need to be able to Bowl Smart. We've explained what is happening on the lanes, what causes what, and how you can change that outcome. We've explored common conditions, problems, and variables that can affect performance, and provided you with the ammunition you will need to address them. We want you to take that knowledge and make it your own. We want you to trust yourself and make your own decisions, and to stop looking to others for easy answers.

This book isn't about dazzling you with our brilliance. It is about sharing hard-won knowledge and experience. It is about giving you tools that can improve your game, and about helping you learn how to assess the situation on the lanes and to make better decisions. Whoever finds the pocket first, and figures out how to stay in the pocket the longest, wins the game. We have tried to arm you with everything you will need to win the game.

Our last goal is to inspire further research into what really happens on the lane, and how our tools and equipment really work. We've said repeatedly that neither of us are engineers, physicists, or mathematicians. While this book is the most thorough and rigorous look at the sport of bowling to date, we hope it is not the last word. It is our sincere wish that those with better skills and credentials in the relevant fields will pick up what we have started and run with it. The sooner we purge the voodoo and supposition and replace them with fact, the faster our sport will progress.

APPENDIX A

CALCULATING DEFLECTION

WHEN A BOWLING ball hits the headpin it creates a more or less *elastic* collision.[63] Isaac Newton tells us that both momentum and kinetic energy are conserved in an elastic collision. Since the pin is stationary before the collision, it adds nothing to the collision in terms of momentum or kinetic energy. Therefore, all of the momentum and energy entering our collision derives from the ball. Once the ball hits the pin, some of that energy and momentum will be transferred to the pin, with the ball retaining the balance. The laws of conservation of momentum and conservation of energy tell us that the amount of energy and momentum remaining with the ball after the collision, plus the amount assumed by the now moving pin, will equal the amount originally carried into the collision by the ball.[64] In an idealized system no energy or momentum are lost during the collision, they are merely redistributed. We can use these facts to help us determine the path that the ball will take following its collision with the headpin, which we bowlers know as deflection.

We need to set up our problem within a coordinate system. We will call the axis that runs down the lane in the direction of the boards the X-axis, and the axis that runs across the lane parallel to the foul line and perpendicular to the boards will be our Y-axis. We can now describe the position of our pins and our ball, and their movement, in relation to this X-Y coordinate system (Figure A.1).

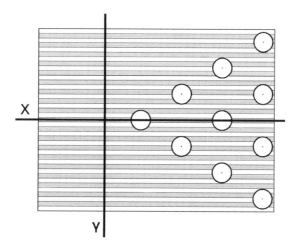

Figure A.1: X-Y coordinate system

Some physical characteristics of our ball and the pins exist independent of their motion or position. For example, our 15 pound ball has a mass of 15 pounds whether it is rolling, sitting still on the lane, or spinning in a circle. Such factors that do not rely on motion are called *scalars*, and they remain unchanged no matter what happens in our collision system. Our ball will still weigh 15 pounds after it hits the headpin. Scalars are considered to be one-dimensional in that they possess a magnitude only, and not a direction.

Somewhat confusingly, kinetic energy is also a scalar. Even though kinetic energy is created by the fact that the ball is moving, it does not have a direction. It just sort of exists within the ball, waiting to be transferred to whatever the ball hits.

Other physical factors only exist because of an object's motion. For example, our ball will only have a velocity when it is moving. Since the ball is moving, its velocity will have both a magnitude and a direction. Such factors that must be described by both a magnitude and a direction are called *vectors*, and they exist in two or more dimensions. Momentum is a vector, so its magnitude and its direction will both factor into our computations. The direction component of momentum will be described within our lane-based X-Y coordinate system.

When our ball travels down the lane on its way to the pins, its path defines the direction in which its momentum operates. Suppose our ball is hooking, or is traveling straight but on an angled path from the corner of the lane to the headpin. Because of the angled path, the ball will have a very large X- component of motion down lane, but it will also possess a small Y- component of motion across the lane as it travels from the right side of the lane toward the center (right-handed bowler). Since the angled or hooking ball travels in both the X- and the Y- direction, it will possess momentum in both directions. This compound motion adds additional complexity to what are already rather complex computations. In order to simplify our calculations, we will therefore look at a ball that rolls straight up the lane with no hook or curve. With such a straight "up the boards" shot, all of the ball's motion before the collision, and therefore all of its momentum, will be confined to the X- direction. Since the ball is not moving side to side, its momentum in the Y- direction will be zero.

For our test subject we will again use Brian, whom we introduced in Chapter 2. Recall that Brian's delivery produces 91.26 newtons of force, so sends his 15 pound ball down the lane at 16 miles per hour. This provides us with two know values or *givens*, the mass of the ball, and its initial velocity. We will denote the mass of the ball as Mb, where M stands for mass, b for ball, so Mb—which would be read as "M sub b"—means *mass of the ball*. We know that Mb, the mass of the ball, is 15 pounds. We also know that the velocity of the ball before the collision, which we will call Vb, is 16 miles per hour.

We also know a couple of things about the headpin. The USBC specifies that bowling pins must weigh between three pounds, six ounces, and three pounds, ten ounces. We shall use the average value of three pounds, eight ounces, or 3.5 pounds. We also know that since the headpin is standing still, it's initial velocity is zero. We shall call the pin's initial velocity Vp. We now know all of the information pertaining to the ball and the headpin before the collision occurs, which are summarized below:

Mb (mass of the ball) = 15 pounds
Vb (initial velocity of the ball) = 16 MPH
Mp (mass of the pin) = 3.5 pounds
Vp (initial velocity of the pin) = 0

We will also specify in this particular example that Brian's ball enters the pocket on board 17-1/2.

In order to figure out what is happening on the lane as we bowl, we need to determine what happens to the pin and the ball after they collide. This gives us four unknown values; the velocity and direction of the pin after the collision, and the velocity and direction of the ball after the collision.

Velocity is ordinarily denoted as "V", as we did when describing the initial velocity of the ball and pin. Physics convention is to call the velocities after the collision V' (V prime), but the prime mark is easy to miss when working through the equations, making things very confusing. To avoid confusion we will instead employ the letter "U" to denote velocity after the collision. Thus, Up will be the velocity of the pin after the collision, and Ub will be the velocity of the ball after the collision.

Deflection angle is denoted by the Greek letter Θ, pronounced *theta*. Continuing with our naming convention, Θp will be the deflection angle of the pin to the left, while Θb will be the deflection angle of the ball to the right. Our four unknowns are therefore:

Up (final velocity of the pin) = ?
Θp (deflection angle of the pin) = ?
Ub (final velocity of the ball) = ?
Θb (deflection angle of the ball) = ?

CONSERVATION OF KINETIC ENERGY

Let's start setting the stage. We have already agreed that both momentum and kinetic energy will be conserved after the collision, but what does this mean? Let's look first at Conservation of Kinetic Energy.

The Law of Conservation of Energy states that the total amount of energy entering our collision will be equal to the total amount coming back out. This simply means that the kinetic energy of the ball before the collision plus the kinetic energy of the pin before the collision will equal the kinetic energy of the ball after the collision plus the kinetic energy of the pin after the collision:

Ek-ball-before + Ek-pin-before = Ek-ball-after + Ek-pin-after

Since kinetic energy, Ek, is equal to 1/2 x Mass x Velocity², or $1/2MV^2$, let's substitute this more complete definition into our equation:

$1/2MbVb^2 + 1/2MpVp^2 = 1/2MbUb^2 + 1/2MpUp^2$

This equation is rather complex, so let's see if we can simplify it a bit. We know that the velocity of the pin before the collision is zero. We also know that any number multiplied by zero yields zero, so we know that the kinetic energy of the pin before the collision, $1/2MpVp^2$, is also zero. The *additive identity property of algebra* tells us that any number plus zero is equal to just the original number, so we can completely drop the pin's kinetic energy expression from our equation without altering anything:

$$1/2MbVb^2 + 0 = 1/2MbUb^2 + 1/2MpUp^2$$
$$1/2MbVb^2 = 1/2MbUb^2 + 1/2MpUp^2$$

The *multiplication property of equality* states that we can multiply both sides of an equation by the same number, and the equation will still be true. Thus we can eliminate all of the "1/2" expressions from our equation by multiplying both sides of the equation by 2. Our formula now reads:

$$MbVb^2 = MbUb^2 + MpUp^2$$

Now let's see if we can get rid of some of those Mass values. We said that our ball has a mass of 15 pounds, while the pin has a mass of 3.5 pounds. It does not matter in what units we express the mass of the ball and the pin in our equation so long as both units are the same. We could express both in pounds, in ounces, in grams, or whatever unit we wish. The *multiplication identity property of algebra* states that any number multiplied by 1 is equal to just the original number. If we express the mass of the ball and of the pin in a made up unit called "ball weights," then the ball will of course weigh one "ball weight," meaning that the Mb term would drop out of our equation. Since the ball in this example weighs 15 pounds, let's set one "ball weight" at 15 pounds. The ball therefore weighs 15 pounds divided by 15 pounds, or 1, while the pin weighs 3.5 pounds divided by 15 pounds, or 0.233 ball weights—just shy of 1/4 of the weight of the ball. Let's substitute these numbers for Mb and Mp in our formula:

$$MbVb^2 = MbUb^2 + MpUp^2$$
$$1 \times Vb^2 = 1 \times Ub^2 + 0.233 \times Up^2$$
$$Vb^2 = Ub^2 + 0.233Up^2$$

That's a whole lot simpler! We shall call this modified version of the Conservation of Kinetic Energy formula, *Equation 1*:

1. Vb2 = Ub2 + 0.233Up2

CONSERVATION OF MOMENTUM IN THE X- DIRECTION

We know that Momentum will also be conserved in our collision, but the implications of the Law of Conservation of Momentum go a bit deeper than that. We learned that Momentum is a vector, meaning that it has both a magnitude and a direction. We have also learned that any motion of the ball or the pins involves both an X- and a Y- component. That is to say, as the ball or the pin moves on the lane, some portion of that movement will be in the down lane X- direction, and some will be in the cross lane Y- direction. The Law of Conservation of Momentum tells us that the X- component of momentum will be conserved in the X- direction, and the Y- component will be conserved in the Y- direction. Let's look first at conservation of momentum in the down lane X- direction.

The Law of Conservation of Momentum tells us that the momentum going into the collision in the X- direction will equal the momentum in the X- direction coming out of the collision. The momentum entering into the collision is equal to the momentum of the ball plus the momentum of the pin before the collision. The momentum coming out of the collision is equal to the momentum of the ball after the collision plus the momentum of the pin after the collision. Momentum is denoted by the letter P. Thus we can write this as:

Pball-initial-x + Ppin-initial-x = Pball-final-x + Ppin-final-x

Recall that in our example our ball is rolling straight down the lane, parallel to the boards. Since all of its motion is in the down lane X- direction with no cross lane movement, then all of its momentum will likewise be in the X- direction. We know that momentum is defined as Mass multiplied by Velocity. Since all of the ball's velocity is in the down lane X- direction, the X- component of the ball's momentum is simply the ball's Mass multiplied by its Velocity, or MbVb.

We also know that since the pin is initially not moving, its initial velocity is zero. Since Mass multiplied by zero is zero, the pin's initial momentum is zero. Let's substitute these two initial momentum values into the left-hand side of our formula:

Pball-initial-x + Ppin-initial-x = Pball-final-x + Ppin-final-x
MbVb + 0 = Pball-final-x + Ppin-final-x

Our ball's straight path down the lane greatly simplified matters on the left-hand *initial value* side of our equation. Things are not so simple, however, on the right-hand *final value* side. After the collision, our pin will deflect off to the left at some angle, while the ball deflects on an angled path to the right. This means that after the collision the motion of both the pin and the ball will be made up of some motion in the down lane X- direction, and some motion in the cross lane Y- direction. Since we are only dealing in this particular equation with the X- component of momentum, we need to figure out a way to divide up the ball and the pin's total momentum after the collision into their respective X- and Y- components. While Isaac Newton has been helping us out so far, this time it is Pythagoras to the rescue! Let's look at a diagram of what happens after the ball strikes the headpin (Figure A.2).

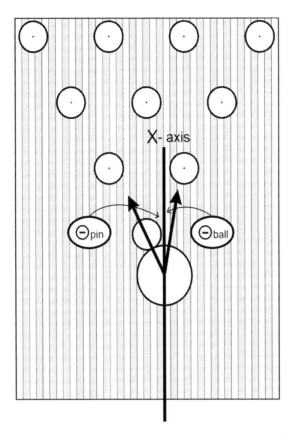

Figure A.2: Collision System

In Figure A.2, the ball impacts the headpin on board 17-1/2. The pin deflects to the left along the indicated vector line. The angle formed between the pin path and the X- axis parallel to the boards is our pin deflection angle, which we have called Θp (*theta sub pin*). The ball will deflect to the right along the right-hand vector line. The angle formed between the ball path and the X- axis is the ball deflection angle, or Θb (*theta sub ball*).

Let's look first at the ball. We see that the ball will travel on an angle toward the right, so its momentum will also operate in this direction. The length of the ball's momentum vector represents the magnitude of that momentum, and we need to separate this angled momentum into its X- and Y- components. We can do so by employing the Pythagorean theorem and a bit of trigonometry.

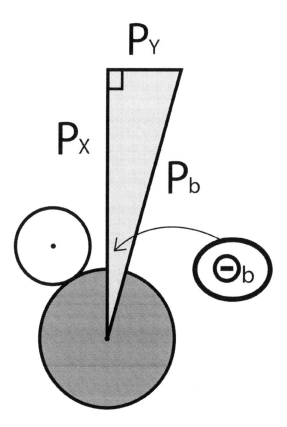

Figure A.3: Ball Deflection Angle (Θb)

In Figure A.3, above, we see that the ball's rightward momentum vector Pb forms a right triangle with vectors drawn along the X- and Y- axes. The length of the X- vector represents the magnitude of that portion of the ball's momentum operating in the down lane X- direction after the collision. Likewise, the length of the Y- vector represents the magnitude of that portion of the ball's momentum operating in the Y- direction. How can we calculate the length, and therefore the magnitude of these vectors from the information at hand?

Trigonometry tells us that the cosine of angle Θb is equal to the adjacent side of the triangle—which represents momentum in the down lane X- direction (Px)—divided by the hypotenuse of the triangle, which in our case is the final momentum of the ball (Pb). We write this formula as:

CosΘb = Px / Pb

We solve for Px by multiplying both sides of the equation by Pb, yielding:

Px-ball = PbCosΘb

Since Pb, the momentum of the ball after the collision is equal to the Mass of the ball multiplied by the final velocity of the ball, or MbUb, we can substitute this expression into the formula in place of Pb, yielding:

Px-ball = MbUb CosΘb

This formula tells us that the momentum of the ball in the X- direction after the collision is equal to the ball's mass, times its velocity after the collision, times the cosine of its deflection angle.

In like fashion, we can calculate the X- component of the pin's momentum after the collision.

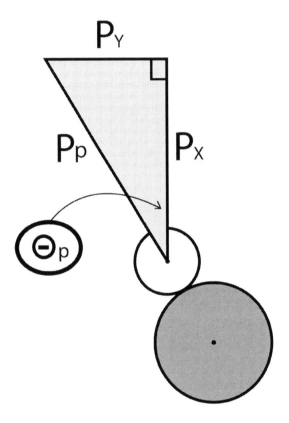

Figure A.4: Pin Deflection Angle (Θp)

Figure A.4, above, illustrates the pin deflection angle, Θp. Just as momentum in the X-direction for the ball was momentum of the ball after the collision multiplied by the cosine of angle Θb, the momentum of the pin in the down lane X- direction after the collision will be the momentum of the pin after the collision multiplied by the cosine of angle Θp:

Px-pin = PpCosΘp

Again, since the momentum of the pin, Pp, is equal to the mass of the pin multiplied by its velocity after the collision, we can substitute this expression in our formula to yield:

Px-pin = MpUp CosΘp

Hang on, we're almost there! Let's refer back to our formula for Conservation of Momentum in the X- direction:

Pball-initial-x + Ppin-initial-x = Pball-final-x + Ppin-final-x, or
MbVb + 0 = Pball-final-x + Ppin-final-x

Now let's substitute in the new expressions we just created for the ball's and the pin's final momentum in the X- direction on the right-hand side of the equation:

MbVb + 0 = MbUb CosΘb + MpUp CosΘp

Eliminating the zero on the left-hand side:

MbVb = MbUb CosΘb + MpUp CosΘp

Once more substituting in our "ball weight" values of 1 and 0.233 respectively for the mass of the ball and the mass of the pin yields:

Vb = Ub CosΘb + 0.233Up CosΘp

We can solve the equation for Ub CosΘb, the momentum of the ball in the X- direction after the collision by subtracting the X- momentum of the pin from both sides. We will call this *Equation 2*:

2. Vb - 0.233Up CosΘp = Ub CosΘb

CONSERVATION OF MOMENTUM IN THE Y- DIRECTION

OK, Conservation of Momentum in the X- direction was pretty hairy, but we promise Conservation of Momentum in the Y- direction will be at least a little bit easier. Just as the momentum going into the collision in the down lane X- direction was equal to the momentum in the X- direction coming out of the collision, so too with momentum in the Y-, or cross lane direction:

Pball-initial-y + Ppin-initial-y = Pball-final-y + Ppin-final-y

As in our X- direction calculation, the pin's initial momentum is zero, so it drops out of our equation:

Pball-initial-y = Pball-final-y + Ppin-final-y

Here's where things get a bit simpler. Since our ball was initially traveling straight down the lane parallel to the X- axis, it had no movement at all in the cross lane Y- direction. This means that all of the ball's velocity was in the X- direction, so its velocity in the Y- direction was zero. Since the ball's initial momentum in the Y- direction is equal to its mass multiplied by its velocity in the Y- direction, and since that velocity is zero, so too the ball's initial momentum in the Y- direction is zero. Because the ball's initial momentum in the Y- direction is zero, it too can be dropped from our equation, which now becomes:

0 = Pball-final-y + Ppin-final-y

Referring back to Figure A.3, which depicted the ball deflection angle Θb, we see that the Y- component of the ball's final momentum is the side of the triangle opposite to angle Θb. Trigonometry tells us that the sine of angle Θb is equal to the opposite side of the triangle, the ball's final momentum in the Y- direction, divided by the hypotenuse of the triangle, which is the ball's total final momentum:

SinΘb = Py / Pb

We solve for Py by multiplying both sides of the equation by Pb, yielding:

Py-ball = PbSinΘb

Since Pb, the momentum of the ball after the collision is equal to the Mass of the ball multiplied by the final velocity of the ball, or MbUb, we can substitute this expression into the formula, yielding:

Py-ball = MbUb SinΘb

Likewise, the pin's final momentum in the Y- direction will be:

Py-pin = MpUp SinΘp

We need to be careful here, as our bowling problem set a little trap for us. Following the collision, the pin and the ball will travel in opposite directions along the cross lane Y- axis, the ball traveling to the right, and the pin traveling to the left. Since we arbitrarily declared the ball's rightward motion to be in the positive direction, the pin's movement, and hence its momentum along the Y- axis will be in the negative direction. This means that the value we just calculated for Py is actually a negative number. The true value for Py is therefore:

Py-pin = -(MpUp SinΘp)

Let's substitute these new expressions into our formula:

o = Pball-final-y + Ppin-final-y
o = MbUb SinΘb + -(MpUp SinΘp)

Adding a negative number is mathematically equivalent to subtracting a positive number, so we can rewrite this formula as:

o = MbUb SinΘb - MpUp SinΘp

Once more substituting in our values of 1 and 0.233 "ball weights" for the mass of the ball and of the pin, we get:

o = Ub SinΘb – 0.233Up SinΘp

Adding 0.233Up SinΘp to both sides of the equation transforms it to what we will call *Equation 3*:

3. 0.233Up SinΘp = Ub SinΘb

Okay, that was fairly brutal. I'd like to tell you that we were getting close, but sadly we are only about a quarter of the way there! We now have three equations that describe various relationships within our collision system, but recall that we have four unknown properties:

Up (final velocity of the pin) = ?
Θp (deflection angle of the pin) = ?
Ub (final velocity of the ball) = ?
Θb (deflection angle of the ball) = ?

It is not possible, at least by any method with which we are familiar, to solve for four unknowns given only three equations. We either need a fourth equation, which is again well beyond our pay grade, or we need to find the value of one of our unknowns by some other method. Fortunately for us, there is a relatively simple way to determine the deflection angle of the pin, Θp. Let's dive right in.

CALCULATING HEADPIN DEFLECTION

When our ball impacts the right-hand side of the headpin, the pin will deflect off to the left while the ball will deflect more or less to the right. The angle at which the pin deflects is purely a function of where on its surface the ball impacts the pin. This impact point is determined solely by the board upon which the ball entered the pocket. Note that the deflection angle of the pin is not affected by the angle upon which the ball was traveling before it hit the pin, nor upon whether the ball hooked or was traveling straight. At the risk of anthropomorphism, the pin does not know at what angle the ball was traveling before it got hit, and it does not care. All the pin knows is, "I just got hit on this certain point with this certain force," and that is the only thing that affect's its post-collision path.[65]

Determining the deflection angle of the target pin is therefore a relatively simple matter. When two round objects collide, in our case the ball and the pin, the point of impact will fall on a line drawn through the center points of both objects, and the force of the collision will act along this same line regardless of the path the ball took before the collision. Since the pin will deflect away from the collision along this center line, determining the angle of this line with reference to the lane will tell us the direction of the pin's travel (Figure A.5).

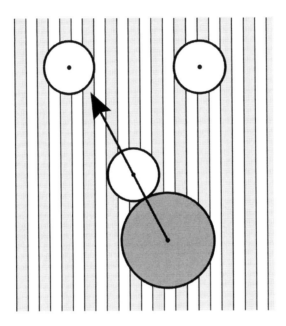

Figure A.5: Ball impacting headpin

We can see from Figure A.5 that the line along which the pin deflects forms a right triangle with a line drawn from the center of the headpin perpendicular to the lane boards, and a line drawn parallel to the lane boards from the center of the ball. Since we are dealing with a right triangle, the Pythagorean Theorem tells us that if we can figure out the lengths of two of the sides of the triangle, we can determine all of the remaining sides and angles (Figure A.6).

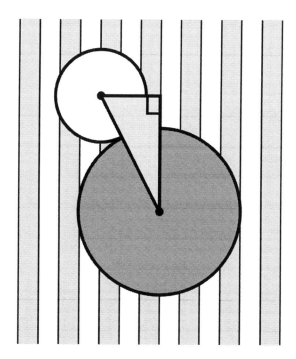

Figure A.6: Determining pin deflection angle

The line connecting the center points of the ball and the pin, the *pin deflection path*, forms the hypotenuse of our right triangle. We see from Figure A.6 that its length is simply half the diameter of the ball plus half the diameter of the pin. The diameter of a bowling ball is approximately 8.595 inches. At its widest, a bowling pin has a diameter of 4.766 inches, but the ball contacts the pin a bit below this wide point, where the pin's diameter is only 4.72 inches. If we add 8.595 inches and 4.72 inches, then divide the result by two, we find that the length of our hypotenuse is 6.66 inches.

The length of the base of our triangle, the horizontal line between the center of the pin and the board that the center of the ball is located on, is likewise easy to determine. We know that the headpin is centered on board 20. We also know as a given that our ball entered the pocket on board 17-1/2, which means that the center point of the ball is directly over the seam between board 17 and 18 when the ball contacts the headpin. Thus, we know that the length of the base of our triangle is 2-1/2 board widths—all of boards 18 and 19, plus half of board 20. We further know that a bowling lane is 41.5 inches wide, and is comprised of 39 boards. Each board is therefore (41.5 ÷ 39) inches wide. Since our base line is 2-1/2 boards long, we can compute its length as 41.5 / 39 x 2.5, or 2.66 inches.

Look back to Figure A.6. We now know the length of two sides of our triangle, the hypotenuse and the base. With this information, plus the knowledge that the angle between our base and the third side is 90°, we can employ a bit of trigonometry to determine the pin's deflection angle.

Since the pin will deflect along our hypotenuse, the pin's deflection angle is that formed between the hypotenuse and the line drawn along the lane boards. This angle, which we have called Θp (theta sub pin), is at the bottom of our triangle. Trigonometry tells us that the sine of any angle Θ is equal to the length of the side opposite the angle—

the base of our triangle—divided by the length of the hypotenuse. Since we know that the length of the base is 2.66 inches, and that the hypotenuse is 6.66 inches, then the sine of our pin deflection angle is:

SinΘp = opposite side / hypotenuse
SinΘp = 2.66 / 6.66
SinΘp = 0.3994

Okay, that tells us, well... pretty much nothing! In order to obtain useful information, we must somehow convert sine into some recognizable unit. The actual computations involved in converting the sine of an angle into degrees is quite complex. Fortunately, there exist several shortcuts. In days of yore, one would look up 0.3994 in a published sine table. These tables, computed and compiled by folks much smarter than you and I, typically do not contain every value, requiring us to interpolate between the closest published number above and below our own value.

An easier method of converting sine to degrees is to employ a scientific calculator, either of the actual physical variety, or any of the various and sundry computerized or web application versions. The function that converts sine to an angle measurement is called *inverse sine* (Sin⁻¹), or more commonly, *arcsine*. One can punch the sine value, in our case 0.3994, into the calculator, then hit the arcsin button to obtain an answer. There is, however, one big caveat with this method. Arcsine returns the answer not in degrees, but in a less arbitrary though highly confusing unit called *radians*. We needn't discuss what a radian is, but while a circle contains 360 degrees, it contains only roughly 6.28 radians. Thus, to convert the arcsine result from radians to degrees, we must multiply the result by 360, then divide it by 6.28.

The calculator method was fine back in the technologically backward days when we were watching the Jetsons on TV and dreaming of owning a flying car, but it's a brave new world we live in, and today there exists a far simpler method (though, sadly, still no flying cars). Through the good graces of the magic pixies employed by Google, we need only type into the Google search bar on our computer, phone, tablet, or Internet-connected toaster, "arcsin 0.3994 in degrees," and *voila!*, we find that our pin deflection angle when our ball strikes the headpin on board 17-1/2 is 23.55 degrees. Table A.1, below, contains the result of similar calculations performed for pocket entry points on boards 15 through 19-1/2.

Pocket Entry Board	15	15-1/2	16	16-1/2	17	17-1/2	18	18-1/2	19	19-1/2
Pin Deflect Angle	53.05°	46.00°	39.74°	34.01°	28.65°	23.55°	18.64°	13.88°	9.20°	4.58°

Table A.1: Θp relative to the lane

The values in the above table represent Θp, our pin deflection angle. Since we have specified in our example that our ball enters the pocket on board 17-1/2, we can simply grab the proper value for Θp from the table and plug it into our calculations as a given. This brings our four unknowns down to only three, so with three unknowns and three equations, we can now solve our problem. We're finally getting somewhere!

SOLVING THE EQUATIONS

Before we dive in, let's restate our givens, our unknowns, and our three equations:

Given:

Mb (mass of the ball) = 15 pounds
Vb (initial velocity of the ball) = 16 MPH
Mp (mass of the pin) = 3.5 pounds
Vp (initial velocity of the pin) = 0
Θp (deflection angle of the pin) = 23.55°

Unknowns:

Up (final velocity of the pin) = ?
Ub (final velocity of the ball) = ?
Θb (deflection angle of the ball) = ?

Equations:

1. $Vb^2 = Ub^2 + 0.233Up^2$
2. $Vb - 0.233UpCos\Theta p = UbCos\Theta b$
3. $0.233UpSin\Theta p = UbSin\Theta b$

Since all of the terms in equation 1 are squared, our life will be simpler if we likewise square equations 2 and 3 so that all of the terms will be raised to the same power. This is allowed by the *equivalency property of algebra* which states that if a=b, then $a^2=b^2$. Let's square Equation 2:

$Vb - 0.233UpCos\Theta p = UbCos\Theta b$
$(Vb - 0.233Up \, Cos\Theta p)^2 = (Ub \, Cos\Theta b)^2$

Since squaring just means multiplying an expression by itself, we can expand both sides of the equation. Let's start with the left side:

$(Vb - 0.233Up \, Cos\Theta p) \times (Vb - 0.233Up \, Cos\Theta p) = (Ub \, Cos\Theta b)^2$

Further expanding the two binomials on the left side yields:

$Vb^2 - 0.233VbUp\ Cos\Theta p - 0.233VbUp\ Cos\Theta p + (-0.233Up\ Cos\Theta p)^2 =$
$(Ub\ Cos\Theta b)^2$
$Vb^2 - 0.467VbUp\ Cos\Theta p + (-0.233Up\ Cos\Theta p)^2 = (Ub\ Cos\Theta b)^2$
$Vb^2 - 0.467VbUp\ Cos\Theta p + 0.054Up^2Cos\Theta p^2 = (Ub\ Cos\Theta b)^2$

Let's now expand the right-hand side of the equation:[66]

$Vb^2 - 0.467VbUp\ Cos\Theta p + 0.054Up^2Cos\Theta p^2 = (Ub\ Cos\Theta b)(Ub\ Cos\Theta b)$

Via the *commutative property of multiplication* applied to the right side, we get *Equation 4*:

4. $Vb^2 - 0.467VbUp\ Cos\Theta p + 0.054Up^2Cos\Theta p^2 = Ub^2Cos\Theta b^2$

Again, equation 4 is simply equation 2 after we have squared it. Next, we will square both sides of Equation 3. This one will be easier:

$0.233Up\ Sin\Theta p = Ub\ Sin\Theta b$
$(0.233Up\ Sin\Theta p)^2 = (Ub\ Sin\Theta b)^2$

Expanding both sides of the equation yields:

$(0.233Up\ Sin\Theta p)(0.233Up\ Sin\Theta p) = (Ub\ Sin\Theta b)(Ub\ Sin\Theta b)$

Commuting both sides of the equation gives us:

$0.233^2\ Up^2\ Sin\Theta p^2 = Ub^2\ Sin\Theta b^2$

Squaring 0.233 yields *Equation 5*:

5. $0.054\ Up^2Sin\Theta p^2 = Ub^2\ Sin\Theta b^2$

Okay, if we haven't lost you yet, hang on tight. Things are about to get really ugly!

We've already employed the *additive property of equality*, which stated that if a=b, then a+c=b+c. We are going to use this tool again. Think for a moment about what an equation means. If we state that a=b, we are saying that a and b are the same thing, just stated in a different way. That is, the expressions on either side of the "=" sign in an equation have the same value even though they look different. Since this is so, the additive property of equality allows us to add two equations together. Let's add Equation 4 to Equation 5:

Equation 4: $Vb^2 - 0.467VbUp\ Cos\Theta p + 0.054Up^2Cos\Theta p^2 = Ub^2Cos\Theta b^2$
Equation 5: $0.054Up^2Sin\Theta p^2 = Ub^2\ Sin\Theta b^2$

Adding them together gives us:

$$Vb^2 - 0.467VbUp \; Cos\Theta p + 0.054Up^2Cos\Theta p^2 + 0.054Up^2Sin\Theta p^2 = Ub^2Cos\Theta b^2 + Ub^2 Sin\Theta b^2$$

Now it's time to try to simplify this absolute mess of an equation. Let's look for a moment at only the third and fourth expressions on the left-hand side of the equation: $0.054Up^2Cos\Theta p^2$ + $0.054Up^2 \; Sin\Theta p^2$. Since both expressions consist of $0.054Up^2$ multiplied by some other number, this portion of the equations has the form of ab+ac. The *distributive property* states that ab+ac is the same thing as a(b+c). Thus, we can restate that portion:

$$0.054Up^2Cos\Theta p^2 + 0.054Up^2Sin\Theta p^2$$

..as:

$$0.054Up^2 \, (Cos\Theta p^2 + Sin\Theta p^2)$$

substituting this new expression back into our equation in place of the third and fourth expressions yields:

$$Vb^2 - 0.467VbUp \; Cos\Theta p + 0.054Up^2 \, (Cos\Theta p^2 + Sin\Theta p^2) = Ub^2Cos\Theta b^2 + Ub^2 \; Sin\Theta b^2$$

This formula is still quite hairy, so Pythagoras is going to help us out again. In trigonometry, *identities* describe certain relationships between trigonometric functions which are always true. Probably the most important of these is the *Pythagorean Identity*, which states that for any angle, the cosine of that angle, squared, plus the sine of that angle, squared, will always equal 1. This identity is written as $Cos\Theta p^2 + Sin\Theta p^2 = 1$. We can use this identity to further simplify our equation.

Notice that the above formula contains the Pythagorean Identity as part of our newly created third term on the left-hand side:

$$0.054Up^2 \, (Cos\Theta p^2 + Sin\Theta p^2)$$

Since $Cos\Theta p^2 + Sin\Theta p^2 = 1$, we can rewrite this expression as:

$$0.054Up^2 \, (1)$$

...and since any number multiplied by 1 is just the original number, we can reduce this expression to:

$$0.054Up^2$$

substituting this back into our formula yields:

$$Vb^2 - 0.467VbUp \; Cos\Theta p + 0.054Up^2 = Ub^2Cos\Theta b^2 + Ub^2 \; Sin\Theta b^2$$

We can use the same trick on the right-hand side of the equation:

$$Vb^2 - 0.467VbUp \; Cos\Theta p + 0.054Up^2 = Ub^2Cos\Theta b^2 + Ub^2 \; Sin\Theta b^2$$
$$Vb^2 - 0.467VbUp \; Cos\Theta p + 0.054Up^2 = Ub^2 \; (Cos\Theta b^2 + Sin\Theta b^2)$$
$$Vb^2 - 0.467VbUp \; Cos\Theta p + 0.054Up^2 = Ub^2 \; (1)$$
$$Vb^2 - 0.467VbUp \; Cos\Theta p + 0.054Up^2 = Ub^2$$

Well, that's a lot simpler! We will call this *Equation 6*.

6. $Vb^2 - 0.467VbUp \; Cos\Theta p + 0.054Up^2 = Ub^2$

With our new equations, we can start to wrap this mess up. This will go quickly, so stick with us! Let's recall Equation 1:

$$Vb^2 = Ub^2 + 0.233Up^2$$

We can begin to solve our complex equations by trying to eliminate some of the terms. Since equation 1 tells us that Vb^2 is the same thing as $Ub^2 + 0.233Up^2$, we can substitute this expression into Equation 6 in place of Vb^2:

$$Vb^2 - 0.467VbUp \; Cos\Theta p + 0.054Up^2 = Ub^2$$
$$Ub^2 + 0.233Up^2 - 0.467VbUp \; Cos\Theta p + 0.054Up^2 = Ub^2$$

subtracting Ub^2 from both sides gives us:

$$0.233Up^2 - 0.467VbUp \; Cos\Theta p + 0.054Up^2 = 0$$

Notice that on the left-hand side we have $0.233Up^2$ and $0.054Up^2$. Since they are both some number multiplied by Up^2, we can add these two together, yielding:

$$0.287Up^2 - 0.467VbUp \; Cos\Theta p = 0$$

If we add $0.467VbUp \; Cos\Theta p$ to both sides of the equation, we get:

$$0.287Up^2 = 0.467VbUp \; Cos\Theta p$$

Both Vb, the initial velocity of the ball, and Θp, the pin deflection angle, are givens, so we can plug their values into our formula.

$$Vb = 16 \; MPH$$
$$\Theta p = 23.55°$$

$$0.287Up^2 = 0.467VbUp\ Cos\Theta p$$
$$0.287Up^2 = 0.467 \times 16 \times Up\ Cos23.55°$$

We can find the cosine of 23.55° by typing "cosine of 23.55 degrees" into the Google search bar (or any of the other methods mentioned earlier).

$$Cos23.55° = 0.917$$

Plugging in this value yields:

$$0.287Up^2 = 0.467 \times 16 \times Up \times 0.917$$
$$0.287\ Up^2 = 6.852\ Up$$

Dividing both sides of the equation by Up yields:

$$0.287\ Up = 6.852$$

We can solve for Up by dividing both sides of the equation by 0.287:

$$Up = 6.852 / 0.287$$
$$Up = 23.88\ miles\ per\ hour$$

Woo hoo! We've found the value of one of our unknowns! Up, the velocity of the pin after the collision, is 23.88 miles per hour! Let's take this further.

Recall Equation 1:

$$Vb^2 = Ub^2 + 0.233Up^2$$

We can solve for Ub^2 by subtracting $0.233Up^2$ from both sides of the equation:

$$Ub^2 = Vb^2 - 0.233Up^2$$

Since we know the values of both Vb and Up, let's substitute them in:

$$Vb = 16\ MPH$$
$$Up = 23.88\ MPH$$
$$Ub^2 = Vb^2 - 0.233Up^2$$
$$Ub^2 = 16^2 - (0.233 \times 23.88^2)$$
$$Ub^2 = 256 - (0.233 \times 570.254)$$
$$Ub^2 = 256 - 132.87$$
$$Ub^2 = 123.13$$
$$Ub = \sqrt{123.13}$$
$$Ub = 11.1\ MPH$$

Another unknown solved! Ub, the velocity of the ball after the collision, is 11.1 MPH! Two down, one to go, and this last one is the holy grail. Our last unknown is the deflection angle of the ball following the collision, or Θb. Let's finish this thing!

Let's start with Equation 3:

0.233UpSinΘp = UbSinΘb

We can solve for SinΘb, the sine of our ball's deflection angle, by dividing both sides of the equation by Ub:

SinΘb = 0.233UpSinΘp / Ub

Since we now know both Up and Ub as well as Θp, let's substitute in their values:

Up = 23.88 MPH
Ub = 11.1 MPH
Θp = 23.55°
SinΘb = 0.233UpSinΘp / Ub
SinΘb = 0.233 x 23.88 x Sin23.55° / 11.1

Looking Up the sine of 23.55 degrees, we find that it is 0.40. Plugging in this value yields:

SinΘb = 0.233 x 23.88 x 0.40 / 11.1
SinΘb = 2.22 / 11.1
SinΘb = 0.20
Θb = Sin⁻¹0.20

Looking Up the arcsine of 0.20, and remembering to specify that we want the answer in degrees rather than radians, we find that:

Θb = 11.54°

There it is, and after only about 347 pages of work and a horrible migraine! The ball, after striking the headpin on board 17-1/2, will deflect to the right on its way toward the 3-pin at an angle, Θb, of 11.54°!

Let's summarize everything:

Brian throws his 15 pound ball with 91.26 newtons of force, sending it straight up board 17-1/2 at 16 miles per hour.

The ball strikes the headpin, sending the pin off to the left at an angle of 23.55 degrees and at a velocity of 23.88 miles per hour.

The ball deflects to the right at an angle of 11.54 degrees, and at a velocity of 11.1 miles per hour.

Whew!

APPENDIX B

CALCULATING SPARES

In Chapter 17, we presented the specific boards your ball must cross at the foul line in order to target all of the possible single pin spares over the third, fourth, and fifth arrows. This appendix explains the computations involved in arriving at those numbers.

SETTING THE STAGE

If we were to draw a line from the pin we wish to hit out to our chosen targeting arrow, we could continue that line all the way back to the foul line. This line would show us precisely where our ball *must* cross the foul line in order to cross our target arrow and hit the pin. By gathering information on the placement of the pins and arrows and the standardized dimensions of a bowling lane, and applying a bit of trigonometry, we can determine just where that crossing point on the foul line is for any given pin and target arrow combination.

In addition to our imaginary line from the pin to our arrow, we can draw a second line from the pin straight back toward the foul line, parallel to the lane boards and the gutter, and a third line across the lane from our targeting arrow toward the gutter, perpendicular to the lane boards (Figure B.1). These three lines form a right triangle, with the pin-to-arrow line, which is our desired ball path, being the hypotenuse. If we can figure out the lengths of two of those lines, trigonometry will provide us with the length of the remaining side and tell us what the other two angles are.

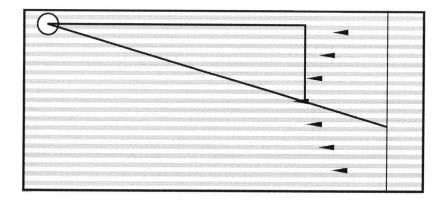

Figure B.1: Ball path from foul line to pin

CALCULATING WHERE THE BALL PATH CROSSES THE FOUL LINE

The placement of the pins on a lane is governed by United States Bowling Congress (USBC) regulations, and is nearly identical on every lane and at every bowling center. These specifications give us the side-to-side location of every pin with reference to the gutter. There are seven targeting arrows on every lane, and we number them starting at the right gutter for right-handed bowlers and at the left gutter for left-handed bowlers (for simplicity, this discussion will be from the perspective of a right-handed bowler). For a right-handed bowler the arrow closest to the right gutter is the first arrow, the center arrow is the fourth arrow, and the one farthest left is the seventh arrow. These arrows are always on boards 5 through 35, at five board intervals. The USBC specifies that all lanes must be 41-1/2 inches wide (plus or minus 1/2 inch) and be comprised of 39 boards. We can therefore calculate that each board is 41-1/2 inches ÷ 39, or approximately 1.064 inches in width. Knowing the width of a board will also let us determine side-to-side distances from any arrow to any pin. The difference between the side-to-side location of our target arrow and of the pin we are trying to hit determines the length of the short, perpendicular side at the base of the right triangle we drew in Figure B.1. We will call this the *pin offset distance*, since it is the distance by which our target pin is offset to the left or right of our target arrow.

Determining the long leg of the triangle, the one we drew parallel to the gutter, is only slightly more problematic. The USBC specifies the distance from the foul line to every pin, but the location of the target arrows is not standardized, requiring only that they fall somewhere within a 12 to 16 foot band beyond the foul line. Bowlers often say that the arrows are 15 feet from the foul line, but a quick glance at any lane will tell you that this can't be so since the arrows are not set in a straight line. The center arrow is very clearly farther from the foul line than are the arrows adjacent to it, and each subsequent arrow is closer still.

At the time of this writing, the USBC has certified and approved 42 different synthetic lane surfaces from 21 different manufacturers, and there are subtle differences in arrow placement between many of them. Brunswick's Pro Lane, one of the most common lane surfaces, places the tip of the center arrow 190 inches from the foul line. Since the arrow is six inches in length, the center point of that arrow is 187 inches from the foul line, and each subsequent arrow is six inches closer to the foul line than the one ahead of it. We will base our calculations on these figures. Since most other lane surfaces are fairly similar, the differences will be negligible and our calculations should be well within the margin of error regardless of the surface you bowl on.

By subtracting the known distance from the foul line to our chosen target arrow from the total distance from the foul line to the pin, we can determine the down lane distance from our pin to our target arrow. This measurement, which we will call the *pin to arrow distance*, forms the long side of our right triangle. Since we know that the angle between the long and short sides is 90 degrees, we now have enough information to proceed with our calculations.

To help clarify all of this, let's look at the example of shooting the 10-pin over the center, or fourth arrow. Since our lane is 41.5 inches wide, we know that the middle of the fourth arrow, being in the center of the lane, is 20.75 inches from the right gutter. We know that this is also the distance from the center of the headpin to the gutter, since it too is located on the center board. USBC specifies that each subsequent pin must be six inches to the right or left of the one in front of it. Thus the 3-pin is six inches to the right of the headpin, the 6-pin is another six inches right, or a total of 12 inches from the headpin, and our 10-pin another six inches right, or a total of 18 inches to the right of the headpin (Figure B.2). This 18 inch distance from the headpin to the 10-pin, our pin offset distance, forms the short side of our right triangle.

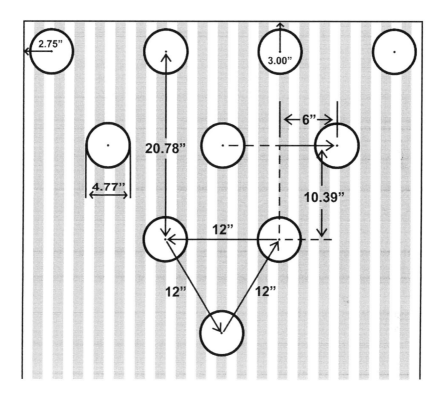

Figure B.2: Pin layout diagram

The USBC specifies that the headpin must be 60 feet, or 720 inches from the foul line. Each subsequent row of pins is roughly 10-3/8 inches farther down lane from the row in front of it. Thus the 10-pin, being three rows back, is roughly 31.125 inches beyond the headpin, or a total of 751.125 inches from the foul line. This is our *pin to foul line* distance. We have already determined that the center of the fourth arrow, our target in this case, is 187 inches from the foul line. Subtracting the foul line to arrow distance from the total 751.125 inch distance to the 10-pin tells us that the pin to arrow distance from our target arrow location to the 10-pin is 564.125 inches, which forms the long side of our right triangle.

Trigonometry tells us that the ratio between the sides of any right triangle will remain the same no matter how far we might extend those sides. Therefore, if we know what the ratio is between the short leg of our triangle—our pin offset distance at the arrows—and the longer leg—the down lane pin to arrow distance—this ratio will remain the same as we extend the triangle out to the foul line . This extended triangle defines what we will call the *foul line offset*, which is the cross-lane distance between the location of our target pin and the point where our ball path must cross the foul line (Figure B.3).

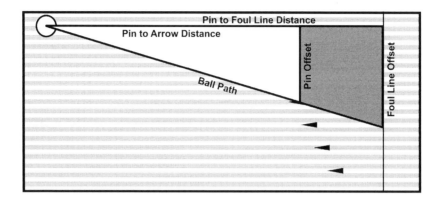

Figure B.3: Triangles formed by our ball path and the lane boards

To calculate the ratio between the pin offset distance and the pin to arrow distance, we simply divide the former by the latter.[67] Since we know that this ratio must be the same as the ratio between the foul line offset and the pin to foul line distance, we can say that:

Pin Offset Distance ÷ Pin to Arrow Distance = Foul Line Offset ÷ Pin to Foul Line Distance

Since we've already determined the value of three of the numbers, let's plug them in:

18 Inches÷ 564.125 inches = Foul line Offset ÷ 751.125 inches

We need to determine our foul line offset distance, so we must isolate it by multiplying both sides of the equation by the pin to foul line distance, or 751.125 inches:

Foul Line Offset = 18 Inches ÷ 564.125 inches x 751.125 inches

Doing the math yields:

Foul Line Offset = 23.97 inches.

Our ball must therefore cross the foul line approximately 24 inches to the left of the 10-pin position. The USBC specifies that the 10-pin must be 2.75 inches from the right gutter (+/- 1/4"), which means that our ball must cross the foul line at a point 24 inches plus 2.75 inches, or 26.75 inches from the right gutter. Since each board is 1.064 inches wide, we can divided 26.75 inches by 1.064 inches to determine that our ball must cross the foul line at a point roughly 25 board widths left of the right gutter if we are to hit the 10-pin dead center while targeting the fourth arrow. Be careful here, though, as this does not mean that our ball must cross *on* board 25. The peculiar way we bowlers count boards sets a little trap for us.

Think of the very first board, right next to the gutter. If our ball rolls directly over the center of this board at the foul line, we say that our ball crossed the foul line on board 1. Notice though that in actuality the ball was only half of a board *width* from the gutter, since it was on the center of the board. Thus, in order for our ball to cross the foul line at a point which is 25 board *widths* from the gutter, it will actually be rolling on the line between boards 25 and 26, which bowlers define as board 25-1/2. Since our numbering system starts counting half a board greater than the actual position (calling half a board width "board 1"), we must add the missing half board to our calculated distance in order to make our numbers and our language comport.

We've now calculated that if we are to shoot the 10-pin, targeted over the fourth arrow, our ball has to cross the foul line on board 25-1/2. We can easily perform a similar calculation for every other single pin spare and for every useful target arrow. Table B.1, below, presents the required foul line board for every pin, shot over the third, fourth, and fifth arrow, and for both right- and left-handed bowlers.

Pin		Lay-down Board at Foul Line		
Right hander	**Left hander**	**3rd Arrow**	**4th Arrow**	**5th Arrow**
10	7	19	25.5	32
6	4	17	24	30.5
3 or 9	2 or 8	15	22	28.5
1 or 5	1 or 5	13.5	20	26.5
2 or 8	3 or 9	11.5	18	25
4	6	9.5	16	23
7	10	8	14.5	21

Table B.1: Spare shot lay down board when targeting the arrows

To verify our math and to prove that the lay down boards in Table B.1 are correct, we placed actual tape lines on a bowling lane running from the pins to the foul line, correlating to every shot denoted in the table. As examples, Figure B.4 depicts the 10-pin and the 7-pin, both targeted over fourth arrow. In both cases you can see that the physical lines agree completely with the calculated foul line positions in Table B.1, board 25-1/2 for the 10-pin, and board 14-1/2 for the 7-pin.

Figure B.4: 10-pin, fourth arrow, and 7-pin, fourth arrow

APPENDIX C

SPARE SYSTEM WORKSHEETS

SELECT THE PROPER worksheet for a left or right hander.* Choose a target arrow for each spare. Copy the foul line lay down board number from the appropriate column of the table on the left. Fill in your lay down distance and your drift, either left or right. Note: If you drift by different amounts or in a different direction when shooting right side versus left side spares, make note of this on the worksheet and fill in the appropriate drift and direction for each individual spare.

Add your lay down distance to the foul line board number, then add or subtract your drift, as appropriate. Write the resulting board number in the column labeled "Stand On Board" for each spare, and you're done!

BowlSmart Spare System Worksheet: Left-hander

My lay down distance is _____ boards.   My drift is _____ boards R / L (circle one)

Pin	Target Arrow	Lay-Down Board at Foul Line	+ Lay Down Distance (boards)	+ Drift Left (boards)	– Drift Right (boards)	Stand On Board
10						
6						
3 or 9						
1 or 5						
2 or 8						
4						
7						

Lay-Down Board at Foul Line

Pin	3rd Arrow	4th Arrow	5th Arrow
10	8	14.5	21
6	9.5	16	23
3 or 9	11.5	18	25
1 or 5	13.5	20	26.5
2 or 8	15	22	28.5
4	17	24	30.5
7	19	25.5	32

BowlSmart Spare System Worksheet: Right-hander

My lay down distance is _____ boards.   My drift is _____ boards R / L (circle one)

Pin	Target Arrow	Lay-Down Board at Foul Line	+ Lay Down Distance	+ Drift Right (boards)	− Drift Left (boards)	Stand On Board
10						
6						
3 or 9						
1 or 5						
2 or 8						
4						
7						

Pin	Lay-Down Board at Foul Line		
	3rd Arrow	4th Arrow	5th Arrow
10	19	25.5	32
6	17	24	30.5
3 or 9	15	22	28.5
1 or 5	13.5	20	26.5
2 or 8	11.5	18	25
4	9.5	16	23
7	8	14.5	21

NOTES

Chapter 1: Luck *Is* a Factor in Bowling

1. Rescher, Nicholas. *Luck: The Brilliant Randomness Of Everyday Life*. University of Pittsburgh Press, 2001. 28.

2. Ben-Ze'ev, Aaron. "Are Negative Emotions More Important than Positive Emotions?" Psychology Today. https://www.psychologytoday.com/blog/in-the-name-love/201007/are-negative-emotions-more-important-positive-emotions (accessed November 26, 2017).

3. Baumeister, R. F., Bratslavsky, E., Finkenauer, C., & Vohs, K. D. "Bad is stronger than good." Review of General Psychology 5, no. 4 (2001): 323–370.

4. Frijda, Nico H. "The Laws of Emotion." American Psychologist 43, no. 5 (1988): 349-358.

5. Wason, Peter C. "On the Failure to Eliminate Hypotheses in a Conceptual Task." Quarterly Journal of Experimental Psychology 12, no. 3 (1960): 129–140.

Chapter 2: Does a Heavier Ball Really Hit Harder and Carry Better?

6. Our calculation of momentum yields results in the somewhat bastard units "pound-miles per hour." Momentum is ordinarily measured in units called kilogram-meters per second, also known as Newtons. Employing proper units would require us to convert our ball's weight from pounds to kilograms by dividing by 2.205, and also to convert our ball's speed from miles per hour to meters per second by multiplying by 0.447 (1609.34 meters per mile divided by 3600 seconds per hour). Let's recalculate our momentum numbers using proper units:

8 pounds ÷ 2.205 = 3.628 kilograms
16 pounds ÷ 2.205 = 7.256 kilograms
10 miles per hour x .447 = 4.47 meters per second
20 miles per hour x .447 = 8.94 meters per second

3.628 kg x 4.47 meters per second = momentum of 16.217 kg-m/sec. Doubling ball weight to 7.256 kg = momentum of 7.256 x 4.47, or 32.432 kg-m/sec, or precisely double the momentum. If we instead double the ball speed to 20 miles per hour, our momentum is 3.628 kg x 8.94 meters per second, which is 32.434 kg-m/sec, again doubling the momentum (the very slight difference is due only to rounding errors). Thus, while converting to proper units rather than using our bastard mixed units changed the absolute numbers computed, they're relationship to one another is unchanged. We are therefore justified going forward in employing our simplified mixed units in this and other examples. While the absolute numbers so produced are not terribly meaningful, their relationships are precisely the same as if we went through the many extra steps involved in converting all of our variables to proper units.

7. Kinetic energy is ordinarily measured in units called kilogram-meters^2 per second^2, also known as Joules. As was the case with Momentum, in order to express our Kinetic Energy results in Joules we would have to convert our mass units from pounds to kilograms, and our velocity units from miles per hour to meters per second. While our unconverted units of pound-miles^2 per hour^2 aren't terribly useful, they are nonetheless accurate and comparable. Since converting units requires extra steps, and since units aren't important for our purposes, we will continue employing our bastard units.

8. In reality, our starting velocity is not zero. Since we are physically traveling down the approach at some rate of speed, the ball is likewise traveling at this rate at the top of our backswing. However, since our travel speed is the same for all examples, we can simply ignore it for the sake of simplicity and assume that our entire ball speed derives from our arm swing.

9. The speed examples cited herein are those indicated by the down lane sensors on the bowling lane. They do not represent actual "off the hand" delivery speed, which is typically a mile or two per hour faster.

10. A bowler's swing and release occurs much too quickly to time it in any conventional way, such as with a stopwatch. To determine the duration of Brian's swing, we employed a video of his approach. We were able to analyze the video frame by frame, and determined that his swing, from the top of his backswing to the point of release, occurred over 16 frames. We can convert frames to seconds by dividing the number of frames by our camera's frame rate. Since our camera shoots video at 30 frames per second, Brian's swing occurred over 16 frames divided by 30 frames/second, or .533 seconds.

11. 16 miles per hour ball speed.
    1609.34 meters per mile
    3600 seconds per hour

    16 miles per hour x 1609.34 meters per mile = 25,749.44 meters per hour.
    25749.44 meters per hour / 3600 seconds per hour = 7.153 meters per second.

    15 pound ball

2.2 pounds per kilogram

15 pounds / 2.2 pounds per kilogram = 6.8 kilograms.

12. One might think that the heavier ball would slow down Brian's swing, thereby slightly increasing time T, such that his ball speed would be a tiny bit faster than the 14.95 miles per hour which we calculated. In actuality, the mass of a pendulum bob, in our case the ball's weight, has no effect on the period (swing time) of the pendulum. Even if Brian's swing did slow down a bit due to the extra ball weight, the change in ball speed thus calculated would be minimal, so can be ignored for our purposes.

Chapter 3: Does a Lighter Ball Really Deflect More?

13. The "mass" we discussed in our previous chapters, the ball's weight, is properly called gravitational mass. Gravitational mass is a measure of how much "stuff" is in an object; "stuff" which can be acted upon by the force of gravity. Weight is simply the gravitational mass of an object in some particular gravitational field, say that of Earth. As such, since most of our bowling takes place on Earth, we were able to simply substitute weight for gravitational mass in our earlier calculations.

Inertial mass is a related concept, but which also incorporates the energy obtained from the object's acceleration and velocity. At extremely high speeds, those approaching the speed of light, an object's inertial mass will actually be significantly greater than its gravitational mass. At all lower speeds, an object's inertial mass will be precisely the same as its gravitational mass. Since very few bowlers throw the ball at the speed of light, we are safe in simply employing gravitational mass, or weight, as our unit of measure of an object's inertia.

Chapter 4: Follow the Bouncing Ball

14. In actuality, since the ball strikes the headpin off to the right side rather than head on when it enters the pocket on board 17-1/2, it will make contact roughly half an inch behind the front edge of the pin. Likewise, after the ball deflects over to the 3-pin, it will strike the 3- a bit behind the front of the pin. These two distances will be slightly different, and will vary a tiny fraction as the deflection angle changes, but the differences are small enough to simply ignore for the sake of simplicity.

15. In actuality, our calculated results are not as precise as they seem, due not only to slight rounding errors and issues with significant digits which we introduced for the sake of simplicity, but also to the simplifications we made when constructing our collision system. In an actual on lane scenario, energy would be lost to both heat and sound, and to the fact that our collision is not in actuality perfectly elastic. Further, we reduced the collision to two dimensions. In an actual collision, the shape of the pins causes them to be launched into the air to one degree or another, and this motion in the third dimension also draws off some of the energy and momentum which the moving ball delivers. Despite these shortcomings, the results nonetheless allow comparison between differing ball weights on a ceteris paribus basis.

Chapter 5: You Say You Want a Revolution

16. Torque is technically not a measure of force, but rather a measure of the efficiency of the system under examination to convert force into spin. We will be employing the term torque in a more colloquial sense, thinking of it as a spinning or twisting force.

17. M.S. Hallbeck. "Flexion and Extension Forces Generated by Wrist-Dedicated Muscles over the Range of Motion." Applied Ergonomics 12, No. 6. (1994): 379–385.

18. R.V. Gonzales, T.S. Buchanan, S.L. Delp. "How Muscle Architecture and Moment Arms Affect Wrist Flexion-Extension Movements." Journal of Biomechanics 30, No 7. (1997): 705-712.

19. Waldemar Karwowski. International Encyclopedia of Ergonomics and Human Factors, Second Edition. New York: Taylor & Francis Inc., (2001).

20. Technically, fingers do contain tiny little muscles called arrector pili, which are attached to our hair follicles and serve only to make our hairs stand on end. Standing our hairs on end will not add significantly to our rev rate, so we'll just ignore the arrector pili.

21. Peter N. Chalmers, et al. "Glenohumeral Function of the Long Head of the Biceps Muscle: An Electromyographic Analysis." Orthopaedic Journal of Sports Medicine 2, No 2. (2014): 2325967114523902.

22. A.S. Levy, B.T. Kelly, S.A. Lintner, D.C. Osbahr, K.P. Speer. "Function of the long head of the biceps at the shoulder: Electromyographic analysis." Journal of Shoulder and Elbow Surgery 10, No 3. (2001): 250-255.

23. Technically speaking, the Frisbee thrower must abduct his or her shoulder in the transverse plane, but this motion is the equivalent of extension of the joint, just in a horizontal direction.

Chapter 6: My Rev Rate Is...

24. We realize that the phrase "CATS system" is redundant (Computer Aided Tracking System system). We employ the phrase in spite of this shortcoming to conform to common usage, and in order to avoid confusion with the idea of the feline variety of cats being the cause of some discussed bowling issue.

25. David G. Sprager, Larry M. Vezina, Daniel R. Speranza, James M. Donovan. "Apparatus and method for analyzing bowling technique.", U.S. Patent US6110052A (February 14, 1996).

26. K. King, N.C. Perkins, H. Churchill, et al. "Bowling ball dynamics revealed by miniature wireless MEMS inertial measurement unit", Sports Engineering (2011) 13: 95. doi:10.1007/s12283-010-0054-z.

27. Ebonite Powerhouse Bowler ID Presentation, "Bowlers ID Presentation", YouTube video, 5:52, posted by Ronald Hickland Jr, January 15, 2015, https://www.youtube.com/watch?v=dnXOm3cXSs0

28. This is a simplification. In truth, our fingers impart a force vector tangential to the surface of the ball, and this force vector, combined with certain physical properties of our ball/hand system creates Torque within the ball.

29. An actual release typically occurs far more quickly than this, much too quickly to time with a stopwatch or even with our video frame counting method unless our camera has a high frame rate, but since we are keeping this number constant throughout our calculations, and since we are concerned with comparative values rather than actual values, the particular number we use here changes nothing.

Chapter 7: Does a High Rev Ball Really Hit the Pins Harder?

30. This definition of RG is not precisely accurate but it is close enough for our purposes, and the simplification makes the concept of RG much easier to visualize.

31. 15 pound ball = 6.804 kilograms
2.60 RG = 0.066 meters
16 MPH = 7.153 meters per second

Bowler A:
200 RPM = 20.944 radians per second

Translational Kinetic Energy (Kt) = 1/2 x Mass x Velocity^2
Kt = 1/2 x 6.804 x 7.153^2
Kt = 1/2 x 6.804 x 51.165
Kt = 174 Joules

Rotational Kinetic Energy (Kr) = 1/2 x Mass x RG^2 x Angular Velocity^2
Kr = 1/2 x 6.804 x 0.066^2 x 20.944^2
Kr = 1/2 x 6.804 x 0.0044 x 438.651
Kr = 6.57 Joules

Total Kinetic Energy (K) = Kt + Kr

K = 174 + 6.57

K = 180.57 Joules

Bowler B:

400 RPM = 41.888 radians per second

Translational Kinetic Energy (Kt) = 1/2 x Mass x Velocity^2

Kt = 1/2 x 6.804 x 7.153^2

Kt = 1/2 x 6.804 x 51.165

Kt = 174 Joules

Rotational Kinetic Energy (Kr) = 1/2 x Mass x RG^2 x Angular Velocity^2

Kr = 1/2 x 6.804 x 0.066^2 x 41.888^2

Kr = 1/2 x 6.804 x 0.0044 x 1,754.604

Kr = 26.26 Joules

Total Kinetic Energy (K) = Kt + Kr

K = 174 + 26.26

K = 200.26 Joules

32. 14 miles per hour x 63,360 inches per mile ÷ 60 minutes per hour = 14,784 inches per minute.

Chapter 8: Why Does My Ball Hook?

33. Neil Stremmel, Paul Ridenour, and Scott Sterbenz. "Identifying the Critical Factors That Contribute to Bowling Ball Motion on a Bowling Lane.", United States Bowling Congress (2005).

34. Ibid.

35. Shun Wang, Yuan-zhong Hu. "Effects of Surface Roughness on Sliding Friction in Lubricated-Point Contacts:Experimental and Numerical Studies.", Journal of Tribology 129 (2007): 809-817.

36. Ibid.

37. Ibid., 812.

38. Bo He, Wei Chen, Jane Wang. "Surface Texture Effect on Friction of a Microtextured Poly(dimethylsiloxane) (PDMS).", Tribology Letters 31 (2008): 187-197.

39. Nick Siefers. "Marketing vs. Physics: The truth about axis migration and core dynamics." United States Bowling Congress (2007). http://www.bowlingdigital.com/bowl/node/2836 (accessed 31 October, 2017).

Chapter 9: Track Flare, or Much Ado About Nothing?

40. There are, of course, no parallel lines in spherical geometry. We use the term here very loosely, for want of a better word.

41. "How to find the PSA of a bowling ball using a washing machine." YouTube video, 6:13. Posted by "Sprocket454" on October 23, 2013. https://www.youtube.com/watch? v=-WIfDXDAloQ (accessed 17 September, 2017).

42. Neil Stremmel, Paul Ridenour, and Scott Sterbenz. "Identifying the Critical Factors That Contribute to Bowling Ball Motion on a Bowling Lane." United States Bowling Congress (2005).

43. "Brunswick Extra Hole Demonstration." YouTube video, 11:11. Posted by Eric Morrett on August 7, 2015. https://www.youtube.com/watch?v=f1e8VeZf4WA (accessed 17 September, 2017).

44. Cliff Frohlich. "What makes bowling balls hook?" American Journal of Physics 72 no.9 (September 2004): 1170-1177.

45. Stremmel, op. cit.

46. Frohlich, op. cit.

47. Joydeep Banerjee, John McPhee. "A Volumetric Contact Model to Study the Effect of Lane Friction and the Radii of Gyration on the 'Hook Shot' in Indoor Bowling." Procedia Engineering 72 (2014): 429-434.

48. Frohlich, op. cit.

Chapter 10: The Pocket Isn't the Pocket, and It's Nowhere near Where You Think It Is!

49. United Stated Bowling Congress. "Pin Carry Study." *Bowl.com.* https://www.bowl.com/Equipment_Specs/Equipment_Specs_Home/Research,_Articles_and_Presentations/ (accessed July 22, 2017).

50. United States Bowling Congress. "I left what where." *Bowl.com.* https://www.bowl.com/Equipment_Specs/Equipment_Specs_Home/Research,_Articles_and_Presentations/ (accessed July 22, 2017).

Chapter 11: I Was Robbed!

51. Kegel LLC. "Kegel Sport Series - DEAD MAN'S CURVE - 3043 (40 uL)." Kegel Pattern Library. http://patternlibrary.kegel.net/PatternLibraryPattern.aspx?ID=663 (accessed September 18, 2017).

52. In actual practice, oil is only applied to the brush for the first 21.3 feet on the forward pass, and then buffed out to 43 feet. On the reverse pass the machine applies a second layer of oil beginning at the 32 foot mark, and spraying or buffing all the way back to the foul line.

53. Neil Stremmel, Paul Ridenour, and Scott Sterbenz. "Identifying the Critical Factors That Contribute to Bowling Ball Motion on a Bowling Lane." United States Bowling Congress (2008).

54. Actually, though the ball travels 16 inches back to the pocket from the 2-board, it hooks far less than this distance. The ball hooks only a short distance, after which it is then traveling in a straight line toward the left rather than straight along the boards or out to the right. After completing its relatively short hook phase, the ball simply rolls the remaining distance to the left since that is the way it is now pointing.

Chapter 12: So Why Did I Leave *That*?!?

55. United States Bowling Congress. "I left what where." Bowl.com. https://www.bowl.com/Equipment_Specs/Equipment_Specs_Home/Research,_Articles_and_Presentations/ (accessed July 22, 2017).

56. There are other changes to your line that are also effective in certain situations. These will be discussed in later chapters.

Chapter 13: Create a Bowler's Tool Kit

57. King, K., N.C. Perkins, H. Churchill, et al. "Bowling ball dynamics revealed by miniature wireless MEMS inertial measurement unit", Sports Engineering 13 (2011): 95-104. DOI:10.1007/s12283-010-0054-z.

Chapter 14: Applying Your Tools

58. Kegel LLC. "Topography Study." Kegel.net. http://www.kegel.net/topography-study/ (accessed February 4, 2018).

Chapter 17: Spare Change

59. United States Bowling Congress. "Oddities-Miscellaneous." BOWL.com. http://usbcongress.http.internapcdn.net/usbcongress/bowl/recordsstats/pdfs/OdditiesMiscellaneous.pdf (accessed March 10, 2018).

60. One of your coauthors coaches a large number of highly competitive PBA and national team caliber bowlers. Amongst such bowlers, he has observed an almost universal five board lay down distance. Your other coauthor works with mostly high school and recreational bowlers. The bowlers he has observed tend to have lay down distances of five or six boards. The most extreme that he has encountered in a recreational bowler was 12 boards, which is quite excessive.

61. Directional walking is an intentional act, and is one we do not condone for a number of reasons. Walking diagonally across the approach toward one's spare actually adds complications to the game, the most important of which is that it renders any simple mathematical targeting system inoperative and requires the bowler to make either guesses or separate calculations for every possible shot and for every different starting distance on the approach.

62. As an example of tweaking the Calculated Spare System, I shall outline my own adjustments. I target all of my spares over the 4th arrow. I have a five board lay down distance, and little or no drift. Since even a polyester spare ball may occasionally hook a small amount if the lane conditions are very dry, and to provide a bit of wiggle room away from the gutter, I adjusted the table's stated board 14-1/2 lay down position for converting the 7-pin to board 15, and my standing position therefore moved to board 20. I left the positions for shooting the 4- and 2-pins unchanged from those calculated in the table, so my own moves from my 7-pin spot for left side spares are one board left for the 4-pin and two more boards from there, or three in total, for the 2-pin.

For right side spares, I made a similar adjustment for the sake of simplicity. I adjusted the table's stated board 25-1/2 position for targeting the 10-pin to board 26, making my standing position board 31. I left the calculated positions for the 6- and 3-pins unchanged, so my moves for right side spares are two and two to the right from board 31.

Appendix A: Calculating Deflection

63. Collisions can be categorized into two types; elastic, and inelastic. An elastic collision is one in which the colliding objects bounce off of one another, as would, say, billiard balls following the break. An inelastic collision is one in which the objects "stick together" after colliding, continuing on as one larger combined mass. Think, perhaps, of a car and a truck becoming entangled after colliding, becoming one large mass of twisted metal. In both types of collision, momentum and energy are conserved. In our elastic collision, each billiard ball continues on with some portion of the combined energy and momentum that each brought into the collision, while in an inelastic collision our smashed together "car-truck" skids along carrying the sum total of the energy and momentum each vehicle brought into the crash. Bowling, of course, represents a more or less elastic collision.

64. This is not precisely true. The laws of conservation of energy and momentum state that both will be conserved, but not necessarily in the same form. For instance, in the example of a bowling ball hitting the pins, the kinetic energy the ball brought into the collision will indeed be shared amongst the pins, but some of it will be converted to sound energy, and some will be converted to heat due to friction. The total of all of these forms of energy will equal the amount brought into the collision. For our purposes, however, assuming a completely elastic collision in a frictionless environment will greatly simplify our discussion without introducing any meaningful errors.

65. One might think that a spinning ball, with the axis of rotation severely tilted Up near the top of the ball like a child's spinning top, would affect the deflection path of the pin and indeed of the ball after the collision, much like a "cut shot" in billiards, but there may or may not be enough friction between the ball and the pin to allow for such an effect. Though the "Asian helicopter spinner" bowling style attempts to make use of this idea, in conventional tenpin bowling there is in most cases very little axis tilt and therefore very little vertical spin imparted to the ball to begin with, and even when there is, all or nearly all of it is lost to friction long before the ball hits the pins. Thus, for the purposes of this discussion spin is not an issue.

66. When one squares a trigonometric function such as the cosine of angle Θb, the proper way to express it is $Cos^2\Theta b$. In order to make our presentation a bit easier to understand we have strayed from this convention, employing instead the more straightforward sounding $Cos\Theta b^2$. Since we are talking about "the cosine of angle Θb, squared," our unconventional presentation is closer to the way we read the expression for we non-mathematicians.

Appendix B: Calculating the Spare System

67. The ratio between the short leg and the long leg of either triangle can also tell us the actual angle to the lane that the ball must travel on its way to the target pin, should we desire to know this. In trigonometry, this ratio is called the tangent of our ball-path-to-lane angle. In our case, the ratio or tangent is 18 inches divided by 564.125 inches, or 0.032.

The computation to convert tangent to degrees involves some complex calculus, but there are two simple ways to reach a reasonable approximation. The first method is to look up our 0.032 tangent on a published tangent table. A more accurate method is to compute the arctangent of our 0.032 tangent using the ArcTan function on a scientific calculator (or any of the many online calculators). Be careful here, as arctangent can be displayed in either degrees or radians, so make certain you have specified degrees. Either method tells us that our 0.032 tangent corresponds to an angle of just over 1.8 degrees. Thus, in order to hit the 10-pin targeting over 4th arrow, our ball must travel on a course that is 1.8 degrees to the lane.

GLOSSARY

- **active release**—A release characterized by a wrist that extends backward prior to release, and then flexes powerfully forward after the bowler's thumb exits the ball. An active release generates the most possible torque, resulting in a relatively high rev rate.

- **Abralon**—A brand name of sanding pads used to resurface bowling balls

- **acceleration**—The rate at which an object changes its velocity. How quickly it speeds up.

- **angular move**—Moving your target line to a different part of the lane while also changing your angle of attack. Accomplished by moving both your feet and your target, but moving each a different number of boards or in different directions.

- **arrows**—The diamond-shaped markings on the lane approximately 15 feet past the foul line, commonly used for targeting.

- **arsenal**—The array of bowling balls a bowler assembles for a particular league or competition. Functional equivalent of a set of golf clubs.

- **axis migration**—The change in the location of the ball's axis of rotation with each revolution. Caused by a weight imbalance within the ball.

- **axis point**—See PAP.

- **axis of rotation**—The axis, imaginary or real, that an object spins around. Also called the spin axis. When you hear "axis," think "axle."

- **axis rotation**—A release variable the bowler imparts to the bowling ball to change the skid distance and the shape of the ball's path. Axis rotation is the rough equivalent of turning an automobile's front wheels to make it round a corner. All forward roll is zero degrees of rotation, and all side roll is 90 degrees. As axis rotation increases from zero toward our optimal level, the ball hooks more and skids less. Once we go beyond our optimum rotation, the ball skids farther and hooks less, though the hook we do get will become sharper in shape.

- **axis tilt**—A release variable the bowler imparts to the bowling ball to change the skid distance and the shape of the ball's path. Measures how far the ball's spin axis—its "axle"—is tilted up from horizontal. Zero degrees of tilt indicates a horizontal spin axis. A vertical spin axis, like a spinning top, is defined as 90 degrees of tilt. As tilt increases from zero degrees, the ball will skid farther and hook less.

- **baby split**—The 3-10 for right handers, and the 2-7 for left handers.

- **back-up ball**—Also called a reverse hook. A back-up ball hooks in the opposite direction of the traditional hook most bowlers use, to the right for right handers and to the left for left handers. A back-up ball is caused by a wrist that turns outward during the release.

- **balance hole**—An extra holed drilled into a bowling ball, originally used to adjust the ball's static weights to meet USBC specifications. Now used to slightly alter the RG of a drilled bowling ball to subtly adjust ball reaction. Balance holes have been outlawed by the USBC beginning in 2020.

- **ball down**—Switching to a weaker ball due to changing lane conditions. Balling down means changing to a bowling ball with a chemically weaker coverstock, a shinier surface preparation, a higher RG, or a combination of these factors.

- **ball up**—Switching to a stronger ball due to changing lane conditions. Balling up means changing to a bowling ball with a chemically stronger coverstock, a duller surface preparation, a lower RG, or a combination of these factors.

- **ball start**—See push away.

- **benchmark ball**—A ball in a player's arsenal that is used to "read the lane" the first few shots of practice before a tournament. The best choice is a medium strength, medium RG ball with a smooth and predictable reaction, usually with a solid coverstock, although it does not have to be. If the benchmark ball over- or underreacts, the player can move up or down in their arsenal.

- **big four**—The 4-6-7-10 split. Also known as "double bedposts," or "grandma's teeth."

- **blocked lane**—See walled up.

- **board**—The individual strips of wood that make up the lane surface. On synthetic lane surfaces, the overlay is printed with a pattern that imitates individual boards. Lane boards are approximately 1 inch in width, and there are a total of 39 boards on a lane.

- **breakpoint**—The area down the lane where the ball makes the sharpest portion of its hook back to the pocket.

- **Brooklyn**—An errant shot that crosses the center of the lane and hits on the wrong side of the headpin. A Brooklyn shot hits in the 1-2 area for a right hander, or the 1-3 for a lefty. Often referred to as "Jersey" by bowlers in New York.

- **bucket**—A diamond-shaped cluster of four pins left standing, comprised of the 2-4-5-8 for right handers, and the 3-5-6-9 for left handers.

- **burn**—A part of the lane where there is increased friction due to a lot of bowling ball traffic, resulting in the ball hooking earlier than desired. Also refers to the generally dry conditions resulting late in a tournament block, especially when the lanes are not re-oiled.

- **burn up**—See roll out. Can also refer to a condition where the lanes that get progressively drier through repeated shots thrown in the same area, especially with dull bowling balls.

- **burnt heads**—Excessive friction in the front part of the lanes. Burnt heads are more common on wood lanes. Burnt heads will cause the ball to hook early, and will significantly decrease the skid portion of ball motion.

- **carry down**—A condition where bowling balls pick up oil from the front part of the lane and redeposit it on the back ends where the lanes are supposed to be dry, resulting in a longer skid phase and decreased hook.

- **CG**—The center of mass within an object. Think of it as the balance point where the weight of the object is centered, which may be different than the geometric center. Bowling balls are slightly lopsided. The center of mass is ordinarily roughly 1/16th inch away from the geometric center of the ball. The CG—the center of mass—will be marked on the surface of the ball.

- **center of gravity**—See CG.

- **channel**—See gutter.

- **chop**—When a bowler picks off one or more pins from a combination spare, leaving one or more pins standing. For example, knocking down only the 6-pin following a 6-10 leave.

- **closed (stance)**—The orientation of the bowler's body when the feet, hips, and shoulders are angled toward the left for a right hander, and toward the right for a lefty. Can refer to the bowler's stance either on the approach before beginning the delivery, or at the foul line.

- **closed frame**—See filled frame.

- **clothesline**—See picket fence.

- **coefficient of friction (COF)**—In physics, coefficient of friction is the relationship between the friction between two objects and the amount of force pushing those two objects together (frictional force ÷ normal force). In bowling, think of coefficient of friction as the amount of friction between the ball and the lane.

- **conventional grip**—A bowling ball grip characterized by a very short span between the finger holes and the thumb hole. The fingers are inserted deeply into the ball, up to the second knuckle, resulting in a shortened lever arm and decreased rev rate.

- **core**—See weight block.

- **coverstock**—The material making up the outer shell of a bowling ball. By far the greatest influence on ball motion. Coverstock frictional characteristics can be manipulated to a degree by altering the surface finish.

- **cranker**—A bowler who employs a heavily muscled and powerful delivery and release, often resulting in a relatively high rev rate. Sometimes less accurately used to describe any bowler with a high rev rate, regardless of their bowling style.

- **deadwood**—Pins that have been knocked down but remain on the lane or in the gutter after the pinsetter has reset the other pins.

- **deep**—Playing a part of the lane that is far to the inside, left for right handers and right for left handers. Bowlers typically move deep inside when they are "opening up" the lane, or when the pattern and lane environment favor this area of play.

- **deflection**—Change in an object's speed and direction of travel following a collision.

- **differential**—See RG differential.

- **dots (approach)**—Two or more rows of circular markings on the approach. Bowlers use these dots as reference marks when determining where to stand, both laterally and longitudinally. The center dot in each row is often larger, and denotes board 20. The remaining dots are spaced in five board intervals. There may be a total of 5 or 7 dots in each row.

- **dots (foul line)**—A row of circular markings just inches from the foul line. Like the approach dots, the foul line dots are centered on board 20, and are spaced at five board intervals. They are typically used to determine foot position following delivery in order to monitor drift.

- **dots (mid-lane)**—A row of circular markings, ordinarily five on each side of the lane, and located roughly halfway between the foul line and the arrows. These dots are not on the same boards as the approach or foul line dots, and are not spaced evenly. Though they are not well suited as targets, we believe that may have been their original purpose. There is no USBC requirement that these dots exist, no specification as to their number (so long as it is 10 or less) or their cross-lane position, and only a very general specification as to their distance from the foul line.

- **double**—Two strikes in a row.

- **double wood**—See sleeper.

- **down and in**—A ball path that is relatively straight up the boards from release to breakpoint, with all of its lateral motion occurring after the breakpoint. The ball path crosses few if any boards until after the breakpoint is reached.

- **drift**—An angled variation in a bowler's footwork on the approach, resulting in a slide that ends on a different board than his or her starting position.

- **early timing**—A situation where the ball has already left the bowler's hand before the bowler reaches a solid position at the foul line. Early timing is characterized by a loss of leverage on the ball, resulting in a lower rev rate.

- **entry angle**—The angle of the ball's final path toward the pocket relative to the lane after completing its hook. A ball that travels straight up the lane has zero degrees of entry angle. A maximum entry angle of around six degrees is theoretically possible, though the length of oil patterns typically enforce lower angles.

- **face, through the**—See nose.

- **fast 7-pin**—See ringing 7-pin.

- **fast 10-pin**—See ringing 10-pin.

- **fill ball**—The last ball in the tenth frame, following either two strikes or a spare. If the game is not close, the fill ball is often used to experiment with something new before the start of the next game.

- **filled frame**—A frame in which the bowler had a strike or a spare.

- **fingertip grip**—A bowling ball grip characterized by a span sufficiently long that the fingers can only be inserted up to the first knuckle. This results in a long lever arm, creating greater leverage and increased revs.

- **flare**—See track flare.

- **flat (oil pattern)**—An oil pattern having very little difference in oil volume from side to side on the lane. While a house pattern can have an oil ratio of 10:1 or more, meaning that there is 10 times as much oil in the center of the lane as on the sides, a flat pattern often has a ratio of 3:1 or less. Sport patterns are generally considered flat. Flat patterns require far greater accuracy, and result in a lower scoring pace.

- **flat 7-pin**—A 7-pin left standing by a left hander, characterized by the 4-pin falling lazily into the gutter. Ordinarily caused by a light hit on the headpin.

- **flat 10-pin**—A 10-pin left standing by a right hander, characterized by the 6-pin falling lazily into the gutter. Ordinarily caused by a light hit on the headpin.

- **flat hit**—See hit flat.

- **flush**—A shot where the ball impacts the headpin in the true pocket, on board 17-1/2.

- **force**—An interaction between two objects resulting in a change in the state of motion. Think of force as a push or a pull exerted by one object upon another.

- **foul**—A foul results when any part of the bowler's foot crosses the foul line either before, during, or after the release. A foul also results if any part of the bowler's body touches the lane, a wall, or any other part of the bowling center beyond the foul line. Note that if the ball is not released, no foul has occurred. A foul results in a "dead ball." Any pins knocked down are reset, and the bowler receives a score of zero for that ball.

- **foul line**—The line separating the approach from the lane. The bowler must remain behind the foul line.

- **friction**—a force that acts against the motion of one object sliding over another. Friction inhibits sliding by converting motion to heat.

- **fried heads**—See burnt heads.

- **full roller**—An old school release style that results in a ball track that passes between the finger and thumb holes. Full rollers require a special drilling layout to prevent the ball from rolling over the gripping holes.

- **Greek church**—The 4-6-7-9-10 split for right handers, or the 4-6-7-8-10 for lefties. A variation on the "big four" split, and caused by the same through the nose hit, plus a dose of bad luck.

- **gutter**—The gully-shaped areas on either side of a bowling lane designed to collect any ball that leaves the lane surface, channeling it back to the pit. A ball that enters the gutter results in a score of zero.

- **hand**—Slang term for a release that creates a lot of revs, as in "She put a lot of hand on that shot," or "He has a lot of hand."

- **handicap**—Pins given to a player or team to compensate for the opponent's skill advantage and create a more even playing field. The equivalent of giving a slower runner a head start. Handicap is usually set as a percentage of the difference between a bowler's average and a target score chosen by the league or tournament director.

- **heads**—The front part of the lane, between the foul line and the arrows.

- **heavy**—See high.

- **high**—A ball that hits left of the pocket for right handers or right of the pocket for left handers. A high hit is anywhere from board 18-1/2 to board 20, and often results in a split or difficult spare.

- **high flush**—A shot that hits the headpin on board 18, which is the highest position that is still considered "in the pocket."

- **high RG axis**—The imaginary axis running through the ball 90 degrees to the low RG axis, and around which its mass is the most spread out, resulting in the highest possible RG for that particular ball. The high RG axis is located through an undrilled ball's PSA, and will end up in the vicinity of the thumb hole once the ball is drilled.

- **hit flat**—A term used to describe a light hit that failed to carry and seemingly had no energy, but where the observer mistakenly believed the shot was in the pocket.

- **house ball**—The array of brightly colored polyester bowling balls that are available at the bowling center for anyone to use. They are drilled very generically, and don't properly fit any bowler's hand. The collection may also include older personal equipment that was abandoned at the lanes.

- **house shot**—A relatively easy oil pattern put out by most bowling centers for league and recreational play. House shots have very high oil ratios, often 10:1 or more, featuring very dry boards toward the outside of the lane and a flood of oil up the center. House shots are designed to produce artificially high scoring by funneling errant shots back toward the pocket (see "walled up"). Often called a "typical house shot," and abbreviated to THS.

- **inertia**—The tendency of an object to maintain its state of motion, including speed and direction, unless acted upon by an outside force. Described by Newton's first law of motion.

- **initial spin axis**—See PAP.

- **inside**—Playing the part of the lane that is toward the left for right handers or toward the right for left handers. The opposite of playing an outside line. Inside lines often require greater angles of attack.

- **intermediate RG axis**—An imaginary axis running through the ball 90 degrees to the high and low RG axes. Exists only on an undrilled ball with an asymmetric weight block. USBC testing has shown the intermediate RG axis to have no measurable influence on hook or ball motion.

- **Jersey**—See Brooklyn.

- **kickbacks**—Technically called kickback plates. Rigid panels attached to the walls on both sides of the pin deck, intended to both protect the walls and to increase rebound and thereby increase pin action and carry.

- **kinetic energy**—The energy an object possesses due to its motion.

- **lane transition**—See transition.

- **late timing**—A situation where the bowler reaches a solid stance at the foul line just before releasing the ball. Late timing results in the maximum leverage on the ball and the maximum rev rate for a given bowler's release. Caution must be exercised though, as timing that is too late often results in over-rotating the shoulders and pulling the shot.

- **launch angle**—The initial trajectory of your ball path relative to the lane.

- **lay down distance**—The distance in boards between the instep of the bowler's slide shoe and the center of the ball at the point of release. Lay down distance is critical information when formulating a spare system.

- **lift**—Adding topspin to the ball by pulling upward on the finger holes during release. Formerly referred to as "hitting up on the ball" and considered a negative trait, it is instead the primary way those who employ a static release achieve their revs.

- **light**—A shot that impacts the headpin too far to the right for right handers, or too far to the left for lefties.

- **lily**—See sour apple.

- **loft**—The act of launching the ball farther out on the lane during the release. Loft is used to effectively shorten the lane to reduce the effect of excess friction, particularly in the front part of the lane.

- **low RG axis**—The imaginary axis running through the ball around which its mass is most concentrated, resulting in the lowest possible RG for that particular ball. The low RG axis is located through or very close to the ball's pin.

- **mark (lane)**—The lane feature the bowler uses as a target. Bowlers typically use the arrows or one of the boards between them as their mark, though others use the dots, the range finders, or other identifiable targets.

- **mark (score)**—A strike or spare.

- **mass**—A measure of how much matter, or "stuff," makes up an object. While mass and weight are subtly different things, they can be thought of as being the same in terms of bowling.

- **mass bias**—See PSA.

- **messenger**—A pin, usually the headpin, that bounces off of one of the kickbacks and rebounds across the pin deck to take out a pin or pins left standing by a bad hit. A messenger is ordinarily the result of an extremely light hit that was thrown with a lot of speed.

- **mixer**—A sloppy strike that results from a very light hit, usually around board 15-1/2.

- **momentum**—Momentum can be thought of as the amount of motion an object has. It is defined as an object's mass multiplied by its velocity. The more momentum an object has, the harder it is to stop.

- **neutral stance**—The orientation of the bowler's body when the feet, hips, and shoulders are aligned square to the lane, angled neither right nor left. Can refer to the bowler's stance either on the approach before beginning the delivery, or at the foul line.

- **neutral timing**—A situation where the bowler releases the ball just as he or she becomes solid at the foul line. Once thought to be ideal timing.

- **nose, through the**—A shot that hits on or very close to the center of the headpin. Through the nose shots typically result in big, ugly splits. Also called "through the face."

- **open (stance)**—The orientation of the bowler's body when the feet, hips, and shoulders are angled toward the right for a right hander, and toward the left for a lefty. Can refer to the bowler's stance either on the approach before beginning the delivery, or at the foul line.

- **open frame**—A frame that did not result in a strike or a spare.

- **open up (lane)**—Increasing launch angle by moving toward the inside of the lane, moving the breakpoint toward the outside of the lane, or both. Often accompanied by an increase in axis rotation, and sometimes requiring increased ball speed or a ball change. Usually a response to higher friction conditions as the lanes transition. Also called "swinging," "wheeling," or "freewheeling."

- **optimal axis rotation**—The degree of axis rotation at which skid is minimized and hook is maximized. Optimal axis rotation is a function of the bowler's rev rate and ball speed.

- **out of bounds**—An area on the lane that is essentially unplayable due to peculiarities of the oil pattern or bad lane topography.

- **outside**—Refers to a line of play out near the gutter. There is no firm definition of "outside." Some bowlers consider it to be any line outside of the second arrow, while others say it is on or outside of the first arrow. Outside lines require straighter angles of attack. "Outside" can also refer to a shot that misses the bowler's mark to the right for a right hander or to the left for a lefty.

- **over/under**—Refers to a lane condition where even a slight miss to one side of the bowler's mark results in the ball skidding too far and hitting too light, while a slight miss to the other side of the mark results in a ball that over hooks and hits too high. Can be the result of a high ratio oil pattern, lane transition, or bad topography. Also called wet/dry.

- **PAP**—Positive axis point. One end of an imaginary axis running through the bowling ball about which the bowler initially spins the ball. Used as a reference point when laying out a ball for drilling. The other end of the imaginary axis is called the negative axis point. These are arbitrary names, though, as physics makes no distinction between positive and negative ends of the axis. In physics, the PAP is referred to simply as one end of the initial spin axis.

- **pair**—Two adjacent lanes, sharing a ball return. Most sanctioned play occurs on a pair of lanes.

- **parallel move**—Moving your target line to a different part of the lane without changing your angle of attack. Accomplished by moving both your feet and your target by the same number of boards and in the same direction.

- **passive release**—A ball release characterized by an uncontrolled, extended (bent back) wrist. Often results in a weak release and a low rev rate.

- **pearl (coverstock)**—A bowling ball coverstock material composed of modified polyurethane, with the addition of a friction-reducing powdered mica filler material.

- **picket fence**—The 1-, 2-, 4-, and 7-pins left standing by a right hander, or the 1-3-6-10 left by a lefty.

- **pin (ball)**—One end of a bowling ball's low RG axis. Marked on the ball's surface with a small, colored dot. The pin marks the location of the device that originally held the weight block in place inside the mold when the ball was cast.

- **pin action**—Randomly bouncing and flying pins that take out stragglers left by a less than perfect pocket hit. Pin action is the result of high kinetic energy, which is mostly dependent on ball speed.

- **pin deck**—The area at the end of the lane and before the pit where the pins are placed by the pinsetter.

- **pin down**—A ball layout where the pin is located below the finger holes. Generally results in an RG lower than that of the undrilled ball, resulting in an earlier and more gradual hook.

- **pin up**—A ball layout where the pin is located above the finger holes. Generally results in an RG higher than that of the undrilled ball, resulting in a later and sharper hook.

- **pit**—The depressed area behind the pin deck where the ball and toppled pins collect before being picked up by the pinsetter.

- **pitch**—The angle at which the gripping holes are drilled into the ball. Pitch is dependent on the flexibility of the bowler's hand and the desired release characteristics. Zero pitch describes a hole drilled directly toward the ball's geometric center. Reverse pitch describes holes angled away from the center, as though gripping a basketball with one hand. Forward pitch describes holes angled more toward the center, as though gripping a baseball. Finger holes will also be pitched right and left so they don't intersect and weaken the ball, and the thumb hole may be pitched right or left due to flexibility issues.

- **plastic**—See polyester.

- **pocket**—A name for the optimal point of impact with the headpin, which is on board 17-1/2. "Pocket" is a misnomer stemming from past belief that the ball should hit in the pocket formed between the 1- and 3-pin for righties, or the 1- and 2-pin for lefties.

- **pocket 7-10**—A 7-10 split left after a shot that the bowler believes was in the pocket. In truth there is statistically zero chance of leaving a 7-10 split on a true pocket hit, so the "pocket 7-10" is a myth. The 7-10 split almost always occurs from a hit that was 1-1/2 to 2 boards light.

- **polyester**—A very hard and dense, low-friction coverstock material, often referred to by bowlers as "plastic." Though once considered a high performance coverstock, polyester does not display enough friction to hook to any meaningful degree on modern lane surfaces. Polyester is now relegated to spare balls.

- **porosity**—Microscopic bubbles in the polyurethane making up a bowling ball's coverstock. Porosity adds greatly to friction, and therefore hook, because the physical structure of the pores act like tread on a car tire. The downside to porosity is that it leads to oil absorption which causes the ball to lose friction and hook over time.

- **positive axis point**—See PAP.

- **post**—To maintain your finish position and posture at the foul line, and to hold that position until your ball hits the pins. Posting your shot is a sign of good balance.

- **power player**—Also called a "cranker." Power players employ a great deal of muscle in their swing and release, often resulting in high ball speed and a very high rev rate.

- **PSA**—Preferred spin axis, also known as the "mass bias." A bowling term used to describe one end of a bowling ball's high RG axis. The PSA is marked on the surface of an undrilled ball. Once the ball is drilled the PSA will shift from the marked spot, and will ordinarily be located in the vicinity of the thumb hole.

- **pull**—An errant shot that misses the bowler's mark toward the inside of the lane, often resulting in a high hit. Pulling is caused by a flaw in the bowler's delivery. Beginners often pull their shot by trying to "help" the ball hook. More accomplished bowlers typically pull their shots due to timing issues or a fault in the direction of their arm swing.

- **push (noun)**—The distance between where the oil pattern ends and the bowler's breakpoint.

- **push (verb)**—Used as an exclamation when a bowler misses their mark toward the inside, and wants their ball to travel farther down the lane before hooking to compensate for the miss. Synonyms are "hold," and "sit."

- **push away**—The initial motion a bowler makes with the ball when beginning the approach. The ball is literally pushed forward, away from the body, in order to initiate the arm swing. The push away usually occurs simultaneously with the first step of a four step approach or the second step of a five step approach.

- **rack**—The initial cluster of 10 pins set by the pinsetter. A "bad rack" is a cluster of pins where one or more pins is set significantly out of position.

- **radius of gyration**—See RG.

- **reactive resin**—Marketing term for a highly modified form of polyurethane used as a bowling ball coverstock. Such polyurethane formulations typically feature plasticizers, "blowing agents" to create porosity, and other compounds intended to increase the chemical friction of the coverstock.

- **rev rate**—How fast the ball is spinning when the bowler releases it. Rev rate is measured in RPM, or revolutions per minute.

- **revolutions**—See revs.

- **revs**—Short for revolutions per minute. Used to describe the amount of topspin the bowler imparts to the ball.

- **RG**—Radius of gyration. A measure of how the mass is distributed within a spinning object, in our case a bowling ball. RG is measured in inches. A high RG means the weight is spread out. A low RG means that the weight is concentrated more toward the center.

- **RG differential**—The difference between the RG of the ball's PSA and the RG of the pin. RG differential is thought to influence the amount of track flare. See high RG axis and low RG axis.

- **Rico**—An ultra-low RG drilling layout, characterized by the ball's pin being located in the center of the grip.

- **ringing 7-pin**—A 7-pin left standing by a left hander, characterized by the 4-pin flying rapidly around the 7-pin. Ordinarily caused by a light hit on the headpin. Also sometimes called a wrap 7-pin or a fast 7-pin.

- **ringing 10-Pin**—A 10-pin left standing by a right hander, characterized by the 6-pin flying rapidly around the 10-pin. Ordinarily caused by a light hit on the headpin. Also sometimes called a wrap 10-pin or a fast 10-pin.

- **roll out**—Premature loss of ball speed and axis rotation due to excessive friction. Results is an early but abbreviated hook phase, and a light hit and low entry angle. Caused by using a ball with too much surface texture or chemical friction for the lane conditions.

- **rotation**—See axis rotation.

- **rotational kinetic energy**—The energy an object possesses due to its spin. In bowling, it is the energy the ball possesses due to its rev rate.

- **RPM**—Revolutions per minute. See revs.

- **Sarge Easter grip**—A hybrid bowling ball grip wherein the middle finger is drilled with a fingertip grip, the the ring finger is drilled conventional. Intended to create an intermediate lever arm falling somewhere between that of fingertip and conventional.

- **scout**—See messenger.

- **scratch**—A league or tournament in which no handicap is given. Every bowler competes on a level playing field.

- **siaair**—A brand name of sanding pads used to resurface bowling balls. Pronounced as two words, "see-ah air."

- **sleeper**—A pin left standing directly behind another pin. The three possible sleepers are the 8-pin when part of the 2-8, the 9-pin when part of the 3-9, and on rare occasions the 5-pin when part of the 1-5. These leaves are also know as "double wood."

- **solid (coverstock)**—A bowling ball coverstock material composed only of modified polyurethane, with no filler materials added.

- **sour apple**—The very rare 5-7-10 double split.

- **span**—The distance between the thumb hole and finger holes on a drilled ball. Span is dependent on the bowler's hand size, desired grip type, and desired fit. Care must be taken because span can be measured in two ways, actual, or cut-to-cut. Actual includes the thickness of the finger inserts and thumb slug, while cut-to-cut does not. Actual and cut-to-cut will be the same if no finger inserts or thumb slug are used.

- **spin**—Technically, spin describes the amount of topspin the bowler puts on the ball, so would be synonymous with revs. In conventional bowling lingo, however, spin usually refers to an excessive amount of axis tilt, resulting in a ball that spins like a top as it skids down the lane rather than hooking and rolling.

- **spin axis**—See axis of rotation.

- **split**—Describes groups of one or more pins left standing that are not diagonally adjacent to one another, leaving a gap between the groups. If the headpin is among the groups left standing then the leave is not technically a split, and is instead classified as a wash out.

- **static release**—A ball release characterized by a rigid wrist. Often the result of a slower but powerful wrist, or of a wrist device that restricts movement. Significant revs can be generated by a static release depending on how forceful the arm swing is and on how powerfully the bowler flexes their fingers during release.

- **stone 7-pin**—A 7-pin left standing by a right hander on a pocket hit, as though the pin were made of stone and resisted the carnage. Stone 7-pins are rare, as most 7-pins are actually left by shots that hit 1-1/2 to 2 boards light.

- **stone 10-pin**—A 10-pin left standing by a left hander on a pocket hit, as though the pin were made of stone and resisted the carnage. Stone 10-pins are rare, as most 10-pins are actually left by shots that hit 1-1/2 to 2 boards light.

- **stretched grip**—An old school bowling ball grip where the finger holes are drilled as far as possible from the thumb hole. The goal of the stretched grip was to increase the amount of leverage the bowler could get on the ball, but the downside was damage to the hand, especially at the base of the thumb. The stretched grip has largely fallen out of favor.

- **stroker**—While the term "stroker" is often applied to any bowler with a relatively low rev rate, it really refers to a style of approach and delivery. A stroker delivery is characterized by long and smooth motions and a lack of obvious muscular effort.

- **surface finish**—The texture applied to the surface of a bowling ball with various grades of sandpaper, rubbing compounds, and polishing compounds. Surface finish may be dull, glossy, or satin, and is distinct from the microscopic surface texture created by the polymer chemistry.

- **synthetic lanes**—Bowling lanes made of panels of melamine laminate, similar to Formica countertop material or Pergo laminate flooring. Though printed to look like wood, synthetic lane surfaces are much harder than wood and display far less friction.

- **tap**—A single pin left standing on what the bowler believes is a solid pocket hit. In actuality, most so-called taps are the result of a light hit. While there is a very small chance of leaving a single pin on a true pocket hit (almost always a 9- or 10-pin for a right hander), the odds of leaving a single pin standing are 23 percent on a hit that is one board light, and 40 percent on a hit that is two boards light.

- **three-bagger**—Three strikes in a row. Also known as a turkey. The "bagger" suffix can be appended to any number of consecutive strikes, such as a four-bagger, five-bagger, et cetera.

- **tilt**—See axis tilt.

- **timing**—Refers to the relationship between the bowler's footwork and arm swing. The most important aspect of timing is where the bowler's swing is when he or she reaches the foul line. See early timing, neutral timing, and late timing.

- **top spin**—Forward rotation of the bowling ball. Required for hook.

- **topography**—Specifically, a description of a bowling lane's surface features, including dips, rises, and tilt. In general, topography refers to the lane's deviations from true flatness.

- **torque**—Torque can be thought of as a twisting or spinning force.

- **track (ball)**—The band of coverstock that the ball rolls over as it travels down the lane. The track is generally adjacent to the thumb and finger holes.

- **track (lane)**—The path down the lane that receives the majority of traffic. This is often in the vicinity of the second arrow, but can vary from one bowling center to another. The track area will generally show increased wear and friction.

- **track flare**—Migration of the ball's track from one revolution to the next. Track flare is highlighted by the fanned out pattern of oil rings left on the ball's surface after a trip down the lane, created as the ball reorients itself with each revolution because of weight imbalances.

- **transition**—A change in the playing characteristics of a lane as the oil is moved around, removed, or redeposited by players' bowling balls.

- **translational kinetic energy**—The energy an object possesses due to its linear motion. In bowling, it is the energy the ball possesses due to its travel down the lane.

- **turkey**—Three strikes in a row. Also known as a 3-bagger.

- **tweener**—A contraction of "betweener" (so should technically be written as 'tweener). A catchall description that refers to a bowler who displays a bowling style somewhere between the smooth and relatively free delivery of a stroker, and the heavily muscled and powerful delivery of a cranker. Sometimes less accurately used to describe any bowler with a medium rev rate regardless of their bowling style.

- **typical house shot**—See house shot.

- **urethane**—Short for polyurethane. In bowling, urethane refers to a ball with a coverstock made of an unmodified or minimally modified polyurethane resin. Urethane balls typically exhibit a more gentle and gradual path than do highly modified polyurethane "reactive resin" balls.

- **USBC**—United States Bowling Congress. The national governing body for the sport of tenpin bowling in the United States.

- **velocity**—Similar to speed. While speed only describes how much distance is covered in a given time period, velocity describes the distance covered *in a certain direction* in a given time period. Speed just says your car is going 40 miles per hour; velocity says your car is going *north* at 40 miles per hour. Since bowling balls travel in pretty much in the same direction every time, we can think of speed and velocity as being the same thing.

- **walled up**—Lane conditions usually associated with very high ratio house shots, where there are very dry boards on the outsides of the lane and a very oily, roughly triangular patch running up the center of the lane. The outside dry boards form a figurative wall, giving extra hook to errant shots toward the outside, allowing such shots to make it back to the pocket area despite the miss. The figurative wall of oil in the center of the lane serves the same purpose, decreasing the hook of shots that miss to the inside, allowing them to slide into the pocket area rather than hitting high. Walled up conditions result in what many consider to be gratuitous strikes and artificially high scores.

- **wash out**—Similar to a split. Describes groups of one or more pins left standing that are not diagonally adjacent to one another, but where one of the pins is the headpin. The most common washouts are the 1-2-4-10 for right handers and the 1-3-6-7 for lefties.

- **weight block**—A very dense, often oddly shaped block of polymer located near the center of a bowling ball. Weight blocks are loaded with rock or metal dust to increase their mass. The weight block creates the imbalances within the ball that encourage both track flare and hook. Weight blocks can be "symmetric" or "asymmetric" in shape. Many bowlers believe that symmetric weight blocks create a smoother and more gradual hook while asymmetric weight blocks create more angularity, but the physics disagree, and see no difference between the two.

- **weight hole**—See balance hole.

- **wet/dry**—See over/under.

- **wrap 7-pin**—See ringing 7-pin.

- **wrap 10-pin**—See ringing 10-pin.

- **WTBA**—World Tenpin Bowling Association. International governing body for the sport of tenpin bowling. A part of World Bowling, which governs both tenpin and ninepin.

- **zebra**—Because every word list ends with zebra.

REFERENCES

Al-Samarai, Riyadh A., et al. "The Influence of Roughness on the Wear and Friction Coefficient under Dry and Lubricated Sliding." *International Journal of Scientific & Engineering Research* 3, Issue 4 (2012): 1-6.

Baggenstoss, Alois C., et al. "Bowling Ball." U.S. Patent 3248113 (April 26, 1966).

Banerjee, Joydeep, John McPhee. "A Volumetric Contact Model to Study the Effect of Lane Friction and the Radii of Gyration on the 'Hook Shot' in Indoor Bowling.", *Procedia Engineering* 72 (2014): 429-434.

Baumeister, Roy F., et al. "Bad is Stronger than Good." *Review of General Psychology* 5, No. 4 (2001): 323-370. DOI: 10.1037//1089-2680.5.4.323.

Bengisu, M.T., A. Akay. "Relation of Dry-Friction to Surface Roughness." *Journal of Tribology* 119, no. 1 (1997): 18-25. DOI: 10.1115/1.2832457.

Brancazio, Peter J. *Sport Science*. New York: Simon & Schuster, 1985.

"Brunswick Extra Hole Demonstration", YouTube video, 11:11, posted by Eric Morrett on August 7, 2015, https://www.youtube.com/watch?v=f1e8VeZf4WA (accessed 17 September, 2017).

Caruso, Mary M., et al. "Mechanically-Induced Chemical Changes in Polymeric Materials." *Chemical Review* 109, no. 11 (2009): 5755–5798. DOI: 10.1021/cr9001353.

Chalmers, Peter N., et al. "Glenohumeral Function of the Long Head of the Biceps Muscle: An Electromyographic Analysis." *Orthopaedic Journal of Sports Medicine* 2, No 2. (2014): 2325967114523902.

Dreyfus, Stuart E., Hubert L. Dreyfus. "A Five-Stage Model of the Mental Activities Involved in Directed Skill Acquisition." *United States Air Force, Air Force Office of Scientific Research*, 1980.

"Ebonite Powerhouse Bowler ID Presentation", YouTube video, 5:52, posted by Ronald Hickland Jr, January 15, 2015, https://www.youtube.com/watch?v=dnXOm3cXSso

Fischhoff, Baruch, Paul Slovic, Sarah Lichtenstein. "Knowing with Certainty: The Appropriateness of Extreme Confidence." *Journal of Experimental Psychology: Human Perception and Performance* 3, No. 4 (1977): 552-564.

Frohlich, Cliff. "What makes bowling balls hook?", *American Journal of Physics* 72, No.9 (2004): 1170-1177.

Funderburg, Mick. "Plasticizers in the Polyurethane Industry." Polyurethane Manufacturers Association. http://www.pmahome.org/files/4714/1884/4820/2014_PMA_PTS_ Funderburg.pdf (accessed October 1, 2017).

Fuss, Franz Konstantin. "Design of an Instrumented Bowling Ball and its Application to Performance Analysis in Tenpin Bowling." *Sports Technology* 2, No. 3-4 (2009): 97-110. DOI: 10.1002/jst.104.

Gonzales, R.V., T.S. Buchanan, S.L. Delp. "How Muscle Architecture and Moment Arms Affect Wrist Flexion-Extension Movements." *Journal of Biomechanics* 30, No 7. (1997): 705-712

Guevin, Paul R. Jr. "Castable Urethanes in Leisureland.", Polyurethane Manufacturers Association (1986).

Hallbeck, M.S. "Flexion and Extension Forces Generated by Wrist-Dedicated Muscles over the Range of Motion." *Applied Ergonomics* 12, No. 6. (1994): 379–385.

He, Bo, Wei Chen, Jane Wang. "Surface Texture Effect on Friction of a Microtextured Poly(dimethylsiloxane) (PDMS).", *Tribology Letters* 31 (2008): 187-197.

Hopkins, D.C., J.D. Patterson. "Bowling Frames: Paths of a Bowling Ball." *American Journal of Physics* 45, no. 3 (1977): 263-266.

"How to find the PSA of a bowling ball using a washing machine", YouTube video, 6:13, posted by "Sprocket454" on October 23, 2013, https://www.youtube.com/watch?v=-WIfDXDAloQ (accessed 17 September, 2017).

Huston, R.L., C. Passerello, et al. "On the Dynamics of a Weighted Bowling Ball." *Journal of Applied Mechanics* 46 (1979): 937-943.

Jayhawk Bowling Supply & Equipment, Inc. "Weight Removal Chart." jayhawkbowling. com. http://www.jayhawkbowling.com/Pro_s_Corner/Pro_Shop_Forms/ weightremoval.pdf (accessed 22 September, 2017).

Karwowski, Waldemar. *International Encyclopedia of Ergonomics and Human Factors, Second Edition*. New York: Taylor & Francis Inc., (2001).

Kegel LLC. "Kegel Sport Series - DEAD MAN'S CURVE - 3043 (40 uL)." *Kegel Pattern Library*. http://patternlibrary.kegel.net/PatternLibraryPattern.aspx?ID=663 (accessed September 18, 2017).

King, K., N.C. Perkins, H. Churchill, et al. "Bowling ball dynamics revealed by miniature wireless MEMS inertial measurement unit", *Sports Engineering* 13 (2011): 95-104. DOI:10.1007/s12283-010-0054-z.

Kruger, Justin, David Dunning. "Unskilled and Unaware of It: How Difficulties in Recognizing One's Own Incompetence Lead to Inflated Self-Assessments." *Journal of Personality and Social Psychology* 77, No. 6 (1999): 1121-1134.

Landin, Dennis, Melissa Thompson, Meghan R. Jackson. "Actions of the Biceps Brachii at the Shoulder: A Review." *Journal of Clinical Medicine Research* 9.8 (2017): 667–670.

Levy, A.S., B.T. Kelly, S.A. Lintner, D.C. Osbahr, K.P. Speer. "Function of the long head of the biceps at the shoulder: Electromyographic analysis." *Journal of Shoulder and Elbow Surgery* 10, No 3. (2001): 250-255.

Liu, Yun, Izabela Szlufarska. "Chemical Origins of Frictional Aging." *Physical Review Letters* 109, no. 186102 (2012): 1-5. DOI: 10.1103/PhysRevLett.109.186102.

Mathiowetz, Virgil, et al. "Grip and Pinch Strength: Normative Data for Adults." *Archives of Physical Medicine and Rehabilitation* 66 (1985): 69-72.

Menezes, P.L., S.V. Kailas. "Role of surface texture and roughness parameters on friction and transfer film formation when UHMWPE sliding against steel." *Biosurface and Biotribology* 2, no. 1 (2016): 1-10. DOI: 10.1016/j.bsbt.2016.02.001.

Methenitis S., N. Karandreas, K. Spengos, et al. "Muscle Fiber Conduction Velocity, Muscle Fiber Composition, and Power Performance." *Medicine & Science in Sports & Exercise* 48, no. 9 (2016):1761-1771. doi: 10.1249/MSS.0000000000000954.

Ridenour, Paul. "Unlocking the Mysteries of Particle-Ball Performance." BowlingChat.net Wiki. http://wiki.bowlingchat.net/wiki/index.php?title=Ridenour_Mysteries_Of_Particle (accessed November 27, 2017).

Rogers, Martin E., Timothy E. Long. *Synthetic Methods in Step-Growth Polymers.* Hoboken, NJ: John Wiley & Sons, 2003.

Schorah, Dave, Simon Choppin, David James. "Investigating the Relationship Between Swing Weight and Swing Speed Across Different Sports using Historical Data." *Procedia Engineering* 34 (2012): 766-771.

Sedlacek, M., B. Podgornik, J. Vizintin. "Influence of Surface Preparation on Roughness Parameters, Friction and Wear." *Wear* 266 (2009): 482–487.

Siefers, Nick. "Bowling Ball Shell Chemistry 101: Basic Coverstocks & Reactive Polymerization." *International Tenpin Bowling Coaches Association.* http://www.itbca.bowlingknowledge.info/index.php/winter-2013/85-bowling-ball-shell-chemistry-101 (accessed September 27, 2017).

Siefers, Nick. "Marketing vs. Physics: The Truth About Axis Migration." *Bowlingdigital.com.* (2007). http://www.bowlingdigital.com/bowl/node/2836 (accessed October 14, 2017).

Siefers, Nick. "Understanding the relationship between core and coverstock." *Bowlingdigital.com.* (2007). http://www.bowlingdigital.com/bowl/node/2324 (accessed October 14, 2017).

Sprager, David G., Larry M. Vezina, Daniel R. Speranza, James M. Donovan. "Apparatus and method for analyzing bowling technique.", U.S. Patent US6110052A (February 14, 1996).

Stremmel, Neil, Paul Ridenour, and Scott Sterbenz. "Identifying the Critical Factors That Contribute to Bowling Ball Motion on a Bowling Lane.", United States Bowling Congress (2005).

Stremmel, Neil. "Entry Angle, Part 1, 2, 3." *IBPSIA.com.*
http://www.ibpsia.com/go/article/url_name/Entry_Angle,_Part_1/
http://www.ibpsia.com/go/article/url_name/Entry_Angle,_Part_2/
http://www.ibpsia.com/go/article/url_name/Entry_Angle,_Part_3/
(accessed May 8, 2014).

Taylor, Ronald P., Jeffrey A. Dodge, Hartmut Nefzger. "Plasticizers For Bowling Ball Coverstocks." U.S. Patent US6407201B1 (June 18, 2002).

Thomas, David L., Ed Diener. "Memory Accuracy in the Recall of Emotions." *Journal of Personality and Social Psychology* 59, No. 2 (1990): 291-297.

United States Bowling Congress. "I left what where." *Bowl.com.*
https://www.bowl.com/Equipment_Specs/Equipment_Specs_Home/Research,_Articles_and_Presentations/ (accessed July 22, 2017).

United Stated Bowling Congress. "Pin Carry Study." *Bowl.com.*
https://www.bowl.com/Equipment_Specs/Equipment_Specs_Home/Research,_Articles_and_Presentations/ (accessed July 22, 2017).

Wakuda, Manabu, Yukihiko Yamauchi, Shuzo Kanzaki, Yoshiteru Yasuda. "Effect of surface texturing on friction reduction between ceramic and steel materials under lubricated sliding contact." *Wear* 254 (2003): 356–363. DOI: 10.1016/S0043-1648(03)00004-8.

Walker, Jearl. "Why Sidespin Helps the Bowler—and How to Keep Scoring Strikes." *Scientific American* (March, 1988): 110-113.

Wang, Shun, Yuan-zhong Hu. "Effects of Surface Roughness on Sliding Friction in Lubricated-Point Contacts:Experimental and Numerical Studies.", *Journal of Tribology* 129 (2007): 809-817.

Yamaguchi, Kazuma, Chiaki Sasaki, et al. "Effect of Surface Roughness on Friction Behavior of Steel under Boundary Lubrication." *Journal of Engineering Tribology* 228, no. 9 (2014): 1015-1019.

Young, Hugh D., Roger A. Freedman. *University Physics Volume I*. California: Addison Wesley, 2004.

Zecchini, Edward J., Gary L. Foutch. "The Bowling Ball's Path." *Chemtech*, December, 1991: 731-735.

Zierath Juleen R., John A. Hawley. "Skeletal Muscle Fiber Type: Influence on Contractile and Metabolic Properties." *PLoS Biology* 2, no. 10 (2004): e348. https://doi.org/10.1371/journal.pbio.0020348.

INDEX

Made in the USA
Middletown, DE
04 August 2018